# Rural development

T0328936

# Rural development

## Knowledge & expertise in governance

Kristof Van Assche

Anna-Katharina Hornidge

*Wageningen Academic* Publishers

EAN: 9789086862566
e-EAN: 9789086868124
ISBN: 978-90-8686-256-6
eISBN: 978-90-8686-812-4
DOI: 10.3920/978-90-8686-812-4

Photo cover: Zerafshan Valley Tajikistan,
Photographer: Anastasiya Shtaltovna.
© ZEF/ University of Bonn, Germany

First published, 2015

© Wageningen Academic Publishers
The Netherlands, 2015

The content of this publication and any liabilities
arising from it remain the responsibility of the
authors.

The publisher is not responsible for possible
damages, which could be a result of content
derived from this publication.

# Acknowledgements

This book was published with the financial support of the Federal Ministry of Education and Research, Germany and the Foundation Silk Road Research. The authors would like to acknowledge the support by both organisations and express their gratitude.

# The words of others

*[We are] marching with confident steps towards the creation of [...] a globalization with no policies of injustice, oppression, discrimination or tyranny, and a world full of partnership and cooperation, dialogue and coexistence, and acceptance of others.*

Tawakkol Karman, Human Rights Activist from Yemen, accepting the Nobel Peace Prize, 2011

*[...] the Roman people was aggrandized, not by chance or hazard, but rather by counsel and discipline, to which fortune indeed, was by no means unfavourable.*

Cicero, quoting Africanus Scipio 236-183 B.C.E.

*Instead of looking on discussion as a stumbling-block in the way of action, we think it an indispensable preliminary to any wise action at all.*

Pericles' Funeral Oration as recorded in Thucydides' History of The Peloponnesian War, Book II, 2.40, written 431-428 B.C.E.

*We should concentrate efforts towards finding ways to harmonize the generation of social and economic benefits with the balanced use of natural resources, [... and this must] not be addressed by the government alone, but through direct engagement of society in the formulation, implementation and monitoring of public policies.*

Marina Silva, Brazil's former Minister of the Environment, accepting the 'UNEP Champion of the Earth' award, 2007

*To root oneself in the present demands an image of the future.*

Gustavo Esteva, 1992

*It is not the possessions but the desires of mankind which require to be equalized. [...] The beginning of reform is not so much to equalize property as to train the nobler sort of natures not to desire more.*

Aristotle, 384-322 B.C.E.

*Buen Vivir demands a thorough review of the lifestyle of the whole society, starting with dismantling the current lifestyles of the elites, which act as models for others – one that is unattainable for most of the population.*

Alberto Acosta, 2012

*'It is my view', [Otanes] said, 'that we should put an end to the system whereby one of us is the sole ruler. Monarchy is neither an attractive nor a noble institution. [...] How can a monarchy be an orderly affair, when a monarch has the licence to do whatever he wants, without being accountable to anyone? Make a man a monarch, and even if he is the most moral person in the world, he will leave his customary ways of thinking. [...] I propose we abandon monarchy and increase the power of the people, because everything depends on their numbers'.*

Herodotus, 484-425 B.C.E.

*Good governance, including the elimination of corruption and the development of participatory decision-making approaches, is of critical importance to the eradication of poverty and hunger.*

Per Pinstrup-Andersen, 2003

*'There, Master Niketas', Baudolino said, 'when I was not prey to the temptations of this world, I devoted my nights to imagining other worlds. A little with the help of wine, and a little with the green honey. There is nothing better than imagining other worlds', he said, 'to forget the painful one we live in. At least so I thought then. I hadn't yet realised that, in imagining other worlds, you end up changing this one'.*

Umberto Eco, 2000

*Many have imagined republics and principalities which have never been seen or known to exist in reality. For how we live is so far removed from how we ought to live that he who abandons what is done for what is ought to be done will rather bring about his own ruin than his preservation.*

Niccolo Machiavelli, 1513

# Table of contents

# III. Combining and concluding

# List of examples

# List of figures

# 1. Introduction

Development is many things for many people. And in recent years, the whole enterprise of development has been questioned from many sides. In this book, we take stock of many of the critiques of development discourses and recipes, while aiming to preserve some of the insights we still deem valuable. We take a look at many approaches to development, some of them under that name, others not usually labelled as 'development' but de facto influential approaches to it.

We focus on rural development, that is, the development of rural areas, including villages and small towns, and consider the rural in its global aspect. Rural development, in other words, is not restricted to the developing world; it is a highly relevant topic for Europe and North America as well. And it is not restricted to reflections on agriculture, or recipes for it. Rural areas have never been purely agricultural, we argue, and in the last century or so, they have become more and more multi-functional: people do many things in rural areas, land is used for many purposes. We will show that mono-functional land use is an exception, usually the result of very open and globalized markets and/or very strong government policies.

Within this still broad field of rural development, we are mostly interested in the various roles of knowledge that can play a role in bringing a community further on a path it finds desirable. We start from the premise that there are always several development options for a given community or area: there is no ideal goal for a certain community or area, and no single path towards such goal. Communities change, their context changes, what is seen as desirable varies and the same holds true for what is possible. Development efforts are, in essence, political, and politics can still be described as the art of the possible.

We further state that local and expert knowledge of various sorts can play various roles in these different options. Some might rely more on local knowledge, others more on expert knowledge, and the kind of expertise privileged will influence the type of intervention chosen later. Local knowledge is not opposed to expert knowledge, can include elements and traces of current and former expert knowledge, and similar things can be observed in the other direction. Indeed, some development options and routes are more knowledge-intensive than others. Some appeal more to government or governmental actors to incorporate knowledge in policy or more direct community decisions, while others think more of including knowledge already pertaining to 'actors', to players present in the decision process.

Last but not least we assume that any chosen path and expertise has a better chance of success if it acknowledges the path already taken. A chosen development option can more easily become reality if there is an awareness among decision-makers of the current and historical context of the community, of previous decisions and their impact, of the relation between decisions, on the type of tools and goals that might work better given this path and environment. This does not entail an easy give-in to path dependency, conservatism or cultural determinism: it does not mean that one past leads to one future, nor that the present organization of the community is the only viable one, nor that similar cultures always end up in the same situation. Rather, it means that a careful analysis of the governance path in a given community provides clues for the development models and implied knowledge forms that are more likely to succeed.

For that reason, our perspective is an evolutionary perspective. What evolves for us is the community and its governance; the state of affairs at one moment can be considered input for the next step in the evolution. Governance we understand as the taking of collectively binding decisions in a community, by governmental and non-governmental actors. Who is an 'actor' cannot always be easily discerned, and it is not always visible in formal procedures. A group that can be considered a real actor in one community can play no role in another. Governance evolves; its structures, procedures, participants, content changes, as well as the tools it counts on. Development cannot be a matter of implementing a form of organization or institutional structure that has evolved somewhere else.

This brings us to a fourth assumption of this book: development cannot be copied from a recipe deemed universal. One approach might have worked in one place, because of a specific history, but this does not guarantee success anywhere else. Even in the same place, an old recipe might not work. The context has changed, and the community has changed. One important aspect of community change is that the kind of polity that is deemed desirable, also varies over time. One moment, a democracy based on representation seems to work well, next day, problems occur, and either a new form of representation or a higher measure of participation is glorified.

Science cannot be an easy escape. It cannot give us the recipe, independent of the always changing polity. There will always be discussion in a community and beyond on good governance, on the right form and measure and time of participation, and new forms of democracy are likely to sprout for a very long time. Development studies are therefore to be considered governance studies, and studying rural development is studying evolving governance. Science, as a collection of different forms of expert knowledge, can be helpful in many ways in governance, and can inspire the choice for and substance of certain development paths, but, we argue, it can never prescribe the way to go.

In more and more scientific disciplines, including many versions of development studies, what we call post-modernism, has become generally accepted: we can summarize it here as the perspective that says there is no universal perspective on things. We know the world through concepts, and those concepts make the world for us. Science cannot neutrally uncover the world as it is, let alone prescribe the way it should be. The world can be understood in many ways, using different sets of concepts, all human-made, and it can be made and remade in many ways. For that reason alone, it would be strange to assume there is one way forward, one ideal political organization, and one set of knowledge that can help to move in such direction, and help in the daily functioning of governance later on.

The primacy of this or that model of government and the primacy and objectivity of any form of knowledge has proven to be disputable. One can safely assume that knowledge can play different roles, and that useful knowledge can stem from many disciplines. That insight, underpinned by research in many disciplines, renders it necessary to take a distance from any disciplines promising a clear path to an ideal model of governance, underpinned by one supposedly objective sort of knowledge.

In other words, one cannot embrace and believe simple recipes for rural development and simple prescriptions as to the type and role of expertise involved.

Each governance path implies a different destination, a different implied model of governance and a different form and role of expertise in governance and its transformation. This first analysis can already be useful to criticize some earlier answers to the problems of development and expertise already mentioned. One important example is that of 'participation' as a supposed improvement to older development approaches. Participation has been touted as the answer to expert-driven development approaches, based on models imported from elsewhere, and dominated by scientific expertise deemed irrefutable. Indeed, participation forms can bring in forms of local knowledge, and other forms of scientific knowledge, which might enable governance to envision alternative paths and destination. Yet participation itself cannot be reduced to a simple formula, and all of its forms, as we shall see, have side-effects. Besides, participation cannot work without representation, while it can simultaneously undermine it.

Analyzing the issue of expertise in rural development thus requires cutting through many layers of old promises and mythologies. The promise of a simple recipe for development was in many cases tied to other promises, which in many cases look questionable now. One can summarize these promises as the promise of simple worlds and the promise of steering. The promise of simple worlds we define as the promise of transparency in reality, brought by scientific means. Science can make reality transparent, and this process also includes a revelation by experts of a single structure, a single essence in the political, economic, legal and cultural realities of communities, the deficiencies in empirical case, the ideal model to strive for, and the path towards that model. Many economists define markets as the essence of society, and a certain structure of markets as ideal, and often they believe the recipe to come to a well structured market – a 'rational' market – is clear.

The promise of steering we define as the promise of powerful intervention: the simple world allows for analysis recommending possible interventions, and the steering promise tells us that indeed within society, within government in most cases, one can find or produce the tools that can 'implement' the policies, plans and other decisions that are taken. Belief in 'development' in many of the old definitions was therefore belief in the power of steering (mostly by government, or international organisations, sometimes by non-governmental organisations (NGOs)), the power of prediction and planning, and the power of Western science, economy and politics to project their reach to the rest of the world and transform that world in their image.

The very understandable backlash both in the west and the developing world against these entangled assumptions does not, however, need to lead to cynicism or an outright rejection of any Western concept in politics, economy and law, or to any role of scientific expertise in development. Neither does it warrant an outright rejection of all concepts of development, or an unmasking of the whole development enterprise as oppressive and neo-colonialist.

Many rural communities, in the west and the rest, do want change. They want transformation, are aware of transitions, of unwanted evolutions and missing opportunities, and for many communities, 'development' is not something to be feared or distrusted (while 'the development industry' at least in the developing world in fact is). In general, local communities do want more say in deciding their own fate than a few decades ago, while often, environmental problems are worse and the faith in expert knowledge to deal with issues in general has been reduced.

Against this general background, this book develops a perspective on rural development that redefines development and rethinks the roles of knowledge and expertise in development. We start from the unicity of communities and their governance paths, paths that require an analysis which can in turn inspire tailor-made strategies for development as envisioned in the respective community. The work is based on various strands of theory, including social systems theory, post-structuralism, and development and institutional economics, and empirically on a wide array of case studies in four continents. Besides case studies, we enrich the analysis and readability by means of shorter illustrative narratives, vignettes and comparisons. A dialogue with selected classics from political theory, among whom Machiavelli is prominent, adds to the reflection on expertise in governance and development.

In our perspective, the concept of governance paths is thus central. We will argue that these paths are unique, marked by three dependencies, and yet leaving room for contingency, path creation, and intervention. What is seen as desirable development is shaped by narratives, and the path towards the desired model of society and governance structured by both discourses on the good life and the good community, and by modes of coordination that formed in prior evolutions. This brings us to two further concepts which structure the book: actor/institution configurations and power/knowledge/configurations. It will be demonstrated how actors and institutions shape each other, how power and knowledge are entwined, and that how these two configurations relate underpins the form of governance in a community, as well as its transformation options.

Figure 1.1. Local knowledge with global antecedents. Coconut oil processing in Eastern Indonesia. Photo: Anna-Katharina Hornidge. © ZEF/University of Bonn, Germany.

Understanding a governance path can then help to craft an approach to development in a community that is more context-sensitive, in the sense that it is more likely to have effects in that context but also in the sense that it is more sensitive to the relations, desires, fears, qualities and hopes in the community.

The approaches to rural development we present in the following chapters, are thus all imperfect, yet all had benefits under certain circumstances and these benefits can be better understood if one traces their histories. Understanding a specific path of governance has to be coupled to understanding the trajectories of different proposed solutions to development. Then, we believe, it might become slightly easier to link properties of situations with properties of tools. It might become more realistic to combine elements of different approaches, into a strategy that deserves to be tried here and now.

The kind of knowledge that is expected to be useful in a development effort, can only then be determined. It cannot be discovered a priori. And, we would add, the definition of knowledge and expertise one chooses, also becomes visible only then, after these different analyses. What is knowledge in general then? Anything that helps to understand the world and ourselves in it, anything that gives insight and the insight itself. That is the starting definition we take in this book. All other distinctions between sorts of knowledge, between expertise and local knowledge, between disciplines, between experts and laymen, are contingent, can be drawn in different ways, and the way you do that has implications for your perspective on development. So, we do not draw such distinctions now, but will look at ways this is done in different development models.

All this being said, we believe this book can be helpful in several ways:
• It can help the reader to get an overview of influential approaches to rural development, their lineage, their pro's and con's.
• It can show ways to map out the governance evolution of a community in such a way that it reveals clues to possible future interventions and transformations.
• It shows manners to evaluate patterns of decision-making, and reflect on possible improvements. This in turn can bring up alternative visions of the future.
• Finally, it can assist in bricolage, in combining elements of different approaches to development in a way that makes sense given the path of governance and the vision of and for the community.

We hope this book finds its way to a readership that extends beyond academia, and beyond the usual suspects in the development industry. As we hope to contribute to ongoing discussions, and take a polemical tone here and there, we are open to comments and suggestions. Please note that this book is also conceived to be used in different manners: it can be read as a whole, with a narrative connecting the different parts, or in parts. If you want to delve deeper into some of the discussions and proposed solutions, there are sections with literature notes at the end of each chapter. The different sections can also be the basis of classes, workshops, and public debates, while many of the examples can serve as an entrance to more thorough, and maybe comparative, case study work.

Whatever form of action or insight it may inspire, we do hope the book establishes connections between different ways of understanding, and, in the end, between knowledge and action.

*Kristof Van Assche and Anna-Katharina Hornidge*

# Empirical issues and theoretical orientations

*Whoever desires continuous success and prosperity,*
*must change his conduct with time*

Niccolo Machiavelli, 1509

In this first part, we take a closer look at the rural, its issues, and we develop a theoretical frame to look at these issues, to understand them in such a way that links between knowledge and action can be created more easily. We reflect first on rurality, then on development, analyse development as necessarily part and parcel of governance, and then present a way to understand governance. To break open many of the practical and theoretical discussions on development, we draw the attention to the existence of many forms of polity that were apparently acceptable and desirable at different times and places. Also a reference to 'democracy' is not enough to legitimize a certain approach to development, or to governance in general, as there are a number of different models that emerged over time, each with their pro's and con's.

In the analysis of governance, we structure the reasoning around two configurations: actor/institution and power/knowledge. It will be shown that actors (the players) and institutions (the rules of coordination) shape each other in governance evolution, and that the same holds true for power/knowledge configurations. What is recognized as knowledge and as useful knowledge is shaped in a history of shifting power relations, and those power relations partly spring from access to, use of, privileging of, certain types of understanding of self and environment. What looks like an attractive community will look attractive based on a selection of knowledge which partly reflects histories of power relations, of domination and marginalization, but also of mutual benefit, shared understanding and synergies.

# 2. Rural communities and their governance

## Abstract

In this chapter, we address the question why a separate treatment of rural development issues would be needed. We look at rural communities in general, and undertake a first investigation of the issues addressing them. These issues and possible answers to them will be dealt with in detail in later chapters. We notice patterns of convergence and divergence in rural development issues across the world, and argue for an approach which does not a priori distinguish between the developed world and the rest. Also in the developed world, many rural development issues arise. The importance of various contexts is highlighted, and this plea is specified by introducing the concept of differentiation: functional, organizational and segmentary. An analysis of these forms of differentiation is presented as an essential step in the analysis of rural issues and their possible solution. We underline that rural areas cannot and could never be reduced to agriculture, that mono-functional land use is a modernist exception, and that any rural development strategy has to start from a multiple land use perspective. As in later parts of the book, each subsection consists of a theoretical discussion and one or more illustrations, examples or short case studies.

## 2.1 Rurality and the need for development?

What is rural and why does it need development? Poignant questions for a book on rural development. Obviously, many have perceived a need for development in rural areas, and many approaches have been developed. Later in the book, we look in detail at some of these approaches, and in the next chapter, we reflect on the concept of development itself. First, we want to ask the question of rurality. What is it? Often, the answer has been: agricultural areas. Others have seen the rural as not-urban, and, often in the same line, as somewhat backward, since innovation and citizenship were for many theorists and other people located in the cities. Cities were seen as multi-functional, as vibrant, as knots in networks of markets, as drivers of social innovation, of scientific change, as places where new social identities could be developed under less pressure of tradition. In the 20th century, the city also became the place for artistic and cultural innovation, and a place where innovation and change could be observed and enjoyed, as a cultural practice. They became places to see what it means to be modern and cosmopolitan, and to learn and become it oneself.

The countryside was often positioned as the city was not: stagnant rather than innovative, constrained by tradition, and suffocating from conservative identity politics. If the countryside is backward, and if innovation is good, then development is good and the rural areas need development. The need for rural development seems apparent from this point of view.

But, of course, not all cities are the same and not all countrysides are the same. There are different ways to understand cities, and there are different ways of relating cities and countrysides. One can also understand rural areas without a specific reference to cities, as areas where population density is rather low. However, rural areas are mainly perceived as being connected to cities with rare exceptions. Cities are seen as products of the countryside, which, once they exist, reshape the countryside.

The pleas for rural development in policy and theory are often informed by an understanding of rural areas as earlier in evolution, as lagging behind, and as less multi-functional. Development can then mean improving agriculture, or moving towards multi-functional land use and a diversified economy. It does not entail necessarily that rural areas are expected to become cities in the long run. The visions for the future can differ, and there can be room in such future for countrysides, with specific combinations of functions: agriculture, resource extraction, conservation, recreation, retirement, etc. In poorer countries, in what was seen as the developing world, the accent was usually on improving agriculture. Also in Western and/or richer countries, rural development pleas came up early though, often already in the 18th century, when some parts of the European nation-states were perceived internally as lagging behind, and requiring intervention by the state. Since the 20th century, Western countries have noted very often a similar set of issues in their own rural areas. These issues recur in discussions of countrysides in countries as diverse as Canada, Sweden, the Netherlands, France and Brazil.

The main recurring issue in Western discussions of rural development seems to be *access*: access to services, to markets, to schools, to information, to everything. Access is coupled with infrastructure: in rural areas, densities are lower, distances greater, so all sorts of infrastructure are more expensive to build and to maintain. Also in richer areas, even basic infrastructure maintenance can become a problem in the more remote and sparsely populated rural areas: roads, electricity, sewage, and, nowadays, internet. The services that are expected in rural areas are highly context sensitive: when a Western European village complains about failing resources, infrastructure, services, a similar situation in most of the US would not be seen as problematic and in Brazil it looks prosperous.

Problems of access can reinforce each other, and some speak of negative feedback loops: if population densities go down (people leaving the countryside), there is a smaller tax base to maintain infrastructure, services, and if certain types of business leave, others do, too, and below a certain level of service provision more residents will be inclined to leave, etc.

In the Western world, the big evolution behind much of this is the declining importance of agriculture in the overall economy, the growing importance of cities as hubs of activity, but also the so-called 'green revolution', the mechanisation of agriculture, coupled with an enlarging scale of farming, which led to more mono-functional rural areas, focusing more on agriculture, on one specialty in agriculture, and relinquishing much of the ecological and visual diversity of older rural landscapes. Fewer jobs were available on these farms, more in urban areas, and in many parts of the world, depopulation of rural areas is seen as a major problem. Thus, pleas for development, in practice, redevelopment. In many Western countries, the 20th century trend towards a more mono-functional countryside led to environmental problems, to a less attractive countryside, one can also say to a less resilient countryside: if in the modernisation drive ecological and visual diversity got lost, in many cases also local knowledge, skills, local products, schools, associations, it becomes harder to reinvent the countryside later on a new basis. It becomes harder to bounce back.

In the last few decades, many have called for such reinvention, for a return to a more multi-functional rural space, a larger role for nature conservation, recreation, retirement housing, care, and for a new localisation of agriculture, with product again more tied to the place, soil, community, culture they emerged from – as opposed to the global economy where agricultural practices everywhere respond to global market pressures. Places that have modernised the most sometimes suffer the most in the reinvention towards multi-functional space: if all the land is structured to optimise one type of crop, it is harder to choose other crops, integrate tourism into local economies and generally to diversify the local economy. If all local knowledge has been forgotten because it was deemed useless and of no economic value, it becomes harder to credibly rethink and sell products as local and traditional. We can call this a rigidity in governance evolution; once certain choices are made, a path is taken, it becomes harder to steer in a different direction.

Yet, as we all know, countrysides are not only problematic areas, not only places of despair and migration. They are also attractive, for many reasons. Cities and the industrial revolution have spawned a desire to escape from cities, towards nature and rural areas. Rapid changes in economies and societies have created desires to go back to more stable times, when rules and roles and futures where more predictable. To times when ambiguity was less prevalent: one's place in society was more clear, and reflected an order of things that was not questioned to the same extent. With the loss of certainties of modern society, culminating in the post-modern questioning of everything, one can reinvent oneself, and ones community more easily, one can enjoy more freedom than in the old days, but that freedom comes with risks and burdens.

And before the industrial revolution, the Renaissance elites already enjoyed vacations in the countryside, not too far from the city, and were proudly cultivating (or pretending to) their own vegetables and fruits, emulating some of the Roman and Greek writers they admired. In painting, poetry, philosophy since the Renaissance, idyllic images of the rural have been conjured up, with the countryside standing for a wide range of virtues: simplicity, honesty, a slower pace, clarity, closeness to nature, industry, etc. Usually, what was projected in the countryside as attractive, was the opposite of some problems encountered in city life. If the city was dirty, rural areas could look desirable because clean; if crime was high, the countryside was good since safe. These positive rosy images of rural life were circulated more widely when more people could read, had access to images, later moving images.

These positive images are idealizations, but they have real effects, just as the negative images. We call this *performativity*. If people believe that there is no future in their village, even if this belief inspired by movies produced the other end of the world, they might move, leave the village empty, and set in motion the negative feedbacks just described, so after a while it does look like the end of the world. If people see the same place in the positive light of a popular novel, they might renovate abandoned homes, make them nicer than ever before, replant hedges, add flowers, organize farmers markets, trace and preserve local knowledge, and create a community that is closer to the world of the novel than to the previously existing community on the same spot. Images, and stories, can become reality, and even when they do not produce the reality they describe, they can change the reality they are lived in. We call this *reality effects*.

Figure 2.1. Medieval pharmacy garden in Bruges, Belgium. In the middle ages, the distinction between urban and rural was harder and harsher than now, with cities enjoying more freedoms, a higher degree of self-organization, than the countryside. Yet, the cities, and religious institutions residing there, as here the St. John's hospital, played an important role in rural development, e.g. land reclamation projects, and in the development of expertise pertaining to it. Photo: Monica Gruzmacher. © ZEF/University of Bonn, Germany.

Reality effects can be discussed in relation to negative and positive images of rural areas, but also to definitions of them. And, as we know, definitions and values cannot always be separated. A certain definition of a rural area, or of rural areas in general, can easily produce negative associations, and in some cases a positive or negative value is already part of the definition. We believe it is clear now to the reader that defining the rural is not easy, but also that this is not a problem at all. The rural is changing all the time, is different in different places, can be defined differently, and certainly not reduced to a set of variables. Communities can look very rural, as in small, remote, green, but filled with people living very globalized lives; cities can be large but isolated; one village can be focused on agriculture, in a high-tech manner, linked to global markets, the next one can be empty, and one further is resettled by a combination of artists and tourism entrepreneurs. The networks and cultures that make a community, give it a character one could then call urban or rural, and are not always easy to discern. How one sees the rural will however have effects, will influence thought and action, and this is all the more true for governments: once certain images of the rural become embedded in policy, they are likely to have stronger reality effects.

Recapturing some of the points made in this section, we can say that the rural can be defined in many ways, that positive and negative images have co-existed for centuries, and have had real effects. Choosing a version of rurality is not neutral, has effects on your analysis and decisions later, in all likelihood. And associating a version of rurality with a wider web of positive and negative associations is likely to further shape action. When governments pick up ideas, they can become more influential, acquire a greater influence on governance. Even with the socially constructed nature of 'the countryside', one can easily see recurring themes that cut across places and contexts; almost always, there is distinction between city and countryside. Places are usually not seen as both at the same time. What is seen as problems of the countryside are usually issues of access, of links to cities and to networks deemed important for a contemporary community. The way the relation between city and countryside is structured and perceived will differ however; understanding this relation means understanding the social networks, knowledge networks, economic networks in an area, and the specific forms of multi-functionality these networks allow and reproduce. Rural areas have always been multifunctional, but old and new forms of multi-functionality have to be grasped and distinguished, in order to figure out how a certain rural area 'works', and further along the line, how governance could be structured to move it in a slightly different direction.

## Further reading

Scott, J.C. (1998). Seeing like a state. How certain schemes to improve the human condition have failed. New Haven, CN, USA: Yale University Press.

Slicher van Bath, B.H. (1963). The agrarian history of Western Europe, AD 500-1850. New York, NY, USA: St. Martin's Press.

Van Assche, K., Beunen, R. and Duineveld, M. (2014). Evolutionary governance theory. An introduction. Heidelberg, Germany: Springer.

Van Schendel, W. (2002). Geographies of knowing, geographies of ignorance: jumping scale in Southeast Asia. Environment and Planning D: Society and Space, 20, 647-668.

## 2.2 Development as redevelopment

Development is always redevelopment. And where this tends to be forgotten, we should remind the forgetful that it is the case. One can never start from scratch, because there is always something. Even when one thinks the old was bad and has been destroyed, one can never be sure that it was wholly bad and that it was entirely destroyed. Even the memories of older times can turn into ideas of glories past and a desire and push to return to the previous state: social memory can influence images of the future, by recreating images of the past and these images can be performative.

What exists in a community deserves careful study, and even in undesirable situations, it is important to think what can be saved, reinterpreted, reused, and how a desirable development path can be initiated without wiping out the past. The past will come back to haunt those who ignore it. This very general statement can be substantiated in many ways: erasing the past can create unstable communities, unsure about their identity, about present and future. It can create a cynicism and lack of trust in government and science that can make it hard to envision any future, let alone coordinate actions towards it. Heritage can be defined in many ways, but in general, people cherish some traces of the past in the present, in the form of landscapes, buildings, histories, practices. Erasing the old landscape is also likely to create environmental problems, since ecosystems that exist are finely tuned systems of relations, and cannot easily be designed in their complexity and variety. The same holds true for esthetics: with the exception of maybe a small group of architects and planners, people generally prefer older environments with a diversity of times and elements asserting its presence. Designs cannot easily create the esthetic quality of old living environments, and one can say the same for the functioning. A newly designed area is likely to be less intricately used than an older environment, where different groups have found a balance, found their way to use a space in various ways.

Ignoring the past can haunt the present in more ways. If we mentioned functionality, we refer not only to the actual uses of spaces, but also to the coordination of that use. We will come back to this topic later, but it is worth mentioning already that such coordination always takes place in formal and informal ways. Understanding a community, its use of a place, its organization, is understanding both formal and informal rules. Development efforts overlooking these informal rules can drastically reduce the quality of life in a community; destroying informal coordination mechanisms can make it impossible to implement any development policy (as a set of formal rules) later on.

We dwell on these points of ignoring the past precisely because such ignorance has been a point of faith in development studies for a long time, and even more in associated fields as public administration and planning. Even now – as we shall see in Part II – certain approaches to development want to completely replace the past with the future, and/or believe the good future does not ask us to dwell much on present or past. We call such approach *blank slate* approaches, or *tabula rasa* approaches.

Tabula rasa approaches are approaches to policy that believe one can start from scratch. Some versions believe it is best to get rid of everything which existed before. Modernist planners in the 1950's and 60's often believed it was best to demolish old neighborhoods to get rid of social problems associated with them. Improving conditions was best done by extreme redesign: get rid of the place, clean it up, then build a new neighborhood, which can be clean, functional, healthy, safe, and prosperous. The reader will notice a strong belief in the power of engineering and the power of policy to remake society.

We speak of *social engineering*. In the case of spatial planning, that meant that spatial design was thought to have great powers to solve social and economic issues. Later we will touch on this more in detail, and investigate some of the strengths of design in development issues, but now most experts would say the belief in social engineering was too big in the post-war period.

We can place the origin of social engineering thinking, and of blank slate approaches in the 18<sup>th</sup> century European enlightenment, a period of strong belief in the power of reason, and of science, the most reasonable activity, to understand the world as it is, and to fix it. The 19<sup>th</sup> century nation-states, often with democratising tendencies and bureaucratic tendencies, incorporated enlightenment values in their structure and function. The state, the bureaucracy and its experts were expected to oversee society, to get a clear and neutral overview of the state of things, the issues remaining, and see which knowledge and which policies would be needed to further perfect society. Enlightenment ideas thus produced ideas of progress, and the road to progress is development. Progress is easier to achieve when less discussion is needed on the goals and the tools, and the very confident nature of young science was welcomed by government: it offered the promise to see clearly, and to solve objectively the problems at hand: poverty, safety, health. Fixing these issues was good in and by itself, and, it was also seen by ruling elites as a way to appease the working classes, who had been living since the industrial revolution in worse conditions than before.

Development is easier when the analysis of the current state is deemed easy: if you know exactly what is wrong, then it is easier to come up with ideas to fix it. Transparency and direct access to reality, holds the promise of social engineering already. The next step in the promise is the actual engineering: we can remake society. The science that gives a clear picture, also can paint an alternative, better picture, and can suggest the tools to move in that direction. Another element of that promising of social engineering was the blank slate mentioned: if you can ignore the current state, and its past, it is easier to redesign things. It becomes easier to rethink society on the drawing board, without spending too much time looking at minute details of that society, and without studying previous attempts to change things in that society. If you look in detail at how societies, communities, work, you will notice that they change in complex patterns, that an attempt to 'develop' is probably not the first attempt to induce change, and that there are patterns in the response to these change attempts.

The philosophy underpinning the blank slate thinking we call *modernism*, and the version where government can redesign society high modernism, after James C. Scott, an influential writer on this topic. Modernism emerged in the 18<sup>th</sup> century, as a product of the enlightenment, and it became more entrenched in the daily lives of people when the nation-states became more centralized, more science-driven, and more inclusive of many topics: states started to interfere with, eventually structure, the behavior of people in more and more ways. New laws, rules, policies, plans came up, covering more topics, and behind those, one could find more and more scientific research.

Modernism came up in Europe, as did high modernism. European countries started to look at their own regions and cities, and countrysides, some more prosperous than others. 'Development' was perceived as something desirable in general, and needed in those 'backward' areas. In many cases, there was a moral aspect to the endeavor: backward areas were somehow deficient in morality, and while communities needed investment in infrastructure and 'cleaning up', the people living there could not be considered mature, full citizens. They needed more education, re-education, in some cases punishment, based on the assumption that the government knows what's best.

This brings us to another point of critique of modernist approaches to policy and development (besides the blank slate idea): lack of *participation*. Indeed, the 'correct' form and level of participation in governance cannot be determined in advance or in general (which would also be a modernist assumption), but one can say in general that a modernist philosophy tends to radically reduce public participation. More power

Figure 2.2. Macin National Park, lower Danube area, Romania. The fertile lowlands in the river valley are the product of highly coordinated intervention, by the communist regime, before that encouraged by the European Danube Commission and before that by the existence of old multi-ethnic riverports Braila and Galati. Meanwhile the Macin mountains were scarcely populated, left for grazing, quarrying, and recently, after the example of the nearby Danube Delta, for eco-tourism. Photo: Kristof Van Assche. © ZEF/University of Bonn, Germany.

goes to bureaucracies and their experts since they know exactly what's wrong and how to proceed. If science can determine what's the issue, and the development recipe, and government can organize the development process, then local input is not needed. Locals can vote, elect people, those representatives have administrations, which include and hire scientists, and not other form of action is needed. Modernism thus tends to reduce the importance of local knowledge and it tends to reduce the scope and size of citizenship. Indeed, as we shall see, democracies have many shapes and forms, and being a citizen, an active member of a democracy (or more broadly a polity) can mean different things in different models.

The low importance of participation and local knowledge brings us to a third point of critique of modernism: *rigidity*. Policies in general are less likely to adapt to local circumstances when local knowledge is neglected and this is more likely to happen when participation is low. Participation can thus be seen as one way to keep policy making adaptive and flexible. When talking about development, this seems all the more important, because development always includes an image of a desirable future, and a development policy or plan will be more persuasive when the locals affected can at least recognize themselves in this future. We will see later how the persuasive force of plans and policies is essential for their implementation; people do not simply follow rules or plans because they exist, and also sheer force, coercion, does not work for long. We can see here how the different assumptions of modernism entangle, and make this ideology stronger, keep it in place: if we know best, we do not need to include others. What others say is irrelevant, because we know best. The existing situation does not need study, since we can better start from scratch. Knowledge of that situation is less relevant, and people with that knowledge are not relevant for the process. Those people would only make us stumble, as they are not enlightened yet, and need re-education, which best takes place in an environment that is the result of the plan.

The critique of rigidity became recently more important again, as more and more people started to speak of governance, as opposed to government, and of adaptive governance. While the modernist approach to development, and to policy in general, did not feel the need to include citizens, and thus relied much on the principle of power by representation, especially since the 1990's, a variety of disciplines saw a greater call for participation again. People started to use the word governance and opposed it to government, as the more central and context-insensitive steering under the modernist banner. We will see later that in practice, governance always existed, that non-state actors were always important in decision-making and implementation, in stabilizing society, and that there were always forms of participation, but we already have an explanation now why these calls came up: modernist ideologies and practices had shrunk participation, increased rigidity, excluded local knowledge, wishes and desires in many places, and this caused a backlash, in theory and practice, a backlash under the banner of participation.

This rallying under the participation cry happened not only because voters felt excluded, because of issues with democratic legitimacy. Another source of dissatisfaction was the lack of implementation of many modernist-inspired policies and plans. Many things simply did not work, hit some wall of reality in the process. Many high hopes were dashed, many plans never implemented. Hence the call for more adaptive governance. Implementation was thought to become more easy when locals could speak more directly, so their resistance could disappear, but also because the plan could be adapted to local circumstances. A third aspect of adaptation is adaptation to locally changing circumstances, an aspect becoming more important in theories of governance for sustainability, resilience, and (climate) change. We come back to this.

Most of what was described in this section took place in the developed world, from the 18th to the late 20th century. The developed world was developed in its own eyes, according to its own definitions, and those definitions were imposed in many places in a colonialist enterprise which reached its peak in the late 19th century. Enlightenment ideas of progress and development, derived from modernist ideologies of steering and social engineering, were projected on the colonized areas, often poorer areas, often more rural. Since many things normal in the European states were missing in the colonies, these absences were linked with deficient development. Development became the catching up with the west, becoming more similar, and the knowledge needed is the scientific expertise embedded in Western bureaucracies at that time. The question of alternative paths of development, of non-Western knowledge as an integral part of such paths, will come back often in this book, but right now, we want to draw the attention to the fact that new knowledge was assumed to be important for the colonies (and other poor countries) to develop.

Yet this was not the knowledge that actually played a role in the development of Western countries themselves. De Soto and others (such as ourselves) have argued that, besides the obvious problem of imposing your development recipe on the rest of the world, the lack of insight into the own history of development has been a structural issue for Western economists, and Western development experts in general. What has made the west richer, it was argued, was not a philosophy like high modernism, and neither was it an extremely free market (as many economists believe, see below), but a slow path of development, in which a series of co-evolutions can be discerned: new forms of organisation, new forms of knowledge, networks, legal and political systems. And in some cases it was good luck. So, in other words the own path of development is not well understood, as a complex path of evolving governance, and this made it easier to project a misunderstood recipe of the own success on the rest of the world.

When, after World War II, the colonial world order disintegrated, the old powers did not have the same influence anymore on the development path of the former colonies, but many of the modernist elements of ideology persisted. The successor states to the colonies were often shaped in the image of the old country, the new elites copied parts of the old ideologies, and foreign aid or investment was in many ways tied to a push for policies in the same direction. Also in science, and in the applied science of development studies, modernist ideologies were not dead, and 'development' became an important topic of investigation exactly in the time when many colonies became independent, had to get on their feet, and experienced a wide array of issues. Most of these places had not been nation-states before, had not seen something akin to the rule of law in the Western sense, were not dominated by one ethnic group, and all these differences with the Western starting point of modern development created more complications on the path to become more Western.

The answers were sought by Western scientists in the development of rational models of community development, of market reform, of infrastructural engineering, of health reform (see below). The point here being that, although several paths were explored, there was usually the assumption that current Western expertise would provide the objective solution; it just needed 'implementation'. Issues with implementation were then often analyzed in terms of local resistance, ignorance, etc. This was presented as one classic development trap: people don't know they have a problem, they don't recognize the solution, so they undermine the solution, which keeps them trapped in a miserable situation. We recognize here some of the interwoven assumptions of modernism, mixed with the condescension of neo-colonialism. Although development thinking and practice have evolved beyond this perspective, for some, in poorer and richer places, the unpleasant association between 'development' and modernist-colonialist thinking was strong enough to get rid of the whole development concept; we speak of post-development thinking (see below). The search for alternative development paths is an ongoing one, and this issue will be revisited in this book many times, linked to different models of democracy, to governance paths, to varying forms of expertise that might or not have an influence on development visions.

This section dwelled on the emergence and distribution of modernist ideology, its importance for development thinking and practice, and its links with colonialism and colonialist legacies. We discussed the problems with modernist development ideas, practical, theoretical, moral problems, and analyzed briefly a few of the main responses to these critiques. Modernist development approaches we considered problematic because of their rigidity, tendency to reduce participation and local knowledge, and tend to think in terms of an ideally clean slate – tabula rasa. We politely disagree with this ideology, without replacing one simple recipe with another one (e.g. participation). Later, we will talk more about a set of influential approaches, their relation to modernism and participation. Now, we emphasise that development is always redevelopment. It always has to take into account context, in order to come up with policies, plans, interventions, strategies that might work.

## Further reading

Ferguson, J. (1994). The anti-politics machine: 'development', depoliticization, and bureaucratic power in Lesotho. Cambridge, UK: Cambridge University Press.

Scott, J.C. (1998). Seeing like a state. How certain schemes to improve the human condition have failed. New Haven, CN, USA: Yale University Press.

Jamali, H. (2013). The anxiety of development: megaprojects and the politics of place in Gwadar, Pakistan. Crossroads Asia Working Paper Series, 6.

Van der Ploeg, J.D., Renting, H., Brunori, G., Knickel, K., Mannion, J., Marsden, T., De Roest, K., Sevilla-Guzmán, E. and Ventura, F. (2000). Rural development: from practices and policies towards theory. Sociologia Ruralis, 40(4), 391-408.

## 2.3 Context and its importance – patterns of differentiation

It is one thing to say that context is important, that recipes for development, for policy in general, cannot simply be copied or imported, and it is another thing to define which context is important in which manner. '*Context*' is many things, and not everything can be relevant, can be considered when tailoring a policy to a time, place, community. 'Context' comes from linguistics, where it refers to those things outside the text that influence the interpretation of texts. Yet, as in linguistics, in policy and development, context is potentially unlimited: does the whole history of Spanish literature resonate in Garcia Lorca's poems? Does the Roman conquest of Belgium influence its current governance and development? In some ways yes, for both questions, but the whole point is to figure out in which ways. Otherwise crafting a policy would mean sinking in a morass, mapping out every possible aspect of every layer of context.

What about rural development? Which context can we consider relevant? We already filled in one piece: the history of governance itself can be considered an important context to study, the history of collectively binding decisions, the tools used, the actors included. We will develop a theoretical perspective to analyze governance evolutions below. Independent of this, if one does not intend to use such frame, we can distinguish very broadly types of context which will shape the development path, and the impact of development policies or plans.

One can usually find relevance in economic, political, legal contexts, but also in physical and cultural contexts. Each of these can be more or less relevant, and these different contexts influence each other. Political structure affects economic developments, in turn affecting the resources available for investment, which affects infrastructure development, in turn leading to economic effects. None of these contexts can be mapped exhaustively, and the same can be said about their interactions. This means that context mapping is always a matter of selection and interpretation. The observer, the scientists, community group, politician, business person, activist, always relies on interpretations of context to get an understanding of governance paths and development options. This is not a problem, it just points to the need for self-awareness, for reflexivity. Looking at these different contexts can be useful to structure the analysis, to guide the thinking.

There is usually an *economic context* to consider: a plan might assume resources that do not exist. It might be too expensive, rely on taxes that are not steady, it might have long term effects that weaken the economy. It might lead to overexploitation of resources that brings ecological disaster or economic collapse in the long term, or it might be so much focused on long term stability that short term economic incentives are forgotten. There is usually a *political context*: a certain policy might be political suicide for one party, might be watered down because it rests on a coalition of parties, or it might be accepted, then die on a shelf after a new government takes power. It can be used by the powers that be, or by administrations that de facto took over power from the politicians. One can usually look for a *legal context*: laws make policies possible, they can stop them, they can help in implementation. If local democracy is very strong, higher level development initiatives are more vulnerable to legal attacks from below, while in very centralized political systems, local initiatives might be quashed with new laws written in the center.

*Cultural context* can refer to the ways groups of people see themselves and the world, and the way this affects their mode of organization, their manners of decision-making. This too is potentially unlimited, and requires interpretation and selection. Groups might be aware of some cultural influence on their governance, but not of everything. Outside observers can play a useful role here, in analyzing how world views, rituals, values, stories, images, obsessions and fears, permeate governance. Awareness of cultural influences on governance can help to reform it, to see more openings for change, broaden the scope of options.

Physical context, or *material context*, can refer to everything that is not discursive, that is not a matter of concepts, stories and interpretations: the physical landscape, the weather, the material properties and aspect of trees, rocks, water, soil, the tangible influence of hard physical borders on development, the presence or absence of material infrastructure. If we believe that such physical context completely decides on paths of economic development, we can call ourselves physical determinists. We, personally, do not subscribe to this line of thought, but we do believe the influence of geography, of the material world, on the formation and implementation of policy is often underestimated. Often, plans, policies, development recipes, travel across the world, and often, one of the contexts most overlooked is the physical context. Rediscovering the importance of this context is often called the 'material turn' (in geography, in anthropology, sociology).

The governance process itself should be considered an important context in studying the evolution of governance: what happens in governance, refers to previous decisions in governance, and to decisions elsewhere. We will refine this idea later.

Another way to categorise context, one useful for the analysis of governance and rural development options, is to look at sorts of differentiation. Societies are always differentiated, from the smallest scale to the highest level, they are not homogeneous. Groups always exist, social groups, professional groups, ethnic groups, clans, etc. Following social systems theory and world systems theory, we distinguish between functional, organisational and segmentary differentiation. Usually, all three can be found in a community, and getting an understanding of these forms of differentiation can be helpful in figuring out what 'development' can mean in a community, and how it could be pursued.

*Functional differentiation* refers to the categories of law, politics, economy already mentioned, and one can add here science, religion, education. Over time, in many societies, a process of specialisation took place, in which people could specialise in legal, political, etc. professions, but also, more fundamentally, in which specialized forms of communication, of thought and action developed. A doctor can analyse a patient and understand the ailment, so he participates in scientific thinking, and he can think how much to charge for it, which is economic thinking. Each form of thinking can be seen as a functional domain, marked by its own logic: economic thinking boils down to profit and loss, political thinking to calculations of power, scientific thinking to learning, being right and wrong. Functional domains are important contexts for governance, and understanding governance can require an understanding of the influence and specific entanglements of these ways of thinking. As said, this can mean the presence and importance of people clearly associated with law, or politics, or science, but it can also refer to the importance of these perspectives for people not so clearly specialised or labelled.

If the legal system is weakly developed, this means that it does not follow its own logic, and that its decisions are taken somewhere else, often by politics, but this could also be economics or science, religion maybe. If legal reasoning is not allowed to be followed, it means that another form of reasoning took over somewhere. One can apply this to all the functional systems. Governance, the taking of collectively binding decisions, can be placed now in the domain of politics, it is politics. But different functional domains contribute to it in unique ways, different per community. The same plan will have different effects in places where the relations between law, politics, economy, science are different; and they are always different. If a specific discipline is not very developed in a community, it will not play a significant role in governance; if it is developed in academia, but not deemed relevant by politics, it will have little influence on governance; if specialists in the discipline are important in the administration, and the administration is important in carrying out development policies, the actual influence of its perspective, of its knowledge will still depend on legal, economic, political factors later on.

As important context, then, it is best to refer to the relations between the functional domains.

*Organisational differentiation* has to be understood as well. Governance is not only a matter of the large functional domains, as perspectives on reality, as different logics. And it is not simply a matter of individuals wanting or doing something. The 'actors' around the table in governance processes are usually not individuals but organizations: political parties, governmental organizations, non-governmental organizations, community associations, economic interest groups. A business is also an organization, and a farmer also stands for a farm as an (economic) organization. Just as the functional domains, organizations reproduce themselves following a specific logic. Each organization has a distinct identity, an image of self and the world, of identity and goals, that guides the internal decision-making, and the possible participation in governance. The world is in other words also a puzzle of organizations following their own logic of reproduction, developing their own perspective on things, and defending their own turf. This applies not only to business organizations; the same applies to all types.

How is this an important context to governance and rural development? Because, as said, even very inclusive, participatory forms of governance, rely on representation, and the form of representation that is often most important is representation of an organization. Proposals that go against the perceived interests or identity of organizations around the table will be met with fierce resistance, and this is magnified by the difference in perspective that is cultivated within organizations. A public good, or a common cause, will always be perceived through a variety of lenses, some lenses pertaining to functional domains (what does this mean legally?), some to organizations (is this affecting our bottom line? What does this mean for the relation with the other ministry?).

If we want to articulate a vision for the future of a rural community, as a rural development effort, such vision, in a democratic polity, is expected to pursue a common good, is expected to produce a future which is good for the community. But, as stated above, 'the' community is always fractured, divided, segmented. Even without referring to power struggles, double agendas, corruption, etc. (see below), a common good is never unambiguous, just as win-win situations for all actors are rarely easy to achieve. Communities are functionally differentiated and organizationally differentiated. Political pleas for a unity vision will meet resistance from other political factions with a different idea of unity, by legal reasoning, by scientific obstacles, economic interests. The map of organizations around the table of governance, their relations with similar and dissimilar organizations (e.g. government-business relations, but also business-

**Example 2.1. Functional, hierarchical and segmentary forms of differentiation in Uzbekistan.**

Uzbekistan is a region of world society that is – since its independence in 1991 – undergoing tremendous socio-economic transformation processes which nurture, while at the same time being further fostered by, the coexistence of varying forms of structural differentiation. These range from (earlier) forms of differentiation along lines of age, sex, ethnicity/region of origin, to social stratification by means of political and economic hierarchies, overlapping with center/periphery-differentiations, to functional differentiation. The existing forms of functional differentiation nevertheless appear to be continuously challenged. Despite ongoing attempts to develop into a market economy, spontaneous interpenetration by the state and of function systems such as the market, education, agriculture as well as judiciary is widely observable. As such, function systems are closely interlinked and autopoietical closure is hardly given. The ongoing socio-economic processes of change leave this region of world society in a situation characterized by institutional opaqueness and fragility. Formerly formal regulatory frameworks have partly been informalised, partly continue to be in place, while at the same time informal but widely followed institutions are partly formalized, partly remain in the sphere of informality but gain importance in everyday livelihood provision. What is left are varying formal/informal configurations, exemplifying that the formal/informal distinction as originally introduced by Douglas North and others in some regions of world society is only of value for the purpose of analytic distinction. In practice institutional configurations are followed that are neither 'formal' nor 'informal', but often a combination of both. In consequence, the observable coexistence of varying forms of differentiation (ranging from social fragmentation and stratification to (mostly eroding) forms of functional differentiation) little reduces complexity. Instead the ongoing change processes seem to create a fertile ground for the further development of these varying forms of differentiation and, despite moderate forms of functional differentiation, diversity and with this diversity also complexity increases.

**Further reading**

Hornidge, A.-K., Van Assche, K. and Shtaltovna, A. (2015). Uzbekistan – a region of world society (?) Variants of differentiation in agricultural resources governance. Soziale Systeme (Special Issue edited by Rudolf Stichweh).

Van Assche, K., Shtaltovna, A. and Hornidge, A.-K. (2013). Visible and invisible informalities and institutional transformation. Lessons from transition countries: Georgia, Romania, Uzbekistan. In: Hayoz, N. and Giordano, C. (eds.), Informality in Eastern Europe. Frankfurt< Germany: Peter Lang, pp. 89-118.

business relations) will affect the thought and actions of the players around the table of governance, their willingness to subscribe to a common good or at least to a development policy that proclaims it.

Further complications stem from a third form of differentiation: *segmentary differentiation*. This is probably the most basic form of differentiation, to be found where the others are weakly developed. But it can also persist where the others exist. Segmentary differentiation refers to the differentiation of society in groups of belonging; ethnic groups, clans, extended families, subcultures. Sometimes (e.g. clans), a segmentary group can also be an organization, and its reasoning can become primarily economic, or political (if they're trying to gain power, or get rich, or both). We said that governance is influenced by culture, and here segmentary differentiation comes in. If we see governance as participation in decision-making of government and non-government actors, then it become easier to understand how segmentary differentiation can influence governance. It can be very difficult, if not impossible, to discern precisely how an actor thinks, how she participates in governance, how actors relate in the process, because they are framed by and respond to all forms of differentiation. This means that one position taken, one tactic, or a larger strategy, can be largely inspired by economic thinking, but not by the organization one is supposed to represent, and that this disconnect has something to do with a clan network one adheres to. These combinations of identities, of allegiances, of ways of thinking is complex and shifting per actor, and even more complex if one tries to map a process of governance.

As with the other contexts, this is not necessarily a problem. One does not need a complete map of differentiation in a community to get an understanding of its governance evolution. But the concepts of segmentary, organizational and functional differentiation can help to guide the analysis of a process. The forms of differentiation can thus be seen as an important context to take into account. If businesses are behind several supposed government actors or supposed community activists, one can look for an economic logic in their participation in governance. If one clan de facto has political control over one community, this will hamper the inclusion of non-members in governance, and it could mean that inclusion remains a paper reality. The different forms of differentiation also affect each other: if clan belonging is the main form of differentiation, it will be difficult to develop anything resembling the 'rule of law' (functional differentiation, law doing its job), and it will difficult also for organizations to follow their own logic (business perspectives will be abandoned if they conflict with clan interests or clan identity). Organizational and functional differentiation imply each other to a certain extent: it becomes more difficult for organizations to pursue their goals when function systems are weakly developed. And a primacy of segmentary differentiation undermines both functional and organizational differentiation in the long run. Understanding these forms of differentiation in a given society is thus not only context mapping, but also useful in identifying mechanisms of change, and possible roadblocks.

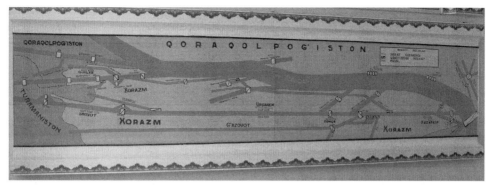

Figure 2.3. Pride in public works. The main irrigation canals in Karakalpakstan, Uzbekistan, on display as a work of art in the water and irrigation department of the provincial government of Khorezm, Uzbekistan. Photo: Anna-Katharina Hornidge. © ZEF/University of Bonn, Germany.

Where the previous section emphasized the problems of forgetting the past and forgetting context in general, in this section we provided a few simple ways to look at context that might be relevant for understanding governance and development. The type of context mapping one engages in, ideally depends on the goal of the exercise, the time and resources available. In a one day workshop on rural development, a participatory exercise, one can rely on first sketches produced in the group, on research carried out beforehand, on an existing self-study of the community.

The emphasis on context, on context-sensitivity, on unique governance paths and tailor made development plans, does not mean that everything is different, that every community is incomparable, and that nothing can be learned from other times and places. Certainly, this, too is a very general statement, and a big topic, which will be further explored in this book. In the following section, we provide a first analysis, in terms of similarity and dissimilarity of rural areas. We speak of *convergence* and *divergence*. Convergence and divergence can be studied in communities, their issues, but also in the development approaches taken.

## Further reading

Lister, S. (2009). Changing the rules? State-building and local government in Afghanistan. Journal of Development Studies, 45(6), 990-1009.

Luhmann, N. (1995). Social systems. Stanford, CA, USA: Stanford University Press.

Rose, G. (1997). Situating knowledges: positionality, reflexivities and other tactics. Progress in Human Geography, 21(3), 305-320.

Van Assche, K. (2007). Planning as/and/in context. Towards a new analysis of interactive planning. METU JFA, 27(1), 110-119.

> **Example 2.2. Coffee heritage in Ethiopia and the revival of pasts for development (with thanks to Catherine Reynolds).**
>
> The Environment and Coffee Forest Forum (ECFF), an Ethiopian NGO, coordinates an international 'Participatory Forest Management' project aimed at preserving cultural and ecological heritage on a local and global scale. The project began by exploring ecological and social systems that were working well, even if in a threatened and fragmented manner, and build on them.
>
> Montane rainforests in SouthWestern Ethiopia harbor an abundance of resources that have long been integrated into local strategies for maintaining livelihoods: spices, honey, timber and wild coffee, among others. Ethiopia's montane rainforest is also of global significance as a unique habit for wild coffee arabica, which has been used to breed coffee cultivars the world over. Unfortunately, only about 2.5% of original montane rainforest coverage remains intact (25,000 km).
>
> Recognizing not only the forest's cultural value on multiple scales, but also the important ecosystem services provided by it, including erosion control and regulation of water flows, ECFF set out to preserve what forest remains and reforest additional areas. ECFF's main strategy has been to encourage the harvesting, certification and marketing of forest grown coffee, both locally and internationally, as well as to etablish gene banks for conservation of and easier access to coffee varieties. The project evolved out of a long-standing cultural affinity to the forest and builds on local knowledge of harvesting, preparing and marketing coffee. By scaling up sustainable cultivation of coffee and facilitating international certification, this project has helped to expand economic opportunities for growers – for years to come. Projects aiming at the conservation of forest and genetic resources have the best hope of longevity if integrated into existing local and global systems.

## 2.4 Convergence and divergence in rural issues and solutions

If we understand development efforts as in essence governance, and if we understand governance best by looking at paths of governance, it becomes interesting to compare *governance paths* of various communities, small and large, cities, villages, countries. One very general observation one can make is that there is convergence and divergence between governance paths. This can be observed over time, and everywhere, at every scale. Units at a comparable scale, of a comparable nature (say municipalities in one country, or in several countries) become over time more and less different from each other, and their governance, which tools are used, which rules, procedures, who is included/excluded, which knowledge is used, in all these aspects they become sometimes more similar, sometimes less similar. Two villages can become closer to each other, then more dissimilar, then closer again, in a different respect.

Figure 2.4. Coffee production in Ethiopia. Photo: Till Stellmacher. © ZEF/University of Bonn, Germany.

**Further reading**

Kelboro, G., Stellmacher, T. and Hoffmann, V. (2013). 'Conservationists' and 'local people' in biodiversity conservation: the case of Nech Sar National Park, Ethiopia. Ethiopian Journal of Social Sciences and Humanities, 9(1), 29-55.

Because this is a very general observation, the reasons can be manifold. What was said about context just above should not be forgotten. The different contexts just mentioned can shape the way communities learn or not learn from each other, copy or rather try to be different, to distinguish themselves, in substance or in procedures of governance. If one is interested in understanding rural development, one can focus on context mapping of one entity, or one can start with looking at patterns of *convergence* and *divergence* of several communities, to get a larger picture, or to get a deeper understanding of one community, around which you see a group of similar/dissimilar places.

Becoming similar can have many reasons. We list below a number of driving forces, each of which will recur several times later in the book. The mechanism of change however can also be of different natures: simply copying, simply distinguishing (becoming different), social learning (a communal learning process), learning of a few influential actors, following steps of small incentives that come from larger driving forces (e.g. changing forms of capitalism), with reflection or without reflection. Change can come by design, or by accident, or by following the current, and change creates similarity or dissimilarity with others, convergence and divergence. The presence of the others can be important (what and who do we like/dislike, what do we want to learn/achieve) and it can be not so relevant (we happen to follow a path, are not aware others are on a similar path). More about this later.

Regarding the driving forces of convergence and divergence of governance paths, we want to distinguish:
- economic models and ideologies;
- political and legal models;
- colonialist legacies;
- migrations/flows/mobilities;
- political shifts;
- resources/material differences.

This list can be written in a few different ways, and, as with other things presented above, it can be used in a few different ways. One can focus on one driving force in one case, one can quickly sketch a series of possible driving forces, then zoom in on one or two, or one can link more on one context of governance and processes of becoming similar/dissimilar to others. In other words: this list, too, is a tool that can structure your analysis of a particular case, a tool that can be used in a few ways and combined with other tools.

*Economic models* and *ideologies* are often tied to political and legal models, but not necessarily. One can focus on 'economic development' in a community and pretend this is a technocratic effort, that there are no links to politics and law. Of course, this is a fiction, but it is a fiction that is prevalent, in the development studies world and in many communities. One can also see the economy as the center of social life, with politics and law and the rest following the demands of the economy. Then, there is the type of economy one is proposing: 'capitalism' is not enough for an answer; there are many varieties, and each assumes a different embedding of markets in society, or, to refer back, a different pattern of differentiation of law, politics, economy and science. Economic models thus are always tied in a way to *political* and *legal models*, but communities are not always aware of this. Development efforts are not always linked to politics and law, while they should. 'Development' cannot take place in isolation, even if the proclaimed goal is only economic development.

The chosen or inherited economic ideology, the form of market (or non-market) economy one is dealing with, will affect the way a community learns from others, the way it interacts with others, the way it changes, becomes more or less similar to others. In the former USSR, communist political ideology had a strong idea on a way to organize markets (based on no private property and on collective efforts) and the spread of the political ideology also brought other places in the orbit of their economic ideology; Cuba became more similar to the USSR after it embraced communist market principles. In the other direction, trade policies of large countries can push others to become more similar, or their economic ideology can be admired and copied in other places. What is seen as a success breeds emulation, and if one shares already certain traits of ideology, a situation elsewhere will more easily be seen as a success, studied, and copied elsewhere. As we know already, the result of a copying effort will produce something different than the original, but we can likely still speak of convergence in governance. Cities can influence each other, as do villages, larger rural areas, or whole countries.

In the case of rural economies, they can become more similar to others more easily if there is a strong focus on one economic activity, on one land use. That makes the community more vulnerable to changes elsewhere affecting that land use; particularly, in globalized, interconnected markets, in a very free form of capitalism, prices of one commodity can affect the economy of many communities focusing on that commodity crop. If there's nothing else, these communities will be less resilient and they will tend to become more and more similar to others, in appearance and likely in governance: once a path of specialization in one crop is chosen, it is likely that this will be optimised, more and more of the same, and more similar to others. If prices crash, the alternatives envisioned then, will likely be another cash crop, so different yet the same.

These introductory examples already show that political and legal models are always entwined with economic models. Sometimes the main driver of convergence/divergence is economic ideology, sometimes it is rather political or legal. Sometimes (as with the USSR) cause and effect are hard to distinguish: did economic ideology come with political ideology, the other way around, or should one speak of one package? In many practical analyses, it does not matter much; rather, one needs a starting point of analysis, to grasp governance evolution, and this starting point, e.g. economic ideology, can then reveal its linkages with political, legal models. In the next section, we discuss in detail five models of democracy, theoretical models with real world following. Development is governance is politics, so they deserve attention. Here, we simply make the point that the form of political and legal organization one chooses, the practical organization and the mental model of an ideal organization (the ideology) is important for the patterns of learning, copying, distinguishing with other communities, for becoming dis/similar.

If the politics of your community is different from the neighbors, you are less likely to learn from their solutions. Or, you can be inclined to pick a small part of their solution, but disregard the connections with their politics. One can speak then of *technocratic reduction*: a solution is copied and presented as a purely technical thing, disconnected from political and legal assumptions. If you admire the neighbors, you might be inclined to learn more, maybe even to copy without much thinking what you consider a success. This approach, too, can lead to blindness, to overlooking weaknesses in the neighbor's approach, or to overlooking the way their success is rooted in local conditions and histories, or even to overlooking that their success is not really a success. The measuring and defining of success in governance and development is always framed by ideology, by what is liked or disliked, and what one thinks one knows already.

*Colonialist legacies* also shape the convergence and divergence of governance. Colonialism is considered by some theorists a largely homogenizing enterprise, making the rest the same as the west. This, we believe, is not entirely the case, as the forms and models of colonialism were quite different per country and period. The idea of the colony, its use, its planning, the relation with locals and local elites, the attention to education and science in the colonies, but also in the colonization process, differed greatly. The social, economic and political effects of colonization also differed greatly, in the colonies and in the colonizing countries. Some colonizers became more or less absorbed by local cultures or elites, others merged into something new, others remained distant and saw the colony purely in extractive terms.

This difference is important because it also created huge differences in the post-colonial era, and in the convergence and divergence of governance there. One has to think here

Figure 2.5. Ancient windmills in Nashtifan, Khorassan province, Iran. Photo: Shahnaz Nadjmabadi. © Institute of Ethnology, University of Tübingen, Germany.

Rural development

of convergence/divergence between former colonizer and colony, and between several former colonies. In general, one will see more divergence after independence, in the post-colonial period, but still many similarities can be observed. The reasons can be manifold, but similarities in governance between former colonizer and former colony are often related to the role of local/regional elites. Usually, the current elites still have something to do with the former non-white cadres, the groups more participating in colonial rule, more educated, more familiar with the functioning of the state. Often, the nation-state itself was a colonial imposition, but after independence of this colonial construct, those who were most familiar with it were more likely to take it over, to make it work, to use it for their benefit or the collective benefit. If a collective benefit was strived for, if the state did not become an extractive machine for a small group, the way this was pursued showed many marks of Western, in this case colonial approaches, often tied to the version of state and development espoused by the former overlords.

In analyzing convergence and divergence of governance paths through the lens of colonialist legacies, one has to be careful however. We come back to this theme as well, but can say here that some patterns of convergence are not simply colonialist: the colonizers themselves were often following larger patterns of change, e.g. broader ideologies of modernism that permeated much of the Western world, and much of the rest too. In some cases, this modernism in public administration and planning was clearly imposed on the colony and seen in the colony as such, associated during that time and later as a colonial ideology itself, but for other cases, this is not so clear. Indeed, colonizing powers were often, at some stage, embracing a modernist ideology for development of the colony – not only of itself-and one could look at it as a tool of colonization, but on the other hand, one can also say that both colonizer and colonist were in the grip of the same ideology, with harmful effects for both. The more the colonizer saw the colony as part of itself (not simply extraction), the more similar the effects of this modernism could become.

After independence, patterns of convergence with the former colonizers can similarly be ascribed in some cases to broader patterns of change, to policy fashions, development fashions, to the influence of international organizations on both former colonizer and colony. Several of the development approaches we will discuss later in this book are applied in various parts of the world, poor and rich countries, colonizers and colonies. Also the former colonizers have to deal with rural development issues, and use ideas and mixes of ideas coming from different times and places. One could analyse every case of convergence of governance as a negative legacy of colonialism, as internalized colonization. We believe this does not explain much. It all depends. In general, yes, it seems beneficial in former colonies to reflect on the legacies, on patterns of convergence and divergence in governance, but not every similarity with the former rulers is a colonialist legacy, not every colonialist legacy has to be automatically rejected, and not every real preference or desire in former colonies can be dismissed as unreliable because of being distorted by internalized colonialist concepts. If we take that angle, it becomes very hard to think of reinventing governance in former colonies, to think of development in general. (We dwell more in detail on this in the section on post-development thinking).

Certainly, there is not only convergence as a result of colonization. After independence, divergence can be observed. This seems natural, as a form of natural drift in evolution, as colonies decide more on their own fate, take their own decisions in different directions. Sometimes, there is a negative correlation with former rulers, in the sense that a course was taken as different as possible from their systems of governance. Yet, in most cases, the idea of a nation-state was not abandoned, and the new regime needed to be a regime of a nation-state. It needed some ideology, some expertise, forms of organization, etc. that could run a nation-state. Sometimes, a really localized alternative came up, but often (this took place mostly in the 20$^{th}$ century) the different ideology was also imported, from Western countries with their own colonialist histories or ambitions. Most notably, there was communism, imported by many former colonies as an alternative to (negatively experienced) market economies. One should not forget democracy: most former colonies were not fully included in the decision-making of supposedly democratic overlords, and once independent, the alternative was not usually an alternative to democracy but a fuller realization of democracy, at home.

The previous paragraphs already pointed at the importance of *migrations, flows, mobilities* to understand patterns of divergence and convergence in governance. Colonization itself is a form of mobility, also the spread of ideology, of goods that inspire desire and accumulation and similarity. We use the word mobilities here, taken from geographers. Mobilities, again, is a general term designed to look for general, broad patterns of relations. Mobilities refer to movement, of people, of things, goods, of ideas and the larger narratives and ideologies they are embedded in. The word is useful to draw attention to the linkages between moving things, people, and ideas. For understanding convergence and divergence in governance paths, this is useful.

People moving have an influence on the place they end up. A mass migration might lead to a political shift, to a new state even. A slower migration of many people can change the political climate of the new country, the new community. The migrants can bring old identities, values, preferences, but even when they change, become integrated, they do change the receiving community. New arrivals can become the most zealous defenders of the ideology of the new country, especially if they didn't like much what happened at home (quite likely, as they moved away). Or they can embrace the ideology of the new country, but give it a new twist, reinterpret it. They cannot openly embrace a grand ideology, but slowly transform governance by participation at the local scale. Or they can slowly transform it because political entrepreneurs see a new market there, new people with new preferences as potential voters, so a new program to write for them.

**Example 2.3. Mobility as a factor in development – the case of Uzbekistan.**

The break-up of the Soviet Union has led to a variety of mobilities in Central Asian states. These emerge out of or have contributed to the growth of networks of informal institutions. The existence of informal institutions, which shape and are shaped by formal institutions, can be seen as a legacy of the Soviet era across many successor states (convergence). This, in turn, is due to the fact that the dissolution of the Soviet Union caused a vacuum of economic opportunities and led to oppressive forms of governance. Successor state governments are eager to extract financial/material benefit from what limited economic activity exists. Because they lack the infrastructure for effective taxation, they exert inordinate control. This, along with the fact that formal work migration between successor states of the Soviet Union is heavily restricted (with residency permits hard to obtain), contributes to making the mobility taking place in the former USSR difficult to track. It has been called 'hidden' mobility.

Mobility here refers not only to spatial mobility (moving from one place to another), but also to social mobility (an increase or decrease in social standing) and knowledge mobility (crossing of epistemic boundaries). In Uzbekistan, for example, decreased opportunities for social mobility following the disappearance of Soviet structures for learning and career advancement (knowledge mobility) have led to increased physical mobility. Former employees of communal farms (*kolkhoz*) have been driven to seek economic opportunity abroad, in Russia, Kazakhstan, the Ukraine, or even China, usually as seasonal laborers. This is a type of spatial mobility that fails to lead to upward social mobility – a phenomenon referred to as the 'mobility trap'. Given the disappointing prospects of physical mobility in this context, other agriculturalists in Uzbekistan today choose to attempt social mobility in a fixed place. They face a significant obstacle to mobility in the form of a state plan that dictates how much of which crops (foremost cotton) is to be grown, and regulates farm incomes and expenses to the extent that farmers have no access to their earnings. Circumventing these barriers, however, a number of farmers grow other crops (e.g. rice) for sale in informal networks. This is enabled by restricting the visibility of such endeavors to at most a handful of state officials who can be trusted or inspired to cooperate.

Thus, mobility in Uzbekistan (in many ways representative of other former Soviet states) is influenced by existing economic and political models, as well as access to resources (including personal relationships), while having the potential to affect distribution of resources (knowledge, power and material wealth) and create new social and physical boundaries. Hence, mobilities in Uzbekistan have a strong effect on governance paths. Successful development strategies will take into account all the mobilities and related political configurations that exist in Uzbekistan. Many attempts at development also define development goals in part in terms of enhancing or restoring mobility.

**Further reading**

Urry, J. (2007). Mobilities. Cambridge, UK: Polity Press.

Van Assche, K. and Hornidge, A.-K. (2014). Hidden mobilities in post-Soviet spaces. Boundaries, scales, identities and informal routes to livelihood. Crossroads Asia Working Paper Series, 20.

People bring goods, people bring ideas. But also good can bring ideas and people. Ancient trade routes have not only moved goods across great distances, but also science, religion, philosophy, forms of political organization (based on moving ideas). Trade could establish links used by larger groups to move around, not just because of the physical connection, but also because of the knowledge of other places, their riches, but also the knowledge of other cultures and political cultures (which might be attractive to settle in, or to overthrow). Buddhism and Greek philosophy, but also sculpture moved along the ancient silk roads, from Europe to China and northern India. Methods of warfare traveled the same road. Nomadic groups traveled, became settled, while settled groups became nomadic or simply moved somewhere else. New ethnic identities were created in the process: the 'we' that moved become different, integrating new people, new ideas, and new material practices.

Sometimes it starts with goods, sometimes with people, or with ideas, but these different flows of things, these different mobilities, are usually connected: if people move, they bring their ideas and goods, or preference for certain goods. If ideas move, people might follow, or move out, and people will change, alter material practices. Communist ideology brought very different material practices, different flows of goods and people, inside the USSR, but it also sparked changes in mobilities elsewhere in the world (see above, on communism in former colonies).

Both the people moving and the receiving community will change in and by mobilities. Many new goods can also bring new material practices, new social identities and new forms of governance. Mobilities can be slow and fast. They can be very visible (a new party starts, a new political ideology dominates governance, a new region becomes prominent because of suddenly valuable goods) or not so visible. They can be slow or fast, restricted to a small spatial scale or encompassing the globe.

Mobilities can be tied to *political shifts*. Political shifts in a community, as fast and dramatic changes in governance, can be brought about by them, by ideas, things and people moving, and the connections between these flows. Political shifts are another important driver of convergence/divergence in governance. Shifts in one path can occur, making it suddenly different from another community which seemed to be traveling along the same road. These shifts can be induced by mobilities, but also by the internal accumulation of small changes, leading to a tipping point. The term comes from ecology, where, e.g. a pond can suddenly change its ecology when accumulated nutrients suddenly have a strong effect. It refers to a sudden and dramatic change resulting from many small changes, often unobserved. A social democracy can subsidize many social services, at some point it cannot be afforded, services stop, taxes reach a certain level, and the community moves into a different state, with different actors involved in governance, believing in different ideologies, a different idea of the common good, a new vision of 'development'.

Figure 2.6. Central Asia reveals very beautifully how infrastructures structure mobilities and drive development. The region was very rarely one of contiguous centralized states aiming to develop their whole territories, but rather a network of roads and routes connecting cities, agricultural areas, nomads, and faraway markets. Flows of people, goods and ideas entwined, as in the famous example of the Silk Road bringing silk to Europe, Buddhism to China and the Mogul dynasty to India. Silk, Buddhism, and the dynasty all changed on the road. Photo: Katja Mielke. © ZEF/University of Bonn, Germany.

Thus, political shifts can be externally and internally induced. Communities can sometimes see it coming, sometimes not. In general, communities cannot be completely aware of the mechanisms of its own governance. It is never entirely transparent to itself, so that also means that not all political shifts are expected. Even in the case of a clear tipping point, however, there can still a combination of design and contingency: it can be predicted by some, engineered by some, to pursue their interests or because they believe it is good for the community. Political shifts are not always to be interpreted as negative, as a crises, a dramatic move from one ideology to another one; it can also be that the community itself slowly changed, and suddenly realizes that it does not fit its own governance system anymore, that its current policies do not fit the changed identity anymore. It can e.g. realize that it does not want the countryside anymore that developed under the regime of an old identity which it rejects now. Even when there is no real change in identity, some desires can change in a community, or the balance of power between certain factions wanting different things, leading to shift which might bring a new stable state. In the most prosaic case, a community can simply be bored, tired of leadership, of a form of governance, and, without reflecting much on its benefits, reject it, in favor of something new, fresh, fashionable. That, too, is possible, and can create new differences with the governance paths of surrounding communities (hence, their interactions, and possible collaborative development policies).

Finally, another source of convergence and divergence we want to highlight here, is the *material world*: differences in material conditions, in resources. Elements of the natural world can become resources in a given community, in a given economy and a given culture. Gold has no value unless communities assign value to it; trees are not a resource unless communities use trees, so it acquires a value. Once something becomes a resource, is seen as valuable, it starts to circulate in communities and between communities in a different way. If other communities also assign a similar value to the same thing, a market is born, which can be more or less open, affecting again the circulation of the thing in question. What happens next, and becomes very relevant for governance, is how much people want the thing and how scarce it is. Next, if scarcity is local scarcity or scarcity somewhere else. If the whole world wants something, and it is scarce (say, oil), this resource, if abundant, clearly creates opportunities in the places where it is abundant. It can create wealth, the desire to accumulate wealth, to protect it, the desire to make governance more local, to reduce influence of other levels (say, federal) on decision-making and redistribution of revenues. It can create actors (e.g. oil companies) that want to influence and have means to influence local politics, and it can invite envy from less fortunate places, which again can translate into politics, tensions, war, and changing governance in tough times.

The resource does not cause these changes in simple way: as said, things become a resource because people assign value to them, and the governance effects of oil or gold depend on economic and political systems at several scales. When gas was found in northern Alberta in the 19th century, Ottawa (the federal government) decided not to pursue its development since too far from anything, so the effects locally were virtually nothing. Only the memory of possible value in the future was kept alive, and this memory did have a strong impact in recent times.

Resource abundance and scarcity, leading to resource competition, thus affect governance paths, as well as patterns of convergence and divergence. A whole region, originally more diversified, can become organized around one resource economy, creating a web of interdependencies in economic but also in governance terms; a clear convergence. If only one place has the resource, depending on the relations between local and regional government, it could also change the whole region (preserving a diversified economy; redistributing and reinvesting resources in this), or, if localism is very strong, it could affect only the local economy, and local governance, in term making this quite different form the surrounding communities. We come back to our remark on resilience and mono-functional land use, and would argue that any community focusing on one resource, takes a substantial risk in the long term. We would further argue that such situation also necessitates a deeper reflection on the long term than in other places, a reflection on a future post that resource, and on reinvestment to make such future more likely.

Besides those elements of the material world that become resources, there are other effects of the material on governance, as mentioned before. The opposite of resources could be obstacles: elements of nature which hinder the community in its development. A village up north might be abandoned after a while because the peat bogs could not be reclaimed, a village on the fringe of the desert might be abandoned because the sand dunes are blown in the wrong direction; a hamlet in old Europe always struggled, was always poorer and more poorly governed than it neighbors because its fields were full of rocks exuding the wrong kind of minerals. Also here, we do not want to suggest material determinism: the same obstacles might be dealt with differently in different communities, and some ingenuous places might even turn the obstacle into a resource. Just as resources, obstacles only become this in a community, which wants certain things, is organized in a certain manner. The same nasty rocks are no obstacle in a village in Southern Europe, where the land would be used for grazing goats.

More generally, the landscape and climate are material conditions that can affect governance. Communities can change landscapes and even climate, as we know now, but landscape and climate also shape communities. It is not always easy to discern the full extent of this. Landscapes can be obstacles and resources in an obvious sense, they can be analyzed also as material systems, of elements and relations, that as a whole enable a certain type of economy and community. Changing some elements might create difficulties for the whole community. Sometimes a resource does not need the landscape context to be mined, to have a value, to be used, sometimes it does; sometimes it does not need a certain organization of the community to support it, sometimes it does. So, one can say that in some cases the landscape as whole should be considered a resource, in other cases the resource is part of the landscape but requires that material context, and in yet others it is found in a landscape but does not need links with it to be extracted.

Landscapes can be altered on purpose, to pursue economic value, to do things that are otherwise seen as important in a community. And it can change as a series of unintended consequences of other decisions and actions. People produce garbage, and that needs a place; they pollute water, and that moves around; they cut trees, but don't realize the effects on neighboring lands. The sum of all these changes can be an ecological tipping point, maybe even followed by a tipping point in governance, but even when this is not the case, it can affect the economy and the community at large. Changed material conditions, altered landscapes, can scare tourists away, can make the production of certain things difficult, affect the quality of others, can scare away residents, looking for a better quality of life elsewhere; if this happens for a while, consequences in governance will become visible.

The same material conditions can thus be seen as positive in one place, negative in another place, and even in places where they are seen as positive, the governance effects will differ. Yet, similarities in material conditions, in resources, obstacles, landscapes and climate, deserve close scrutiny when analyzing governance paths and development options. Convergence can be observed under material similarities; sometimes this will be directly inspired by the material conditions (cold places do ask for similar things in governance), sometimes by similar resources found there (oil extraction has similarities across the world) and sometimes one can speak of a broader learning process, in which communities under similar material conditions observe not only the ways to survive under these conditions, but also to make money off a place or resource, and how to organize themselves to do this. Rural development we can consider as more linked to material conditions than urban development, so this aspect of governance deserves special attention.

Summarizing some of the points in this section, we can say that looking at patterns of divergence and convergence between governance paths of different communities can be helpful to understand a specific community, in its context, but also to see larger patterns of governance, at larger scales. Development efforts can rarely be undertaken

Figure 2.7. Attabad Lake, Pakistan – formed in consequence of a landslide blocking parts of the Karakorum Highway through Hunza Valley. Physical landscapes can create path dependencies in development. By scarcity or abundance of resources or, as here, by allowing and suddenly disallowing for certain infrastructure combinations. Photo: Andreas Benz. © Andreas Benz, ZELF/Freie University of Berlin, Germany.

in isolation, so obtaining an understanding of several scales can be useful to figure out which approaches might work in a given place. The study of convergence and divergence can further be useful in understanding the drivers of change in community, what works to push them in this or that direction, to become more similar or dissimilar to another one. Part of the pattern is design (learning), part is accidental, and there is the gradual accumulation of small actions, and the floating on big currents, that can bring places closer together or not. If a local effort has to fit larger scale efforts, convergence becomes essential to understand: what kind of convergences between communities are required to make a regional development policy work? Some forms of convergence, as in uniformity and reliance one resource, are less desirable, others, like broad convergence on ideology, on principles of good governance and sustainability, are very useful in whatever development vision one wants to entertain.

We showed that mobilities of people, things and goods affect patterns of convergence and divergence in governance, that these patterns are also affected by changes in political, legal and economic systems, dramatic politic shifts, colonial legacies, material conditions. Each of those drivers of convergence and divergence deserves more study. The examples given above already indicate that they interact; mobilities can bring political shifts, political changes can bring different economic practices, affecting material conditions, etc. Each of them separately can create new divergences and convergences with other communities; sometimes such one factor can be clearly pointed at as the main driver, sometimes it is more the interaction between several factors.

We do need to deepen this analysis, and this can be done by looking more closely at governance, and distinguishing models of governance and models of development. We already distinguished drivers of divergence and convergence, but need more insight in the fine mechanics; we need to understand better how and why communities construct visions of a good future, and how they learn in this from other communities. We posit here that one way to do this is to look at different models of the good community, and good development that were influential, that pushed communities in a certain direction, and made certain transformations more likely than others.

Models in each case are conceptual structures, which can affect reality, become performative, if they are embraced in actual governance. Different forms of democracy, marked by different relations between law, politics, economy, and science, will respond differently to their environment. They will learn differently, distinguish themselves differently, use expertise differently, and grasping this can help in explaining patterns of convergence and divergence in governance. Categorizing sorts of democracies can help in finding out how and why certain communities embrace certain development models and what effects these models might have. Later in the book, we will zoom in on rural development approaches, where we take the insights of general governance analysis and general analysis of development approaches with us.

## Further reading

Ismailbekova, A. (2013). Migration and patrilineal descent: the effects of spatial male mobility on social female mobility in rural Kyrgyzstan. Crossroads Asia Working Paper Series, 12.

Jung, L.S. (1988). Feminism and spatiality: ethics and the recovery of a hidden dimension. Journal of Feminist Studies in Religion, 4(1), 55-71.

Massey, D. (1994). Space, place and gender. Cambridge, UK: Polity Press.

Mielke, K. and Hornidge, A.-K. (2014). Crossroads studies: from spatial containers to interactions in differentiated spatialities. Crossroads Asia Working Paper Series, 15.

Sheppard, E. (2002). The spaces and times of globalization: place, scale, networks, and positionality. Economic Geography, 78(3), 307-330.

Urry, J. (2007). Mobilities. Cambridge: Polity Press.

Van Assche, K. and Hornidge, A.-K. (2014). Hidden mobilities in post-Soviet spaces. Boundaries, scales, identities and informal routes to livelihood. Crossroads Asia Working Paper Series, 20.

Van Assche, K., Beunen, R. and Duineveld, M. (2014). Evolutionary governance theory. An introduction. Heidelberg, Germany: Springer.

# 3. Development

## Abstract

In this chapter we systematically link governance and development concepts. We underline the centrality of governance by discussing five models of democratic governance and, briefly, their historical antecedents. We discuss liberal democracy, socialism, civic republicanism, communitarianism and civil society models, emphasizing that neither of them can be identified as an ideal form of democracy; all had specific contexts in which they emerged or were promoted, and have pro's and con's. The discussion of these models we then link with [concisely presented] development theories, associated with discourses of development, and often with specific forms of expertise that are expected to play an important role. We reflect on various assumptions in these development models and narratives and argue for inter-and trans-disciplinary approaches to development questions. The specificity of focus of the disciplines should not be abandoned, but in development studies and projects, they ought to complement and correct each other. Not doing so makes academic and project politics more important than the envisioned rural community and its issues.

## 3.1 Models of democracy

In this section, we talk about five models of the good community that had a real influence on the development of communities across the world. This is not the only possible typology, way of distinguishing; there are others. But this one is helpful in establishing links between governance, development and expertise. Each real world community had a history in which different models were preferred at different times, and at one point in time, one can observe a combination of features of different models. Sometimes, this can be interpreted as traces of models that used to be dominant, surviving together with structures stemming from more recently applauded models. Sometimes, coexistence between different models can refer to a history of different factions living together, vying for power, finding accommodation. In our first descriptions of these models, we are especially interested in the connections between these models and development approaches, and in the roles of expertise and other knowledge in governance. In later sections, these links will be further analyzed.

*Socialism* and *communism* can be mentioned in one breath. In the socialist model of democracy, the people's interests are embodied in the state. The state serves the people, who all have equal rights and opportunities. Private property does not exist, as this would rig decision-making in favor of the rich, and reduce equality, which is seen as a value in and by itself. Individual rights are less important than collective rights, and common goals are more important than individual goals or ambitions. Production, including agricultural production, is collectively organized, with the role of the farmer distributed over a number of different specialists.

Communism does not believe in a strong differentiation of law, politics, economy and science: politics is at the helm of society, decides how the economy will be organized, how legal decisions will be taken (they ought not to contradict politics) and how science will be conducted. Religion is seen as a relic of the past, standing in the way of a real understanding of society, how it works, how it can be improved.

And it can be improved: communism starts from the assumption that people do not know what is good for them, since they are dazed and blinded by ideologies that protect the rich and powerful. Others have to tell them, the communists. Communism requires revolution, since those in power want to keep it, and most others are blinded by them, not realizing how oppressed they are. Revolutions need to be pushed, engineered, but they are likely to come about across the world, as they are the result of a logical evolution of capitalism. Capitalism is expected to succumb to its own contradictions. After a period of globalization and consolidation of power and capital, it will use all resources, create internal unrest, and overly free markets will create bubbles that in the end destroy the market. Once communists take over, they need to remake society, first as socialism, and when that reaches its apex, we can call it communism.

Communism believes in social engineering to the extreme: society can be remade, in every way. Infrastructure can be built, factories, cities, but also people and mentalities. Stalin asserted that engineers are needed, but also engineers of the soul: writers, artists, thinkers. Both the structures and the elements of society can be constructed. 'Soviet man' is not a starting point of Soviet society, but a result of its construction. Once communism is fully realized, history will stop. Communism is perfection, so history ends. Development then is the building of communist society in places where socialism already arrived, and it is the spreading of socialism across the world. Once the whole world is communist (ultimate goal of socialist development), then it is a question of maintaining the machine, keep finding resources, keep an eye on equality, maybe improving quality of life.

Governmental actors define long term and short term goals and strategies. They rely on planning, economic planning and spatial planning to achieve these goals. Citizens are supposed to have an input through local councils (Soviet), regional councils, state level councils, and through various associations per profession. On paper, communism is a highly participatory democracy, where the collective decides everything. In most practical examples, the state took over the role of the collective, the community, and the party decided many things for the state.

Scientific expertise plays a crucial role in this form of development. Communism glorifies progress, and science and engineering provide the insights and the tools. For Lenin, communism was 'electrification of the country'. Natural science especially was promoted, but mostly when practical applications were expected. Science was helpful in cleaning up obstacles to communism, and in achieving the goal of a communist society. Agriculture had to become collective, nomads had to be settled in towns, religions stamped out, social identities broken and erased, infrastructure built, and in all these efforts, science could show the way. The whole society had to be re-engineered, so who else to turn to than engineers? As said, planning played an essential role in this: science was expected to plan for the future, to define a future and the path towards it. In that sense, communism can be called a highly modernist ideology. Local knowledge was in most cases deemed irrelevant, since belonging to old lifestyles associated with despised regimes, and since not scientific. (In some cases, Soviet science and Soviet governance were more sensitive to local context, and to local knowledge).

In many ways the opposite of communism, as a big government and social engineering oriented model, is *liberal democracy*. For liberal democracy, the unit to look at is not a collective, but the individual. Society is not a collective, but a collection of individuals. Essential feature of these individuals is that they are the bearers of individual rights, which are seen as rooted in or representative of natural rights. Central individual right is freedom, including freedom of oppression by the state. Government is ideally small, not very powerful, and its main task is to protect the rights of individuals, against each other and against the state. Solving conflicts between citizens, protecting property rights (seen as natural right), organizing elections, streamlining representation of interests and desires are the work of government. Government does not define and pursue collective goals; what government strives for, if there is goal-oriented policy at all, is something considered aggregate of many individual desires. Desirable futures for the community are usually not envisioned, as the community itself is not seen as a whole, and common goals are a priori suspicious. Behind common goals and visions for the future, individual interests will be suspected.

**Example 3.1. Innovation, development and a critique of linear thinking.**

The belief in linear development processes (from underdeveloped to developed) encouraged by successful innovation diffusion goes back to the expert knowledge focused development paradigm of the 1950's to 1970's, as well as innovation theory of the 1940's to 1980's. As examples, the pioneering works of diffusion theory by Ryan and Gross (1943), as well as later the Transfer of Technology approach by can be mentioned. Similarly to 'development' in development theory of that time, this 'linear model' to innovation diffusion postulates that introducing a new idea, technology/technique, or method – an innovation, in a 'recommendation domain' can lead to a wave of adoption along an S-shaped 'diffusion curve': the diffusion process starts slowly, then gathers momentum and finally peters out when all users for whom it is feasible have adopted the innovation (Rogers, 2003). Similarly to the assumed superiority of (Western/donor) expert knowledge in development, scientific knowledge is implicitly regarded here as being superior to the problem owners' knowledge, independent of context (Robertson and McGee, 2003).

This, from the 1980's onwards, was answered by a wide range of critique, pointing to the 'lack of fit' of externally developed technologies with the problem owners' needs, due to an undervaluing of the problem owners' knowledge of their own situation (e.g. Biggs, 1978, 1980). Consequently, and together with participatory approaches increasingly influencing development discourse and practice, also innovation and diffusion theory turned to joint experimentation and transdisciplinary approaches to innovation development – in itself again not without problems. Here, the importance of innovations being each time deployed in a specific social, political and cultural context and by the problem owners themselves for getting them to work is especially underlined. By stressing the socially constructed character of innovations, the innovations' social embeddedness is emphasized as determinant for their diffusion.

Building on these decades of contested approaches to the linkage between 'innovations' and 'development', the STEPS Center at the University of Sussex, UK, forty years after the original Sussex Manifesto, prepared for the UN-Report 'Science and Technology for Development: Proposals for the Second United Nations Development Decade' and

Power is power by representation. Participation is low, and reduced to voting. Voting is the way for citizens to show what they want. They elect politicians, based on a program, and politicians carry out the program, assumed to be a fair representation of an aggregate of desires. This is seen as the best way to bring all the voices in society to the surface, and to give them a place in decision-making. Interestingly enough, the idea of delegation of power by citizens to government, and after that a hands-off approach by those citizens, comes close to one of the ideas underlying communism. In that sense, the two models are not opposites. Both share a social contract idea, an (imaginary)

rejected by the UN in 1970 (The Sussex Group, 1970), published a new version with the title 'Innovation, Sustainability, Development: A New Manifesto' (STEPS, 2010). The group turns against the linear technology focused development model of the UN second development decade and instead proposes a combination of constructivist and positivist approaches to innovation development and diffusion within a globalizing and an ever faster changing world (Leach *et al.,* 2007). It furthermore emphasizes the need for more integrative and open innovation conceptualizations, fostering the integration of much wider stocks than the narrow technology focus reaffirmed above. The manifesto states on its opening page:
'By innovation, we mean new ways of doing things. This includes not only science and technology, but – crucially – the related array of new ideas, institutions, practices, behaviors and social relations that shape scientific and technological patterns, purposes, applications and outcomes. Central to this, is a move away from progress defined simply by the scale or rate of change – about who is 'ahead' or 'behind' in some presumed one-track race' (STEPS, 2010: 1).
As such, the contestation of 'knowledge' in development as captured under the term 'innovation' continues. The actors (and acting organizations) are determined by their legacies, path dependencies and of course strategic interests.

### Further reading

Leach, M., Scoones, I. and Stirling, A. (2007). Pathways to sustainabilitiy: an overview of the STEPS Centre approach. STEPS Approach Paper. Brighton, UK: STEPS Centre.

Robertson, H.A. and McGee, T.K. (2003). Applying local knowledge: the contribution of oral history to wetland rehabilitation at Kanyapella Basin, Australia. Journal of Environmental Management, 69, 275-287.

Rogers, E.M. (2003). Diffusion of innovations (5 ed.). New York, NY, USA: The Free Press.

Ryan, B. and Gross, N. (1943). The diffusion of hybrid seed corn in two Lowa Communities. Rural Sociology, 8, 15-24.

STEPS Centre (2010). Innovation, sustainability, development: a new manifesto. Brighton, UK: STEPS Centre.

contract between rules and ruled, in which the ruler is chosen, then given power over the ruled. The difference with communism being that the scope of power delegated to government is much wider.

Liberal democracy does not ask much from citizens, and it does not ask from the state. This is tied to the already mentioned idea of absent community: if government only sees a collection of individuals, it cannot and ought not to impose a vision of the whole, and a future for that whole. 'Development' looks very different than in communist ideology then. There is no objective progress, government cannot steer in a desirable direction, and cannot decide what such direction is. A community moves in different directions, depending on what most people want at the moment. If common goals are not articulated, planning plays a minor role in policy, and would be seen to conflict with the (property) rights of some.

Scientific knowledge can be useful for policy when it serves the limited purposes of the state: finding what people want, if they are safe, healthy, if property is protected. It does not assist in the finding and articulation of common goals, public goods, or of visions in which these would be furthered. Local knowledge can play a role in policy formation, if it becomes incorporated in the voting behavior of people: if people believe the earth is flat, they vote for me, this can become part of our program. If locals find that a regional plan disregards specific ecological conditions in town, then local elections can lead to an adaptation of that plan.

In *civil society* models, there is a similar absence of community and of common goals in decision-making. As liberal democracy, it is a small government model, but, different from it, it finds the basic element of society not in individuals but in organizations. More specifically, in non-governmental organizations, for profit (business) and non-profit. The plurality of voices in society is expected to be unearthed and synthesized into policy by membership of people in organizations. Individuals can be member of several organizations, some for profit, others not, and this can lead to a representation of several of her interests in politics. Government is imagined as a little desk in a little room, with representatives of various organizations coming to court, asking for favors, expressing views, vying for influence on the rule-making process. Government is expected to listen to all, weigh the voices, for profit and non-for profit, and come up with laws, policies, plans.

Participation in governance is most of all participation be organizations. If people do not express their interests in this manner, governance will captured by those most active. Another element of critique could be that the little room of government is never entirely visible for the rest of society; it is hard to know exactly what happens there, who is representing what, promising and asking what. The actual influence on policy-making is hard to render transparent, and this leaves room for corruption. This seems all the more true because not every organization is as tightly organized as others, has the same government connections, resources. There is a real difference in this respect between for profit and non-profit organizations. A traditional strategy of non-profit organizations is to leave the little room of government, use the detour of media, scandal, demonstration, to show government that a lack of resources does not mean a lack of support. Also votes are important, and public image.

Development in this model can be many things, and hinges on what is organized, and how it is lobbied. Visions and common goals can be formed, often under the influence of non-profit players. World Wildlife Fund can shape nature conservation policy in a country, GreenPeace actions can bring about environmental policies. If organizations form coalitions, and their stories resonate, reinforce each other (we can speak of discursive coalitions), then it is more likely that visions for the future emerge and are translated into policies and plans. If homeowners plus the tourism sectors plus nature organizations and small farmers come together first, come up with a plan, then government is more likely to listen. Civil society models are thus not necessarily pro small government. And not necessarily against planning and broad development visions. They are more likely to emerge than in liberal democracy, less likely than under socialism.

The role of science and of local knowledge in this all depends on the sorts of organizations, coalitions and visions that emerge. Long term development policies are more likely to hold when the coalitions underpinning them are very stable.

*Communitarianism*, fourthly, is a model of democracy that pays most attention to local democracy, to the small scale of a town or village. It positively values mutual help and interdependence in communities. Community becomes a central concept again, a view of the whole, an identity, and an idea about a desirable future. Development comes more into the picture again and becomes community development. Dense social networks, localized economies, active citizenship make it possible to rely on each other in various ways, to create safe and nurturing environments in which benefits and burdens are distributed widely. It takes a village to raise a child.

Governance is expected to be highly participatory. Individuals are members of organizations, help each other as individuals, and participate directly in politics, in various councils. You go to the local bakery, know the baker from your church choir, his wife from the gardening club, and from city council, and you know their kid because he mows your lawn. Schools are under local control, and the teacher knows what happens at home, so she can help the children better.

There is something very nostalgic about communitarianism, an idealized version of small town life in the 19th century. But there are reasons why so many people ran away from those towns. For some, they can indeed be very safe and nurturing environments, where collective values can be embodied and visions of good development realized. For others, they can be suffocating places, where all are tied to pre-existing identities. It can be hard to reinvent yourself in a place of such extreme interdependence, in a place where all know about all. Such communities can also become easily dominated by small groups, factions, that seem to embody best the proclaimed values of the community, or, more prosaically, because they know best how to play power games in an environment with very complex and layered rules of behavior and constant monitoring.

One can also question the viability of such communities, if they would be fully realized, in the contemporary world. In a globalized world, a world in which very large corporations exist, and nation-states, extreme versions of communitarianism seem anachronistic. In addition, if the focus of local governance is too local, then other relevant scales are forgotten, while they do influence what happens in one place. If taken very far, the local focus, and emphasis on shared identity, can create negative images of the outside world, of other communities, of the nation-state. Internal oppression can be combined with external aggression.

**Example 3.2. William Easterly's legends of development.**

- The poorest countries are stuck in a poverty trap from which they cannot emerge without an aid-financed big push.
- Whenever poor countries have lousy growth, it is because of a poverty trap rather than bad government.
- Foreign aid gives a push to countries to achieve a takeoff into self-sustained growth.

William Easterly, development economist, formerly at World Bank, now New York University, demonstrates that indeed these theses are legends, but also that this stubborn survival of the legend of the Big Push (towards development) has continued to foster a planning approach to development, by which he means, an approach that believes the final goals and the best tools can be observed and picked here and now by bureaucrats and experts. For Easterly, this downplays the importance of good governance, and of what he calls the searchers, the people and organizations, who, with local knowledge and by trial and error, find new ways to old problems, and see new qualities and opportunities where planners (and their scientific minions) didn't.

**Further reading**

Easterly, W. (2006). The White Man's burden: Why the West's efforts to aid the rest have done so much ill and so little good. New York, NY, USA: Penguin Press.

Science in this picture plays little role. Development paths are envisioned locally, local knowledge tends to be dominant. One can imagine new versions of communitarian small societies, open to science and technology, closed in other respects.

*Civic republicanism*, finally, expects the most from citizens and government. This model assumes a very active government and very active citizens. Public goods and visions for the future are articulated in a complex interplay between organizations, governmental actors, active individuals. Private property exists, but taxes are high. Entrepreneurship has to be encouraged, but redistribution of wealth is essential, to allow others to become entrepreneurial, or for them to become active in civil service, helping the community in pursuing the common good. Machiavelli spoke of 'strong citizens in a strong state'.

Development in this perspective is not a problematic concept, on the contrary, a community finds itself in common enterprises, in expanding, in improving in ways that are continuously discussed. The common good is never unproblematic however: different opinions always exist, and these differences should be seen as productive. More strongly: conflicts have to be accepted, as long as they do not undermine the institutions that guarantee a stable state. Conflicts can be good because they allow all different ideas to be fully shown and developed, to allow for a clear comparison between many different policy options and also because in the conflicts new ideas can be born. Essential here is active citizenship, but also information. Citizens can only be productively active if they are well-informed; the quality of media and education determines the quality of governance. Public debate, discussions in bars, around the dinner table, all these things contribute to the quality of democracy.

For civic republicanism, a perfectly stable community, and perfect laws, ideal tools to stabilize a community, do not exist. Corruption will recur every now and then, internal strife and external danger will hollow out a regime, laws will lose their teeth, so communities every now and then have to reinvent themselves. As long as citizens and state remain active, as long as there is some form of checks and balances, and rules to change the rules, this cycle of stability and instability, of regular reinvention, does not pose a problem. Laws are not perfect, timeless or universal, as laws are to be understood as expressions of what a certain community finds it important, how it wants to organize itself. Natural rights can therefore not be the basis of a community; natural rights, in this view, are a fiction, an idea proposed by a group that believes its own values are universal.

Development paths are thus to be seen as highly particular to a community, and the chosen tools are also specific. Recipes cannot be copied from somewhere else, and science cannot prescribe an ideal path of development. Local knowledge is not glorified either, but it is naturally included in the continuous discussion that is governance, just as bits and pieces of scientific knowledge, when they fit the purposes and the narratives of the actors.

As a point of critique we can mention that civic republicanism expects much from everybody. Nowadays, many citizens in developed countries criticize liberal democracy (when that is the dominant model) but are very comfortable with its minimal engagement requirements. Or they are critical of their social democracy, a European, tempered version of socialism, in which government, aided by administrations and their scientists, articulates common goals, visions and plans. But they appreciate the fact that they do not need to be involved very much. Machiavelli, a prominent theorist of civic republicanism, might answer that, indeed, this might be true, but that then citizens have to accept that in the shadows, shadows created by non-observation and non-participation, corruption will flourish, that rules will be written to suit the interests of those that are active, and close to power.

Summarizing this section, we can say that none of our five models of democracy is perfect, that none of them can be perfectly embodied in one real world community. These models did have, however, a very strong influence on the way communities have seen and reformed themselves in the last few centuries. We did not go into historical detail in our descriptions, but one can say that by the late 19$^{th}$ century, all five models were matured and became alternative options in many places. Each model of the good democracy has implications for the type of development preferred, in terms of substance and procedure. The role of government in development, of individuals, organizations, media, education, of science and local knowledge, all these things look different if seen from within this model rather than that one. An advantage of real people and real communities is that they are usually not completely subsumed by conceptual models. They are more hybrid, more complex, and, most important, they can take a distance, reflect, and see that there are alternative forms of governance and alternative paths of development. In this light, the only essence of democracy is rules to change the roles, to switch governance models and/or development approaches.

In the next section, we switch perspectives too, and this time start reasoning from influential approaches to development, looking from there to forms of governance. We list and analyse a series of important approaches to development, and try to link them with forms of governance they might fit best, and ferret out the implications for sorts of expertise and local knowledge that might be prominent. For the analysis of concrete cases, each perspective can be useful by itself, and they can be combined. One can reflect on the models in and behind governance in a community, think of development paths from there, and one can analyze existing development approaches there, place them in the context of known ones, and then link back to existing governance, and reflect on fit or non-fit.

Later in the book, we will refine the analysis, bring it closer to rural development approaches and the governance of rural areas. For analysis of concrete cases, the rural development approaches presented there might be more easily recognized, but we believe it can also be worthwhile in some cases to take even more distance, and see connections over larger conceptual distances, then bring them back to the ground. Understanding general theories of development can be important, because sometimes the rural aspect turns out to be not so important in the end, and because what really helps you in understanding a development path can sometimes be the recognition of a general development approach (with its own assumptions, links with forms of governance). More simply: sometimes you'll have to take one step back, sometimes two or three steps, and we present you some maps and schemes to make sense of what you can see at different distances.

## Further reading

Held, D. (2006). Models of democracy. Stanford, CA, USA: Stanford University Press.

Huntington, S.P. (1971). The change to change: modernization, development, and politics. Comparative Politics, 3, 283-322.

Scott, J.C. (1998). Seeing like a state. How certain schemes to improve the human condition have failed. New Haven, CN, USA: Yale University Press.

Sen, A. (1999). Democracy as a universal value. Journal of Democracy, 10(3), 3-17.

## 3.2 Development theories and narratives of development

Ideas on good ways to develop cities, countrysides and countries have existed for centuries, since at least ancient Greece, and since the 18th century Enlightenment, there has been a scientific reflection on the public administration, political organization, scientific knowledge, how to use and organize them to benefit the community, to facilitate progress. The goal of progress has been defined in many ways, but a common denominator of development thinking has always been that progress is possible, that communities can improve themselves, work on their issues, create new qualities. 'Development theory' however is not that old, and usually it came up in the latter 20th century in the context of de-colonization. After the colonizers withdrew, we suddenly spoke of developing countries, and Western scientists came up with various development theories. This created a lot of confusion, because the existing ideas on development in the west were disconnected from development thinking for poorer countries. That is a pity, since Western ideas on public administration, planning, sociology, economics, could have inspired many more ideas on possible development paths in other places. If connections were seen between poor and rich, they were too direct: let us try to copy what we see in the west now (without studying the way Western histories produced Western tools and results).

**Example 3.3. Aristotle, democracy and causality.**

Aristotle (384-322 B.C.E.) was a Greek philosopher, scientist and policy advisor, who wrote on almost any topic imaginable in antiquity. We know his work through notes made by his students, and it is likely that much has been lost. What survives is still impressive, and, interesting for us, he devoted treatises to politics, rhetoric, ethics and the art of reasoning. His political theory is best represented in his book on ethics (the actual political theory) and the book on politics (illustration and elaboration in a wide range of examples, polities analyzed). His teacher Plato believed in a perfect state, under the leadership of a philosopher-king, but the disastrous results of an experiment in that vein in Souther Italy convinced Aristotle that it is better to understand first the variety of political forms, the reasons for their coming into being, and the pro's and con's of each form. Democracy he understood as a rather radical democracy, where citizens (not all residents) were directly involved in the making of many decisions, in large assemblies. He was not charmed by what he saw of democracy in the Greek world, assessed it as too volatile, too susceptible to populism, conspiracies, flaring passions, and uninformed and unrealistic visioning.

One should aim for the best possible constitution, meaning the best possible organization of the community, and that is usually a mixed form, a combination of democracy and aristocracy or monarchy. Monarchies and aristocracies can be deemed virtuous when the leader or elite envisions the common good, not private or group interests. For Aristotle, elites (aristocratic features) are useful to stabilize a democratic polity, and he believes and illustrates in many 'case studies' that the formation of elites in democratic polities is hardly avoidable. In modern terms, interest groups will form, money will accumulate, some will organize, network, get more access to power, influence rule-making, become more prosperous, influential, etc. But he also shows how aristocracies can 'degenerate' into democracies, and more broadly, how political forms can morph into each other. As Machiavelli later, Aristotle didn't believe that pure stability in politics was possible, that no set of formal institutions could guarantee such stability.

Development in the long run is thus always a set of transformations of one regime type into another. In the shorter run, it is possible, in a regime aiming at the common good, to give substance to and multiply the common good, into a variety of causes to strive for.

Over time, the influence of modernist thought diminished, and simple development recipes were more and more distrusted. Also, the links between recipes 'the west' created for itself and for 'the rest', between reflection on 'the west' and reflection on 'the rest', became stronger and stronger. Last but not least, many developing countries became developed, and many poorer countries acquired their own voice in political and academic debates on development. In recent years, as reflected in some of the

Development cannot be reduced to the accumulation of wealth, since this leads to oligarchies, and not to the accumulation of power or military might, since this will also lead to a strong rigidity, to missing important things inside and outside the community that can represent danger or opportunity. An eroding economic basis can be overlooked (as in Sparta), a lack of technological innovation (as in Sparta), shifting power balances (as in Athens).

Aristotle also sees the evolution of governance in terms of causes. He distinguishes four causes: material, formal, immediate and final cause. A blacksmith (immediate cause) makes a sword based on an idea, design of a sword (formal cause), using steel (material cause), in order to defend or attack (final cause). The community for Aristotle has a formal cause, a constitution, as an institutional design, a material cause, its territory, an immediate cause, the leadership, and a final cause: the set of goals that is associated with the common good. Development as evolution is the interplay of the different causes, while development as substantive visioning is the reflection on and impact of the final cause.

We can link the four causes to our three dependencies (see Chapter 4). Goal dependencies can be understood as the final causes observable in their impacts on the transformation of actors, institutions and the other governance configurations. Material causes can be seen as one type of path dependence, whereas the formal causes can be found in the structure of the institutional configuration. Immediate causes can be associated with the actors moving governance forwards, in an interdependence partly caused by the overall idea of the institutional configuration, partly by its contingent evolution. The idea is never perfectly embodied because of imperfections in actors, territory, institutions (made by actors in a territory). Things always change, and if one wants this change to be managed, one needs to see and manage the interplay between the four causes as much as possible. Perfection is likely impossible, but coming close to a common goal requires understanding this interplay, or, in our framework, the interplay between the three dependencies.

### Further reading

Barker, E. (1995). The politics of Aristotle. Oxford, UK: Oxford University Press.

later approaches, the discussion on development in Western countries became more intense, because serious problems asserted themselves there: economic crises, ecological crises, identity crises. We come back to this. Now, we can already mention that such reflection on the own need for (re-)development created new links with the reflection on development in poorer areas, and a new impetus for general development theories, this time with fewer colonialist overtones.

If we take one step further back, in time and space, we can see that democracies, in their different versions, are not the only types of polities, and that the 18$^{th}$ century Enlightenment, with its progress concept, was not the earliest era where development ideas came up. In terms of types of polities, we can distinguish: theocracies (religion at the helm), authoritarian regimes (leaders dictate rules), oligarchies (small groups rule), clan rule (networks rule), monarchies (kings in charge), and failed states (disintegrated polities; entities that never integrated). Of course, in practice, some communities are part of something that can be described in many ways, and what is 'failed' is not always clear-it depends on what you consider 'normal' in a functioning state, more than boundaries and a capital on paper. If we look at the history of development approaches, looking at a wider variety of political systems is important, and it is also relevant when analyzing or working on situations in some parts of the contemporary world.

Whatever the polity, we can say that development models, types of polity, and used expertise interact. One polity is not always aligned with a development model, or with a model of knowledge use and inclusion. But there are preferential links, more likely combinations. That some development approaches, forms of governance (polities), and uses of knowledge are more related, have more affinity, has to do with the nature of the political ideology, the power relations in situ, with contingent evolutions. In the following sections, we will introduce new concepts to explain these links more precisely. The existence of such links, is however universal: we can look for them in poor and rich countries, warm and cold, new and old.

What you think of as development will inspire the way you want to move forward, the goal and the way to that goal, the tools. This includes the role assigned to this and type of expertise, this and that form of local knowledge. While it is influenced by broader political ideologies, ideas of the good community, the right role of the government, the definition of the good citizen. It is further influenced by seeing other places (we spoke of learning and distinguishing), by knowing other ideologies and theories.

If we look beyond the Enlightenment for development concepts, we can see them more easily when we look for concepts of growing complexity in human societies. For some Greek and Roman philosophers (some of them revived in the middle ages), societies did originate from simple beginnings, becoming more complex over time, and allowing to be improved. Aristotles 'Politics' and Livy's 'Dawn of the Roman Empire' are famous examples. For some, the nature of individual living things was similar to the nature of society: they move towards complexity as they grow, and this growth is guided by a plan, where the mature being has realized its blueprint.

Interesting for us is that for most times and places in European history, ideas of time as arrow and time as cycle coexist. This means that for some, development means going through the cycles, ups and downs of history, times of building and times of destruction, with communities coming and going, while for others (time as arrow) time points in one direction, moves on, and at least allows for the idea of progress, of communities that survive and improve themselves. A third current (represented e.g. by Ovid) was one of pessimism, of decay, a golden age situated in a mythical past. Everything we see now is already inferior to the past, so why even bother thinking of development. We could possibly to go back in time, bring back the good old days, but usually, this is seen as futile.

So, development ideas where present in times before the Enlightenment, but in the company of very different ideas of time and society, not very compatible with development thinking. Also the grip of humans, as individuals and communities, on things, was understood to be very slippery. Fate decides what happens; we cannot control faith. And if we fail here in this life, there might be redemption later. So maybe we do not have to try very hard. This life is misery anyway, and our suffering might be rewarded later. Individual autonomy and control became prominent concepts in the Renaissance (16$^{th}$ century), when science slowly emerged from the medieval darkness, when political theory was reborn, and the here and now, the individual achievement, became slowly more important than the afterlife, and the will of the ruler (at least these narratives became more influential and widespread). The Renaissance person is expected to be versatile, learned but practical, adaptive, aware of fate but still trying to make his own life, his own identity. And communities can be made and remade as well, if we want to and work together. Humans became the center of the universe.

Success in life is possible, and is ok, is acceptable. Being rich is not immoral, and trading is not stealing. We can define what success is, which strategies we use. God accepts us to do our best, and if we use all our faculties and powers, we use what God gave us. Fate can be modified in its effects. In the theories of these days, we see a clear break with the preceding middle ages, but in practice, what we just said about the Renaissance started earlier, in the merchant cities of the late middle ages, where autonomy was slowly increased.

What the 18$^{th}$ century added then was, as we know, the idea of progress, and the link between progress and rationality. What makes us, humans, unique, is our intellect, our rational capacity, and this is also what brings us closest to God. Ratio is not opposed to religion. On the contrary: God made a ordered universe, gave us the capacity to see that order, through science, and wants us to order our societies according to the same rational principles. That also means that all people have to be free, to be allowed to think, to work together towards a better society. Freedom is thus not a goal in itself, but a condition for working together on development. Rationality also gives a clear picture of the deficiencies of self and community, and helps to figure out which tools to use to fix them. Ration and science can thus illuminate and improve society.

The state, the nation-state, can help with this. The state can make people more rational and can make itself rational. Therefore, it needs the help of the most rational of all: scientists. Here we meet again the birth of Modernism. This happened at a time when nation-states consolidated, when their reach increased, to include more and more types of policies, including education, health, city planning, infrastructure, a military, etc. Consolidation of power meant centralization of power, and larger bureaucracies at the centre. They needed to know what happened, and scientists became more important. We can mention the Habsburg Empire in the 18$^{th}$ century as an example, but also the Prussia of Frederik the Great, and, last but not least, France, as the most centralized early nation-state.

**Example 3.4. World Bank and technocracy.**

The World Bank was established in 1944 at the Bretton Woods conference, a conference organized by the Allies who thought they were close to winning World War II (it turned out, correctly). World Bank was seen as part of an international political-economic-military order which could stabilize the post-war world, foster development, and deal with lingering issues, such as colonialism. It was expected to provide both financing and expert advice to the poorer countries, and, to colonies expected to become independent soon. World Bank was to include national aid agencies, NGOs, representatives of other international agencies, all assisted by development experts. Article IV, Section 10 proved esssential for the technocratic character displayed later, and for the ignoring of human rights issues. It stated: 'the Bank and its officers shall not interfere in the political affairs of any member; nor shall they be influenced in its decisions by the political character of the government of the member or members concerned. Only economic considerations shall be relevant to their decisions'.
Politics and economy where thus considered as distinct realms, and economic assistance was deemed possible without looking at the type of regime, ideology, market, rule of law in place. The clause allowed to cooperate with the USSR, and gave a technocratic (modernist) perspective central place. World Bank was going to focus on the 'Third World', and this was defined as the leftover, what was not US and its democratic allies, or USSR and its European satellites. The internal diversity of the Third World was initially not recognized, diversity in political, economic, legal and cultural sense. Latin America became suddenly a collection of third world countries, after being seen as close to Europe. World Bank started thinking of development planning as necessary for the Third World, including Latin America. Most Latin American intellectuals initially disagreed, doubting the power of governments to devise and implement such plans. In Latin America, in British Africa, in China and in other places, World Bank struck deals with authoritarian governments to assist them in planning the economy towards development, and de facto to reform society in ways they, not citizens, wanted. International politics in a late colonialist and post-colonialist era collided with

These early nation-states developed central policies for road development, canals, improving agriculture, tax collection, raising the education level, and slowly an idea of progress spread. The state was supposed to improve itself and uplift the people. In the 19th century, against this background, new philosophies of progress and development saw the light. Hegel expected time to end when society was fully rational, but before this is needed some further education and rationalization, while, a bit later, Marx saw the end of time in a perfect communist society (see above). Darwin, in the natural sciences, also saw evolution, but no end to it, no final goal. Ideas of evolution were coupled with ideas of progress: things change by themselves, in a direction of greater complexity, but they also need our coordinated action to improve. For some thinkers, the state was the

a strongly modernist technocratic belief in economic development experts. This allowed economic expertise of one sort to become deeply institutionalized in World Bank, to see it as disconnected from other forms of expertise, from local knowledge, and from political ideology. Third World countries were considered a blank slate for development experts to do their work. Context was forgotten. William Easterly, a development economist formerly at World Bank, argues that the supposed high tide of development theory in the 1950's and 1960's, was in fact stuck in the technocratic consensus formed in the 1940's. Even before World Bank was formally established, drafts circulating in the US administration (oriented towards economic planning and technocracy itself) pointed in that direction.

In recent decades, 'evidence based policies' are a new manifestation of technocratic thinking at World Bank (sometimes in league with a neo-liberal agenda, sometimes not), but some things have changed. The role of NGOs in driving the agenda has been acknowledged, but, since the 1990's, a recognition of self-organization, local knowledge and context, can be observed. The shift from government to governance, and the call for more local participation did not go entirely unnoticed. In our own research, we noticed a high level of reflexivity and self-critique with World Bank in post-socialist countries, where many projects were assessed negatively internally, because of lacking participation, lack of embedding in local governance, and lack of capacity to 'absorb the funds' (i.e. lack of transparent channels, of checks and balances, of entrepreneurship, of ideas, and reliance on self-serving, often corrupt elites). Often, follow up projects were not approved for these reasons. At the same time, one can still see a strong focus on large scale policies and technical infrastructure (think dams, irrigation), and on the sorts of projects embodying dreams of technocrats and autocrats employing them.

**Further reading**

Easterly, W. (2013). The tyranny of experts. Economists, dictators and the forgotten rights of the poor. New York, NY, USA: Basic Books.

bringer of progress (e.g. Hegel), for others, the state has to be overthrown first (Marx) and then replaced by a superior version.

Since the Renaissance, Europeans had looked at the rest of the world not simply as non-Christian, but also as less developed. Similarly, Muslim countries looked down on the rest, and for the Chinese everyone else was barbarian too. Yet, the specific colonialist histories of Europe gave a different impact to their manner of looking down on the rest. In later stages of colonialism, some colonies became seen as part of the colonizing power, and others were seen as in need of, and deserving 'development'. After colonialism, helping, and aid, came to be seen as a moral imperative. Sometimes, helping towards development was an excuse for colonization, sometimes for intervention in post-colonies. As we described earlier, in early development approaches, we were dealing with Western scientists assuming the former colonies had to become more like themselves, without fully understanding their own path of development.

In some of the development theories we present in the following paragraphs, this attitude is still present, and so is the modernist idea that science can produce a simple recipe for development. In the next part of the book, we will study approaches to rural development, and you will notice that the development theories and rural development approaches do not fit one on one. Some rural development approaches are more embedded in general development theory than others, and some rural development styles are influenced by discourses and practices coming from unexpected places.

In the following, we thus discuss:
- modernist models of development (including community development, structural adjustment);
- structuralist economics/industrial policy/science policy;
- dependency theory;
- livelihoods approach/asset-based development;
- sustainability/resilience perspectives;
- innovation/transition management;
- participatory development/resource management;
- institutions;
- post-colonial/post-development approaches.

On each of those, an enormous literature exist, and we can only sketch them here. We provide a quick assessment, and establish links with the potential roles of expertise and local knowledge, and the relations with governance models discussed before.

## Further reading

Deleuze, G. and Guattari, F. (1987). A thousand plateaus: capitalism and schizophrenia. London, UK: Continuum.

Easterly, W. (2006). The white man's burden: why the West's efforts to aid the rest have done so much ill and so little good. New York, NY, USA: Penguin Press.

Esteva, G. (1992). Development. In: Sachs, W. (ed.), The development dictionary: a guide to knowledge as power. London, UK: Zed, pp. 6-25.

Tipps, D.C. (1973). Modernization theory and the comparative study of societies: a critical perspective. Comparative Studies in Society and History, 15, 199-226.

Van Assche, K., Beunen, R. and Duineveld, M. (2012). Performing success and failure in governance: Dutch planning experiences. Public Administration, 90(3), 567-581.

### 3.2.1 Modernist models

Modernist models of development are strongly expertise driven. That does not mean that a lot of expertise, of science, is necessarily involved, but it does mean that the correct formula for good development comes from experts. The formula itself can be simple. Different modernist theories focus on different scales or units to improve: household, individual, community, region, state. As we know the general approach is a product of the 18ᵗʰ century Enlightenment, and spread through colonialism and growing bureaucracies.

The dominant version takes a nation-state as a unit, reduces development to economic growth and economic growth to increasing GDP. Later, versions emerged with a wider variety of development indices, become more inclusive: health, environment, well-being. Still, the idea is that development can be measured, captured in a few numbers by scientists, shaped into a set of macro-policies, mostly of an economic nature. In recent versions of this model, law, legal frames, get more in the picture: 'rule of law' becomes seen as a precondition for economic development, as an institutional frame that can also be captured in a formula, or better, in one 'correct' design. We will argue that 'the rule of law' can be many different things, with different assumptions and different effects. In some case 'the rule of law' is linked to 'good governance', also conceived as a matter of following correctly a neutral recipe. Good governance and rule of law are still often seen as tools to increase GDP, as final goal.

We can mention as related the concepts of structural adjustment and *shock therapy*. In which poorer countries are regarded as requiring adjustment, that is, try to change a few macro-economic parameters so they can afterwards quickly evolve into capitalist democracies. Some version of capitalist democracy, usually liberal democracy, is seen as the best state model, and macro-economic policy indicators (debt ratio, currency value, import/export ratio, foreign investment numbers, GDP, etc.) are the elements of the formula for faster evolution towards the final goal. For some economists, it's better to do this fast, to devalue currency fast, sell unprofitable state companies, privatize as much as possible, and such shocks are expected to be the best way forward; delaying only makes it more painful later.

A Western defined model of society is still seen as superior, a model inviting imitation/emulation. The approach is related to an older, evolutionist current in anthropology and sociology: from family to tribe to big men to state and finally, to democratic/capitalist state. Often, even in narratives where the goal is a very free market and small government, there is a strong social engineering assumption, and when the Western experts look abroad, the engineering approach seems to be reinforced: there, in poor countries, not much happened, not much (we want to observe) exists, and much has to be done. Let's get started!

Not all modernist models of development focus on large scale economic reform. Sometimes, the approach is more comprehensive, with different policies aiming at different scales. One can then speak of nested policies. Small projects fit macro policies in a larger rational development scheme. Micro and macro are based on the same modernist assumptions.

Or, in less ambitious and more disillusioned versions, the nesting of policies is given up, and only the micro scale remains as object of engineering and social engineering. One gave up the idea of reforming the state from outside, by foreign experts, with foreign expertise, but at the local level, projects can still be carried out that can make a difference, and where control is still possible. Maybe there is still a farther time horizon, when the idea remains that many projects over time can bring bigger change, through changing mentalities, setting examples, building capacity (educating and training locals), showing alternatives, providing piecemeal for necessary infrastructure.

Smaller scale policies and projects more quickly evolved away from modernist approaches, in general, but also in the case of individual, long lasting projects. In many cases, things start more technocratic, with foreign experts deciding what to do, later, local knowledge becomes more important, local participation, a strengthening of local government. One can draw a parallel here with the American tradition of 'community development', an approach targeting mostly smaller communities, with a comprehensive vision for development, working on many aspects of community life. After World War II, there was a strong belief in a comprehensive recipe to be applied in developing countries, a recipe defined by American scientists (so many pumps, so many sheep). In recent decades, the approach became more inclusive of other sorts of knowledge (environmental, e.g. local knowledge), more participatory, and lost in general the belief in a perfect formula. Since the 1990's, the reinvented community development approach, was exported back to the USA, where it has become more context-sensitive again (starting from analysis of various community assets, with asset analysis becoming more and more refined context and path analysis).

## Further reading

Bird, G. (2007). The IMF: a bird's eye view of its role and operations. Journal of Economic Surveys, 21(4), 683-745.

Booth, D. (1985). Marxism and development sociology: Interpreting the impasse. World Development, 13, 761-787.

Easterly, W. (2013). The tyranny of experts. Economists, dictators and the forgotten rights of the poor. New York, NY, USA: Basic Books.

Gay, P. (1996). The enlightenment: the science of freedom (Vol. 2). New York, NY, USA: WW Norton & Company.

Hornidge, A.-K. (2010). An uncertain future – Singapore's search for a new focal point of collective identity and its drive towards 'knowledge society'. Asian Journal of Social Sciences, 38(5), 785-818.

Rostow, W.W. (1956). The take-off into self-sustained growth. The Economic Journal, 66, 25-48.

Rostow, W.W. (1959). The stages of economic growth. The Economic History Review, 12, 1-16.

Wade, R. (1996). Japan, the World Bank, and the art of paradigm maintenance: the East Asian miracle in political perspective. New Left Review, 3.

## 3.2.2 Structuralist economics

Whereas modernist models of development led in most cases to macro-economic prescriptions, structuralist economics sticks to the expertise of economics for development, but does not believe that one should attempt to copy the present state of developed countries, the functioning of markets there.

Structuralist economics emerged in Latin America in the 1950's, in a continent with serious economic problems but also a highly educated population (in most countries). Capacity development looked different there from Africa. Local experts stood up early and questioned the authority of Anglo-Saxon economic prescriptions that were presented as the only remedy and the only way forward. Structuralist economics asked to consider unique structures which marked the position of developing countries. Opening markets too quickly, and without working on various sorts of infrastructure, was not considered a good option. Developing countries need time before they open their markets, reduce their deficits, and follow rule sets that work in developed countries. If the doors open too fast, then local producers will be wiped out, the terms of negotiation on any economic transaction, small and large, will be unfair. What a developing country does will for a long time be dictated by the developed countries with most clout in international politics.

The time bought before following a Western recipe, should be used for further improvement in education, infrastructure improvements, growing local business in a more protected environment, studying foreign models of business, innovation, and possible roles of government to spur the economy.

Structural economics is not entirely unrelated to Western traditions though. It is in essence not very different from industrial policy, applied in France, Germany and other European countries in much of the 20th century, and sometimes before that. Many European nation-states decided that they should focus on certain industrial sectors they considered strategic; this included import restrictions but also positive encouragement and support, in terms of infrastructure, subsidies, training, export coordination, research & development. The German auto industry is an example, but also French banks, and (we will discuss this later) Dutch agriculture (not industry in the narrow sense, but a sector similarly treated in post-war Holland).

Industrial policy and structuralist economics can be translated in macro economic policies, but also in different ways of geo-political positioning and diplomatic activity (different patterns of links, finding coalitions to support each other in resistance to Western development recipes). It can become visible in science & education policy, spatial planning, energy policy, and other policy domains.

## Further reading

Adam, C. (1995). Review article: adjustment in Africa: reforms, results and the road ahead. World Economy, 18(5), 729-735.

Dorosh, P.A. (1994). Structural adjustment, growth, and poverty in Madagascar. Ithaca, NY, USA: Cornell Food and Nutrition Policy Program.

Lopes, C. (1999). Are structural adjustment programmes an adequate response to globalization? International Social Science Journal, 51(162), 511-519.

World Bank (1988). Targeted programs for the poor during structural adjustment. A summary of a symposium on poverty and adjustment. Washington, DC, USA: World Bank.

### 3.2.3 Dependency theory

Structuralist economics is furthermore closely related to dependency theory, which also emerged in Latin America, a bit later. Dependency theory is a more clearly political version of structuralist economics, stating that the current structure of the world political economy keeps poor countries poor, and their development recipes will keep poor countries in that positions. The benefits of the currently dominant forms of capitalism (usually understood as a form of liberal democracy) are reaped by the developed countries, who followed different paths to get rich, than what they preach, and who keep developing countries poor by retaining them in the position of

Figure 3.1. Selling honey from an ancient car, Uzbekistan. Assets can be very hard to assess for outsiders. Honey can be a by-product of a weed invasion, an old chestnut forest, of a mono-culture crop, of bees mainly pollinating orchards, and it can be a big business in itself, a main occupation. It can also be a marginal activity with great cultural significance. Photo: Anna-Katharina Hornidge. © ZEF/University of Bonn, Germany.

commodity producers. Finished products are imported from developed countries, raw materials are exported in their direction. Often, the relation between the US and Latin-America was the underlying example for theory development.

Poor countries, for dependency theorists, are not caught in primitive stages of development. They are in a condition created mostly by colonialist legacies and other first mover benefits for the west. They took a different path, and a path they did not entirely create themselves. Moving on from the current position cannot entail copying Western rhetorical or practical recipes, but rather restructuring the world economy. Following Western (understood as modernist, macro-economic) recipes would amount to a forced integration into an unjust world economy.

For many of the authors of dependency theory, the developing countries, seen as a periphery used by a center, do not need capital in the first place, but rather autonomy and autonomous innovation processes. Innovation in a more protected environment can lead to product which can be exported, and to hopefully a slow change of economic relations, of the unfair order. Industrialization is ok as strategy, an export focus is also fine, but before that, the focus should be on replacing imports (by local/regional products). After that, one can think again of export orientation. In some versions of the theory, radical socio-political change within the developing countries is seen as a precondition and usually this is seen in a Marxist or socialist perspective. F.E. Cardoso should be mentioned as a theorist with important real-world political experience (in Brazil). Dependency theory was quite influential in development studies in the 1960's and 1970's, although within the discipline of economics it remained marginal (or 'heterodox' in economists' lingo).

## Further reading

Cardoso, F.H. (1977). The consumption of dependency theory in the United States. Latin American Research Review, 12, 7-24.

Escobar, A. (1985). Discourse and power in development: Michel Foucault and the relevance of his work to the Third World. Alternatives, 10, 377-400.

Escobar, A. (1995). Encountering development: the making and unmaking of the Third World. Princeton, NJ, USA: Princeton University Press.

## 3.2.4 Livelihoods approaches/assets

In the 1980's and 1990's, several livelihood-focused approaches to development became quite popular in development studies. It focused on the small scale of family, and village community, and is in some ways an offspring of the broader political model of communitarianism. Livelihoods approaches were/are mostly promoted in sociology, but were also picked up in the larger community of development studies and development practitioners (working for NGOs, international organizations, Western governments, university outreach, etc.).

Some versions are strongly linked to sustainability discourses: development interventions and support ought to target sustainable livelihoods. This can mean livelihoods that could also be available for the children and grandchildren, it can refer to the sustainability of the environment one looks for a livelihood (not depleting resources, altering the landscape too much), or a combination of both (protecting the environment, maintaining assets, so livelihoods can be continued).

Other versions are strongly linked with anti-colonialist discourses (so sometimes with the anti-colonialist dependency theory and its emphasis on different paths and protected environments). This, in turn, often means there is an underlying disappointment in macro-economic and modernist approaches, and in engineering-driven smaller scale projects. One can say that the livelihoods approach usually assumes that the older small and large scale strategies did not work, that most attention should go to the small scale, to local knowledge, and to local assets. Assets become assets in a given community and a given environment, and in this perspective, the physical environment is often seen as the context which links the various assets that make a community and its economy possible. Assets are thus assets in a local context, and the context provides linkages between assets that make them elements of a functioning local economy. Changing the landscape can undermine the links between assets, and destabilize local economies and communities. 'Development' is tightly coupled to the physical and social environment, and interventions can only take place after a thorough analysis of physical and social contexts. Almost all existing methods were seen as insensitive in every sense: political, cultural, physical.

The livelihoods approach is theoretically quite open and hybrid, and often includes concepts also present in other theories (inside and outside development studies): strategies should be asset-based (as in community development, social work), focus on capacity development (similar), local knowledge, be conscious of local networks (actor-network theories), aim at sustainability (see below). In some versions, assets are presented as capitals, in the tradition of sociologist Pierre Bourdieu and political scientist Robert Putnam, and authors distinguish between economic, social, cultural and political capital, as different sorts of assets that need to be mapped, networked, developed, built upon.

The Gross Domestic Product (GDP), other economic indicators, and the macro-scale as such should not be the main focus of development efforts and the main measures of success in development. The importance of a macro scale is usually acknowledged, but the relations between the scales are not always clearly theorized. Often, there seems to be an assumption that the local social and physical environment can be slightly and subtly reorganized, to stabilize traditional economies, or move them in a slightly different direction. Livelihoods have to be understood first of all, before prescribing anything or intervening at all. They are diverse, do not always allow for a separation of economy and the rest of society as in the west, and concepts such as progress, development, poverty, well-being, should always be considered against the background of local livelihoods. GDP might increase, but many local livelihoods might be disturbed or interrupted, and people might feel less satisfied and poorer than before.

Some versions of the livelihoods approach are more sensitive to larger political and economic contexts than others. Some are more interested in uses of the physical landscape, others more in social or cultural change. Some are more interested in the positive uses of landscapes and their resources (assets for sustainable development), while others are looking to minimize risk posed by certain landscapes and climates, by landscapes and climate change, for sustainable development, or, more bleakly, for causing poverty and disease.

The American tradition of community development, in its recent versions, since the 1990's, shares many of the concepts of the livelihoods approach: asset-based development, capacity building, a combination of top-down and bottom-up strategies, and the tendency or the moral imperative to save places, communities.

## Further reading

Scoones, I. (2009). Livelihoods perspectives and rural development. The Journal of Peasant Studies, 36(1), 171-196.

### 3.2.5 Sustainable development/resilience/adaptive governance

Also related to the livelihoods approach, also conceptually hybrid, but even more productive, and widespread, is the sustainable development approach. The Brundtland Report (1987) on the perils of our current path of development (with 'us' being the world community) paved the way for an impressive stream of research and policy trying to address the sustainability question: how can we develop in a way that can be sustained in the long term, without depleting resources, destroying our environment, destabilizing societies? The Club of Rome offered similar warnings in the 70's, seeing limits to growth, and looming environmental and resource crises, but its warnings did not have the same impact.

Emerging scientific knowledge on climate change gave more weight to the sustainability approach, and the rise of China and India, greatly increasing the use of fossil fuels and mineral resources, contributed to the resonance of sustainability rhetoric. If indeed we already caused climate change, and we were not even aware of it, then not only our development path but also our expertise has to be questioned. We should be in general more cautious with our environment. If our expertise turns out to be false, overlooking major risks, then maybe we should not base too radical decisions on that expertise, when it affects the use of resources, and changing our environment. We cannot experiment too much with the earth. If it fails, we cannot try again.

In this light, rich countries cannot be seen as good examples for 'the rest'. A sustainability perspective offers different arguments not to trust Western development recipes. Poor countries cannot take the same path and rich countries have to change. Sustainability thinking forces Western countries to rethink their own development; they now have new development work to do by themselves. And, in most accounts, they have responsibility for much of the damage done to the environment, and should somehow be held responsible. One way of bearing that responsibility is to support poorer countries in taking an alternative path, e.g. by paying them for not logging rain forests, for not mining in protected areas, for sticking to environmental rules they didn't think of themselves during and after the industrial revolution.

Critics quickly said that things always change, and that sustainability cannot be used to trap a society in a current situation. Nothing is sustainable in the end, if sustainability is taken to mean that everything can change as is. Too many factors are unpredictable, and both communities and their environments change all the time (cf civic republicanism). Another recurring critique has been that sustainable development perspectives tend to pay too much attention to environmental factors, to a narrow set of topics such as resource depletion and climate change. Critics also asked for more clear recipes for good, correct sustainable development practices and policies (a modernist critique).

Since the 1990's, the *sustainability* discourse has been refined, new versions have emerged, science has progressed. This provided some answers to the afore mentioned critics. Sustainability has been redefined as a combination of social, ecological and economic sustainability. A community and society is only sustainable when all three aspects are considered, and certain investigations and policies can target one of these aspects separately, to gain deeper insight. With these distinctions, new questions came up about prioritizing the aspects of sustainability and the best ways to relate these aspects, in theory and in practice. A univocal answer does not exist yet, and we argue that it cannot exist, because the sustainability question is in essence the question about the good society, and this always has many answers. How stable do we want a society to be? How much do we rely on science, politics, economy, on innovation, to deal with shocks, to change when is needed? Different answers are linked to the different models of democracy we discussed above.

In general, giving a clear answer in the positive sense is very difficult, indeed impossible: we cannot say what sustainability 'is'. We can however more easily deal with the negative versions of the concept: we know that we don't want to deplete resources (at least not without very seriously thinking and acting on alternatives), that we don't want to destroy the environment, that we want to reduce the options for future generations to change their community and the world in a direction they might prefer. The climate change debate made this aspect of responsibility more important, and it showed more clearly how everything is linked: domains of policy, different parts of the world. This forces a new reflection on cooperation, and on the difficulties in giving simple answers. It forced a global perspective on many policy decisions on smaller scales, and it gave an ethical dimension to more policy discussions (since we already caused problems, and what we decide now causes problems later and somewhere else).

Elements of positive answers to the sustainability question are represented by concepts such as footprints (the full impact of decisions, actions), of cycles, and of many possible equilibria (in stead of one correct one, the sustainable state. We refer to the specialized literature for more detail.

Another response to the critics of sustainability can be found in the *resilience* approach to development. Resilience is a concept that came up in the 70's in ecology (e.g. in the work of Holling). It originally referred to the idea that there is not one equilibrium point in ecosystems. They do not evolve and tend towards a stable point. Several equilibria are possible for ecosystems, as always dynamic systems. Resilience here means that a system can refer to a previous state after disturbance. High resilience means a high capacity for bouncing back. More recent evolutions of this ecological resilience story include the concept of tipping points, points in the evolution of systems where many small changes suddenly produced a big shift, a new state and sometimes structure of the ecosystem (see above).

Resilience concepts were welcomed in more general sustainability thinking because of this option of several equilibria but also because of the promise of bouncing back. It liberated sustainability from achieving one goal, one correct state, and it implied a promise of maybe cultivating resilience in society. Resilient societies could then bounce back more easily from catastrophes, e.g. economic crises, but also ecological crises and more weather drama associated with climate change. Resilience was picked up in development studies, planning, environmental studies, public administration because of this way out and this promise.

Within these disciplines, it also made it clear that no blueprint approach to development was sensible. Rather, one needed to work on the capacity to deal with issues. In these disciplines, it also linked up with recent versions of complexity theory and systems theory, which emphasized that there are limits to steering, that policies cannot be simply 'implemented': the effects of policies later on are too complex to product. There is no linearity. Policies, and policies as part of societies, are subjected to feedback loops, positive and negative, that can magnify or minimize the effects of policies, or send the impacts in different directions. Policies can affect landscapes, which affect people, which affect policies, etc. These chains of effects can never be predicted, and should inspire less planning, less certainty about development goals and the path towards these goals.

Complexity and systems approaches also work well with the resilience thinking because they see the world as a set of interconnected systems, where the actions in one place and one system, have complex effects in other systems, and in the whole. Such extreme connectivity of subsystems is not only an obstacle for policy and planning. It also means that answers to issues, such as climate change, can come from unexpected places: technological innovation can have an impact, but also social innovation, law, interdisciplinary work, cultivating entrepreneurship, in general cultivating reflection on resilience. Whatever undermines the capacity of systems, of organizations and individuals, of communities, to bounce back, should be rejected as policy option, even if the intentions are good and the immediate outcome seems promising.

Within the context of sustainability and resilience approaches, we want to introduce a few more concepts which will recur in this book. Resilience can be studied in *socio-ecological systems*. If we give central place to the concept of socio-ecological systems, the attention tends to go to the relations between social systems and ecological systems, as two subsystems of a larger whole – which can cause shocks to each other. Resilience can thus be studied and possibly promoted in social systems and in ecological systems, and it makes sense to study the way the two are connected, since this gives insight in the channeling of shocks in the direction of the other subsystem, and in the amplification of effects of small events in one system, causing major damage in the other one. Small social change can lead to ecological disaster, and small ecological change (say, a few degree difference) can cause major shocks to social systems. One can also focus on

Figure 3.2. Technology can bring stories of other realities into the living rooms of rural communities everywhere. Yet, whether this in itself leads to 'development' can be debated. Photo: Anna-Katharina Hornidge. © ZEF/ University of Bonn, Germany.

the whole, as opposed to the subsystems, and try to grasp the principles governing socio-ecological systems as such, their evolution, their response to shocks. This comes conceptually close to pantheistic theories, where people and nature are considered to be similar in essence, closely tied together. For some, this means that people are part of ecosystems just as lichens and crabs, for others, it means that animals and plants are spiritually closer to us than we think, and yet other versions personify the Earth, as one tightly integrated system of which we are part, possibly a sentient being.

In less radical versions of the theory of socio-ecological systems, *adaptive management* or *adaptive governance* becomes important. If we can cultivate resilience in social systems and ecological systems, this means we can manage both ecosystems and social systems. If resilience entails the absorbing of shocks, this can be translated as the capacity to adapt. Absorbing shocks in the literal sense requires just surviving, with adaptive capacity already internalized, present in the structure and functioning of the system. If resilience also refers to change, then we can speak of management of ecosystems and governance of social systems to change more easily. Adaptive governance then requires acute observation of environmental change and internal, social change, the availability of internal options to understand that change and translate it into policy options, and the power to implement these policies.

Even some recent versions of adaptive management and governance are quite modernist in nature (see e.g. below where discussing environmental approaches to rural change): one assumes that there is one ideal structure of governance that can absorb shocks the best and/or can introduce a form of flexibility that works best to address environmental change (often: climate change). In these modernist versions of adaptive governance, it is often assumed that one form of expertise (environmental sciences) should be improved, to know exactly how and when to adapt policies, in response to environmental change; the analysis of social systems, of steering and implementation limits, is usually less developed.

In less modernist versions, there is more attention to *local knowledge*, to *co-management* of resources (including locals, more diverse stakeholders, more diverse sorts of knowledge), but there seems to be a lingering belief that this diversity of voices can be synthesized in one correct form of expertise inspiring one correct form of adaptive policy. The hope seems to be that inclusion of more voices is inclusion of more perspectives, leading to more adaptation options, and a more refined adaptation mechanism. Sometimes, scales of governance are distinguished, and scales of ecosystems.

### Further reading

Redclift, M. (2005). Sustainable development (1987-2005): an oxymoron comes of age. Sustainable Development, 13(4), 212-227.

### 3.2.6 Transition/innovation

Usually within a modernist paradigm operate transition & innovation approaches to development. As opposed to most of the approaches discussed above, this one did not emerge as a perspective on developing countries. In fact, it emerged as a response to a perceived crisis in the west (somewhat similar to the sustainability approach). In this case, the perception was, in the early 80's already, that the west was lagging behind in innovation. Not all developed economies were growing, not all were capable of supporting welfare systems (as in many European social democracies), and a discourse became influential among many government that innovation was the solution, that lack of innovation was the cause of the problem. Innovation was mostly understood as high tech development, and the silent or not so silent reference was what was happening in Silicon Valley (California, USA). That sort of development was seen as the future, it didn't exist yet in the rest of the world, so the rest tried to copy Silicon Valley in every possible way. High tech innovation was understood to be the essential form of innovation which would bring economic growth. In Europe, there was an additional focus on, expectation of, job creation.

Every country inspired by Silicon Valley (and a few other places, such as Boston's tech corridor), had a different interpretation however of the functioning of Silicon Valley, of the reasons for its success, and they had a different manner of following the example. Copying is never copying, and in the new context, the Silicon Valley idea becomes something different, linked to other ideas, translated into policies in different ways. It meets other positions of power in and around government, other modes of industrial production, other ideas of science and applied science. So, the outcomes were very diverse. In particular, most foreign observers did not notice that government played a small role in the rise of Silicon Valley, that spatial planning played no role at all, that risk was perceived very differently in the Valley than elsewhere, that it was no shame to go bankrupt, that there were little expectations of creating employment. Finally, it was often not noticed that the different social network of the Valley, with its different combinations of roles, people doing science, then starting a business, then becoming venture capitalists, supporting risky investments, that this structure of roles and network made it possible to come to a much more refined analysis of what was really scientifically innovative, and what among those could lead to commercial success.

Somehow, management schools, but also some people in social sciences, derived from the success of Silicon Valley the idea of a formula for innovation. European versions of that formula were more attuned to European ears, that is, the ears of European governments, who believed on average more in ideas of steering and social engineering, of visions of the future that could be articulated and implemented by government. In those versions that believe in the potential to steer innovation, to link innovations in a structured and programmed way, one often finds the ideas of transition and transition management. If a government has a comprehensive perspective on innovation, how to promote it, which kind of innovation, how to link them, how to bring them to implementation, to business, how to support those businesses, then one can say they have a transition management approach.

Innovation and transition management exists in many versions, with different ideas on the susceptibility of innovation to steering by means of policy. And there are very different perspectives on the types of policy that are most relevant: economic policy, fiscal, science and education policy, and spatial policy and planning. In that last version, there is the assumption that redesigning space is an important driver for redesigning the economy, in a manner more favorable for innovation. The transition management approach in its extreme versions rests on a strong belief in social engineering, since there is the idea that government, assisted by scientists (and business, often) can identify where innovation is needed, how it can be coupled, what is most promising, how to bring it to commercial success, and how this can benefit not just the company in question, but society as a whole. Sometimes, there is an assumption that society itself has to change, so it can become more innovative, engender economic growth, which can benefit itself. We come close to the Soviet idea of engineered society, in its structures and elements (people).

**Example 3.5. Impact and assessment: recurring modernism.**

Expertise and local knowledge can have influence on policies and plans, and those can have impact on the community. Impact is many things however. In most cases, it does not mean that the policy is exactly implemented as intended by decision-makers, while the result is rarely what was envisioned. Still, there is likely to be impact. A special form is what we called goal dependencies: impact of new institutions envisioning a new future on the current configurations of actors and institutions, on the way these evolve. Ideas on the future affect what happens now, how it transforms. The impacts of policies and plans are visible and understandable only later: a development plan might have been considered a disaster, but it can reappear with better effects in a changed context. Resistance can reinvigorate governance, and lead to the formulation of new ideas, new players, and more effective or appropriate policies. Impact hinges on informal institutions embedding the formal institutions, and on informality in the implementation process. The assessment of impact is always colored by the perspective of the actors assessing, their position in power/knowledge configurations, their understanding of measurable, visible and relevant effects, of causality, and of success and failure.

The same issues affect a series of assessment types, which pretend to be technical but are not: environmental impact assessment, ecological indicators, wetland delineation, heritage or cultural impact assessment, swot analyses, cost-benefit analyses. None of these can be disconnected from assumptions, and the discourses and ideologies they are embedded in. The point of all of these was initially to force a conversation on the impacts of policies or proposed policies and to keep the conversation going. Reducing them to a small number of quantifiable parameters defined and measured by usually mono-disciplinary experts, undercuts this idea of embedding in governance, of a community reflection on a specific aspect of a shared future, the best tools to get there, the price and side effects of these tools. Each of these assessment methods has merit, but cannot be decoupled from this discursive context, of narratives about community and environment where values are defined and impacts are measured. A SWOT analysis (looking for strengths, weaknesses, opportunities, threats) is more honest and helpful when it is explicit about the values and threats recognized: threat in which perspective? To what exactly? Opportunity for whom? Did we talk about this? A cost-benefit analysis can be misleading for similar reasons: benefits under which conditions? What counts as benefit? Is it ok to measure possible benefits of a measure (say, a new school, or road) without thinking about flanking measures, about synergies of policy integration (e.g. a new school with a new school bus and a park; or revised planning of towns around train stations)? Same for ecological indicators: what is measured, how is value attributed, which unity, which relation, which process, is valued, which spatial and temporal reference is used for an optimal state? How hard do you look for a threatened snail? Or with environmental impact assessment: what model of the environment is used here? What is valuable and why? Which combinations of variables is deemed an acceptable or good environment, and what can possibly compensate for what? Can slightly cleaner water offset cutting a variety of trees, and can cutting tree A be the same as tree B? For heritage: who decides what is heritage, how valuable it is, and whether the context contributes to that value? Is a ruin the same as the ruin in a landscape? For wetlands: wasn't the whole idea of wetland protection to make people think about the interconnected nature of water resources, and the value of protecting that web of linkages, rather than trying to pseudo-objectively isolate the wetland?

Each of the methods has to be seen as a tool to make impacts of policies visible and susceptible to discussion, discussion in governance. Since almost all of them were reclaimed by technocrats, it seems important to reclaim assessment for governance. Participatory impact assessment (PEI) can be helpful there: in the sense of participation in the assessment, and a participatory discussion of the result in some governance setting. Citizens are not scientists, and they are not elected officials, so PEI needs to fit that space; scientific methods used in the current assessments are useful, and will be carried out by scientists, and decisions in the end are always politics. A decision is never caused by an assessment, otherwise it would not be a decision. There are always options, with pro's and con's. A specialized sub-organization in governance (a heritage council, an economic development task force, an environmental council, a planning board, a downtown association) can follow more closely and be engaged in PEI, and rapport back to a town board.

With the rise in popularity of PEI, formulaic approaches pop up as well: how exactly do we do this? While this is understandable, copying of so-called best practices or standard formula's is not a good idea, since the context will be different, with different actors, institutions, power relations, values, ideas on the future. Again, the whole idea is to force reflection, not to avoid it. With PEI, the added value can lie in the communal structuring of the assessment, the communal reflection on the result, allowing for an interrogation of not only the proposed policy, but also the linkage with other policies: the community can decide what it sees as the most relevant results of the proposal, positive and negative, and how this could be managed in the context of other policies, other values, the kind of environment and community one aspires to. It can also cause a rethinking of some goals, policies, plans. That way, it can become part of the ongoing conversation we call governance.

### Further reading

Walker, G. (2010). Environmental justice, impact assessment and the politics of knowledge: the implications of assessing the social distribution of environmental outcomes. Environmental Impact Assessment Review, 30(5), 312-318.

Sometimes, innovation and transition management is disguised as rhetoric of the 'knowledge economy', which is supposed to refer to a new economy in which knowledge is essential, and a competitive advantage is mostly a difference in the quality, quantity and novelty of knowledge. We have to refrain from a thorough discussion here, but, as with many of the development perspectives discussed, we find it curious that there is so little interest in, understanding of, the actual development path of Western countries, and the role of knowledge and expertise there. 'Knowledge' is, again, often reduced to technical knowledge of high tech production, and this is directly linked to commercial success. Also within management science, there are a wide variety of other explanations of commercial success in the contemporary world, and economic historians will point at the importance of knowledge in most phases and forms of economic development. Only where political or religious power would forcefully open markets, and those communities were not allowed to develop, would the same products, based on the same expertise, remain successful for a long time. One can also say that the agricultural revolution 10,000 years ago required an impressive level of expertise, of refined observation, trial and error, exchange of information, co-development, so wild species of plants and animals would quickly evolve into domestic animals and crops that would support an enormous growth in population and in the sophistication of societies.

One modification of the discourse or one can say an addition by social scientists who saw the success of innovation discourses and policies, was the concept of social innovation. Many definitions exist, but we can say that it is usually a way of non-natural scientists to draw the attention to other forms of innovation as important for economic growth and to bring about broader social benefits (to further more diverse common goals). In some versions, it means that also organizational and cultural changes in society can bring about economic growth, coupled with the technological innovation policies, whereas other versions use the concept more to break open the whole innovation discussion, away from technological innovation, to state that societies are always innovating, evolving, and that in this process there are risks and benefits. Benefits can be seen as common goals that come closer in the next step of evolution, risks as goals that become more removed, and new problems that are introduced. Social innovation could then be the encouraging of benefits and the management of risk. It can be more passive, observing which initiatives come up, with governmental, non-governmental and science and business actors, and it can be more active, encouraging various players to think of new ways of organizing themselves, new ways to coordinate among each other that might bring communal benefits (some of them monetized, others not).

One famous version of transition management is the triple helix model by Loet Leydesdorff. Leydesdorff speaks of a co-evolution, mutual dependence of government, business and science. The interactions between these three can spur innovation in all three, and can lead to scientific innovation with commercial success, without destabilizing society. Transition management is then structuring the interaction between these three parties. Different successive versions of the triple helix exist, responding to critics, but one can still notice that this innovation is curiously de-coupled from politics. Government seems to refer to administration, bureaucracy, but not to politicians elected by people on the base of programs, reflection what voters like, reflecting different versions of the good society. Both participation and representation are out of the picture. Local knowledge does not play a significant role, but also local participatory democracy, institutional experiment (as part of social innovation) is hardly considered, and within the scientific realm, there is little attention to the actual logic of discovery, the way in which pure understanding of issues of different natures can lead much later to economic success. Most of the time, economic breakthroughs cannot be tied to scientific breakthroughs that were managed with the eye on scientific success, either by companies or by government.

Some versions of transition management do become more inclusive, by distinguishing different scales of governance that are relevant for transitions, by allowing some input bottom-up, and, last but not least, by speaking of transition towards other or broader goals: transitions towards resilience, towards sustainability, or social justice. This broadening of scope can lead to a more participatory approach, an openness to social innovation, but it can also maintain the social engineering character of earlier versions, similar to modernist sustainability approaches, but now with a major input of corporate players in policy making on science, education, infrastructure and planning.

## Further reading

Christensen, C. (2013). The innovator's dilemma: when new technologies cause great firms to fail. Cambridge, UK: Harvard Business Review Press.

Leydesdorff, L., Dolfsma, W. and van der Panne, G. (2006). Measuring the knowledge base of an economy in terms of triple-helix relations among technology, organization, and territory'. Research Policy, 35(2), 181-199.

## 3.2.7 Participation as everything

A very different current in development thinking, coming up in various disciplines since the 1990's, sees the practice of participation as the solution to almost anything. The reasons for this turn away from modernism, and in many cases from scientific expertise as the basis of policy, are diverse. Aaron Wildavsky analyzed already in the 1970's how implementation should not be understood as one thing, one concept, one action. Policy tends to rely too much on scientific expertise in policies and plans that are routinely not implemented. Or, it is implemented, but the effects are very different from expected. Or, one aspect is implemented, others not, and the overall result can be the opposite of what was intended. In other words, the idea of 'implementation' was a modernist trick to give the impression that, after policy formulation, just one thing was

**Example 3.6. Projects and organizations in development.**

Much common discourse on public policy and development assumes that things will be organized, and structured in projects. These assumptions are not so natural, and we will briefly highly a few consequences of them.

Organizations are an invention of the middle ages, with companies in our sense emerging, but also guilds, professional associations, and monasteries and universities. Before that, people were organized, but organizations as legal persons and as entities going above individual authority and lifespan, virtually did not exist. Even armies were often tied to the person of the leader and transformed or disbanded after his death.

Organizations can be governmental, non-governmental, and within that category, they can be for profit (business) and not-for-profit (NGO in the narrower sense). 'The' government seen from an organizational perspective, or a governance perspective, does not exist as a unity; it is a cluster of organizations in administration and politics, a set of actors in governance. Organizations can survive for centuries, but their life span can also be intended to be short. Project organizations belong to this category. They are associated with projects, usually short term clusters of activities, decisions, people and resources, aiming at a goal more narrowly defined than that of an organization, aiming to coordinate decision-making towards that goal. Projects can exist only within an organization, or they can be underpinned by a project organization. Such organization can be helpful for complex policy coordination, when a variety of actors, often other organizations, is tied to one goal. If the project becomes a long term policy orientation, the project organization can become a more stable organization, lightly institutionalized, to keep other orgnizations communicating on a topic. Governments can support project organizations through directing funding. They can be useful to bring together actors and perspectives which are usually separated; if that is the case, they can be called boundary spanning organizations. Different scientific disciplines can e.g. be brought together in a project organization, but also governmental actors, businesses and other non-governmental organizations (NGOs).

Organizations are marked by an organizational identity, and procedures of self-reproduction through decision-making. There is a guiding idea on what the organization is, its goal, its members, its procedures. Organizations see the world through their own lens: they interpret it through linking it to goals and identity. A political change can be an opportunity to sell more drinks for a soft drinks company. It can be a reason to change the lobbying strategy for low taxation, etc. A person is a potential consumer. Organizations also try to stay alive: once established, they tend to adapt to their environment, or try to change that environment. Non-governmental organizations in general do not represent a general interest, or if so, they represent something they interpret as a common good, without the checks and balances of democratic governance. NGOs have an agenda which is different from, and more narrow than that of a government. They generally think in shorter term spans, shorter than governments, because of precarious financing and less stable institutional embedding. Often, they are mostly structured along project lines; what they do is projects, and looking for new projects, since this is the way to do things and to find money. The logic of the organization becomes the logic of the project. Managing such organization is thinking continuously in terms of results that might bring new projects, in terms of timelines and expertise befitting projects and in terms of visible and sellable project results. NGOs participating in rural development projects necessarily bring their own organizational identity to decision-making, and if they become influential in governance, that agenda will shape the selection and interpretation of public goods. NGO participation in governance is tricky because of this slant of interpretation and interest, because of time horizons, and lack of inclusivity. Yet NGOs can also be irreplacable, where governments don't work, are too slow, too corrupt, or too entrenched in one way of thinking.

Governments are expected to represent the general interest, but do not always do this. They can represent sections of the community and currents of ideas. Governmental actors do not always represent the government, and the organizational identity can twist a policy, plan, law in a distinct direction. A governmental organization will have its own version of the public good it is supposed to further, and it will tend to make itself important in the process. Competition between governmental actors is in most respects competition between organizations. Governmental actors can think in the longer term, mobilize resources more reliably, and are at least in theory capable to participate in policy integration processes. They can also be tied to political parties, interest groups, to one narrow form of expertise.

Businesses, as organizations, could be in some cases more efficient, as their results are very clearly visible in financial terms, and they are assessed harshly in those not very disputable terms. Their survival hinges in the most direct way on financial results so the motivation is very strong, and a focus is easier to maintain. On the other hand, a financial motivation is not the same as motivation by product quality. The forms of markets, and the sort of corporate organization accountability make a difference. A company can aim at results for shareholders, for the owners, for management, and each form will imply different strategies of investment, different time-horizons, and different participation strategies in governance. If short term returns to shareholders dominate, assigning power to business in rural development is probably not a good idea. If the companies are more capable of long term strategies, and sensitive to the image in a community they can be more sensitive to shared issues and common goods.

Organizations are powerful tools of coordination which cannot be missed anymore from any development effort. Projects and project organizations can provide flexibility, and make governance less rigid in its development path. Yet, understanding the nature of projects and organizations is very useful to understand their limits, and their effects in a certain governance path. They are tools of governance which have their own dynamics, their own identity, so using them changes the governance path.

### Further reading

Seidl, D. and Becker, K.H. (eds.). (2005). Niklas Luhmann and organization studies. Malmö, Sweden: Liber.

Atack, I. (1999). Four criteria of development NGO legitimacy. World Development, 27(5), 855-864.

needed, implementation, and then the policy would change the world. Wildavsky and others showed that usually what happened in the world after the policy was enacted, was quite different from the original intention. They also showed that this was not always bad: what happened later in the process could sometimes be considered a complex and opaque process of participation. Other actors do their own thing with the policy, exert influence, push aspects in a different direction, modify it based on local knowledge and local preferences, or based on different forms of scientific knowledge. Or, other actors, block aspects because they don't agree.

More and more people in policy and science then started thinking: why not include these other actors more directly, why not formalize this as participation process? This could make everything less opaque, less complex, clearly structured, and, who knows efficient. A weaker version of the participation discourse could be summarized as: if locals participate, they will understand us, government and scientists, and then they will follow us. A stronger version: if we include more actors directly, openly, then locals can transform both policy making and implementation, and policies can be based on a combination of expert knowledge and local knowledge. The strongest version of

Figure 3.3. 'No national park'. National parks embody a combination of tourism and nature conservation as a strategy for development. The recognition is per definition formal and by a national government, but the initiative can be bottom up, top down, or by a specific coalition of actors cross-cutting scales. Making a designation more participatory can increase local support but just as well resistance. British Columbia, Canada. Photo: Monica Gruzmacher. © ZEF/University of Bonn, Germany.

the participation discourse would like to rethink all policy making as participatory, to include all the 'stakeholders', all actors affected or interested, and base everything on local knowledge. Expert knowledge in this version is destined to be an exception, only brought in when actors decide collectively to do so. In some variations of this approach, also the science itself, the expert knowledge which can be included, should be the product of a participatory process, with the community not only indicating which issues should be studied, but also participating in the production and evaluation of the research (citizen science; participatory research; evaluation).

Participatory approaches to policy making, and to development, as comprehensive policy making for alternative futures, came up as an answer to problems of implementation, but also as an answer to problems of democratic legitimacy. High modernist public administration and planning, relying on administration and their experts, was seen as not context-sensitive, but also as not accountable enough. The answer was sought in more participation, which would include more in the decision-making, and make it more transparent, but often the benefits and importance of representation for democracies was forgotten. As was the importance of specialization of professions and expertise, and differentiation of organizations and function systems (see above).

If one neglects the representative mechanisms in a democracy, a strong accent on participation can bring 'actors' around the table where it is not clear who they are really representing and if they are representing them well, and it does not give a guarantee at all that all interests, voices and desires in the community are actually around the table. Many people will not be represented at all, because they do not fall clearly under a stakeholder label ('fishermen', 'heritage enthusiasts') or under a label that is vague ('inhabitant', 'local', 'neighbor'). Further, it creates differential access to governance, because some people and groups are not suited to the process: they would be happy to rely on the expertise and procedures already put in place by the people they voted for and do not enjoy the new form of politics and competition, the importance of rhetoric, strategy, and case and policy knowledge that is required to be successful in participatory governance. More communicating does not simply solve problems; it can bring new problems to light, create more problems, and it creates the rhetorical arena which many people want to reserve for the people they vote for, and their experts.

Participation creates new light in governance, but it also creates new areas of shade and darkness. It can undermine mechanisms of representation if the decisions made in the participatory arena e.g. replace those formerly made by city councils, or fill in gaps that were left by councils, without much oversight. If such oversight is taken seriously however, then the work done in a participatory arena (e.g. an environmental local council), can be undone, and many citizens with daytime jobs may find they spent their evenings working for nothing. This can undermine both representation and the next participation attempt. We believe it is better to think in terms of a balance between *representation* and *participation* that needs to be discussed before policy reform towards more participation. The undermining of representation (and specialization) that could otherwise ensue, can bring back shades of the past: old forms of corruption, old networks and clans that were reduced in influence by effective principles of representation. Five 'stakeholders' around the table can represent de facto one old clan, more easily than a group of council members elected in different neighborhoods, by more people.

Extreme participation also has a problem with *scale*: large scale policies would require the participation of many many actors. The mapping of relevant actors, stakeholders, becomes very complex, and questionable, and even if this would be possible, the coordination of the process of participation would be very complex, slow and costly. In addition, there is a good chance that the complexity of the policy issues at larger scales transcends the grasp of people selected only because they are affected, not because they have the time and knowledge that makes them suitable (whether this knowledge is scientific or not). At the large scale, also the issue of democratic legitimacy comes back with more urgency: should these kind of decisions not be taken by voters, or, should the result of the process, a policy or plan affecting a large area, not be voted upon? Different answers are possible, depending on the model of democracy one prefers, but in general, we can say that extreme participation hits limits at the larger scales of policy making, limits of complexity, efficiency, expertise, legitimacy.

We can add another issue: *short-term* vs. *long-term*. Participatory processes can envision both, but for the long term stability of communities and societies, a strong accent on participation vs. representation can undermine the checks and balances that contribute to stability and orderly self-transformation. Small groups of people can take decisions in unchecked participatory processes which can undo the long process of specialization and differentiation that allowed Western democracies to emerge in stable forms: the presence of both politics and administration, of both local knowledge and expert knowledge, of legal, political, scientific and economic perspectives that are separately institutionalized (with different organizations, rules, roles, competition, arena's) has contributed both to the stability and adaptability of Western democracies. That process of specialization, associated with the political mechanism of representation, can thus be understood a the bringer of an elaborate set of checks and balances.

Participation naively understood and implemented in extreme versions, can undo the important separation of arena's, of roles and rules, of expertise forms that was so important in Western development. Simply bringing people together around the table, seeing them as representative of 'the community' and then deciding on short and long term policy issues based on questionable representation and scant understanding of the issues at hand, might solve the problem of a formerly oppressive political elite or bureaucracy, or the problem of a formerly unchecked expert group hiding behind the administration. But it can also destroy the bureaucracies and differentiated roles that make democracies possible, by giving more direct access to power to clans, networks and interest groups and by weakening the checks on that power. The local knowledge that becomes more important in such process, does not necessarily benefit the community.

For all these reasons, we propose, rather than to speak of a discovery of participation as something new, and rather than presenting representation, expert knowledge and administration as necessarily oppressive, to say that both participation and representation have risks and benefits, that they need and assume each other and that they always coexisted. Even before the word participation was invented, there was participation, in forms often not acknowledged. Just as laws cannot work without informal rules embedding them and governing their enforcement (see below) mechanisms of representation cannot work without participation. And the other way around.

In line with civic republicanism, we would propose that the forms of governance in a community change continuously, because of changing internal and external circumstances. One aspect of this is that the forms and balance between participation and representation in a community have to be constantly reflected upon, for governance to be efficient (some procedures don't work anymore after a while) and to be legitimate (some are not believable anymore, or not acceptable anymore). Ideas on the good community and on the good democracy evolve. Continuous reflection on the desirable balance between participation and representation, and new ways to give organizational form to this, without undermining checks and balances, seems very useful to maintain legitimacy while keeping an eye on practical problem solving.

Cultivating such reflexivity, we argue, can be helpful to move closer as a community towards a developmental goal, or a shared vision for the future. It can simultaneously transform the idea of the goal, and of good and acceptable paths towards that. If such reflection does not take place, if there are no ways to adjust the balance mentioned, then there is a very real possibility that new plans do not have the legitimacy of old plans anymore, without administrations noticing, and the real risk that long term plans achieve goals that are not desirable or shared anymore by the community.

## Further reading

Cooke, B. and Kothari, U. (eds.). (2001). Participation: the new tyranny? London, UK: Zed Books.
Easterly, W. (2006). The white man's burden: why the West's efforts to aid the rest have done so much ill and so little good. New York, NY, USA: Penguin Press.

## 3.2.8 Institutions

Institutionalist approaches to development focus on rules and rule making. They can be modernist in orientation (e.g. looking for the perfect institutional arrangement which can underpin development, which can be measured in macro-economic parameters), or not. It can focus on the macro scale, or not. It can be focused on legal/political reform (establishing 'the rule of law'), or not. It can restrict its observation to formal institutions, usually law, or it can have a broader scope of observation, an interest in all possible ways in which people coordinate economic interaction, or interaction in general.

Probably the most influential versions of institutionalism stem from economics (several schools of institutional economics, starting with Veblen in the early 20<sup>th</sup> century), but there are also important examples in political science, public administration, planning, sociology. Depending on the discipline of origin, the emphasis can be on different functional domains, or different relations between functional domains: the relation between politics and economy, or between law and politics, e.g. Some see some form of Western capitalist democracy as a goal of development, others as a precondition, before anything else can work, and yet others try to think of development as possible in a wider variety of political models and context, and a wider variety of paths and forms.

The versions we are most interested, we consider to be most promising, are those where limits on social engineering are envisioned, and where 'the rule of law' is seen as something with many faces and forms. If one assumes there is one form of rule of law that could enable economic development, one disregards most of history and geography, and if one assumes that such rule of law could summarily be created, before any real development policy takes off, one distances oneself from reality. If we look at other times and places, and at the history of Western nation-states themselves, we see that what we call 'rule of law', as a positive institutional framework, enabling stable polities and strong economic development, is not one thing, but a series of differentiations, slow crystallizations of rules and roles. What is shared among most examples is the stability of rules, the predictability of coordination among actors for certain types of transactions, the development of specialized rules for different types of activities, the belief in enforcement of rules. In other words: some kind of coordination needs to be organized, preferably with specialized rules (regulating economic transactions, political action, legal action, scientific work, religious work, art) which is credible for those involved. And, as an important addition: stability is furthered by the existence of rules to change the rules. If those do not exist, adaptation to changing environments, internal and external, will be in the form of shocks, which can destabilize the whole community. In terms of a previous approach: rules to change the rules increase the resilience of social systems.

'The rule of law' is in other words very important for development, but can be many things. The only measure of success is whether it works or not, not whether it conforms to an ideal imposed by Western economists or legal scholars. The rule of law might work without written law, and the rule of law most relevant for economic transactions might be law pertaining to a very different field (environmental law, religious law, etc.).

As long as economic transactions are possible, specialized tools to further them, make them easier, develop new types of them, are possible, can be developed, then one can speak of a rule of law that enables economic development.

If one drops the idea of one ideal institutional configuration, it makes sense also to drop the idea to engineer perfect institutions. Many different opinions on this topic exist, but we believe, with Daron Acemoglu, William R. Easterly, Paul Seabright and Douglas North, that development cannot entirely be planned, that it always includes a measure of experiment. This refers to economic entrepreneurship, trying to find niches and create niches in markets, but it also refers to institutional experimentalism: institutional configurations have to be modified all the time, to adapt to changing circumstances, to make them work better. Easterly speaks of planners versus searchers, and takes the side of the last ones.

Besides the need to experiment, and the need to fit new rules to a context of old rules, there is another limit to engineering of good institutions: *informal institutions*. Formal rules, such as laws, but also policies and plans, only work if they fit existing informal institutions, informal ways to coordinate action, to deal with other rules. If formal institutions, as rules of coordination, ignore informal institutions, they will have either no impact, or a result very different from what was intended. The more evolutionary versions of institutionalism, e.g. Douglas North, Avner Greif, Daron Acemoglu, often see formal institutions as historically emerging from informal institutions. Laws codify something that already worked, or they punish something that exists but which was commonly condemned. If a law punishes something that is considered normal in society, then the law will probably not be enforced, or, if it is, this will lead to destabilization of the polity. (In democracies, to a new law probably). In such historical institutionalism, we can speak of paths of development, guided by institutions created in that path, formal and informal institutions. The form of 'rule of law' that works for a community, is in other words the product of the evolution of that community.

If one drops the idea of one ideal institutional configuration, and adds the idea of evolving configurations, we can also understand more easily some limits to policy transfer: 'good' policies or laws cannot be simply be copied somewhere else. Their effects will vary depending on the developmental path of a community, the formal and informal rules governing that development, and also depending on the knowledge present in the community and its power relations. According to the historical institutionalists, institutions emerge together with actors. Rules and roles co-evolve, and once you have certain actors in place (say: merchant, tax collector, commercial law judge, notary, bank) they will try to maintain themselves, improve their position, become more powerful, makes themselves necessary.

**Example 3.7. What type of 'development'? For who? And by who? The Center for Development Research, University of Bonn, Germany.**

With the decision by the federal government of reunited Germany to move from Bonn to Berlin in 1991, it was also decided to establish Bonn as the capital of development and development cooperation, attract several United Nations Secretariates, leave the Federal Ministry of Economic Cooperation and Development in Bonn and locate several implementing agencies of German development cooperation (e.g. German International Cooperation (GIZ)) in Bonn. As part of this, the Center for Development Research, an interdisciplinary research institute attached to the University of Bonn was found (www.zef.de). In large inter- and transdisciplinary projects, mostly funded by the Federal Ministry of Education and Research (BMBF) of Germany, international teams of researchers study socio-ecological processes of change. Together with their research partners in Central, South, Southeast Asia, the Caucasus Region, Eastern and Western Africa as well as South America, the researchers formulate suggestions for improvement (i.e. social, political, technological innovation packages) to counter locally-pressing, real-life problems (e.g. desertification in North-Western Uzbekistan, climate change in Western Africa, flood risks in urban Indonesia, etc.), posing increasing threats to everyday livelihood provision.

The mandate of the institute is to conduct inter- and transdisciplinary development research and – based on this largely empirical research – formulate 'solutions', potential answers to issues of development. The center's research is thus placed at the verge between applied and basic research, between contributing to the answering of real-life problems in 'the global South' and de-Westernising (de-provincialising, but instead globalising) methodological and conceptual debates within the epistemic centers of the world (still largely located in 'the global North'). A recurring discussion amongst the researchers with disciplinary backgrounds ranging from hydroloy and soil sciences to economics, to geography, political sciences, anthropology and sociology looks at the notion of 'development' itself. Most common definitions of 'development' communicate a linear, progress and economic growth oriented idea, dividing the world in 'the west' and 'the rest', attaching different levels of wealth/poverty to nation states as political as well as geographically fixed entities – a simplistic and hegemonic assessment that in a world characterised by global movements of people, goods and finances decreasingly holds. And yet, how do we define 'development'? As a form of 'positive' social, economic and ecologic change? 'Positive' for who? And defined by who? 'Change' from what? And towards which other state of life? What type of 'change' itself: linear, non-linear, etc.? – In these discussions, 'development' regularly proves its value in acting as a boundary concept – a concept and notion that in its vagueness, its blurriness, its multifaceted characteristics brings together people with very different disciplinary and cultural backgrounds, encourages discussion and opens further questions. One answer regularly found is to agree, to disagree – a fertile ground for future critical, questioning debates.

**Further reading**

Ziai, A. (2012). Postcolonial perspectives on 'development'. Working Paper 103. Bonn, Germany: Center for Development Research, University of Bonn.

Compatible with historical institutionalism is the idea that alternative visions for the future, alternative needs, desires, values can come up in a community and find their own form of organization, in a history of interactions. Communities can change, embrace different ideas on wellbeing, develop new development goals, implicit or explicit, and this will lead to the transformation of rules and roles, based on the existing set of rules and roles. The rule of law will change, by design, but not design with a blank slate. There are rules and roles, there are rules of transformation, of changing the rules, and this will shape the path of change, and the new version of rule of law which comes about. Laws and policies from somewhere else can be used for inspiration, elements can be incorporated, if it fits this path of change, and this pattern of rules and roles.

What develops in a community is therefore more than a version of the rule of law. Each community develops its own form of market, its own set of relations between economy, politics, law, science, religion (its own form of differentiation, as we said earlier). Institutions, rules of coordination, regulate the internal functioning of each domain (law, etc.) but also the relations between the domains. The way law, politics, etc. are coupled, is also a result of the unique evolution of communities and societies.

Forms of ownership are thus always tied to forms of political organization (link between economy, law and politics) and the forms of ownership that work best in one place, do not necessarily work in other places. Elinor Ostrom and many others have studied common property forms in many cultures, and found they can work just as well as private property rights, while private property rights have many shades (see below). Companies can make as much money in big government environments as in small government contexts; as long as the rules are clear, stable, and enforced, this allows for coordinated action, and for profit making strategies.

Historical institutionalism, thus places limits on social engineering, on policy transfer, on planning, but it opens the mind to envision alternative development paths marked by alternative configurations of institutions. Learning between communities between different paths is possible, but requires reflexivity and reinterpretation: where does this come from? Why did it emerge there, and work there? Why would it work here? It also shows that rules and roles co-evolve, that one cannot think of rules separately from roles. Copying a role from somewhere else without looking at other rules and roles, or copying a rule, without looking at other rules and roles, are equivalent sins. It is one of the development approaches that allows for local knowledge, traditions, alternative rule and role sets, alternative development paths, for tradition and change, and for an understanding that what is driving development in a community is never merely economic goals.

Measuring development purely in economic terms is therefore problematic, but also trying to push development merely by economic policy. And, we can add, it also shows the futility to push and guide development by means of quantified goals (such as the economic goals). Development reasoning always has to start from the present, and desirable outcomes cannot be quantified a priori. What is a good number should be allowed to change over time, the kind of parameters considered important could change, and the simple fact of starting with numbers is problematic: what is possible and what is desirable will evolve, will not always be visible or transparent at the starting point.

## Further reading

Greif, A. (2006). Institutions and the path to the modern economy: lessons from medieval trade. Cambridge, UK: Cambridge University Press.

Haggard, S. (2004). Institutions and growth in East Asia. Studies in Comparative International Development, 38, 53-81.

Johnson, C. (1987). Political institutions and economic performance: the government-business relationship in Japan, South Korea, and Taiwan. In: Deyo, F.C. (ed.), The political economy of the New Asian industrialism. Ithaca, NY, USA: Cornell University Press, pp. 136-164.

North, D. (2005) Understanding the process of economic change. Princeton, NJ, USA: Princeton University Press.

Ostrom, E. (2005). Understanding institutional diversity. Princeton, NJ, USA: Princeton University Press.

Seabright, P. (2010). The company of strangers: a natural history of economic life. Princeton, NJ, USA: Princeton University Press.

Thelen, K. (1999). Historical institutionalism in comparative politics. Annual Review of Political Science, 2(1), 369-404.

## 3.2.9 Post-anything

One last approach to development we want to mention in this list is the complete deconstruction and then abandoning of the whole concept of development. Names often quoted are Edward Said, Homi Bhabha, Arturo Escobar, Gayatri C. Spivak, and James Ferguson. In the background often looms Michel Foucault.

Post-development approaches came up in the 90's, in different versions. All embody more radical critiques of development. Development as a concept and as an industry, as a web of interrelated organizations, are both scrutinized and rejected. Post-colonialism is in general more discourse-oriented, meaning here that these authors are trying to study ways of seeing and thinking which underly speech and action, ways of thinking about the world that underpin development discourse. They find many colonial legacies, oppressive mechanisms, and signs of Western hegemony. Post-development perspectives usually dwell more on policy, embark on policy analysis and critique and investigate the functioning of the development industry, finding it so problematic, oppressive, self-serving, led by external interests, that it should better be dismantled.

Figure 3.4. Local knowledge in many places betrays a strong influence of scientific knowledge, although maybe of an older generation, and a different paradigm. We cannot see this as a tainting of the authentic traditional knowledge, but as a reminder that knowledge is always co-produced, and an accumulation of traces coming from different times, places, conceptual realms, through networks that might be lost or forgotten. An experimental lab of the Institute of Botany at the University of Agriculture in Tajikistan. Photo: Anna-Katharina Hornidge. © ZEF/University of Bonn, Germany.

Ways of acting and thinking are connected, and the functioning of the development sector is informed by many of the same Western ideas that structure development discourse by Western authors, donors, policy-makers. Post-development and post-colonialism deserve to be discussed together, in other words.

For post-colonialist Spivak the concept of development is already poisoned by a web of discourses in which positions are taken, images are used. Cleaning the concept would be like cleaning a poisoned well: almost impossible. Better to drop it, dig another well, make new concepts. 'Development' will always be tainted by associations too many people have with enlightenment ideas of progress, Western superiority, failed development attempts, use of development projects to gain political or commercial influence. Development is too much tainted with what Edward Said called *orientalism*, the representation of poorer countries as essentially different, and this opens the door to seeing them as lesser, as less developed, maybe as needing intervention (or colonial takeover). The hard line drawn between 'us' and 'them', 'rich' and 'poor', 'us' and 'the Other' of developing countries, makes it harder to understand 'them' and 'ourselves'. Understanding would be enhanced by seeing the relationships and similarities. Reflecting more on ourselves in an honest way, without using simplistic images of 'the Other' to distinguish from (we are this because we are not that or them) would show our past selves in a different light, our development, and help in relating to other communities and their unique paths. We spoke earlier of lacking insight in Western development paths which created difficulties in understanding other paths, and caused tendencies to project development recipes that didn't apply to ourselves to places where they will certainly not apply.

For Spivak, development efforts, colonialism and its legacies, have created a class of the *subaltern*, those who cannot speak. They have no voice left to speak for themselves, not only because they were not given access to education, and no access to power, but also because the ways they understand themselves and the world now, are structured in and by colonialism. Most developing countries did not exist as countries before colonialism; there were political entities in those areas, but usually either much smaller (tribes, etc.) or much larger (multi-ethnic empires) than the modern nation-state, much less centralized, and without the systems of bureaucracy, education one identifies with nation-states. If India did not exist before (as nation-state), what does it mean to be Indian? It can mean a lot, and without being a fake or self-deceit, but this web of meaning cannot be disconnected from the British colonial past. Even concepts such as oppression, marginalization, the subaltern, are products of a politicized academia that can only be understood as Western rooted and structured.

The solution can therefore not be 'development' as invoked or promoted by the West, but it can also not be found in the liberation of the oppressed, so they could speak an authentic discourse, and choose their authentic path of evolution. Authenticity is impossible, and liberation of some Western-imposed constraints and structures gives more space to others. Identifications and explanations of the poor rely on Western conceptual structures, but they are also shaped by older relations of power, of economic use and abuse. Where to go from here? Not so clear. Avoiding simplistic neo-liberal discourse about opening markets and reducing rules, to promote entrance in the club of modern capitalist democracies, and avoiding similarly simplistic discourse from the political left, on liberation of the oppressed, towards more collective development paths, deemed compatible with 'traditional' ways. Spivak encourages us to reflect deeper on the relations between discourse, action and policy and to understand that there is no way back. There is never an authentic self to return to, we have to start reasoning from individuals and communities that are always hybrid, mixtures of elements coming from different contexts, and results of histories with bright and dark sides.

*Hybridity*, for Homi Bhabha, is a more positive concept, one that can point a way to more actionable futures. For Bhabha, hybridity is more complex, not as in 'a bit of this, a bit of that', but rather a continuous reworking of newer elements of discourse and practice that are being integrated into older structures of individual and society, and slowly transforming those. Western concepts, discourses, modes of action and organization, are always reinterpreted to fit existing modes of thinking and action. Such reinterpretation is often taking place automatically, as a way to make sense of things, of changing selves and circumstances, of making things work in a practical sense. But, as Bhabha points out, hybridization can be mere than passive processing or internalization or practical accommodation. There can be a strategic use of new elements and their modifications, for local goals, and there can be a silent subversion of them (similar to James Scott's idea of everyday resistance). One can pretend to follow rules, but then not, one can follow orders so precisely that they don't make sense anymore, one can selectively interpret rules, use concepts, organizations, to fit existing identities and interests. Old elites can take advantage of colonial newcomers, their structure of organization and administration; old ideas can find a new reach by embeddings in new school systems, administrations.

Hybridity in the sense of Bhabha thus undermines development efforts initiated from elsewhere. Old hybridity will produce new hybridity: colonialism creates neo-colonial hybrids which will reinterpret and hybridize again, when new development efforts are initiated from the west. The direction of reinterpretation and strategic use will always change, and Western observers will never be able to completely see how old hybridity generates new one, how new policies and interventions will be changed locally. Most of Western interventions have either a universal subject assumed (a Western type of person considered the model for 'a' person) or an 'authentic local', of an authenticity that doesn't exist. If we accept hybridity, we cannot insist too much on either global or local citizenship and cannot emphasize the distinction between imposed universal development paths, and authentic, varied, local ones. Development paths will always incorporate local and external elements, ideas, forms of organization, people, and the next step will always be shaped by a previous hybrid state.

Post-colonialism and post-development approaches draw the attention to the fact that the people themselves subjected to development efforts, the people in a community, as individual and social identities, are a product of hybrid evolutions, where we cannot erase colonialist legacies. Those individual and social identities will play a role in governance. The individuals and communities one deals with, are also a product of complex histories, the result of stories they told themselves and others told them, of power relations they defined themselves and others defined by others. 'The community' is always a construct, internally divided and diverse, a set of stories and a set of relations which derive from a history of storytelling and changing relations. The same is true for individual people. Post-development approaches tell us that, for poor and rich countries, one can never start with such stable idea of people and communities, as if they were one and always the same. If one develops policy or project with an idea in mind of a unified subjects, this will always be a blinding assumption, an idea that hides what's really happening, who you are really dealing with, so the outcomes will be very unpredictable. At a more theoretical level, we can say that Spivak *et al.* can make us understand that in governance evolutions all and everything can change: not only rules and roles, but also the ideas on what things are (objects) and should be, and the ideas on what people are and should be (individual and social identities).

Finally, we mention James Ferguson, and his famous argument that development is often a *de-politicizing* enterprise. The development sector itself, with its good intentions, is often not innocent, is interested in maintaining itself, generating new projects, revenue, competing with other sectors. In poorer countries, development organizations can compete with government for functions that should be carried out by government, and subjected to the checks and balances of government (tasks and discussions that should be politicized). They can also be in league with government, national level government, to push for projects and policies which are not subjected to the political controls at local and regional levels. National governments and development organizations can use each other to push each other's agenda's as good for the people and expected by the international community, without really asking locals. Development can avoid real politics, and even undermine real politics. It can undermine the mechanisms of representation and participation that are both needed to ensure both stability and change in future development (see above on institutions and participation).

Post-development thinking can be very useful to deconstruct many of the simplistic myths and ideologies of the development sector and present in development theory. It makes things much more complicated: objects and subjects, action and discourse, power and knowledge, scales of governance, all are linked, all are co-evolving in governance. Authenticity does not exist, neither does complete stability, and colonialist legacies cannot be wiped out. Simple participation is often not possible because of oppressed knowledge and oppressed voices, but modernist development models relying on imported formula's won't work either. The NGOs and other organizations that make up the development sector, which is supposed to encourage development locally, is subjected to the same mechanisms, to the same influences that make them never neutral, and it is often more interested in helping itself.

Enough to make you cynical? Maybe. But ... also these thinkers discern positives. They see great resilience in communities all over the world, new ways in which they adapt to change and use it to their advantage. Dropping easy morality is, we believe, essential here: there is no need to condemn a lack of authenticity, there is no need to only deplore colonialist legacies, there is no need to deplore changing social identities. Things change, all the time, and authenticity is impossible anyway, as there is no core of self in community. There are stories, stories that can harden into identities, which then respond to power relations, to changing environments, which can then absorb, produce, use and abuse, interpret and reinterpret various forms of expertise. Further, we can say that the post-development thinkers do not need to inspire the conclusion that development is impossible; for them, 'development' seems very closely associated with modernism

**Example 3.8. 'Living well' – An alternative concept from the Global South (with thanks to Catherine Reynolds).**

A comprehensive vision of a better life that recently emerged from the Global South, offering a striking counterpoint to dominant development models, is known as Buen Vivir (translated from Spanish as 'living well'). Buen Vivir takes a pluralistic, non-linear view of development, leaving room for each society to advance its own perception of progress and modernity. Such an approach inherently gives more weight to creative, unconventional ways of defining a good life, including those based in indigenous knowledge.

The central imperative of Buen Vivir is to live within the biophysical limits of the planet, and to put an end to the domination and manipulation of nature. It thus rejects defining progress as the accumulation of material wealth, calling attention not only to the ecological costs of economic growth, but also to the social costs. Indeed, a sustained focus on material growth is viewed by advocates of Buen Vivir as being 'collective suicide' (Acosta 2012: 193). This danger is identified even in altered notions of development like sustainable development and green growth.

In place of capitalist economic systems and their exploitative tendencies, Buen Vivir envisions the establishment of social institutions that foster reciprocity, cooperation and solidarity, as well as the cultivation of civilized markets. This requires both state intervention and full participation of society. It also entails the modification of lifestyles that rely on a disproportionate amount of natural resources. Finally, it is predicated on the acknowledgement of reproductive work as being on par with productive work and on an end to all forms of discrimination.

While Buen Vivir can hardly be understood as a fully developed proposal, its overarching philosophical principles of have been translated into action. In 2008, for example, Ecuador's law was amended to affirm the rights of species and their ecosystems to be sustained, representing an institutionalization of Buen Vivir at a high level. This marked the first time in history that a government had granted rights to plants and even indirectly to inanimate objects. However, exploitative, extractive industries still flourish in Ecuador unabated six years later, and these undercut a realization of Buen Vivir.

Cooperative economic models based on reciprocity instead of monetary exchange can work well on a small scale, as evidenced by many indigenous cultures, but they are difficult to implement nationally, let alone globally. Thus, Buen Vivir is best understood – for now – as a framework for sparking productive debate by questioning the assumptions behind prevalent development discourses and highlighting the destructive consquences of consumerism, individualism and the commodification of natural resources.

**Further reading**

Acosta, A. (2012). The Buen Vivir – an opportunity to imagine another world. In: Heinrich Böll Stiftung (ed.) Inside a champion. An analysis of the Brazilian development model. Quito, Ecuador: HBS.

Walsh, C. (2010). Development as Buen Vivir: Institutional arrangements and (de)colonial entanglements. Development, 53(1), 15-21.

and Western hegemony, and rejecting development is rejecting that. If we understand development more broadly, as communities tying to articulate visions for the future and shape their own path towards a preferred future, then, we think we can learn from the post-development thinkers without an outright rejection of development as such.

## Further reading

Deleuze, G. and Guattari, F. (1987). A thousand plateaus: capitalism and schizophrenia. London, UK: Continuum.

Easthope, A. (1998). Bhabha, hybridity and identity. Textual Practice, 12(2), 341-348.

Kiely, R. (1999). The last refuge of the noble savage? A critical assessment of post-development theory. European Journal of Development Research, 11(1), 30-55.

Mkandawire, T. (2001). Thinking about developmental states in Africa. Cambridge Journal of Economics, 25, 289.

Rahnema, M. (ed.) (1997). The post-development reader. London, UK: Zed.

Said, E.W. (1995). Orientalism: Western conceptions of the Orient. Harmondsworth, UK: Penguin.

Spivak, G. (1995). The Spivak reader: selected works of Gayati Chakravorty Spivak. Abingdon, UK: Routledge.

Ziai, A. (2004). The ambivalence of post-development: between reactionary populism and radical democracy. Third World Quarterly, 25(6), 1045-1060.

## 3.3 Development theories and the links with governance models

Approaches to development, ideas and strategies as to how communities and societies should move forward in time, improve their own situation in some manner, are always political. One cannot pretend that development can be disconnected from politics, from how power is organized, how collectively binding decisions are taken by representation and participation. Development is politics, and the kind of knowledge and expertise that will be applied, will be channeled and shaped through the form of governance in place and the form of governance aspired to. Knowledge for development is knowledge for development as seen in a political system.

Civic republicanism, socialism, liberal democracy, communitarianism, civil society models, but also authoritarian regimes, theocracies, etc., all have certain ideas on development and the use of expertise and local knowledge towards development. The approaches to development we discussed, are not directly derived from political models, are not all constructed in the context of policy formation. Some emerged in scientific disciplines, or interdisciplinary fields. Some emerged in even more diffuse fields of science, policy, community activism. The links between development approaches and political models are not one-on-one. Some development approaches are more tightly coupled to political models than others. But the use of certain development approaches, the versions used, the expertise highlighted and applied, will be strongly influenced by political context, either directly, in high level decisions, or indirectly, when bottom up initiatives become more visible and influential, and touch the tasks and interests of politics and administration.

The links between politics, or governance more broadly, and development approach, are more complicated than what might be surmised from the previous lists of political models and development perspectives. One reason is the only partial fit between the two lists, and another reason is that in practice, political systems and development approaches are always hybrid. What we discussed regarding politics were models of democracy, models being presented and constructed in Western political theory since the ancient Greeks, partly derived from empirical examples (existing systems, polities), yet also influencing the actual polities, by offering them models of good organization. Communities might be described as liberal democratic, for example, but have features of the other models, derived from older phases and internal diversity. They might be liberal democratic by design, following theoretical principles espoused by elites, and by default, because what they believe to be good organization, can best be described as such. The same is true for the development approaches: communities can adopt a certain model on purpose, after learning about the theory, or they might be doing in practice what theorists describe as participatory development. And, as with the political models, the development approaches in practice will never completely fit one theoretical model. To add complexity, some of the theoretical perspectives also overlap and influenced each other, and some have versions that can be quite diverse, linking differently with different political models (see above).

Yet, despite all this hedging and all this complexity, we can see some patterns, some clear connections. Let us bring back the development approaches, and consider again links with politics and expertise:
- modernist models of development (including community development, structural adjustment);
- structuralist economics/industrial policy/science policy;
- dependency theory;
- livelihoods approach/asset-based development;
- sustainability/resilience perspectives;
- innovation/transition management;
- participatory development/resource management;
- institutions;
- post-colonial/post-development approaches.

*Post-development* and *post-colonialism* are most critical of scientific expertise and 'expert knowledge' as driver of development. They are very critical of 'development' as a

Western, economic growth focused concept. Yet, Western expertise can also be used to deconstruct other Western expertise, to show how it created colonial subjects with colonized desires and visions for the futures. They will think that technical expertise will bring them something universally good. Or, in other versions, they might cherry pick from Western expertise whatever fits their own goals, while in the goal-setting itself, they cherry pick from what they see elsewhere. There are no clear links with any of the models of democracy, although often there is a silent rejection of liberal democracy, seen as the dominant Western model, driving most unwanted changes in the rest of the world.

*Sustainability/resilience perspectives* can be more or less modernist, more or less open to participation. They can be applied in several sorts of democracy, but seem mostly fitting for the bigger government models, for socialism, civic republicanism, or communitarianism (when things are locally organized), even civil society models (when businesses are not the dominant organizations influencing government). Least compatible it is with, again, liberal democracy. Sustainability/resilience is a

**Example 3.9. Singapore's diversified economy: a path dependency?**

The islands of Singapore evolved from a small assemblage of fishing villages to a global information and commerce hub. Starting from an utter lack of material resources, Singapore has emerged as one of the richest countries in the world, albeit with an uneven distribution of wealth. This development was due in part to Singapore's strategic geographic location and role as overseerer of trade across the Straits of Malacca during British colonialism. However, it is also due to targeted policies on the part of the Singaporian government since independence.

Singapore's transition from isolated and rural enclave to 'Asian Tiger' began with investments in the service sector and later in manufacturing industries. The Singaporian government set up free markets, liberal taxation policies and high penalties for corruption. Finally, a great deal was invested in education and technological infrastructure. All of these strategic moves helped the country to perform economically and develop faster and faster.

In spite of its radid development, however, the fact that Singapore remains a small, exposed island is still reflected in its governance policies and paths. In essence, the same governance strategies outlined above aiming to overcome Singapore's material poverty can be seen as an acknowledgement of the immutability of Singapore's vulnerable position. Precisely in order to help Singapore keep up with advanced societies with greater physical resources, the country's government has invested in human resources, in ideas and services. Developing Singapore into a hive of personal qualifications and skills, what the government calls a 'knowledge society', is the country's path to survival given its eternal uncertain standing.

high expertise approach, assuming much expertise to be present with government, or a government capable of absorbing it. Local knowledge could possibly be added in more participatory processes or by investigating and inserting it. Usually, the expertise derives from environmental sciences, including ecology, hydrology, GIS, geology possibly. Other sciences are seen as assisting these core disciplines to figure out how the people see the issues (really defined by environmental science) and how policies can be more easily implemented (against the resistance or ignorance of people). On the other hand one can mention countless bottom-up initiatives where citizens try to translate a broadly defined sustainability goal in practical action.

*Innovation/transition management* similarly relies on big government models, such as socialism (social democracy), or on civil society versions where government is powerful but in league with business, to prescribe science what to investigate and government what to support (so innovation can flourish and make money for all). It tends not to fit well with civic republicanism, as citizen participation is low on the list of priorities, and

Figure 3.5. Singapore, between Arts Center and Central Business District. Photo: Anna-Katharina Hornidge. © ZEF/University of Bonn, Germany.

**Further reading**

Hornidge, A.-K. (2010). An uncertain future – Singapore's search for a new focal point of collective identity and its drive towards 'knowledge society'. Asian Journal of Social Sciences, 38(5), 785-818.

it is in the interaction between business, government and science (science in the role of listener) that is decided how the next transition should take place, which innovations are needed for that. Local knowledge is often not considered, and scientific expertise considered is usually high tech expertise expected to bring economic benefits. The knowledge of transition management itself is not so clearly located: the experts describe themselves in different ways, but one can speak of a mix of public administration, management, and (very applied) sociology of science.

*Participation* fits the perspective of civic republicanism best: very active citizens and a very active state, with people active in different manners – as individuals, as members of organizations, of political parties, as professionals. it also works well under communitarianism. Participation opens up governance to local knowledge, but also to a wide variety of scientific expertise, depending on the interests of the community, the priorities, and depending on the links between the actors around the table and the scientific disciplines. If participation is extreme, the directions taken can be extremely different, in some cases purely relying on local knowledge, in other cases on one sort of expert knowledge. Survival, in parallel, of lines of representation, elected people and their experts, can temper these wild swings, also in terms of expertise. One can also describe this is a form of checks and balances in expertise and knowledge (avoiding that one type of expertise dominates decision-making).

*Livelihoods/Assets approaches*, just as participation, generally work best at smaller scales. As participation, they fit well with communitarianism and civic republicanism, although most of the practical examples, in very poor countries, are closer to communitarianism, missing the stable institutions, active government, and checks and balances of civic republicanism. There is also a recurring assumption that the state, the larger scale of political decision-making, can be ignored, does not need to function well to make this happen, and that expertise incorporated in state decisions should not be expected and can be missed. These approaches seem to rely most on local knowledge; if expert knowledge is to be inserted, it needs to be at a local level, and, it seems, in a participatory process, with development workers or researchers working with community members. The expertise of this form of assisted governance itself partly derives from sociology, partly from environmental studies (cf sustainable livelihoods), and in some cases combined with concepts found in many disciplines (such as the assets, capitals and networks concepts).

*Institutionalist approaches* can be quite diverse. Some link directly to neo-liberalism, providing recipes for a smoothly functioning neo-liberal capitalism (a recipe for the 'rule of law' that stabilizes markets, allows for their development). Others, especially the historical institutionalists, are interested in local and national scales, in a diversity of development paths, different versions of the rule of law that can work well, different forms of ownership, different relations between representation and participation. Thus, for those versions of institutionalism, there is not strong link with one particular model.

One can say that there is least fit with the biggest government model (socialism) and the smallest government model (liberal democracy). This institutionalism positively appreciates action by government and locals, in co-creating and stabilizing markets, political and legal structures. Which expertise becomes important in a particular case, hinges on a particular evolution. But in general, it is useful to distinguish legal, political and economic systems, and to have specialized rules and roles for them (hence expertise). Local knowledge is essential: it allows for the continuous searching and experimenting that can produce a fit between formal and informal institutions and between different sorts of formal institutions.

*Dependency theory* and structuralist economics are often modernist in inspiration, but politically, they tend to go either in the direction of socialism, or of neo-liberalism (yet insisting on a different path towards it). The essential expertise is macro-economics, yet more sensitive to the position of developing countries. Depending on the version, there can still be place for other forms of expertise and local knowledge. One can see the macro approach as sufficient, but one can also see it as the creation of a frame in which smaller scale initiatives (projects, or local government reform) can take place, in different forms, taking one of the other approaches mentioned, and open to other disciplines and local knowledge (see above, on nested policies).

*Modernist approaches* can be linked to different political models as well, yet are probably least compatible with civic republicanism, where things can go more easily in different directions, and general truths are rarely accepted for a long time. Modernist approaches to development can be distinctly neo-liberal (when offering universal principles for the perfect capitalist democracy), but also socialist (when presenting models for the perfect, not-to-be-improved-upon communist state). In the neo-liberal case, the preferred expertise will be macro-economics, while in the socialist case, the much larger social engineering ambitions will require much expertise, from various disciplines. Local knowledge is, by definition, at odds with modernist approaches, as it is not scientific. In practice, local knowledge can never be completely excluded, just as informal institutions can never be missed; purely modernist approaches, for that reason, can not be found in the real world, and close approximations did not survive for a long time.

In the second part of the book, discussing rural development approaches, these insights in the relations between political models, development approaches and included/ excluded knowledge will be further developed. We will dwell more on the roles of of experts, administrations, organizations, academic discplines and projects in shaping the inclusion and influence of sorts of knowledge in policy, and in the step from policy to implementation. This will help us to formulate a concise general perspective on expertise for rural development.

Before entering into the discussion of rural development visions, we want to introduce some new concepts, and bring back several concepts already discussed, in a frame that can help us to understand the governance paths of communities and societies. The frame leans on a theory of evolutionary governance, which incorporates insights from institutional economics, social systems theory and post-modern philosophy. Reconstructing and analyzing governance paths is useful, we argue, because visions for development, approaches to it, the tools to further it, are the products of evolution in communities. Understanding development in communities is understanding governance evolution, and such understanding is essential if we are even considering giving advice on development, on interventions, on new content or procedure of development efforts. Without understanding these paths, the effects of interventions will be largely unpredictable. It will be very hard to figure out which expertise might be most useful, most appreciated and bring the community closer to the state it wants to be in.

## Further reading

Acemoglu, D. and Robinson, J. (2012). Why nations fail. The origins of power, prosperity and poverty. New York, NY, USA: Crown Business.

Gay, P. (1996). The enlightenment: the science of freedom (Vol. 2). New York, NY, USA: WW Norton & Company.

Held, D. (2006). Models of democracy. Stanford, CA, USA: Stanford University Press.

Pressmann., U. and Wildavsky, A. (1973). Implementation. Berkeley, CA, USA: University of California Press.

Randeria, S. (2007). De-politicization of democracy and judicialization of politics. Theory, Culture & Society, 24(4): 38.

Rapley, J. (2002). Development theory in the wake of structural adjustment. In: Rapley, J. (ed.), Understanding development. Theory and practice in the Third World. Boulder, CO, USA: Lynne Rienner Publishers, pp. 113-130.

# 4. Evolutionary governance concepts

## Abstract

In this chapter, we introduce several key concepts for the further analysis of rural development: governance paths and dependencies, actor/institution configurations and power/knowledge configurations. We link these concepts – and several others already introduced-in such a way that analysis of governance paths becomes easier. The resulting conceptual frame, a perspective on evolutionary governance, can be helpful to reflect on the potential of certain communities to move in certain directions, to transform themselves, and the forms and roles of expertise and local knowledge that might be most appropriate for a given community and a given path. What happened in the governance path, it is shown, determines much of what will happen to new expertise, new plans, policies, laws; it will shape which knowledge is produced, included/excluded, what will have more likely an impact on policy-making and on the community itself.

## 4.1 Governance paths and dependencies

We mentioned before that models of democracy (and of governance more broadly), just as development perspectives, are abstractions. That does not mean they are irrelevant: these are ideas that can guide and did guide political organization and the way polities moved forward. We called this the performativity of concepts and stories: what people and communities imagine and tell themselves can become reality, and if not becoming, it can seriously affect reality. In practice, communities show features of several political models and development approaches. The particular combination of features one can find in a community has to be grasped if we want to see how new knowledge can be introduced, which might lead to policies that can bring positive change. We now argue that this particular set of features can best be seen as the product of a unique *governance path*. We met this concept earlier, will now integrate it more systematically in a theoretical frame.

Governance paths are histories of governance understood as series of sites of collectively binding decision-making in a community. Governance paths are not entirely independent: they are tied to several external contexts, to governance at other scales, and to environments outside governance. Governance is always embedded in societies, and the features of a community inspire the features of governance: who is included, excluded, what are the formal and informal rules at play, what are power relations between actors, their values, what is the balance between participation, which forms of knowledge are used and how, and finally, how does all this play out in the construction of visions for common futures, for development? As we said earlier, the mapping of governance and its context can never be comprehensive; we always need to be selective, impose an interpretation.

Governance paths generally include sites where *object* and *subject formation* takes place: what is talked about, referred to (objects) and who is talking, doing the referring (subjects) is partly the product of governance. 'Actors' change once they become actors, are included in governance, and some new actors never existed outside the structures and content of governance (which might spur new parties, new NGOs, new commercial organizations). The realities of governance (objects and subjects) are partly the product of governance itself: new ideas, new players, new rules, new values, can come in from elsewhere, but they will be reinterpreted, in the context of governance, while others are almost entirely created in the governance process. This can happen in agreement and disagreement: both conflict and consensus can be productive, can produce objects and subjects. Actors in conflict can distinguish themselves more, they can bring in new ideas to help them in conflict, and they can produce ideas. Some objects and subjects will take on a life outside governance, will become part of social and cultural life, will be studied in science.

One can say that governance is *self-referential*. Decisions in governance refer to previous decisions. They are taken by actors that refer to or at least imply the presence of a certain set of other actors, and a certain set of other institutions (see below). They can only make sense in terms of objects and subjects understood. They will only have an impact if they take into account the context of governance, first of all, before any other context, and this form of self-reference makes that governance paths are never entirely flexible. We spoke earlier of *rigidity* and *flexibility*. Rigidity means that governance cannot be with the same ease be reformed in all directions, that the next step in evolution is more likely to go in this direction than in that one. We say that governance paths are marked by path dependence, interdependence and goal-dependencies.

*Path dependencies* are legacies from the past influencing collective decision-making now. These legacies can be manifold. We discuss different forms of path dependency in the following sections, and will find more versions when discussing rural development approaches. The adherence to a certain political model, the belief in a certain development perspective embody path dependencies. Especially when things are organized in a way that reflects this belief. When ideas change in the community, changing this organization can be difficult. A strong presence of one type of expertise, linked to one or more powerful actors, will make it difficult to bring in new forms or make other forms more important. If a municipal organization is devised around an engineering (public works) department, then development planning more inclusive of social sciences, of environmental sciences, will be tough.

*Interdependencies* are links between various players and rules and resources that shape what is possible in governance. If an NGO coalition finally made a difference in governance, because of that coalition, and business interests were curbed, then the parts of this coalition are highly interdependent, cannot simply take positions outside the discourse of the coalition. If government and business community help each other and legitimize each other in a transition management model, then moving away from that model might be difficult, because both powerful actors became more interdependent. Interdependence creates its own form of path-dependence: it is one of the reasons why A leads to B and not to C.

*Goal dependencies* are the influences of imagined futures on present-day decision-making, futures in the form of plans, policies, visions and designs. Most plans and policies will not be precisely implemented as intended but they can nevertheless exert great influence. A policy with an explicit goal, or a plan with a more comprehensive vision of the future, even if not fully implemented, will have effects because it will tend to bind the behavior of some. Because certain parts will likely be implemented. Because it will be selectively implemented, on some occasions, in a selection influenced by the strategies of powerful players. Goals can also have impact by alienating others, by inspiring resistance, creating their own opposition (to something more clearly visible

**Example 4.1. The legacy of the Millennium Development Goals (with thanks to Catherine Reynolds).**

The Rio+20 Conference in 2012 witnessed the launch of a process to develop Sustainable Development Goals (SDGs), which are foreseen as a replacement for the Millennium Development Goals (MDGs) expiring in 2015. Like the MDGs before them, the SDGs define what development is – in this case, sustainable development – and set benchmarks towards achieving it. The SDGs are being formulated by an inter-governmental Open Working Group (OWG) with thirty participants, each representing 1-4 UN countries. In addition, the UN Development Program is organizing global and national consultations with a range of thematic foci, the results of which are feeding into the OWG's deliberations. What is the overall promise of the SDGs? This question is impossible to answer without considering the legacy of the MDGs.

On the positive side, the SDGs stand to benefit from the momentum offered by the MDGs. Although results achieved by the eight MDGs have been and are predicted to remain very mixed, the MDGs can be viewed as a major success insofar as they have become inextricably integrated into development discourses. The SDG process faces the challenge of constructing new goals that not only raise awareness and capture public imagination, but that also represent realistic stepping stones to a global vision of a better world. In doing so, they cannot escape a careful evaluation of what went wrong during the MDG phase.

In part, the SDGs already reflect a critical evaluation of the MDGs. Most importantly, they are less restricted to 'developing' countries than the MDGs were. In just one example,

Figure 4.1. The 8 Millennium Development Goals. © United Nations.

Goal 12.3, as outlined in the final draft SDGs submitted to the UN General Assembly in September 2014, to halve the current rate of per capita global food waste, addresses what is foremost a 'developed' country problem. Increased comprehensiveness of the SDGs can be seen as a deeper realization of what was already aimed for through the MDGs: mutual but differentiated responsibility among individual countries. The SDGs are being positioned to tackle shared global challenges that manifest themselves differently in different parts of the world. This all reflects the broader involvement of a diverse body of stakeholders in the formulation of the SDGs, a significant improvement over the corresponding MDG process. What the SDGs have not yet adequately addressed is underlying contradictions between individual goals, a challenge inherited from the MDGs. A salient example is how to reconcile the goals of economic growth and sustainable use of natural resources. So far, the SDGs make only one reference to mastering this tricky balance: Goal 8.4 includes the intent to 'endeavor to decouple economic growth from environmental degradation'. This deficit in the formulation of the SDGs is particularly striking in light of the overwhelming imbalance in achievement of the MDGs. During the past fifteen years, MDG 1 of halving global poverty came close to being achieved (largely through economic growth in India and China), whereas MDG 7 of ensuring ecological sustainability was one of the most neglected goals.

The SDG process should also explore why rich countries had such difficulty keeping their promises of setting aside a specific amount of official development assistance (ODA) for poorer ones (MDG 8 – A global partnership for development). Without an analysis of what led to past failures, the credibility of SDG 17.2, 'developed countries to fully implement their ODA commitments' is severely lacking. Why should the world believe in the achievability of a goal that went unmet when it was formulated as an MDG, although it appeared to be one of the most straightforward goals at the time?

These examples demonstrate that the past can have both positive and negative effects on ongoing processes – depending on how the past is addressed and integrated into the present. In the case of the SDGs, the more intensively and honestly the legacy of the MDGs is evaluated, the more globally legitimate and thereby binding a set of new goals can be articulated.

### Further reading

Holtz, U. (2013). Die Millenniumsentwicklungsziele. In: Ihne, H. and Wilhelm, J. (eds.), Einführung in die Entwicklungspolitik. Berlin, Germany: LIT Verlag, pp. 41-65.

Loewe, M. (2012). Post 2015: how to reconcile the Millennium Development Goals (MDGs) and the Sustainable Development Goals (SDGs)? Briefing Paper 18/2012. Bonn, Germany: German Development Institute.

Sachs, J.D. (2012). From Millennium Development Goals to Sustainable Development Goals. The Lancet, 379(9832), 2206-2211.

**Example 4.2. Japan and its iconic countryside.**

Japan's path towards modernization has been studied by many. It is seen as a major success story. In the 19th century, Japanese society was stuck in a feudal system, with warlords-landowners (shoguns, led by the Tokugawa clan) controlling politics under the nominal authority of the emperor. They did not favor international trade, higher education, travel, democracy, and the development of cities. After a forced change by American naval power, the Meiji dynasty (1868-1912) opened the doors for rapid modernization. Many foreign advisers were hired, and many Japanese sent out to study abroad, in the USA and Europe, or to learn from different development models. The Japanese quickly noticed that 'the West' did not exist, that many versions of markets and democracies had developed, and that Western ways were not without problems. Japan borrowed and modified selectively from diverse countries, industrial policy and university system from Germany, central bank from Belgium, urbanism and military from France, etc.

Development was understood as mechanization and urbanization, while urban planning was reduced (after an initial design-oriented phase) to infrastructure development. New merchants collided with old land owners and new bureaucrats to form an elite which is, in essence, still in place, visible in large industrial conglomerates with government ties, weak local governments but strong local branches of national bureaucracies, attuned to input from merchant elites.

Rural areas, meanwhile, have been either depopulating or urbanizing. Japan's attitude towards its rural areas has been ambiguous, reflecting a deeper ambiguity concerning its modern identity. Rural areas have been cherished, preserved, mythologized, and associated with the real, traditional Japan, while they have been neglected for the same reason. Few people take up farming, farming itself is heavily subsidized, yet many farmers need second jobs. A second stream of subsidies is important, for the preservation of environmental and cultural resources, sometimes overlapping – a sacred grove, a park, a spring sung in medieval poetry. Rethinking the countryside is tough, because of the association of Japanese modernity with cities, and countrysides as areas deserving little attention, except for preservation. Attempts to transform agriculture, e.g. including land consolidation projects for larger scale rice farming, have often been half-hearted, and met much local resistance as well.

**Further reading**

Murphy, A. and Williams, P.W. (1999). Attracting Japanese tourists into the rural hinterland: implications for rural development and planning. Tourism Management, 20(4), 487-499.

now as not what they want). Plans, policies, laws (and implied goals) can become symbols of larger differences in ideology, in political model and development approach, and catalyze this resistance, thus furthering governance change in possibly direction exactly opposite of what was intended. Policies and plans can shape governance paths also by their selective neglect or lack of insight in the implementation process: the more blind the policy makers are to what will happen during implementation, when new actors might be involved, their interpretations, values, strategies, the more different the effects will be from what they anticipated, but still, the policy itself, the setting of goals, caused governance to go in a certain direction: goal dependence.

We argue that understanding governance paths, why in this direction and not that, requires looking closely at these three dependencies and their interplay, as well as looking at the spaces left for autonomous decision-making. The dependencies do not amount to determinism: a path does not have one outcome, and people influence the next steps. Actors still have a level of autonomy in making decisions, coming up with ideas for the future, and the resulting policies, plans, laws have an influence. Each governance path will have a different delineation of these spaces of freedom, spaces where reform can start. Finding these spaces is very useful, and is in essence the same exercise as mapping the dependencies. Understanding the three dependencies together can also bring a new understanding of each of them. Most notably, it can create a new understanding of the goal dependencies, and the possibility to manage the effects of policies and plans more precisely. That can mean in some cases sticking to a blue print approach, but different from the one previously adopted, in other cases it can mean refraining from decisions, or making policies that are less ambitious in steering, do not intend to steer or predict what cannot be steered or predicted.

In other words, there are several sources of rigidity and several sources of flexibility in governance paths, and this delineates spaces for intervention, for the use of existing and new expertise, for coordinated action towards 'development', however defined.

## Further reading

Beunen, R., Van Assche, K. and Duineveld, M. (eds.) (2015). Evolutionary governance theory: theory & applications. Heidelberg, Germany: Springer.

Hodgson, G.M. (2006). What are institutions? Journal of Economic Issues, 40(1), 1-25.

Luhmann, N. (1995). Social systems. Stanford, CA, USA: Stanford University Press.

Mahoney, J. (2000). Path dependence in historical sociology. Theory and Society, 29(4), 507-548.

Morgounov, A. and Zuidema, L. (2001). The legacy of the Soviet agricultural research system for the republics of Central Asia and the Caucasus. ISNAR report 22.

North, D. (2005). Understanding the process of economic change. Princeton, NJ, USA: Princeton University Press.

Van Assche, K., Beunen, R. and Duineveld, M. (2014). Formal/informal dialectics and the self-transformation of spatial planning systems: an exploration. Administration & Society, 46(6), 654-683.

Van Assche, K., Djanibekov, N., Hornidge, A.K., Shtaltovna, A. and Verschraegen, G. (2014). Rural development and the entwining of dependencies: transition as evolving governance in Khorezm, Uzbekistan. Futures, 63, 75-85.

## 4.2 Actor/institution configurations

In this section, we take another look at governance paths as histories in which actors and institutions are formed. We do not claim that all *actors* are the product of governance, but some are, and most others are thoroughly transformed by their presence [or absence] in governance, a presence which can take several different forms. The same applies to *institutions*, as rules of coordination enabling collective decision-making in governance. They too partly pre-exist a specific governance path, but others emerge in that path, while many are transformed in and through governance.

We already learned that an 'actor' does not exist in nature. The word actor comes from literatures where government is understood as embedded in networks of other organizations and individuals which are needed to get things done. If we assume pure representation, and central steering from administrations and their expert, then there is no need to speak of actors. Governance literature assumes that non-government actors play a role, so they speak of actors. In much of that literature, however, there seems to be the assumption mentioned above, that actors are easy to recognize, gathered around the table, visibly and formally included in decision-making and then all is well. 'Stakeholder' can be analyzed in the same way. Some theorists recognized that government cannot do and does not do everything by itself, and other parties have an interest and an opinion and should be included. Yet, what is a stake? And who is the stakeholder? For both 'actor' and 'stakeholder' we can mention the issues we discussed earlier: who is representing what, and how does this relate to mechanisms of representation in government?

Who is an actor, for what reason, is always a decision, and an interpretation. Sometimes, groups will present themselves as actors or stakeholders, demanding to be included in decision-making. In other cases, actors will be recognized by government, administration, by scientists advising government, by consultancy firms working for government, and included in decision-making. Sometimes, actors will be actors behind the scenes, but in a move to more participatory governance, they will become more openly recognized and present.

When new forums are assembled, as one can often observe in recent years, with more attention to participation, groups can be included with little experience in participation, individuals which have to find their way in and around government. Besides some of the problems mentioned earlier, this situation can also have positives, leading to individual and collective learning, and to initially paper actors become more truly involved, participating in decision-making, and the negotiation and deliberation which precedes it. This is one form of change in and through governance; included groups can be paper actors, but turn into real actors later, by observing and learning, mapping out the terrain, figuring out the possibilities. This learning process can include an improvement of the representative character of the actor; possibly, the association an individual represented, the group she spoke for, did not amount to much, also had to be organized. Or, the group existed but wasn't so sure the spokeswoman was a spokeswoman, and what it meant to take on that role.

Yet this form of change is just one among many, just one of many sorts of transformations that can take place in governance. Existing groups can be included, groups can be created because people see there is a new form of governance emerging, barely surviving groups can be reinvigorated because of a new forum and influence, groups can reinvent themselves because of their participation in governance, their reassessment of their role, their observation of other groups, their substance and strategy.

Once actors exist as actors, they tend to survive, and distinguish between a current and desirable role. Also in participatory governance, roles of actors are not equal. Some have more influence than others, and on different things. This also is true within government, where departments compete, and professional roles spanning different departments ('the engineers' vs. 'the economists'). Actors' roles evolve by their participation in governance, and the competition with other actors is one reason. Adaptation is another mechanism: change can come about by adapting to other actors and to the governance environment itself. Language can change, concepts, self-images. Seeing others can help

Figure 4.2. Not easily recognizable rural development, Sulina, Romania. The water is the middle branch of the Danube, canalized by Sir Joseph Heartley, an English engineer, in the mid-19th century, for the European Danube Commission, and the reeds left are a plantation from the later communist period. Entirely planned 'wild' landscapes, by entirely different actors. Photo: Kristof Van Assche. © ZEF/University of Bonn, Germany.

**Example 4.3. Water management, socio-cultural boundaries and practices in Khorezm, Uzbekistan.**

Water management for the cotton fields in Khorezm, Uzbekistan is increasingly hampered by a number of limitations. Amongst the most pertinent limitations are (a) infrastructural and (b) institutional deficits, resulting in the mismatch of water allocation and water delivery; (c) authoritarian state control, manifest in the agricultural quota system and limiting individuals' innovativeness by side-lining bottom-up development into the sphere of informality/illegality; (d) a vertically structured knowledge system, creating limits to creativity and agency development; and (e) a hierarchically organized society with a complex system of coercive reciprocity. With the aim to overcome these limitations and assure water access, water users employ a range of formal, strategic and discursive practices which result in a strengthening of the boundaries that define two separate spheres of water management, meaning the 'formal' and the 'informal' sphere.

Once water is diverted from the Amudarya into Khorezm's irrigation system, a number of state organizations on different administrative levels (Ministry of Agriculture and Water Resources, lower Amudarya basin irrigation system authority (BUIS), sub-basin irrigation system authority (UIS), main canal management units (MCMs) of UIS, WUAs) are formally responsible for the allocation and delivery of water from the off-takes along the river to the entrance of the WUAs. The set of formal and informal rules that apply in this process demarcate the boundaries around the formal and informal spheres of water management, constantly negotiated during the process of water allocation and delivery. Water allocation hereby refers to the assignment of so called water limits to different units within the irrigation network, determined based on the irrigated area, planted crops and the respective irrigation state norms.

The actual water delivery should, formally, match these water allocations. In reality, however, delivered water quantities regularly differ from the allocated water limits. Especially in averagely water abundant years water management reacts rather effectively to water users' demands, due to different strategies that water users apply to get access to water outside the formal functioning of the water management organizations.

One strategy is the use of small, mobile pumps to lift water into field canals, which is formally considered illegal theft of water but is informally a wide-spread practice. At pumps that are shared between *fermers* and *dehqons*, pump management is a negotiation process in which social relations, such as well-established contacts, play a large role for determining the rules of water use. By catering to individuals' water demands, this delivery according to strategic practice (both with the help of technical means as well as social relations) is a deviation from the formal water management institutions but at the same time effectively compensates for the inadequacies of the formal water management organizations – at least for influential agents.

Water management in Khorezm is thus shaped by two parallel systems of practices: (1) the official system with its practices that reflect clearly formulated formal institutions; and (2) the strategic practices that individual agents apply to pursue their interests and that follow informal institutions. Additionally (3) continuous processes of strengthening and reproducing these two parallel systems of practices through discursive practices by the actors can be observed. While deviation from the formal is commonly taking place, the actors involved spend considerable effort and resources on the discursive compensation of these deviations. When farmers diverge from the rule that cotton as a state crop should be irrigated before the cash crop rice, observations in the case study WUAs have shown that they are very likely to state in any official conversation that cotton needs to be irrigated first.

This behavior (a) to some extent reflects the political risk that openly admitted deviation carries in an authoritative state and (b) illustrates the multiple roles of individual agents in informal and formal (state administrative) networks, the latter creating a stake for them to preserve the status quo of the formal water management institutions. But the very prominence of these discursive practices on all levels of the hierarchy, down to the peasant farmers, suggests that there is a meaning of such practices that goes beyond these motivations. These discursive compensations, basically the verbal references to formal institutions, can be understood as a way to actively reproduce the formal water management discourse instead of formalizing informal practices. Acts of deviation, such as the strategic practices discussed above, are thus concealed by means of discursive practices. They acquire the character of exceptions, special acts in a particular situation – no matter how frequently they occur. They are accepted, applied and do not challenge the formal water management discourse but instead can be regarded as barriers to change.

Formal institutions, while influential, are nevertheless frequently side-stepped and replaced by strategic practices following informal institutions. Even though this deviation from the formal rules, demarcating the boundary of the formal sphere of water management, may be necessary to reach individual goals or cope with malfunctions of the formal institutions, the resulting display of agency and the strategic practices are of a rather applied and situational nature. They are used as coping strategies in struggles over power and water.

### Further reading

Hornidge, A.-K., Oberkircher, L. and Kudryavtseva, A. (2013). Boundary management and the discursive sphere – negotiating 'realities' in Khorezm, Uzbekistan. Geoforum, 45, 266-274.

Oberkircher, L. and Hornidge A.-K. (2011). 'Water is life' – farmer rationales and water-saving in Khorezm, Uzbekistan: a lifeworld analysis. Rural Sociology, 76(3), 394-421.

to understand oneself but in that process one changes too. In the words used earlier: objects and subjects change. The identity of the actor is a subject.

Competition, adaptation, learning, can lead to transformation of the actor, while changes in the constituency, in the link with the constituents (those represented by the actors) in the community at large, can lead to actors coming, going, transforming. The results of governance, the decisions taken, the policies made and unmade, plans, rules and laws decided upon, in form and content, will continuously change the frame of reference for the actors, and this changes the actors themselves.

Which brings us to these policies, plans, laws. We used the word 'institutions' before. Institutions coordinate interactions between players, and are the result of such interaction; they tell people and organizations how to behave in a certain context, in striving for certain goals. Plans are also institutions, as they have a normative aspect, coordinate the behavior of many actors, and can include a variety of more detailed rules. We just described how actors co-evolve in the governance process and how their production of and reference to institutions creates a context that defines them in turn. We can also describe this as co-evolution of actors and institutions in governance. Once included in governance, institutions have more impact on actors, and the other way around. Actors in governance cannot simply ignore the body of policies, plans, laws, of binding decisions taken before. If they try to change one rule, or policy embodying various rules, then they have to rely on other rules to do so. And they have to rely on other actors, which agree on a change of the institution, and agree on the reference to these other rules that make the change possible. But both the set of other institutions making change possible and the other actors needed, make for a different change. The direction things go, will always be influenced by the presence of other actors and institutions.

Change is the rule here, as both the internal environment of governance and the external environment of the community will continuously evolve. Keeping things the same requires pressure, cooperation and is not a matter of being passive. Also a conservative agenda therefore requires reliance on other actors and other institutions, which will change, in substance or in their implementation (also subject to evolution). So, trying to keep things completely the same will not work. It has to follow the same laws of co-evolution of actors and institutions.

If actors remain involved in governance for a long time, their identities can become tied up with certain pieces of legislation, certain plans or policies. These policies, etc. can be seen as major results, major successes of these actors, so, understandably, they identify with them, but such link can also become a liability, when coalitions change, when the community changes, and the link between actor and policy makes it more difficult for the actor to move in a different direction, without losing credibility (i.e. losing identity).

If we want to understand the co-evolution of actors and institutions more in detail, and therefore understand better how this affects the adaptive capacity of the actor, we have to distinguish several types of institutions. We distinguish formal, informal and dead institutions. Under *formal institutions* we understand those institutions that are expected to govern an interaction in a given situation. *Informal institutions* are the alternatives which are present in the situation, for the actors involved; an alternative rule set, not an absence of rules. Formal institutions have been understood as the paper rules, often as the enacted laws, whereas informal institutions where then seen as the actual rules, unwritten, in deviance of the law. We want to distance ourselves from this presentation: also in paperless societies, in societies without legislative bodies, without laws in the Western sense, there are formal and informal institutions, situations where alternative rules are available and where the actors know what is expected. There is an implied authority (on this world or in the spiritual world) that expects something, but there is also a perceived necessity or opportunity (and usually self-interest) to break the rule, and rely on an alternative coordination mechanism. We can be aware that it's not good to bribe a police man, but we can also be aware that he isn't paid, and that if we pay him a bit every now and then, he will still keep an eye on the more important criminal behavior in the community.

What is a formal or informal rule, then, is not stable. Each situation forces a decision on which rules are available, which is formal, and which is used. In modern societies, formal rules can indeed have a paper character, but informal ones too. Sometimes both formal and informal are not written down, as in cultural codes, etc. Some transitional societies had strong formal rules, unwritten, then replaced by written laws with little impact. Informal rules are often linked to the formal rules: rules to interpret the rules, to break the rules, to selectively enforce the rules, etc. The alternatives to choose from are then the intended interpretation of the rule (knowing well what was intended) and another interpretation of the rule (to make things work, out of self-interest).

*Dead institutions* are for us formerly formal institutions that lost impact. Laws that worked for a while, but lost their teeth. Plans that guided the actions of many for a while, but not anymore. Policies that were never officially revoked, but nobody pays attention. In democracies with written laws, the lack of official change, of official dropping of the rule, makes it possible to revive it. If the context changes, if other actors are involved in governance, if other institutions changed the context of decision-making, there might be a window of opportunity to bring back the dead (we will not introduce the word zombie institution here). Old laws, without any influence, not implemented for ages, can suddenly receive a new leash on live, when they become useful as tools in new political discussions, can become something that might underpin a new policy. An old plan might be on the shelve for a long time, but a new minister might see it as a response to a new problem, to new actors making noise and she can decide to give it finally an impact, claiming that she's been doing this all the time.

Figure 4.3. Rural landscape in Zerafshan Valley, Tajikistan. Where regimes came and went but were less ambitious in rural development, local governance in more stable areas can generate landscapes that seem to regulate themselves, but rest on centuries of formal and informal coordination, in a blend simply recognized as 'the normal way'. Photo: Anastasiya Shtaltovna. © ZEF/University of Bonn, Germany.

Formal and informal institutions co-evolve. What is informal depends on what is formal, and the other way around. If an informal rule becomes formal (e.g. after a political change), there is a good chance that new informal rules will come up (as reality never completely conforms with one rule). If formal rules change, the informal ones will respond to the new strategic situation created by that change: sometimes, it will become more attractive to follow the formal rule, sometimes less, and those situations where the formal rules do not work well, might look differently now, might not be well managed with the older informal rule.

Actors do things. They participate in governance, and the main result of this participation is the taking of collectively binding decisions. But they do more. These other things can take place in governance context, but also outside it, in their internal functioning as organization, in their dealing with constituents, in their community activities at large. We can distinguish formal, discursive and strategic practices in this regard. Formal practices adhere openly to the ruling formal institution. Discursive practices rely on the use and creation of discourse, of discursive objects and subjects. Strategic practices are first of all structured around a goal, which then shapes a strategy, a way to get there. An action usually has all three aspects: there is a goal (as reason for the action), there is some acknowledgment of a formal rule (from which can be deviated), and there is some reliance discourse (for it to make sense, for self and others). For the analysis of the way actors and institutions interact and co-evolve, it is useful to distinguish these aspects, because it shows how actors can differently relate to institutions: sometimes following the rule simply, sometimes for display, to be seen as following (highly formal), sometimes using formal and informal institutions, in whatever combination, to further the own goals (highly strategic) and sometimes the content itself, the narratives, arguments, concepts, are what drives an actor most (highly discursive). These different attitudes of actors towards institutions influence how actors and institutions co-evolve in specific cases.

Because of this entanglement of formal and informal and of actor and institution, we like to use the word configuration. Rather than looking at either formal or informal institutions, it is better to get an idea of the configuration of formal and informal, see how they relate, and see how this whole configuration works. What has to be assessed then, is the configuration: does it do what is best for the community? Are there important issues not covered? Are the informal institutions here undermining the formal ones, or the community itself? Or are they rather filling in gaps or providing flexibility? The same can be said for actors and institutions: they shape each other, and what has to be understood is their configuration. The identity of a governance path, of the governance of a community, lies in that configuration, where actors and institutions co-evolve. Once certain roles and rules are crystallized, they tend to remain in place, and represent path-and interdependence. Actors and institutions thus shape each other and formal and informal institutions follow a similar dialectical pattern.

The *actor/institution configuration*, and on the side of institutions, the embedded configuration of formal/informal institutions, the co-evolutions observed in each configuration, have a significant impact on the inclusion/exclusion of knowledge in governance. Actors bring perspectives with them, on governance, the community, the world, what is important there, what is important to know there, and how to produce that knowledge, use it, include it in policies or not. Each actor brings her own perspective on what deserves to be known, studied, included in policies. She brings her own perspective on what the community in the future should be, and which knowledge is needed for that. Some actors harbor a vision of the future that relies more on export knowledge, others on local knowledge, and then there is every combination possible.

The institutions too, have effects on the inclusion/exclusion of knowledge: sometimes, policies can directly say which kind of study is needed. Sometimes, they say who is to be included (actors) in decision-making on a topic (bringing in a selection of knowledge) or who is to be asked for advice (same point). Institutions, and the policies they are embedded in, also bring up a selection of topics and problems, some things are not

**Example 4.4. 'Knowledge': development elixir or hegemonic discourse?**

In the past twenty to thirty years, the notion of 'knowledge' has increasingly shaped development discourses worldwide – as perceived crucial driver for the economic development of nation-states and as key element for successful measures of international development cooperation. Packaged under the terms 'knowledge society' and 'information society', the increasing importance of different types of knowledge for the further development of economies and societies was originally assessed and conceptualised mainly by academics from Japan, the USA and Europe. International organisations such as the OECD closely followed, by sharpening the economic focus of the ongoing debate and arguing for the development of 'knowledge-based economies'. From there – although far from complete – all three concepts entered the national politics of many countries which aimed at the active creation of better futures. Governments worldwide adopted the general idea of 'knowledge society' as well as the manifold terminology originating from the scientific community which resulted in an increased emphasis on science policy-making. In many countries this led to a reevaluation of applied versus basic research and development as well as a widening of the portfolio of scientific disciplines ranging from natural sciences and engineering to economics as well as social sciences and the arts.

In the field of development, the idea of knowledge being a key element of successful activities of development cooperation and poverty alleviation culminated in 1998 in the publishing of the World Bank report with the title 'Knowledge for Development'. With this report, the notion of 'knowledge' as driver of development entered the global development discourse. From there it was taken up by many state governments and linked to (or utilized as a new framing for) ongoing national attempts of strengthening the respective innovation systems (for economic growth) through a stronger emphasis on science policy formulation. Irrespective of their actual comparative advantages and advised by McKinsey, the World Bank and the International Monetary Fund, countries such as Malaysia and Indonesia, just

looked at, some things are not considered as problems, and this selectivity of issues is also a selectivity of knowledge.

If we want to illustrate the impacts of the configuration of actors and institutions on knowledge selection, we can point at the interactions of actors and institutions, linked in a specific pattern, and how this has effects. If 'the developer' did not exist in a Soviet context, then comes up after socialism, and finds a place in local governance, this will be enabled by local institutions (or gaps in institutions, silences) and once in place the new role will influence rule-making, will influence the making of new plans and policies for urban development. The knowledge embedded in these plans and policies will reflect the actor/institution configuration in place. Conversely, when actors are dealing with

as earlier done by the USA, Japan and the EU, identified information and communication technologies (ICTs) and new media, bio- and lifesciences, nanotechnologies, biotechnologies and creative industries including arts and media content production as key sectors for future development.

'Knowledge', as mobilised in the discourses 'knowledge society' and 'knowledge for development' thus took on a normative, yet in the actual implementation of these discourses through national action plans and development projects, a factual character. Additionally, both discourses communicate the images of a knowledge society and a society developed, based on knowledge as realizable options for developing just as for industrialized countries. It is here, where the notion of 'knowledge' takes on a hegemonic character and has to be regarded as part of an ongoing search for simplifying patterns of a global social order and 'magic bullets' for economic growth. Hegemonic as the adoption of the idea of investing into 'knowledge infrastructures', i.e. ICTs, R&D clusters and high-technology knowledge production, was in itself and in the ways it was communicated powerful enough to lead many nations, far off from entering the development phase after the one of the industrial society, to heavily invest into the construction of these 'knowledge infrastructures' as also defined by many countries with better starting positions.

### Further reading

Hornidge, A.-K. (2014). Wissensdiskurse: Normativ, Faktisch, Hegemonial. Soziale Welt, 65: 7-24.

Hornidge, A.-K. (2014). Discourses of Knowledge – Normative, Factual, Hegemonic. Post-Doctoral Thesis, Bonn, Germany: University of Bonn.

Hornidge, A.-K. (2011). 'Knowledge society' as academic concept and stage of development – a conceptual and historical review. In: Menkhoff, T., Evers, H.-D., Chay, Y.W. and Eng, F.P. (eds.), Beyond the knowledge trap: developing Asia's knowledge-based economies. London, UK: World Scientific, pp. 87-128.

certain plans and policies for a while, their selection of topics and knowledge will change too. Because actors and institutions are linked in a specific way in each configuration, the effects of actors and institutions on each other will be different. Which knowledge plays which role in governance, can only be understood when looking at this specific coupling of actors and institutions, at the configuration.

One important factor in this game we did not discuss yet: *power*. In the following section, we locate power in the context of power/knowledge configurations, which can help us to discern how power affects governance and the inclusion/exclusion of knowledge.

## Further reading

Alff, H., Hornidge, A.-K. and Boedeker, J. (in press). The key to the border: boundary production and negotiation at Asia's crossroads. Political Geography.

Hayoz, N. and Giordano, C. (eds.) (2013). Informality in Eastern Europe: structures, political cultures and social practices (Interdisciplinary Studies on Central and Eastern Europe). Bern, Switzerland: Peter Lang.

Hornidge, A.-K. (2011). 'Knowledge society' as academic concept and stage of development – a conceptual and historical review. In: Menkhoff, T., Evers, H.-D., Chay, Y.W. and Eng, F.P. (eds.), Beyond the knowledge trap: developing Asia's knowledge-based economies. London, UK: World Scientific, pp. 87-128.

North, D. (2005) Understanding the process of economic change. Princeton, NJ, USA: Princeton University Press.

Van Assche, K., Beunen, R. and Duineveld, M. (2014). Formal/informal dialectics and the self-transformation of spatial planning systems: an exploration. Administration & Society, 46(6), 654-683.

## 4.3 Power/knowledge configurations

In this section, we investigate the importance of power/knowledge configurations in evolving governance. Power we understand as the fuel of governance, nothing particularly good or bad, not always associated with oppression and domination. Governance cannot be a power-free environment, because governance is about the taking of decision that are collectively binding, so always creating winners and losers, always inducing parts of the community they do something they don't particularly prefer, and always requiring some means of enforcement. Win-win situations are not always possible, and some actors within governance, and groups not included in the decision arena, will get less than others what they wanted. At the same time, the governance process can change the mind and desires of actors, and once implemented, people who didn't like a policy first, might get used to it, or even see the benefits later. Power is always involved, and and not everybody can win all the time.

Power, we believe, has to be understood in a broad sense: the ability to do things, the impact of policies and plans, the ability to persuade. That last aspect makes it clear that power and knowledge are intricately linked: making people see things differently, is exerting influence over them. This rhetorical aspect of power is not simply a matter of deceit, it can just as well be on the basis of rational arguments, or a persuasive alternative vision, or by showing that the vision held by others, or some of their assumptions, are problematic. In the governance arena, this aspect of persuasion, of creating a different understanding of the situation, of the problem, of the tools, is obviously essential. But also after the codification of decision into policies and plans, power is at work. In these resulting institutions, the situation, the issues, solutions, are always framed in a way that was shaped by the governance process, by the actors and institutions present there. Even without thinking law enforcement, without looking at the coercive effects of policies and plans, they exert a power in and on the community by making people look different and think different. Much of this effect comes from normalizing discourse: what was in effect the result of negotiation between actors in governance, is posited as a neutral description of reality, the issues and solutions: 'Of course, there are 7 categories of environmental problems'.

To make this link between power and knowledge more explicit, the link between our views of reality and our relations with and dependencies on others, we introduce the concept of *power/knowledge configurations*. Knowledge creates power and power creates knowledge. Knowledge is power in the literal sense, of access to information that might give you a benefit in negotiations and strategies, but also in the sense just explained, where influencing the understanding of things, is influencing people. Power creates knowledge in the literal sense of authorities telling what is true, what should be

Figure 4.4. A water mill in Tajikistan. In many parts of Central Asia, the appearance of rural areas changed dramatically over time, depending on the capacity of communities to manage water, to use irrigation, control unpredictable rivers, dig and manage underground canal systems. This coordinative capacity came and went, with the ever changing political winds in the region, with waves of political fragmentation and unification and a shifting power balance between nomads and agriculturalists. Photo: Anna-Katharina Hornidge. © ZEF/University of Bonn, Germany.

learned, at school, propaganda on TV, etc., and in the sense hinted at above: relations of influence create the conceptual frames that create understanding. This extends to an understanding of ourselves and the other actors, as they, in essence are also stories told to make sense of things. Power and knowledge cannot be separated, cannot be understood without reference to each other, and when one side changes, it will trigger something on the other side. Because of this type of linkage, we speak again of configurations.

Power/knowledge configurations are thus associated with actor/institution configurations. They shape the inclusion/exclusion of knowledge in governance, and the impact of expertise once included in governance. The last part deserves more explanation. It requires an understanding the governance never stops. Once a policy is enacted, its 'implementation' as said, is not one step, it is a process in which many actors in governance, in the arena considered, and outside it, will be involved. A final decision is never final. It will be reinterpreted, twisted undermined or reinforced all the time, until it is replaced visibly with something else. In that process, power and knowledge are entwined too: the understanding of the policy, the issues, the community by the actors involved later (e.g. opposing community groups, but also silent expert groups in administrative departments, media, political parties now in opposition, etc.) will reframe the policy and modify its effects. The impact of policies on the community is subjected to this whole post-decision process of twisting and turning, of changing power relations and different ways of understanding. Understanding the impact of expertise on communities is understanding the impact of expertise on policy, and of policy on practice.

Power/knowledge configurations are not only visible in the clear inclusion/exclusion of expertise in policy formation and implementation, and the structuring of topics and problems in policies and plans. They are also embodied in the narratives of development, of the rural, of good governance and the good life, narratives which exist both inside and outside the governance arena. In stories about the good future for the community, for a path of development, there is always an image of the good community, ideally, and an image of the community as it is, not there yet. There is also an implied idea of the current role of the actor projecting that image of the future, and of the ideal future role. An architect might dream up a future with beautiful buildings everywhere, for everyone (if it is a socialist architect), but also with a powerful ministry of architecture, and maybe a president-architect. Again, the visions of future and present cannot be disconnected (futures are produced in a present), and those visions always imply a certain web of power relations. A development perspective always implies a power/knowledge configuration, and probably one different from what is observed now. The concepts, images, metaphors embedded in these narratives of the good future already influence the possible forms and impacts of expertise, say on rural development.

Spatial and time scales do not escape the same narrative dynamics. Stories about the good future in all probability imply a different ordering of spatial scales, with some scales becoming more important than now (e.g. requiring more regional policy), and others less. This will affect power relations in the future, and, if actors understand, it will reshuffle the map of actors, create resistance here, support there, new coalitions of pro and contra (of a proposal). Important scales will lodge important actors and policies, and once a scale of decision-making is entrenched, it is hard to get rid of. Actors at an embattled scale of decision-making (e.g. provinces under threat), will mobilize everything they can in the power-knowledge configuration, all the influence they have, as many scientific reports as possible 'proving' they what they do is essential for the well-being of the community. And they will likely project a vision of the future in which the common good is defined in such a way that they, threatened actors at a threatened scale, bring it about.

These mechanisms, the linkage between actor/institution, power/knowledge and certain spatial scales, should, we think, lead to a re-evaluation of territorial (or area-based) approaches: when speaking of development and planning, it is usually assumed that the existing order of governance, the existing layering of scales, cannot be questioned and it is treated as a natural starting point, a natural frame of governance. While we think that 'the community' and 'the common good' should not simply be tied to the units and scales of government that we know now. What is good for a neighborhood is not always best decided at the neighborhood level, what is good for the country not always at the country level, so discussion on development should not automatically be tied to these units. Our stories about the good future are (too much) inspired by the units and scales of government in place now, while new narratives of development can, will and should reconfigure those scales.

The same reasoning can be followed for the analysis of time and policy: the time horizons, episodes, speeds, for change, we assume for development, are part of our stories of development. We do not know if these elements of timing are realistic, will fit with changing realities, but we can say that the way we conceptualize time of and for development will affect other aspects of the development narrative and will affect power relations. They will further affect the map of actors and the relations between actors and institutions. A reflection on the time horizons supposed or required by various policies and plans for development is therefore very useful, and more than an esoteric exercise.

## Further reading

Evers, H.-D. and Hornidge, A.-K. (2007). Knowledge hubs along the Straits of Malacca. Asia Europe Journal, 5(3), 417-433.

Foucault, M. (1968). Les mots et les choses. Paris, France: Gallimard.

Hornidge, A.-K. (2014). Wissensdiskurse: Normativ, Faktisch, Hegemonial. Soziale Welt, 65: 7-24.

## 4.4 Evolving governance, rural development and knowledge

We studied already how models of governance shape the use of knowledge and expertise in development visions and policies. We looked at the ways perspectives on development are linked up with models of governance, and how the use of a development perspective in a form of governance can shape the inclusion/exclusion and implementation of knowledge and expertise. The analysis of these linkages brought us to the central concept of governance paths: analyzing governance paths we see as essential for understanding which development vision can more easily come up here than there, which one makes a better chance here rather than there, and which roles expertise and local knowledge can play. It is in unique governance paths that always hybrid governance forms embrace always hybrid development approaches, with always complex and unique effects, and unique patterns of knowledge use.

In this last chapter, we presented a more cohesive frame to look at these governance paths, and reflect on the way knowledge fits or doesn't fit, and has an impact, or not so much. We discussed flexibility and rigidity in governance evolution, and saw rigidity as the interplay of path dependence, interdependence and goal dependence. The position of knowledge in governance evolution, of concepts, perspectives, narratives, and the information framed by them, we made analyzable by introducing two interlinked configurations, co-evolving: knowledge/power configurations and actor/institution configurations. Which visions for the future emerge, are decided upon, and which knowledge is mobilized and used in the process, hinges on these configurations.

In Part II of the book, these concepts will return, as will the governance models and development perspectives. What has been said this far applies to governance and development in general, not only to rural development. All of it, however, will be useful in our following presentation and dissection of rural development approaches. A silent premise of the previous chapter was that many specifically rural development approaches focus too much on the rural, without paying enough attention to the general development perspective, and the underlying governance models. We believe it's worth the detour. But, of course, the proof of the pudding is in the eating. So, let's move on and see.

## Further reading

Bierschenk T. and De Sardan, J-P.O. (2002). Powers in the village: rural Benin between democratisation and decentralisation. Mainz, Germany: Institut für Ethnologie und Afrikastudien.

Grindle, M.S. (2007). Good enough governance revisited. Development Policy Review, 25(5), 553-574.

Lee, R.L.M. (2006). Reinventing modernity: reflexive modernization vs liquid modernity vs multiple modernities. European Journal of Social Theory, 9, 355-368.

Munnich, L.W. Jr., Schrock, G. and Cook, K. (2002). Rural knowledge clusters: the challenge of rural economic prosperity. Reviews of Economic Development Literature and Practice, 12.

# II Traditions of applied expertise for rural development

In this second part, we examine several approaches to rural development through the lens of the theory developed in previous chapters. The examination is critical, but does not outright reject any of the approaches. We try to discern useful elements, insights and practices, and reflect on the contexts in which they make the most sense. Each of the approaches will be linked to the models of democracy described earlier and interpreted in terms of the governance analysis presented in the previous chapter. The analysis will thereby help position the different approaches and evaluate their advantges and limitations. This part will be richer in examples, as we come closer to real life communities that could be analyzed, and, possibly, advised (by others or by themselves). We cannot cover all approaches and all topics relevant to rural development, and the selection of approaches is not meant to serve as an encyclopedia, but rather as a guide, a way to structure the wilderness of rural development projects, policies, visions. In the examples, the short illustrative cases, and in the literature, we will touch tangentially on a larger variety of topics and cast our nets wider.

## Part II

Some of the approaches we present might not be immediately recognized as rural development, and we have chosen to omit certain approaches present in the scientific literature, which, in our view, are influential in one scientific discipline only and therefore not broadly applicable. The approaches we included all have a far-reaching influence on rural development, in theory and practice, across disciplines and countries – even in the case of approaches not widely regarded as encompassing a rural development perspective. Much of what happens in rural areas and what affects rural development does not result from policies implemented in the name of 'rural development' or from people who perceive themselves as rural development specialists.

In the following chapters we discuss:
- extension models;
- land consolidation and land use planning;
- rural and community design;
- institutional reform;
- environmental and natural resource management;
- innovation and transition management;
- local, local, local.

These are approaches to rural development we find to be influential in many rural areas. We ask the reader to keep this in mind even where there are no direct references to rurality: the perspectives being discussed, in all their dimensions, are being promoted and used in rural areas.

# 5. Rural development: extension models

## Abstract

In this chapter, we look at approaches to rural development that view knowledge as the major driver behind development and therefore focus their attention on education and training of key actors. We start with a brief analysis of models of agricultural extension, in which rural areas are mostly seen as agricultural production zones, and in which farmers are the central actors contributing to development. Extension models emerging at different times and places are discussed, along with their tendencies to assign active roles to universities, administrations and/or farmers' associations or cooperatives. We then look at multi-functional perspectives on rural areas and examine corresponding models of extension. Finally, we look at science and education in a broader sense and reflect on approaches to rural development in which these aspects play a key role.

## 5.1 Rural extension as agricultural extension

Rural extension as an organized practice originated in the 19th century, as agricultural extension carried out by the centralized nation-state, or actors working within the framework of the nation-state. Earlier versions can be found among the French 18th century physiocrats, who saw agricultural production as the basis of economic development, and most farmers and peasants as urgently needing education. In the 19th century, nation-states in various parts of the world embarked on rural education and extension programs, to solve social and economic problems (hunger, 'moral depravity', unrest), and, in some cases, to smoothen the settlement process.

When the word 'extension' is used it usually assumes that rural areas are agricultural areas, and that education of some sort will optimize agricultural production. This, then, is seen as development. We will later see that some more recent versions become more inclusive of other actors and more multi-functional futures. The word usually also assumes a farmer that is autonomous, one entrepreneurial type which has or can create access to land, resources, and labor. Because some perspectives on rural development are closely related in their emphasis on expertise and education, but do not assume the autonomous capitalist farmer, we also use the word expertise systems, with extension perspectives seeing expertise systems as the drivers of rural development.

We distinguish between six models of extension:
- purely individual initiative;
- cooperative extension;
- professional association extension;
- university extension;
- capitalist state extension;
- communist state extension.

Each has different variants and they can be combined to differing degrees. The *individual model* is per definition very localized, while the others can have more centralized and more localized versions. Each model can be infused with different forms of and attitudes to expertise. We call a cohesive set of group attitudes to knowledge, how to produce it and how to use it an epistemic culture. Communities can be marked by a strong and cohesive epistemic culture, or they can be internally more complex and divided. Extension models can reflect an epistemic culture, and can in turn contribute to the reproduction of epistemic cultures. Each can be marked by different degrees of professionalism with the players involved. We do not assume the existence of an ideal model of extension, and do not intend to come to generic prescriptions for intervention. When states or communities transition from one form of governance to another, each will create its own hybrid governance, and, if extension takes place, that will change, too.

**Example 5.1. Mainstream innovation policies: lagging behind (with thanks to Catherine Reynolds).**

International organizations such as the World Bank, the OECD and UNESCO play an important, normative role in shaping innovation policy. The frameworks they set not only determine how resources are allocated at the international level, but also set precedents for national policies.

Currently these policy frameworks demonstrate a strong bias toward technologically focused innovations. This reveals an implicit preference for innovations developed in the Global North (where most technological advancement takes place) and thus for linear models of development that define progress in terms of arrival at a pre-defined, existing state.

This narrow focus comes at a cost to the environment, as well as to resource scarce actors, both in the Global South and the Global North. The inovation policies do not address ways to mitigate the ecological destruction often associated with technology driven, market based economic growth, and they create dependencies on tecnologies that are not affordable for most of the world.

Alternative models like sustainable development and inclusive development, being discussed in other realms of international policy, could inspire more comprehensive and effective innovation policies. These models underscore the importance of fostering context-specific innovations from those who stand to benefit from them, rather than from outside. They also encourage innovation policies that address regulatory mechanisms for internalizing environmental costs, rather than letting them be borne by society as a whole.

Such approaches are emerging, even if they have not yet reached the mainstream. Those aimed at fostering innovations applicable to poverty alleviation are being developed under labels like 'pro-poor innovation', 'social innovation', 'inclusive innovation' and 'grassroots innovation'. Significant innovation schemes for backing sustainable development include 'strategic niche management' and efforts at driving systematic change, i.e. counteracting current path dependencies toward undesirable innovation by altering entrenched constellations of actors and institutions.

**Further reading**

Schwachula, A., Vila Seane, M. and Hornidge, A.-K. (2014). Science, technology and innovation in the context of development – An overview of concepts and corresponding policies recommended by international organizations. ZEF Working Paper, 132.

World Bank (2010). Innovation policy: a guide for developing countries. Washington, DC, USA: World Bank.

UNESCO (2010). Science policy for sustainable development. The power of science to empower society. Paris, France: UNESCO.

OECD (2010). The OECD Innovation Strategy. Getting a Head Start on Tomorrow. Paris, France: OECD.

*Individual initiative* can still be compatible with an expertise system. It can be part of a capitalist society, but one can also think of very communal societies elsewhere where possibilities still exist for the individual to 'modernize' his or her own agricultural practices and where no cooperatives, universities, etc. have a systematic presence. We do not refer here to purely traditional knowledge and/or purely local knowledge, as we do reserve the label 'extension' for activities that somehow intend to insert expert knowledge into the rural economy to modernize it in one way or another.

Experts and knowledge can both be local, but there must be a conscious decision leading to the designation of a particular person and his or her local knowledge as useful expertise in a particular case. Thus, individual initiative, including a measure of autonomy, can be the basis for a form of extension, a form of shopping in local and other forms of knowledge available in the area, even when no systematic attempt has been made to organize extension there. The model is thus a combination of organizational fragmentation and individual autonomy and drive. If knowledge and learning are seen as the major driver of development, and individual farmers have the autonomy to pursue this, we can call this extension based on individual initiative. Over time, individual initiative tends to transition into more organized models, or disintegrate, as the basis underneath individual extension is usually fragmented leftovers of older knowledge and

Figure 5.1. Extension has many faces. It can be an activity in and by itself and it can be part of a larger project with other aims. It can be a matter of listening and reading, or of gaining practical experience. Photo: Anna-Katharina Hornidge. © ZEF/University of Bonn, Germany.

Rural development

other infrastructures, or fragmentary beginnings of new infrastructures. It can be seen as a transitional form of extension, not entirely stable.

*Cooperative extension* can be the next step in such transition. It emerges when several individuals team up to organize extension or the purchase of extension services. That is, the cooperation can focus on the acquisition of expertise somewhere else, or on the production of expertise, or on the dissemination among the members. Implied here that some existing local knowledge might be very useful, but not disseminated or not developed enough, or not linked up well enough with bits and pieces of expert knowledge to be imported from elsewhere.

The model does not necessarily rely on cooperatives sensu strictu, but assumes a group of rural actors that sees a common interest in learning and modernizing agriculture. The useful knowledge can be found, produced, connected together. We can speak here of co-production of knowledge. Cooperatives can be larger or smaller, rich and poor, can have employees or not, can hire professionals or not, and the effects of the extension efforts will vary concomitantly.

Cooperatives can be focused on one crop or on the rural economy in an area. The boundary with the next model becomes less clear when cooperatives merge and acquire more power and influence. Because they produce their own organizational and knowledge infrastructure, cooperative extension forms tend to be more stable than individual extension, but they can still be considered transitional, as they tend either to be integrated into state structures, or link up to and become a functional substitute for state extension (with the state supporting them). Cooperatives can indeed be supported by government, as in Japan, and they play an important role in Japanese agriculture. Also in some post-Soviet countries (e.g. Georgia, Kazakhstan), cooperatives are 'encouraged' by the state, as more cooperation and coordination for agricultural production is considered useful, but it is not always easy to discern whether there is bottom-up initiative supported by the state (actual cooperative) or a state idea pushed down the hierarchy.

The evolution of cooperative extension and cooperatives as such is not always one and the same thing. Cooperatives can become more important, but their extension function can dwindle. The extension function can become separated of other functions. Cooperatives can turn into conglomerates providing marketing, banking, insurance and health care for farmers and get quite close to the role of collective farms in the former Soviet Union (farms as local communities with all local services). And, as in many European countries, these conglomerates can split up again, into private businesses (with shareholders), and properly cooperative organizations, sometimes a spin-off of parts towards government. What is left of cooperative expertise in such dramatic transformations of cooperatives, is different per case. In most European countries, some

**Example 5.2. Belgian Farmers Association: rural development and politics.**

The Belgian Farmers Association (Boerenbond, BB) was founded in 1890 as a national organization, after a series of smaller scale initiatives. In the late 19$^{th}$ century, a wave of globalization, coupled with lower freight prices, caused a serious crisis in European agriculture, forcing it to compete with North American, South American and Asian products. Large land owners were anxious about the value of land, farmers about the value of their production, and politicians about stability in the countrysides. Emigration to the Americas reached new heights. The Catholic Church was worried about all of this, and the Catholic parties were concerned about impoverished farmers moving to the industrialized cities, seen as the cradle of sin and socialism (both dangerous). In 1890, Jacob Ferdinand Mellaerts, a priest, and catholic politicians Joris Helleputte and Franz Schollaert chose the town of Leuven to officially establish the BB, to organize and empower farmers, and to keep them Christian. In the course of a few years, the gentlemen started dozens of local chapters, a magazine, extension services, cooperative purchasing of inputs, a cooperative bank and insurance companies. In 1907, a separate organization for the spouses of farmers was initiated, in 1911 for horticulturalists (seeing themselves as separate from farmers), in 1920 for farmer's children.

In the period before World War II, extension services were an important focus, with BB teaching farmers and horticulturalists modern methods to work the land, seed selection and improvement, animal husbandry, hygiene and processing (especially in dairy farming). BB was largely responsible for improving vocational training and extension, and for increasing profitability of Belgian agriculture in that period. Training was available for farmers, their sons, and for teachers; and trainers could be other farmers, trained teachers, scientists, government employees, university employees, or from the BB itself. In 1930, the cluster of organizations counted ca 130,000 members. The Great Depression hit hard though, especially after 1934. One of the cooperative banks went under, and it would take years to restore confidence and repay members. During World War II, a German model of state-led agricultural planning was imposed, but with little success, because of, indeed the war.

After the war, mechanization, upscaling and globalization took center stage. In 1956, a first version of the European Union saw the light, and BB felt that this was not a threat but an opportunity, for export and for protection on a larger scale. Smaller farms did suffer though, and staying in business required heavy investment, modernization and specialization. The cooperative bank, insurance companies, and BB's specialized retail chain (for all farming and gardening-related things, Aveve) had greatly expanded their activities and clientele, going beyond farming. Social and cultural activities became more prominent, and the impact of BB's organizations on daily life in the countryside increased. Meanwhile, many of the initially cooperative economic organizations grew into larger cooperations dominated by larger shareholders, sometimes by management, and the influence of local branches diminished. The interests of individual farmers, especially smaller ones, were not always met to the same extent.

The number of farmers dropped dramatically, and the countryside became less and less dominated by farming, by BB's organizations and by the Catholic parties. The number of non-farmers among BB members increased, leading to a reorganization in 1971. BB split into two: a professional association and a broader organization addressing issues of rural life. That broader organization ('landelijke beweging') included many pre-existing organizations, such as the youth organization, female farmers clubs, and local chapters, all open for non-farmers. Mechanization and scaling up were intensified in these years; new technologies were introduced. Meanwhile, environmental issues also became more prominent in social discourses on agriculture: topics included herbicides, pesticides, fertilizers, and their impact on soils, water, ecology. Animal welfare became a topic of discussion, as well as overproduction and European subsidies.

The 1990's were turbulent for BB because of internal and external politics. Agriculture was suffering from a negative public image, perceived as neglecting environmental issues, and BB was viewed as conservative and in favor of parochialism in local politics. One controversial issue in the densely populated Belgium countryside was excess manure and its diverse applications. Environmental organizations, community associations and others pushed governments to tighten controls, but the resulting 'manure plans' caused demonstrations and other protests by farmers. At the same time, European Union agricultural policies changed significantly: direct subsidies to farmers and guaranteed minimum prices, which had led to severe overproduction, were gradually reduced, while rural development, aimed at 'maintenance of the countryside' was introduced as a second pillar of EU agricultural policy. BB's leadership sensed the need for reorientation towards sustainability, in an economic, ecological and social sense.

In the years after 2000, BB showed adaptive capacity, aided by its complex organizational structure. It began to promote a broader vision of rural development, inclusive of high tech innovation policies for intensive agriculture but also, in other cases and places, farming as part of a multi-functional rural space, with options for rural tourism, rural health care, farm to table, etc. More different activities were envisioned in the rural areas, and farms became more diversified, from high tech to labor intensive organic farms. A new focus of extension activity became entrepreneurship and rural management, while BB, together with its former insurance and banking branches (now autonomous) established an innovation taskforce, where new ideas can emerge and financing and risk assessment can take place.

### Further reading

Vandermeulen, V., Verspecht, A., Van Huylenbroeck, G., Meert, H., Boulanger, A. and Van Hecke, E. (2006). The importance of the institutional environment on multifunctional farming systems in the peri-urban area of Brussels. Land Use Policy, 23(4), 486-501.

Fernández, E. (2014). Trust, religion, and cooperation in western agriculture, 1880-1930. The Economic History Review, 67, 678-698.

form of cooperative extension is left, but the heydays are in the past, in the early 20th century, when farmers got together and found they had to pool resources, organize their lobby with government, and organize their own learning.

*Professional association extension* can be seen as the organization of expertise production and/or dissemination by associations assembling similar professionals in a larger area. It can overlap with cooperative extension, but does not always rely on cooperative organization or ownership, while cooperatives can come to include many professions. The most common example are farmers associations, often with regional/local branches, but one can also think of vet's organizations, and more specialized associations such as cattle breeder groups, and horticultural associations, or, for that matter, business organizations in greenhouse construction, or food processing. Here, professional association blends into industry association. In historical evolution, many professional associations of farmers have spawned industries and industry groups that became more influential (economically and politically) than the farmers' associations themselves. In many European countries, the professional association model was very important, marked the evolution of extension, and in most cases, a set of national organizations evolved which became involved in educating their own members, in doing research themselves or ordering research with other partners, e.g. universities, state research institutes, or bureaucratic experts (Nagel and Von der Heiden, 2004). This already points at the possibility of a coexistence of several models (Kalna-Dubinyuk and Stanely, 2005).

As might be clear from previous paragraphs, the relations between this model and the cooperative model can be very intricate. Farmers associations can be cooperative in the beginning, private later, become entangled with government, lose their connection with certain types of farming, create connections with other professions, etc. The complex linkages between the different sorts of extension in many cases have to do with the emergence and evolution of an agro-industrial complex, in which farmers played an important role early on, and contributed to the genesis of a web of organizations, private, state and cooperative, to new roles and rules, where farmers eventually became a smaller cog in the machine. (We will see that different paths are possible.)

*University extension* exists in many Western countries. Both North America and Europe have many versions of university extension. Sometimes, the universities themselves took the initiative to become more involved in the development of their region (especially recently), but historically, it was usually state intervention which forced universities to play an active role. In the USA in the 19th century, land grant universities received land and funding from the federal government in exchange for such an active promotion of the rural economy. Later, agricultural extension grew into a more comprehensive regional development package, including also, among other things, environmental education and design, economic development assistance, and public participation courses.

**Example 5.3. Characteristics of local knowledge sharing in Khorezm, Uzbekistan.**

The authoritarian system of state control over knowledge production that can be assessed in the realm of high-level research commissioned by the government of Uzbekistan (Selim, 2009: 80ff), leads to a high level of self-censorship in the realm of local, agricultural knowledge production. Wall (2008: 85ff) identifies 5 characteristics of the local knowledge system of Khorezm. First, local 'masters' with specialized knowledge, embedded in the patriarchal and hierarchical Khorezmi culture, are central to the system and often hold positions of political and economic power. Second, in terms of knowledge dissemination, family based modes of knowledge reproduction and transfer are common. Access to external knowledge and its reproduction in the local knowledge system exists, but to a lesser extent. Third, in sectors of immediate importance to the state agricultural production system, indigenous, local knowledge lies at the interface with formal, university taught knowledge. Wall here assesses a linear, top-down approach to knowledge diffusion with a lack of mutual exchange of ideas (2008: 110ff). Bottom-up approaches to innovation development, involving the ideas, experience and knowledge of local stakeholders as experts, is rather uncommon in Khorezm and in Uzbekistan in general. This interlinks with Wall's fourth point: 'collective knowledge', which is rather unitary in nature, prevails in the Khorezm agricultural knowledge system, leaving little space for creativity-fostering diversity. Fifth, this unitary nature of knowledge is, according to Wall, further exacerbated by ongoing 'knowledge loss' and a 'growth of ignorance' in the post-Soviet era of Khorezm (Wall, 2008: 123ff).

**Further reading**

Selim, M. (2009). Notes from Tashkent: an ethnographic study of Uzbek scholarly life. New Left Review, 55, 73-86.

Wall, C. (2008). Argorods of Western Uzbekistan: knowledge control and agriculture in Khorezm. Münster, Germany: Lit Verlag.

University extension, as the others, can have many different faces. The level of community involvement, the degree of adaptation of scientific questions and answers to local needs, desires and understanding, varies significantly. In some cases, universities defined issues and solved them, after which they told local communities they did it, while elsewhere, state organizations observed issues or thought in pre-defined solutions, then ordered universities to teach the locals. Yet elsewhere, farmers or local governments or cooperatives or professional associations got in touch with universities, or came together with them in a systematic fashion. The signals, the communication, could of course go in different directions, and situations occurred in various European countries in which universities defined issues, discussed with administrations and farmers associations, tried to implement, hit the wall with local governments and individual farmers. Many different patterns can be discerned.

These different patterns, of course, reflect the map of actors, the actor/institution configurations discussed earlier, and the power/knowledge configuration in local, regional, national governance. Scales are relevant. A university can be a local hub with economic and political influence in the region, while another one can be far less so, but more of a central hub in an international scientific network. Some universities have little direct influence in the region, not so many links with local organizations, but a strong impact on certain aspects of national policy, indirectly affecting the rural development in the region (influence on economic development policy, spatial planning, environmental policy, infrastructure development). The possible impact of a university on rural development, through extension or otherwise, hinges on the relations between them and other actors in the community, and these relations will, as said, only be understood when one can sketch the map of actors in governance, and analyze the governance paths. More recently, university extension often wants to transform into a wide variety of community engagement forms, where learning can take place in two directions, where extension becomes more part of a process of participatory development. Yet, which transformations are possible in a given community, hinges once more on the understanding of governance contexts. We will come back to this.

*Capitalist state extension* can include many of these patterns, within a capitalist organization of the economy. In this model, governments can enlist the service of universities, of specialized institutes, of their own expert-bureaucrats, and they can sponsor, subsidize, support professional associations and cooperatives in their extension activities. If government is the driving force in the game, we would use this label, even when universities, etc. are involved. In other cases, when many players play a substantial role and can take initiative, one can speak of a hybrid model. In the USA, one can speak of capitalist state extension, since the federal government initiated the university extension model and also established county extension services with federal government experts posted at the local level. Some version of the capitalist model is usually assumed in the extension literature, and the picture of modernization often includes a gradual introduction into global markets, while the long term goal is often seen in terms of macro-economic indicators.

Capitalist state extension will vary with the form of capitalism which developed, and depending on the map of actors which evolved in a state. If cooperatives became already powerful, then state extension will probably work with cooperatives, induce them to do extension, or support their extension activities, e.g. by linking them to government research institutes. If individual farmers have plenty of land, as in the early USA, have some capital, labor, but miss some knowledge, cooperatives are suspicious and local governments not interested, then, as the federal government thought, it might be a good idea to organize it themselves, at the county level. In the Netherlands, state extension can be seen in a very developed form, with government active in rural development in a variety of guises, including the support of agricultural education at all levels, agricultural research, applied research, extension via government actors, and support of the extension activities of professional associations.

*Communist state extension* is a system of state farms and the expertise in and around them. The farm is de facto local government, a space of economic production but also of political decision making, of local governance, and of knowledge development. It does not start from an individual autonomous farmer taking decisions for an enterprise and its resources, and it does not see extension as the activity of one actor. Agricultural production is taken care of by a web of organizations at local, regional and national level, is highly expert-driven and expertise is specialized and distributed in this web of specialized organizations (focusing on fertilizer, tractors, irrigation, land reclamation, etc.). The collective farms were centers of policy integration and application of the expertise emanating from this network, while it also corrected this expertise where necessary, and contributed to knowledge development in the network.

The goal of extension was often seen in economic indicators, yet different from the Western ones: not macro-economic parameters, but production targets. Plans, at all levels, were supposed to increase production, bringing it to the targets, while enabling the workers to have a good quality of life, improving the welfare of the region. These goals were not always compatible. The reliance on scientific expertise was greater than in the other models, but the actual impact of scientific expertise differed between paper and reality. The communist extension model offered a vision of optimal productivity and optimal spatial organization based on correct mapping, testing, organization, and usage of tools, but the level of expertise integration and policy integration promised by science and bureaucracy alike, proved not very realistic. In other words: it was not always possible to make the expert organizations work together, to make them listen to the farms (and vice versa), to integrate all the expertise into plans, and make those plans work.

## Further reading

Leeuwis, C. (2008). Communication for rural innovation: rethinking agricultural extension. New York, NY, USA: John Wiley & Sons.

Rogers, E.M. (1988). The intellectual foundation and history of the agricultural extension model. Science Communication, 9(4), 492-510.

World Bank (1998/1999). World development report, knowledge for development. Washington DC, USA: World Bank.

## 5.2 The content of extension

What we just described pertains to the form or procedure of extension: how is it organized, which organizations are in place, who is addressed? We can also discuss extension in terms of substance or content. What is being taught or learned? Also in this discussion, the difference between models of democracy becomes visible, the difference between general development approaches, and unique paths of governance. And, as can be expected, form and content are related; the form pre-organized the content, and some content almost asks or a certain form of extension.

If the content is rather local knowledge, we can expect extension to be more cooperative, maybe professional association based. We can expect it to be more local, and, in contemporary times, we can expect extension to be about connecting bits and pieces of local knowledge into a more stable knowledge base, and a more viable base for local-based brands. We can also expect efforts to link local knowledge with new expert knowledge, in science, but also in terms of management and marketing, since the local knowledge can more likely generate a stable local economic basis if this happens. (We come back to this in the discussion of localism). We can also link an accent on local knowledge with more participatory governance, either fully bottom-up, or encouraged by higher level governments.

One form a local knowledge extension strategy can take is an emphasis on sustainability and organic, provided that existing local products, as well as production and processing methods, are understood as organic and commercially promising. Local and organic are two distinct but overlapping categories of agriculture, and conflicts can arise over the organic or sustainable nature of traditional methods. Extension can be focused on enhancing organic production, hence on local knowledge, or it can be focused on local development through the introduction of organic agriculture, hence on a combination of local and expert knowledge. The expertise sought after, and disseminated, can come from several scientific disciplines, and it can be co-produced with organic farmers, building on positive experiences they have had. That knowledge can be adapted to small scale or large scale agriculture. It can be focused on high tech, low tech, or mixed technologies. The accent there hinges on the governance paths, and on the models of governance and development subscribed to by the initiators of extension. Expertise in large scale agriculture is often sought by governments promoting a modernist development approach (from the left or right side of the political spectrum). Local knowledge can be promoted in a communitarian environment, using a participatory development approach.

If we assume a more or less capitalist environment, then we can distinguish four different forms of knowledge extension, focusing on: *production knowledge, processing knowledge, product knowledge* and *marketing knowledge*. In the case of wine, we could say production knowledge relates to growing the grapes, processing knowledge is about making wine, product knowledge enables judgment on the quality of the wine, and marketing knowledge is the assembled expertise that makes something sellable. Wine makers can combine several forms of expertise. In a capitalist environment with well-functioning markets, education, and production and extension infrastructure, we can expect that marketing knowledge restructures the other types: in the end, if something is not sold, it will not be produced anymore after a while. Product knowledge can be considered an infrastructure for the others: without an understanding of the quality of the product, e.g. wine, it is hard to link the other types of knowledge, to understand what the market wants in terms of taste, aroma, color, and to connect that with the traditional product, the soil, the climate, production methods, their efficiency, etc. Marketing knowledge provides goals which can restructure the whole process, while product knowledge can link the types of knowledge in the process, to interpret and transmit the signals that enable restructuring.

Product knowledge and the others can be the target of specific extension activities, depending on the gaps that are perceived, or extension can focus on the whole chain. If this is the ambitious goal of extension, we can expect that a strong organizational infrastructure is needed, or, in a slightly different perspective, an actor/institution configuration that can serve as infrastructure for comprehensive extension: a strong social-democratic government comprising of many actors and willing to invest a lot (as e.g. in the Netherlands), or a combination of government actors, universities/institutes, and professional associations for different parts of the chain, even semi-professional and hobby groups, and media. To continue the wine example, we can then mention wine growers, but also sommelier groups and courses, wine tasting clubs and their magazines, wine institutes and the associations of their graduated vinologists (oenologists). If all these actors exist, are active, have some expertise, then it is easier to coordinate them, and think collectively on gaps and potential in expertise development. The organizational infrastructure can also grow and adapt, with, in the wine example, a new breed of wine consultants flying around the world to tell farmers and wine making cooperative how they could improve their product, to adapt to new markets, in other words, the new role of the consultant makes it easier to link up the types of expertise, in a market and quality orientation.

Discussions on poverty reduction, food scarcity, but also sustainability in the last few decades, when carried out in a neo-liberal and modernist frame, focus on high-tech, large scale solution: large farms, equipped with powerful modern equipment for high productivity, minimal inputs, labor and environmental damage (the package often sold under 'precision agriculture'). The implied farmer requires high levels of capital and expertise, and continuing education (as form of extension) on evolving technology. Because of these requirements, that form of agriculture will work best in an actor/ institution configuration of a low regulation, neo-liberal environment, and dependencies on banks and agro-industrial firms. In the case of high tech focus, extension tends to be production knowledge oriented; what is quality is forgotten or is presumed to be obvious, and processing and marketing expertise are cultivated elsewhere in the chain, with specialized players (food companies, companies processing basic ingredients for food companies, feed companies for animals, etc.).

Extension in recent times has thus been narrowed down in focus in many cases (in highly specialized production and processing chains), but, in other cases, it has also been broadened, to include more than agricultural knowledge. Then, extension becomes part of larger community development efforts and knowledge on many aspects of community assets, as well as how they can be developed and recombined, becomes relevant.

## Further reading

Evers, H.-D., Kaiser, M., & Müller, C. (2003). Entwicklung durch Wissen: eine neue Wissensarchitektur. Soziale Welt, 49-69.

Hitzler, R., Honer, A. and Maeder, C. (eds.) 1994. Expertenwissen. Die institutionalisierte Kompetenz zur Konstruktion von Wirklichkeit. Opladen, Germany: Westdeutscher Verlag.

Hoffman, M., Lubell, M. and Hillis, V. (2014). Linking knowledge and action through mental models of sustainable agriculture. Proceedings of the National Academy of Sciences of the USA, 111(36), 13016-13021.

Lachenmann, G. (1994). Systeme des Nichtwissens. Alltagsverstand und Expertenbewußtsein im Kulturvergleich. In: Hitzler, R., Honer, A. and Maeder, C. (eds.), Expertenwissen. Opladen, Germany: Westdeutscher Verlag, pp. 285-305.

Pretty, J.N., Williams, S. and Toulmin, C. (eds.). (2012). sustainable intensification: increasing productivity in African food and agricultural systems. International Journal of Agricultural Sustainability, 9(1).

## 5.3 Towards extension as community development

If extension turns into community development, the link with the general development perspective of livelihoods and assets becomes very close. We would still call it an extension approach to rural development, if the accent is still on learning and teaching as the driver of development. If community development, rather than agricultural development, becomes the goal, many other forms of knowledge come into the picture. Generally, the focus will shift from teaching to learning, and from individual learning to social learning. This is especially the case when it is part of a move to more participatory governance.

*Social learning* has been defined in many ways, but one can say the essence is that groups learn in and by interaction, by picking up information but more importantly

Figure 5.2. Awards, medals and diploma's in a Canadian winery. They draw the attention of tourists, of buyers, and distinguish the winery, but the system also encourages continuous improvement in product quality, and speeds up learning among producers and consumers alike. Marketing knowledge helps creating product knowledge, processing knowledge and production knowledge. Okanagan valley, British Columbia. Photo: Monica Gruzmacher. © ZEF/University of Bonn, Germany.

by comparing and testing their perspectives, by, in the best case scenario, synthesizing ideas representing a useful perspective for the group. Social learning has been touted as a solution for communities in an impasse, and as a way towards more sustainable resource use. It has been mostly mentioned in that context of resources, and, unfortunately, has often been captured in modernist discourses, where social learning was in fact sustainability teaching by government, in a context where other actors were tied down and forced to listen. All were tied to a learning situation and learning goal. We tend to believe that this leads mostly to local resistance. Social learning is possible, and it takes place all the time, but it cannot be easily steered. It takes place inside and outside governance, on multiple learning sites, including coffee houses, sports clubs, lakeside associations, etc. If we try to influence this learning process, we need first of all to map and understand it: what are the sites, the networks, the methods, the discourses, the influential voices? Or, we come back to the concepts of power/knowledge behind learning in communities. Some goals will never work in a community, others have to be translated and disseminated in very specific ways, and, conversely, the goals might have to be transformed if participatory governance and learning is taken seriously.

If we transform extension into learning-based community development, the question of which approach to development to take emerges again. This question cannot be escaped; pretending not to make a choice is equivalent to making a choice without being aware of it. Often, the not so clear assumption is some form of livelihoods or asset-based approach, in a participatory version, in which community assets are mapped, together with stakeholders, issues defined, and preferences for solutions. The implied governance model can be communitarianism, or sometimes civil society, or civic republicanism. When it is (participatory) communitarianism, a real risk is the forgetting of other scales, and of specialized roles and knowledge. We refer back to the discussion of the risks of communitarianism and of participatory development.

When university outreach was the initial model, and this transforms into learning-based community development, one often speaks of *community engagement*. This, too, has many versions, depending on the context and governance path. The effects, too, will hinge on context and path. If there is already a rather communitarian participatory governance system in place in the community, then the approach may work better, may fit the actor/institution and power/knowledge configurations better, and might be able to transform them in a direction desired by a community missing a few insights to get going. More ambitious, but still possible, is a situation where a community is dissatisfied with something in particular and cannot solve the issue, and then learns from university extension that in fact a restructuring of governance is highly desirable in order to move in the desired direction. A more participatory structure might be suggested and tested in the community, assisted by university extension.

The situation becomes more problematic when engagement implies the de facto reconstruction of local governance based on a model not asked for locally, not decided upon, and maybe only preferred by a small coalition of university and a few local stakeholders closely linked to them. We would argue this is problematic in case of a not locally chosen governance model, but also of development approaches, and extension models. And it can be questionable with regards to content, when certain concepts (e.g. sustainability), or sectors or professions, or certain images of the community and its future are privileged in and by the small university-driven coalition just mentioned. Good intentions do not excuse this. Asset mapping and visioning exercises can be wonderfully effective, but also get on the nerves of participants, and they can attract a very particular selection of actors, leading to a result that will likely be rejected by city council, and probably cause an irritation that means no repeat exercise. In case there is local democratic support, a learning process takes place, and a community vision comes out of it, then the quality of the analysis supported by the university will be crucial to avoid disappointment and rejection of future exercises. We return to the issues of scale and context, in particular the two configurations we highlighted for governance paths. If they are not understood, then locally the vision will not have legs, and if contexts and scales are not understood, what has been decided locally will be counteracted elsewhere.

What was just about risks and benefits of university driven community development applies to other actors taking such initiative. In fact, it is more common that government actors take such initiative, e.g. regional governments or specialized government actors (regional community development offices) embarking on local development initiatives, with the help of researchers, or, also common, NGOs, with the backing of international organizations or governments (e.g. World Wildlife Fund with World Bank support).

The risks mentioned point to the need of reflexivity, already discussed above, and the need to reflect on positionality. Positionality we see as two things: reflection on the roles taken during development activity, support, and secondly, reflection on the path taken through the community, through the networks of actors, perspectives, power relations. Both aspects require, once more, an awareness of actor/institution configurations and power/knowledge configurations in the community. If you have an idea of these configurations, then it is easier to understand how your own perspective on the community, its issues and futures, is shaped by your path of access, and at the same time, the reflection on your own positionality can contribute to the mapping of the configurations. Regarding the first aspect, the reflection on roles, we return to the concept of differentiation: indeed, people, including extension workers and government and NGO workers, can do several things and can be several things, but, when assessing a situation and structuring projects, there is always a structuring perspective, and this perspective will shape what is observed, understood and done.

If we consider the differentiation of science, politics, economy, law, then going to a community, doing outreach or engagement, will always serve a primary goal in one of these functional domains. More simply: if we go to participate in governance, to understand that governance system, we do science, and our activities will be structured along this line. If we participate to solve a problem defined by the community, we do science in the service of politics, which is ok as long as we see the line between science and politics. If we study governance in order to restructure it in line with what was locally decided and desired, the situation is the same. If we go and de facto replace local government, or play the role of activist NGO, we play our own politics, and that seems problematic. If we receive money to study and assist a community, it becomes more complicated. Certainly, organizations need money to function, but it is often the case that the paying party (government actor, industry, large NGO) has an agenda itself, influencing both the research and the politics. Then, for the party receiving funds, and going to a community, the project can easily turn into an economic one (driven, structured or tinged by the main goal of making money), and, if this is not the case, the politics locally becomes more complicated, as, besides the really local governance, the local voices, there are two other agendas involved.

For all these reasons, reflection on *positionality* becomes essential when extension becomes community development. An acute awareness of governance configurations is very helpful, and a continuous reflection on the role one plays. In this regard, it can be further helpful to distinguish between the roles played before, during and after the governance process. It is possible to do basically political consultancy work, in the service of a community, and correctly embedded in local governance, while afterwards (supported by work beforehand), a more scientific reflection takes places – driven by the question what actually happened, how and why. That also means, however, that in this later role, the extension/community development worker/academic will have to say things some powerful or beloved actors in the community will not like to hear. There are no simple solutions.

## Further reading

Hornidge, A.-K., Ul-Hassan, M. and Mollinga, P.P. (2011). transdisciplinary innovation research in Uzbekistan – 1 year of 'following the innovation'. Development in Practice, 21(6), 825-838.

Ison, R. and Russell, D. (eds.). (2000). Agricultural extension and rural development: breaking out of knowledge transfer traditions. Cambridge, UK. Cambridge University Press.

Leeuwis, C. (2008). Communication for rural innovation: rethinking agricultural extension. New York, NY, USA: John Wiley & Sons.

Lovell, S.T., Nathan, C.A., Olson, M.B., Ernesto Méndez, V., Kominami, H.C., Erickson, D.L. and Morris, W.B. (2010). Integrating agroecology and landscape multifunctionality in Vermont: an evolving framework to evaluate the design of agroecosystems. Agricultural Systems, 103(5), 327-341.

Moseley, W.G. (2007). Collaborating in the field, working for change: reflecting on partnerships between academics, development organizations and rural communities in Africa. Singapore Journal of Tropical Geography, 28(3), 334-347.

Roling, N.G., & Wagemakers, M.A.E. (eds.). (2000). Facilitating sustainable agriculture: participatory learning and adaptive management in times of environmental uncertainty. Cambridge, UK: Cambridge University Press.

Van Assche, K., Hornidge, A-K, Shtaltovna, A., Boboyorow, H. (2013). Epistemic cultures, knowledge cultures and the transition of agricultural expertise. Rural development in Tajikistan, Uzbekistan and Georgia, ZEF Working Paper 118, ZEF/Bonn University.

## 5.4 Governance and extension

The points just made about extension turning into community development ought not to surprise the reader. In fact, they directly derive from many of the earlier observations on governance paths and development approaches.

Indeed, if teaching becomes social learning and extension becomes community development, then, in a democratic environment, extension becomes restructuring governance, and takes the responsibilities of such an endeavor. It also means that it will fit better in communities with considerable local controls. This can mean a form of communitarianism, but it can also refer to versions of civil society or civic republicanism with a tradition of localism, of local autonomy. It also fits better where the balance between participation and representation tips more towards participation. Extension in more modest and traditional forms fits more different development approaches and governance models.

The actor/institution and power/knowledge configurations deserve mapping, the more so when extension is more ambitious. When extension focuses on a few technical aspects of agriculture, the coalitions with community actors needed can be relatively simple (except when the offered prescription is not appreciated, of course), while community development extension requires more careful mapping, strategizing, and reflection on positionality. As with the development approaches, the rural development approaches cannot be hermetically separated. Extension is a learning and teaching approach to rural development. These are seen as the essential drivers of development. If we take an expansive definition of teaching and learning, we can call it capacity development. Learning, social learning, and capacity development also play a role in most of the other perspectives we will discuss, but there more in a supportive role. When placing extension in the context of governance, important questions are which actors are involved in the efforts, and who defines the means and ends of extension, which knowledge will be cultivated and how.

## Further reading

Ison, R. and Russell, D. (eds.). (2000). Agricultural extension and rural development: breaking out of knowledge transfer traditions. Cambridge, UK: Cambridge University Press.

Roling, N.G. and Wagemakers, M.A.E. (eds.). (2000). Facilitating sustainable agriculture: participatory learning and adaptive management in times of environmental uncertainty. Cambridge, UK: Cambridge University Press.

World Bank (1998/1999). World development report, knowledge for development. Washington, DC, USA: World Bank.

# 6. Land consolidation and land use planning

## Abstract

In this chapter, we give central place to land and land use as a tool for development. In some approaches to rural development, improving land use is seen as the road towards development, and a recurring tool is land consolidation. Often, this is linked to a clarification or rewriting of property rights, a change in property relations. We discuss the benefits of land consolidation, see them higher and more legitimate when embedded in a spatial planning system which is in turn embedded in governance. An evolution is observed from mono-functional land use to multiple land use, and from land consolidation to comprehensive planning efforts. At the same time, land consolidation in a narrow sense can remain useful, and comprehensive planning has its limits as well. We again discuss the relations with the different models of governance.

## 6.1 Land consolidation in European history

Land consolidation is the reconfiguration of land in rural areas, originally in order to make farming more practical and efficient by bringing farmers' parcels closer to each other. Ideally, all parcels would be merged, or consolidated, in one larger property. In other words, it is the consolidation of scattered farmlands into more productive units. For some sorts of agriculture this is more important than for others (e.g. more for cattle than for vegetables). The most simple and oldest form of land consolidation was the voluntary exchange of parcels by two farmers, a practice documented since the early middle ages in Europe, but probably as old as (privatized) agriculture.

If land consolidation remains restricted to a few individual initiatives, and a few parcels, we would not speak of a rural development strategy. However, we know that, as a policy tool, it can evolve into a broader perspective on the reconfiguration of land, for agriculture and for other activities. Then, land consolidation becomes the core and main tool for a rural planning approach to rural development. Rural planning, or rural spatial planning, is not always tied to land consolidation, but historically, in many cases the two were tied. That's the reason for us to discuss them together.

So, land consolidation can move from small to large scale, from individual initiative to government initiative, from consolidation to planning. And it can change from a tool for agricultural improvement into a tool for comprehensive and multi-functional redevelopment of the countryside. The organization of space is seen as the main driver for rural development. First, for agricultural improvement, later, to solve a variety of issues and create new qualities. Land consolidation has a long history in Europe, under the aegis of social-democratic governments aiming to solve some of the classic rural problems we mentioned in the earlier chapters. It also became important in post-socialist countries, where privatization created in many cases very small farms, lacking the infrastructure of the prior collective farms but also of smaller Western farms, lacking expertise, lacking a web of organizations that would allow them to function and compete in a capitalist environment. So, in old Europe, land fragmentation was the starting point, while in post-socialist places, it was the result of privatization. When these transition countries (first in Central Europe, later also farther east) tried to copy Western-European land consolidation policies, the result of this policy transplant were very uneven.

We would argue that land consolidation has to be part of a larger land management (or planning) strategy to be effective, and that policy transplant will have positive effects only when both the old and new policy environments are mapped and understood (by extension, depending on the exercise, the governance paths). The policies can then be adapted to the new frames in the receiving environment. In the case of land consolidation, this is not hard to understand: if it is government which decides or coordinates,

Figure 6.1. Dutch rural landscape after land consolidation in the mid-20<sup>th</sup> century, Noord-Holland. In most parts of the country, agriculture had since the high middle ages brought a rather geometric landscape, because of the rapid and organized reclamation of peatlands and wetlands. Water boards were de facto the first local governments in many places. Land consolidation often kept the geometry but increased the scale and simplified it by erasing small landscape elements. Photo: Kristof Van Assche. © Kristof Van Assche.

such intervention will find tools and limitations in a variety of other policies, rules, plans: versions of property rights, environmental law, infrastructure policies, general economic development policies, existing zoning forms, nature conservation, heritage policies, etc. The harder the institutional limitations are, the tougher land consolidation will be (if not entirely voluntary); the more power a land consolidation authority (as government actor) can amass, the more it will be able to convince or sideline other government actors (with different ideas on rural futures, or on specific policy topics) and, last but not least, current land owners and users. Even in cases where consolidation was 'voluntary', very often there was a shared understanding that the gathered owners were expected to come to an agreement. Without this pressure by governmental actors bringing them together, there would rarely be agreements. 'Win-win situations' were defined in a context created by government, under pressure of government (which usually had other tools of last resort, i.e. expropriation, taking the land).

Often (as in the Netherlands, the Scandinavian countries, Switzerland, Bavaria), land consolidation became more important when urban planning became more prominent. Countries with a strong urban planning tradition often have strong rural planning traditions, and land consolidation is an important tool there. In some countries (Belgium, Portugal, Spain), land consolidation evolved into an important rural policy tool, but without becoming integrated into a comprehensive rural planning system. After World

**Example 6.1. Land consolidation according to FAO: evolving governance.**

FAO, the Food and Agriculture Organization of the United Nations, established in 1945 and currently headquartered in Rome, has promoted land consolidation and, more broadly, land use policy as a key aspect of agricultural modernization since the early 1960's. Land consolidation strategies fit into its overall objective at that time of helping to trigger a so-called 'Green Revolution' in the Global South, a transfer of Western policies and expertise to developing countries aimed at increasing agricultural productivity. Starting in the 1990's, in response to critiques of the often authoritarian and technocratic character of land consolidation, FAO began to develop new guidelines for land consolidation in a more participatory fashion, ones that were more clearly embedded in discourses on good governance. While still proposing a (modernist) formulaic approach in terms of steps to be followed, the formula became more context-sensitive.

FAO now recommends six steps: (1) initiation, (2) project design, (3) inventory of existing situation, (4) production of a detailed plan, (5) implementation of the plan, and (6) conclusion.

FAO leaves open the possibility of several actors requesting the project (not just government), and recommends participation of a variety of stakeholders in the sketching of a concept plan. Such sketching can be useful to figure out diverging ideas, needs and desires, and can also focus early discussion on financing, on benefits and costs. Participants and the state need to agree on a project proposal, after which a more formalized management team can be formed, with formal representation of the community. In the phase of project design, consultants (deemed necessary) are selected, the area more precisely defined, as is the scope of the project. A more refined cost/benefit analysis is conducted, a cost-sharing formula devised, and a tentative time-table outlined. All these elements are further modified in the next step, a more detailed inventory of the existing situation, including identification of boundaries of parcels, assessing their legal status, lease rights, debts, mortgages, easements, and current status in a variety of land use, zoning and other plans (if existing). This often leads to legal wrangling, litigation and local political struggles (in a democratic environment), so it is not advisable to see all of this as preparatory work; better to keep it for this later stage, when there is a firm commitment.

In a further adjustment to critiques of earlier Green Revolution approaches, FAO recommends the delimitation of important environmental areas. This delimitation makes the land consolidation operation already multi-functional, as does the inclusion of the community (broader than the group of farmers/owners). It forces land consolidation to

War II, the push in Europe for land consolidation could be felt almost everywhere, because of the war damage but also because of the simultaneous modernization drive. In the Netherlands and Sweden, among others, land consolidation became an essential

become part of a more comprehensive planning effort. This becomes visible clearly in the next step, when the detailed land consolidation plan is elaborated. The consolidation plan will have to show new parcel layouts, the location of new roads, other public facilities, and which ones will be moved or removed. Optimizing agriculture, in such more democratic and environmentally conscious environment (now assumed/promoted by FAO), forces broader coordination of decisions of land use: rural space is used by many for many reasons, and changing property lines and configurations affects those many things.

To reflect and accommodate this technical and political complexity, FAO now recommends production, presentation and broad community discussion of several plan alternatives, including public discussion about cost/benefit and environmental impact assessments. The idea is to reduce later objections and lawsuits by making the process more participatory, but space still has to be provided to more formal objections later. Once the detailed plan is approved, it can be implemented, and, as always, implementation is not a simple step but a process where many discussions can be opened again.

Because the implementation process is not only a cost, but also a way to make money for some, one needs to pay close attention to the selection of contractors, subcontractors, engineers, consultants, etc. More ambitious land consolidation schemes can include a wide variety of public works, from leveling, draining, cutting and planting, to demolishing and building, construction of new roads, bridges, culverts and so forth. Critics of older schemes often pointed at the possibilities for graft, corruption, nepotism, and clientelism when (not so democratic) governments and their experts were given central place in land consolidation; ambitious projects were then preferred because of larger graft options. We have to add that increased participation does not necessarily remove these practices, despite the theory of increased checks and balances. If participatory land consolidation takes places without stable embedding institutions (a stable legal and political system with functioning checks and balances), one cannot assume that the internal checks and balances of a project will function. In the final phases, new boundaries have to be drawn by surveyors, compensation schemes worked out (who wins what, who loses what), leading to a new cadastral map (land registry) and new land titles. All of this will be politicized, more so in a more participatory process.

### Further reading

Bullard, R. (2007). Land consolidation and rural development. Papers in Land Management, vol. 10. Cambridge, UK: Anglia Ruskin University.

part of rural economic development efforts; as said, changing the organization of land was understood to be the main driver of rural development. In social-democratic countries such as these, the 1950's and 60's saw a major policy push towards 'modern' countrysides, in modernist fashion thought to be 'correctly' planned and designed by experts. The farmers themselves had to become more enlightened and modern too, so they required re-education (hence agricultural universities, extension services) and scientifically support (hence agricultural research institutes). Governments provided further support in the form of export coordination, energy subsidies, infrastructure development, and planning and development of rural settlements – an improvement from scattered farms, which were not considered efficient, and not conducive to scientific and moral re-education.

In earlier post-war projects of land consolidation (similar things can be said for land reclamation projects), the social engineering ambitions of European governments could rival those of Soviet Republics. Without collectivization. The starting point for rural development was not seen in a rural collective, in collective farms and production units, but in the modern individual farmer. The social engineering efforts then consisted in attempts at the creation of the perfect farmer, and the perfect spatial, social and economic context for that farmer to function. In other words, rural development was the remaking of the countryside for optimal agricultural production. Agriculture increased in scale, became more mechanized, inputs increased, specialization was encouraged. The 'green revolution' relied on land consolidation as policy instrument.

Resistance from different sides, however, caused change. By the 1970's notions of democracy had shifted, so social engineering ideologies were not so much supported anymore, and some of the side-effects of the green revolution became clear: environmental pollution, more uniform, boring rural landscapes, biodiversity loss, more mono-functional landscapes were traces of local identity and heritage were erased systematically. Villages and regions started to look like each other, lost their anchoring capacity of social identities and their quality as residential environments. The mono-functional post-consolidation landscapes became less resilient; they were less able to absorb environmental shocks (e.g. rainy spells) and less capable of economic reorientation. Complete adaptation to a supposedly 'perfect' agriculture made people forget for a while about other aspects of their life, and it made it more difficult to adapt to change, to do something else when market conditions changed, e.g. land consolidation driven by this modernist social engineering ideology thus created rigid environments, in a physical sense. The tool itself, however, was not entirely rigid, and proved that it could be used for different purposes in different circumstances.

Since the 1970's, European governments responded by adopting environmental policies, and making land consolidation projects more participatory. The stakeholders consulted were now not only farmers, but also 'residents' (where were they before?), environmental groups (just invented), but also such new actors as heritage and tourism people. Since the May 1968' revolt, participation had been high on the agenda, and new forms came up (to be forgotten a bit later, to re-emerge in the 90's). The envisioned countryside became multi-functional again. We mentioned earlier that mono-functional landscapes do not exist in nature. They are a product of concerted policies, mostly resulting from a modernist ideology, in centralized nation-states. When these policies stop, places tend to become more multi-functional again by themselves. Probably, however, in a more messy and less attractive state than before, so new and coordinated policy interventions are needed to clean up the mess and bring back a form of multi-functionalism which is appreciated by many and more resilient.

In those coordinated new policies, land consolidation could be important, not with the old narrow goal, but aiming at a more diverse, maybe sustainable, rural economy. While in the 50's and 60's, the young European Union pushed rather relentlessly for agricultural modernization in the sense described, even Sicco Mansholt, European agriculture commissioner, changed his position radically in the 70's, and became a defender of more gradual, sensitive and sustainable rural development. For the 'green' actors in most European countries, land consolidation became a sign of all what was wrong in rural development. And, with a strengthening of property rights and stronger local governments in many countries, farmers joined the anti-consolidation chorus.

The more comprehensive forms of land consolidation, part of comprehensive rural planning, were criticized for other reasons: too slow, and too costly. The costs, indeed, for agricultural 'optimization' had been systematically underestimated, and broadening the scope rendered the projects more democratically legitimate but economically even more questionable. While potential revenues from other uses, such as tourism, new forms of residential and more old fashioned forms of agriculture (coming into fashion again) were not considered. Also the resilience gains were questioned, because very slow processes of land consolidation and planning might produce a more multifunctional landscape, but the slow speed itself creates an adaptation problem. In a 20 year process of rural reconstruction, economies and communities change so much that the whole exercise should start over again. In the Netherlands, possibly the most active country in land consolidation, in the 90's and later, the actors most enthusiastic about land consolidation were environmental groups, who wanted to use the tool to undo damage done in previous rounds of rural development. Creeks were brought back to a more natural state, including meanders, little wetlands, gentle slopes, after earlier land consolidation had straightened them, reducing biodiversity, scenic beauty, and creating water problems downstream.

## Further reading

King, R. and Burton, S. (1983). Structural change in agriculture: the geography of land consolidation. Progress in Human Geography, 7(4), 471-501.

Pašakarnis, G. and Maliene, V. (2010). Towards sustainable rural development in Central and Eastern Europe: Applying land consolidation. Land Use Policy, 27(2), 545-549.

Robinson, G. (1990). Conflict and change in the countryside. Rural society, economy and planning in the developed world. London, UK: Belhaven Press.

Thrift, N. (2009). Space: the fundamental stuff of human geography. In: Clifford, N.J., Holloway, S.L., Rice, S.P. and Valentine, G. (eds.), Key concepts in geography. London, UK: Sage Publications, pp. 95-107.

Van den Brink, A. and Molema, M. (2008). The origins of Dutch rural planning: a study of the early history of land consolidation in the Netherlands. Planning Perspectives, 23(4), 427-453.

Van Dijk, T. (2007). Complications for traditional land consolidation in Central Europe. Geoforum, 38(3), 505-511.

## 6.2 Land consolidation elsewhere?

Land consolidation thus has a checkered track record as rural development strategy, both as stand-alone measure and as part of integrated rural development policies (planning). As a stand-alone strategy, its use will be rare, and the effects will not bring the benefits of coordinated action at community scale. As part of ambitious rural planning schemes, it caused friction with land owners and other actors, and caused a lot of damage to the environment. In defense of land consolidation, we have to say that the damage done owes much to the nature of the plans in post-war Europe, and the nature of the modernist ideology behind them.

We already mentioned land consolidation with reference to post-socialist transition countries and warned against copy-paste solutions. Obstacles to consolidation in many of those places included low land values, little interest in farming as economic activity, incomplete privatization of land (with governments still controlling access to input and access to land), and paper property rights, with de facto little control over land by the owner, and little chance to profit from it. The government control still mentioned contributes to the paper character of property rights; it reduces the autonomy of the owner in using the land. While consolidation could solve some of the problems of privatization, the nature of governance also creates obstacles, as illustrated. Farmers need to be convinced of the need to consolidate, have the right and the means to do so. Consolidation in post-socialist context mostly means concentration of land in fewer hands (which might be opposed for obvious reasons), or it means highly coordinated action and probably cooperative forms of farming and ownership (opposed for reasons of bad memories). Also the benefits of consolidation in such environment can be more meager than elsewhere, since products will have to be sold and processed in the same situation which created the obstacles against consolidation. If property rights of land are unclear, if infrastructure is missing, if bribes are a problem for farming, if the village doesn't like your big farm, the villagers and local government might give you many headaches after land consolidation. This is all the more true because the benefits will be much more substantial when there are flanking measures, such as changing roads, electricity lines, ditches, etc.., which again imply reliance on the same actor/institution configuration.

How and when could land consolidation then be a useful tool for rural development? Can it still be an important tool, the core of a strategy? We would say yes. Land consolidation rearranges the land and the ownership of land, and this can create a new living and working environment for many, and a new matrix of incentives for development. The European experience shows that the flanking measures to reap benefits cannot be forgotten, that consolidation will only be worthwhile when part of a spatial planning strategy. It also showed that these strategies can cause many problems, and have to be more context-sensitive and participatory than most of the post-war examples. The post-socialist experience shows that consolidation can only be the core of rural development strategy when property rights are clear and strong, when there is already an indication that agriculture and other land uses in rural areas can be

Figure 6.2. Regimes come and go, life goes on. Photo: Katja Mielke. © ZEF/University of Bonn, Germany.

attractive enough to restart the economy. And it shows that all of this requires 'good governance', in one of its many guises. It requires local governance with a minimum level of autonomy, not too dependent on elite networks, patronage, corruption. And with this, we are back to governance.

Land consolidation becomes possible in certain governance paths. Governance paths create the actors, institutions and hence incentives and obstacles for land consolidation. Obviously, when there is no institution of private property, there are no owners and no consolidation. One can still rezone or reorganize a rural area. If there are owners and they are not interested in cooperation, one needs a strong government to force consolidation. If there are too many owners, and most are not eager to sell, the initiative will again have to come from government, and the resentment will be substantial. The promising conditions seem to be:
- a stable local government;
- owners with undisputed property rights;
- the perception of a problem of scattering; and
- a promise of benefits after consolidation.

Such promise or hope tends to be tied to:
- a luring market;
- owners with some capital (or access to it); and
- some autonomy.

## Further reading

Benjaminsen, T.A. and Lund, C. (2002). Formalisation and informalisation of land and water rights in Africa: an introduction. European Journal of Development Studies, 14, 1-10.

Djanibekov, N., Van Assche, K., Bobojonov, I. and Lamers, J.P. (2012). Farm restructuring and land consolidation in Uzbekistan: new farms with old barriers. Europe-Asia Studies, 64(6), 1101-1126.

Eichholz, M., Van Assche, K., Oberkircher, L. and Hornidge, A.K. (2013). Trading capitals? Bourdieu, land and water in rural Uzbekistan. Journal of Environmental Planning and Management, 56(6), 1-25.

Van Dijk, T. (2007). Complications for traditional land consolidation in Central Europe. Geoforum, 38(3), 505-511.

Van Huylenbroeck, G., Coelho, J.C. and Pinto, P.A. (1996). Evaluation of land consolidation projects (LCPs): a multidisciplinary approach. Journal of Rural Studies, 12(3), 297-310.

## 6.3 Land governance as the basis

If we want to understand the potential of land consolidation, we have to understand the potential of spatial planning, as the reorganization of space. In fact, we better take one more step back and say that we have to understand land governance. Land consolidation can reach its potential when embedded in planning and supported by good land governance. But what is that? An unequivocal answer is not simple, but we can mention the obvious things, often listed under good governance concepts as well: equal access to laws and policies, equal treatment under them, equal access to enforcement. One could add things such as access to resources and infrastructure which could be reasonably expected to use the land in ways it is allowed to be used.

Good land governance is a sine qua non for rural development, as economic development and community development in rural areas are in most cases tied to land. Rural development paths almost always cross the issue of access to land. In more specialized terms, more applied to the governance of land, we could say that that good land governance entails good land administration: efficient, effective, and competent. A land registry is essential: knowing who owns what, what the use rights are, what property means. It means that property rights have to be defined. This can happen in many ways, and many options are viable, as long as there is consistency and predictability in the rules: if you know this is ok today, it is ok tomorrow. We will return to property rights discussions later.

Land, ownership, permitted uses, should be available, freely. Land policies ought to reflect not the opinion of an elite, but the perspective on land use that was decided upon democratically. Land use is always political; the values in a community ought to emerge in governance and be deliberated; land policies can then be enacted that embody these values and corresponding visions of the common good. Plans, policies and laws pertaining to land should be available, accessible, and the result of a procedure of decision-making agreed upon in the community. In other words, it cannot be separated from governance; it should be part and parcel of it. This political character does not take away the need for consistency: communities can change their mind every day, but some rules regarding land use ought to be decided for the longer term, and not to be changed without hurdles. Indeed, adaptation is important, but so is tenure security, legal security, and the possibility to develop long term perspectives. This is a common problem across developing countries: insecure tenure and absent rule of law make it difficult to think in the long term. Laws, including property rights, are there to stabilize expectations of players in governance, and this makes it easier to coordinate their actions, and translate them into further policies, and into development perspectives. Protection of property rights, in good land governance, requires besides a well-governed land registry also a well functioning legal system, and some form of planning administration.

As with governance as such, it is easier to pinpoint weak land governance than good land governance. There are many versions of good governance, associated with forms of democracy, development approaches, and governance paths, as we know. Yet there are certain things we want to avoid at all cost. In the case of land governance, we can say that most important (besides the positives of organization and rule of law) is the *absence of corruption*. If corruption is prevalent, access to land becomes unclear, the meaning of ownership becomes unclear, as the meaning and value of the products of the land. Corruption can destabilize easily and quickly a well-functioning land governance system. One weak link introduces weak governance. If the land registry is corrupt, the system fails, if the planners are corrupt, the system fails. And the same phrase can be repeated for corrupt policemen, judges, politicians, tax collectors, construction workers, map makers, etc. Nobody can trust the system, and one cannot speak of rule of law, when there are weak links.

Weak land governance occurs in many places, and often the causes are similar. One can refer easily to the rule of law, but as we know there are many versions of this. One does not need a universal reference to see when there is a problem: if the legal system is supposed to work like this, but it works like that, because of corruption, lack of knowledge, resources, infrastructure, there is a problem with the rule of law. With all the diversity of legal systems, and diversity in linkages between politics, economy and law, one can still say there is a problem, when citizens cannot count on rules already made, and when they have no influence on the rule making process.

Some specific issues with rule of law in land governance are the complexity and inconsistency of legal systems. Many things happen on land, so many rules apply, and legal regulations applying to a certain spot can quickly become very complex. Complexity often entails inconsistencies, and law that is inconsistent can more easily be abused by strong players who can advocate for the interpretation that suits them. Land is also often subjected to rules coming from different scales, so fragmented institutional arrangements are often a problem: the authority of each scale is often not so clear, disputed, and the set of rules, policies and plans emanating from them makes, again, inconsistency, and a variety of interpretations likely.

We can add poor motivation, low pay, poor training, but also favoritism, nepotism, conflict, party politics, local networks as causes of weak land governance, of a breakdown of the rule of law with regards to land. Land is subjected to many rules, but also to many interests and powers, because many actors want to do something in a place, or might see a value there. Land easily becomes the center of conflicts, because of this specific nature. Also, conflicts tend to reinforce themselves and create new problems for land governance and the rule of law – leading to a vicious cycle.

Things tend to get worse when there is little transparency, when there is little public scrutiny. Corruption festers in the dark, as Machiavelli (in the tradition of civic republicanism) said, so the light of media, of public discussion, of accessible documents, can be very useful to contain it. Once corruption takes a hold, it can be extremely difficult to weed it out. It can take extraordinary measures, as Machiavelli also observed, to stop conflict and corruption from reinforcing itself. Once corruption becomes part of the governance system, the system no longer works as it was designed, and all actors lose motivation to stick to their initial roles and to the rules.

The consequences of weak land governance are manifold, and show the variety of obstacles to rural development it produces. The list below captures some of the points made in the narrative above. These consequences reinforce each other, and can all be related to an absence of the rule of law, of stabilizing institutions:

- Poverty and social exclusion. If most people do not have access to land, or if access and use are subjected to unclear and unstable rules, then one can expect high levels of poverty and social inequality. Many will not be able to participate in economic development, many talents will be unused. High inequality tends to fuel social instability as well.
- Limited economic development. Economic development tends to be limited in such situations, since weak land governance creates a variety of issues for entrepreneurs. They will either pay too much for land, or will not be able do much on the land, or with whatever was produced there. In macro numbers, the situation might look ok if a small elite monopolizes land and runs efficient plantations there, but such economy is not likely to be resilient. An economy is more resilient when more diverse and more rooted in an inclusive governance system, where the interests of many can be met in economic and land policy, and where the initiative of many can be harnessed in the adaptation to ever changing circumstances.
- Environmental degradation. If the rule of law is not strong, and if long term perspectives are not common, if common goods are not articulated on land laws and environmental laws, or those are not enforced, then one can expect that few people care about the environment. Wise use of resources is not on the agenda, and if some try to follow the rules, they will lose out in the longer run, surrounded by others who stick to short term hit-and-run strategies.
- Reduced public revenues. If land governance is weak, tax collection will be difficult. We refer to the weak links in the chain: if the land governance system does not work as intended, the value of the land and anything done on the land will not be clear. It will likely be underestimated and public revenue (taxes) will be lower. Which means it cannot be reinvested in infrastructure, schools, etc., so development is hampered.
- Tenure insecurity. Weak land governance can affect mostly the access to land, and it can be more problematic for the use of land. In that last case, we speak of tenure insecurity: it is not clear what property rights mean for the actual use. If government, or government cronies, can take away your land, or the water needed

to irrigate, or if use becomes difficult when government blocks the only road, or cuts off electricity, then tenure is not secure. Property rights are always bundles of use rights and restrictions, and when this bundle suddenly changes, when one cannot predict which uses will suddenly become impossible, one can speak of tenure insecurity. Tenure insecurity takes away the motivation to invest in land. It reduces the willingness to invest as such, the motivation to be entrepreneurial, because the initial investment can be lost, the results can be captured (a plantation can be taken). Risk cannot be assessed adequately.

- Land disputes. Weak land governance also creates new risks. If rules are unclear or not fairly enforced, disputes will arise, because, as said, land is always valuable to someone, and in absence of the rule of law, there will always be opposing interests without clear mediation mechanism. As we mentioned before, when disputes turn into conflict, it tends to feed off itself. Conflict will destabilize communities, aggravate social cleavages, polarize groups, make investment even more risky. Escalating conflict makes tenure security even more a fiction.

- Weak land and credit markets. One way weak land governance limits economic development is the link between land and credit markets. Often, rural areas have less access to credit than urban areas, and this reduces entrepreneurship and innovation. If land governance is weak, and land values are low, the motivation to invest can be low, and it also creates a problem when selling land to generate start up capital, and when using it as collateral for loans. Often, the real problem is not the low value of land, but the difficulty in weak regulatory environments to assess value. For long term loans, general instability and lacking belief in rural development add to the banks unwillingness to give them.

- Negative social behaviour. If the rule of law is weak, and land governance is weak, the incentives to follow rules are slight, and social behavior can easily deteriorate. Why not steal from the farm if everybody's doing it? Why not pollute the water if it isn't clear who owns it? Why not chase away people from the land if you were driven out by corrupt officials in their previous village? Why not use violence if it's the only way to get things done?

Weak land governance thus creates a variety of obstacles to development, while good land governance, in one of its guises, can be a driver of development. We started with the analysis of land consolidation since this is the most classic tool of active land governance for rural development. Yet, we mentioned that this too needs to be embedded in some form of a spatial planning system, in the context of the rule of law.

But, what is it that creates an added value when applying good land governance? What are the positive answers one can give, the ways it can trigger development? We already referred to the *rule of law* as a driver in a basic sense, and good land governance can then be a specific form. We also mentioned the efficiency effects of good *land registries*, clear and *simple rules*, and *adaptive rules*, plus the *stabilizing effect* of some rules that are harder to change. Now, we want to add another factor: *linkage with spatial planning*, and planning as policy integration. We will see that this mechanism was an essential condition for success in land consolidation.

## Further reading

Chauveau, J.-P., Colin, J.-P., Jacob, J.-P., Delville, P.L. and P.-Y. Le Meur (2006). Changes in land access and governance in West Africa: markets, social mediations and public policies: results of the CLAIMS research project. London, UK: International Institute for Environment and Development.

Deininger, K. and Binswanger, H. (2001). The evolution of the World Bank's land policy. In: De Janvry, A., Gordillo, G., Sadoulet, E. and Platteau, J. (eds.), Access to land, rural poverty and public action. Oxford, UK: Oxford University Press, pp. 407-440.

Deininger, K. and Feder, G. (2009). Land registration, governance, and development: Evidence and implications for policy. The World Bank Research Observer, 24(2), 233-266.

De Soto, H. (2003). Mystery of capital: why capitalism triumphs in the West and fails everywhere else. London, UK: Basic books.

Grindle, M.S. (2004). Good enough governance: poverty reduction and reform in developing countries. Governance, 17(4), 525-548.

Larson, A.M., Cronkleton, P., Barry, D. and Pacheco, P. (2008). Tenure rights and beyond: community access to forest resources in Latin America. Bogor, Indonesia: Center for International Forestry Research.

Lund, C. (1998). Law, power and politics in Niger. Land struggles and the rural code. Hamburg, Germany: LIT Verlag.

Otto, J.M. (2009). Rule of law promotion, land tenure and poverty alleviation: questioning the assumptions of Hernando de Soto. Hague Journal on the Rule of Law, 1(1), 173-194.

## 6.4 Policy integration and planning/planning as policy integration

*Spatial planning* can be described as the coordination of policies and practices affecting spatial organization. If spatial governance is coordinated for an area, we can speak of *policy coordination*, and this is a first step in *policy integration*.

Policy integration is the search for cumulative effects, synergies and undermining effects, of several policies affecting one topic, one period or one place. Policies, laws, plans, rules (all institutions) indeed affect each other, as the concept of actor/institution configuration already indicated. They can contradict each other, reinforce each other, slowly erode each other, but they can also be combined, to derive more targeted plans and policies for places, times and topics. They can be seen as tools which can be used together to achieve greater goals, to increase effects towards the same goal. Policy integration can increase efficiency (reduce redundancy in intervention, reduce

**Example 6.2. Soviet countrysides and the planning/adaptation balance.**

In the early days of the USSR, the 1920's, the communist leadership deplored the absence of the industrial proletarians who were supposed to shoulder the revolution and lead the development of communist society. Furthermore they were suspicious of rural areas, which they regarded as backward and conservative, with inhabitants too attached to the land and their ownership of it after centuries of slavary/servitude. As a result, industrial development was forced, and the initial capital for it was taken from agriculture. Early collectivization was slowed down when agricultural production dropped, but once industrialization was in full swing, and the grip on the countryside improved, it came back with a vengeance. Existing agricultural areas were collectivized, private ownership abolished, and a system of collective farms was established – kolkhozi and sovkhozi. The kolkhoz was supposedly owned by the local community, the sovkhoz was directly placed under state control, that is, the control of Moscow-based ministries. A sovkhoz was often tied to the production of one crop for essential industries, or for new crops, or to feed an army base. Soviet agriculture was also expanded and reclaimed land where no agriculture existed before, in cold, hot, dry, wet, or otherwise tough regions. In some regions, such as Central Asia, almost everything had to be developed from scratch: enormous irrigation infrastructure, roads, electricity, villages, towns, schools.

Rural governance was distinct from urban and regional governance. Put simply, almost everything (except for the most large-scale infrastructure works) rested with the farms. The kolkhoz cannot be compared to Western farms, and a Western style farmer, as an autonomous entrepreneur – generalist-owner, wasn't there. Ownership was collective, autonomy limited, and the scale and complexity of operations much higher. A cult of the manager developed, somewhat similar to the Western one. Good managers could get things done in the bureaucratic maze of Soviet government, be successful in its internal competition (between many many government actors), and overcome the myriad obstacles locally, of a physical, economic, cultural nature. A kolkhoz could include several villages, and, in Western terms, kolkhoz management has to be compared to a combination of farm management, industrial management and local government. Traditionally, a rais (director) was joined in the board by a chief agronomist, a chief surveyor, a hydro-technical manager, and a representative of the communist party.

The kolkhoz was supposedly responsible for the final step in the implementation of a variety of plans, at several scales, and was surrounded by a web of supportive organizations, providing expertise in water, land, construction management, assistance in pest control, providing inputs and machinery – the famous MTP's (machine tractor parks). They were not much affected by the spatial planning system, but were part of the economic planning system, with regions made responsible for quota's in these and these products, subregions for parts, and then farms for the actual work. All actors knew they needed the farms, and all knew that the comprehensive plans for the farms, including economic and spatial planning, could never follow logically from the series of plans, policies and ad hoc commands at other scales. Former rais told us that sometimes, comprehensive development plans were considered fiction (while formally adhering to all other plans), in other farms they were actually guiding decision-making, but more a product of internal collaboration, and sometimes, while elsewhere, they barely existed. There was also variation in the degree of comprehensiveness: here, there was focus on the quota, and a sketch of the future area's development to get to those quota, elsewhere, there was a concerted effort to think of that future development as furthering collective goods, and along the way, we produce more or less what they want.

There were huge differences in democratic character and quality of life. The negative cliche images of the kolkhoz were true sometimes, with workers stealing left and right, and unhappy workers being coerced into back breaking labor when they couldn't escape it. In many other cases, the collective farms (similarly to protected natural areas) were shelters of a sort, local governments with a relative autonomy, a relative degree of internal democracy, the power to figure out which services would benefit the community. Over the years, most areas developed their own rural lobbies, as aggregate lobbies of the collective farms, and the result was usually a more diverse countryside than initially envisioned by Moscow planners. This often did benefit Moscow as well, since local unrest diminished, a more diverse production could be used for a more diverse economy, and the quota for the staple crop were often not realistic anyway, lacking local knowledge. The nearly black box of the kolkhoz was not only a place where policies were undermined, but also a place where local knowledge (from very local, offered by local workers, to localized technical knowledge, obtained by management) could render larger policies implementable, and modify others so something good would come out of them, for the locals themselves, and for the government. Policy integration took place at this level of local governance. The silently accepted semi-autonomy of the collective farms made Soviet planned governance more adaptive.

### Further reading

Humphrey, C. (1998). Marx went away, but Karl stayed behind. Ann Arbor, MI, USA: University of Michigan Press.

Van Assche, K. and Djanibekov, N. (2012). Spatial planning as policy integration: the need for an evolutionary perspective. Lessons from Uzbekistan. Land Use Policy, 29(1), 179-186.

Figure 6.3. Altit Corridor in Central Hunza, Pakistan. A very planned rural landscape, without formal planning, relying on trial and error, local coordination, slow improvement of certain slopes, a testing of natural boundaries of steepness, fertility, exposure, of access, a careful deliberation of heavy community investments for small additions of land. Path dependence and interdependence as immediately palpable and sustainability requiring close cooperation. Photo: Andreas Benz. © Andreas Benz, ZELF/Freie University of Berlin, Germany.

bureaucracy), and it can harness the power of one policy to fix the problems another policy already targeted. Policy integration can thus lead to solving more problems and creating more qualities.

Policy coordination represents, as said, a minimum level of policy integration, where policy makers are aware at least of the existence of several institutions to target an issue, and aware of possible cumulative effects, positive or negative. It is an elementary form of policy integration, a form not necessarily requiring structural change. Coordination is then the reflection on how to combine these policies, and the attempt to relate and distinguish them in a beneficial manner. This can be a matter of formally designating fields of application for policy A and B, or ways to relate them, but very often, it is a matter of informal institutions, of discussions between actors about rules to interpret the rules, to selectively implement, relate, prioritize ('if this seems the case, then this policy priority sets in, and we link B and C to A and forget provisions 1 and 2 from B'). Policy coordination can eventually lead to further policy integration, e.g. in the case of spatial plans or comprehensive visions, or new umbrella policies.

*Spatial planning* is a logical site of policy integration. Plans themselves are in almost all cases focusing on more than one issue, trying to create new qualities in space, and solving several problems at the same time. As we know, many things take place in space, and plans can alter the pattern of activities there. Planning is always a matter of balancing various institutions and their effects on a place; this is a matter of the complexity of governance, in which many rules apply in a place and require selective and elaborate interpretation. It is also a matter of balancing interests, and forms of expertise. Planning brings power/knowledge configurations close to the surface, because decisions have to be made where many interests become visible, and many understandings of the world. Plans can be made by means of various rules, but also by means of design. Plans rely on a many institutions to become possible, they integrate various institutions, and rely on yet other ones for their implementation. The aim of comprehensive plans is to reorganize space in such a way that various common goals are materialized in or become possible to pursue in the resulting space.

*Spatial design* is a developed form of policy integration, where a reflection on policies and goals is combined with a reflection on the properties of the places aimed at (this far we are still in the domain of planning), and there is at any point in the reflection the possibility to reorganize space in order to link place and policy more appropriately, to pursue several policy goals in one place, by integrating the policies and changing the place, resulting in a new institution, the plan as design. Careful observation of place, of the landscape, the natural and social systems there, makes it possible to see more possible synergies between policies, and to recognize and create qualities, in the light of community values and common goals. Land consolidation is a form of planning as design, in the more comprehensive forms, and its benefits can be reaped best when the policy integration brought by planning extends to land consolidation (when consolidation is not separated, not considered a technical activity outside planning).

We will come back to design as community design in the next chapter. For now, we dwell on the point that policy integration is what makes consolidation and planning possible drivers of rural development, and that spatial design has to be considered one useful form of planning. Linking back, we come to see now that policy integration can take place in administrations (between departments, within a department between policies) or, in governance, when a wider variety of actors is involved, a wider variety of interests considered. Policy integration taken place within administrations, in order to be effective, also has to take into account the broader governance situation, the other parties and their perspectives which will come to bear at some point or another on one of the integrated policies or on the attempt at integration. Calculating the actions of the others affected in policy integration becomes very difficult however, and this constitutes an argument not to conduct policy integration entirely within administration, but rather, in the spirit of participatory development approaches, to bring it to the table of governance, or (to stay in the metaphor), to build such a table, an arena in which policy integration can be discussed and pursued.

In practical terms, policy integration is also a matter of management of a set of organizations (collective actors) each with their own organizational culture, their own idea of a power position and responsibility, their own understanding of topics and realities. All the complexities of governance discussed earlier, and especially of participatory governance, thus are complexities of policy integration. Just as there is no perfect governance model, no correct development model, there is no perfect or correct form of policy integration, a resulting policy in which all interests are perfectly balanced, all collective goals realized to the same extent. There is no such thing as a perfect plan, which will last forever, and satisfies everyone to the same extent. As governance changes, as the set of organizations present changes, policy integration will have to be different. Even if one stays within administration, different sets of state actors, departments, etc., require different forms of integration. As governance at large, policy integration is a matter of organizational learning and adaptation too: policies are usually not integrated by one party, and even if this is the case, the integrating party (say, a planning department working in isolation), still has to grasp the internal functioning, and the relational network of the organizations associated with the other policies (often: other departments, or, courts, or parties backing policies).

Policy integration therefore is *management of interdependencies* between organizations, in an awareness of the path dependencies present in and between them. This understanding can allow to grasp better the goal dependencies which might be introduced by new plans and other integrated policies. For integration of policies is often associated with integration of organizations, and/or with subsumption of the goals and priorities of one under those of another. Integration in a larger whole of policies can be just as scary as integration in a larger organization, and the one is often seen as a sign of the other. Policy integration is possible only when there is a deep understanding of the role of the organizations behind the policies, with role as the contribution to the production of policy in a domain, and the contribution to the outcome of policy. And policy integration becomes much more effective when the path dependencies are understood, the evolution of the organizations involved in policy-making, and their interactions. We come back to the mapping of governance paths, but now in a more specific and technical form, linking the evolution of organizations to the policies they, alone and with others, produce and implement. The idea of policy integration, and the study of obstacles, brings a new understanding of actor/institution and power/knowledge configurations.

Plans can be powerful tools for policy integration, but plans without a base in actual coordination of organizations are likely to remain paper plans. Many spatial plans, and many development visions in a broader sense, remain paper tigers because they simply declare policy integration, without studying the relations and dependencies in the policy environment they rest on. Simply drawing something, and finding it legal, does not mean there is the support to actually tie several actors to the lines. This applies to the actors in governance, but the problem is aggravated when these actors are not really aware of the actual use of the space, and of the actual opportunities and limitations the physical space offers for certain policy goals and certain forms of policy integration.

Policy integration thus requires careful mapping of policy contexts (governance paths, linkages between actors and policies) and careful mapping of spatial contexts, and reflect on how these can be fruitfully related.

When plans remain paper tigers, plans being attempts at formal policy integration, then there is still the possibility of informal policy integration: informal coordination between actors, their policies, visions, needs. Informal policy integration tends to be less comprehensive, less design-based, more short term, closer to the needs of the various actors. In some cases, the physical landscape necessitates informal integration, as people cannot make it on their own, need to work together, pool expertise, labor, capital to survive. In other cases, policy landscapes make it necessary to do things under the radar, to cooperate invisibly, because the formal rules make it hard to make a living, and making a living requires cooperation. If the cooperation transcends the mere practical trial and error, if it involves some sort of deliberation and planning, even if carried out in bars or living rooms, one can speak of informal policy coordination. Highly turbulent environments, volatile policy environment and highly dynamic landscapes, make both formal and informal policy coordination a tough nut to crack.

## Further reading

Cloke, P. (ed.). (2013). Rural land-use planning in developed nations. London, UK: Routledge.

McDonald, G.T. (1989). Rural land use planning decisions by bargaining. Journal of Rural Studies, 5(4), 325-335.

Stöhr, W.B. and Taylor, D.R.F. (eds.). (1981). Development from above or below?: the dialectics of regional planning in developing countries. Chichester, UK: Wiley.

Van den Brink, A. and Molema, M. (2008). The origins of Dutch rural planning: a study of the early history of land consolidation in the Netherlands. Planning Perspectives, 23(4), 427-453.

Van Lier, H.N. (1998). The role of land use planning in sustainable rural systems. Landscape and Urban Planning, 41(2), 83-91.

## 6.5 Expertise, spatial organization and rural development

Organizing space can be an engine of rural development, and so is improving and clarifying the conditions for spatial organization. Land governance, spatial planning and spatial design can be drivers of rural development. We would argue, after the preceding analyses, that design works best when embedded in planning and planning when embedded in good land governance.

What are the limits to this rural development approach? There are limits to each of the nested strategies (land governance, planning, and design). Good land governance can sometimes trigger development, when access to land was the missing piece in a socio-economic puzzle, when there were people with ideas about using the land, some access to resources, some expertise. Planning or design can be the trigger, when they can fix problems or create spatial qualities that make certain uses possible. But this assumes that there is a latent demand for such uses. In the extended discussion of land consolidation, the ideally nested character of the strategies already came to the fore, but also the limitations of this form of spatial policy and design. We won't repeat them all, but can recall simply that the positive effects of reconfiguring parcels hinges on what use people see in them and how the product can be processed, marketed, or distributed. If land consolidation takes place in order to accommodate production of something that nobody wants anymore, neither domestically nor abroad, then efforts were likely in vain.

So, just as with the other approaches to rural development, there are limits to land consolidation and spatial planning, and there are conditions under which it works better. In terms of models of governance, planning and design will probably not work under small government models. In terms of dependencies, the goal dependencies of plans and design will likely have more of an effect if actors are used to policy integration and to being coordinated, i.e. if there is a given path dependency. If actors are used to it, then the actor/institution configuration will not resist new forms of policy integration so much, when the mere idea of planning doesn't already upset them, and when they recognize they can still play a significant role and profit in a setting with high levels of policy integration. This has implications for participatory approaches: indeed, integration can be more stable if it is part of a participatory policy setting, but some participatory settings are more susceptible to policy integration than others. If it is first of all an arena, where competing visions are battling it out, and maybe one wins or a compromise wins, this is not a promising setting for policy integration.

Spatial planning and design can be very useful when aiming at sustainability goals that are more than ecological (therefore requiring policy integration), or at piecing together livelihoods in difficult landscapes (requiring analysis and matching of physical and socio-economic landscapes). Good land governance, without much reference to planning, fits into a broader spectrum of development approaches, including modernist versions of market and legal reform, and works well with the rhetoric of dominant neo-liberal (in our terms: liberal democratic) discourses and actors. We develop the analysis of planning and design further in the next chapter, speaking of community design as a rural development strategy.

With regards to expertise, we can be short. Planning and design as policy integration, and good land governance, are open to virtually any sort of expertise and local knowledge, depending on the form of policy integration, the sorts of policies integrated, the land uses allowed, the priorities of use and of issues, and the framing sort of knowledge. By this, we refer to the form of knowledge which provides the *first ordering principle* of spatial organization. Hydrology can generate a water structure that organizes the plan, in which other forms of knowledge later find a place; agricultural engineering can define a zoning based on soil quality, which offers the first *organizing structure*, ecology can offer an ecological network, in which other things have to fit, etc. (This concept too, will return in the next chapter). In general, more participatory processes will be open to more forms of knowledge, but one can also imagine highly comprehensive administrations in which many forms of expertise (yet not local knowledge) are represented.

We can distinguish *substantive knowledge* and *process knowledge*, or, knowledge regarding the place and the goals, and secondly, on the way to organize and structure the process to get to the goals in that place. Some processes are very open to local and expert knowledge, others not. In some processes of planning and design, certain disciplines, forms of expert knowledge, are privileged, others forgotten. Both process and substantive knowledge change over time, when governance paths create different positions for different actors and their perspectives in planning systems. As one can expect, form and content do affect each other, and process designs are more sensitive to this type of knowledge than to another.

## Further reading

Djanibekov, N., Van Assche, K., Bobojonov, I. and Lamers, J.P. (2012). Farm restructuring and land consolidation in Uzbekistan: new farms with old barriers. Europe-Asia Studies, 64(6), 1101-1126.

Franco, J.C. (2010). Contemporary discourses and contestations around pro-poor land policies and land governance. Journal of Agrarian Change, 10(1), 1-32.

Stöhr, W.B. and Taylor, D.R.F. (eds.) (1981). Development from above or below?: the dialectics of regional planning in developing countries. Chichester, UK: Wiley.

# 7. Rural development: rural and community design

## Abstract

In this chapter, we examine an approach to rural development related to the previous one: design. We acknowledge that spatial design is possible without relation to planning, but emphasize and explain the benefits of design when embedded in planning systems. In the other direction planning can be more flexible, adaptive and beneficial when conceived as design, as more than resulting from rules, laws, procedures. We discuss different traditions, disciplines and actors which can be involved, and analyze the links between design approaches and governance models. Design is presented as particularly appropriate to deal with complex multi-use situations, with rich natural and cultural heritage, where design is necessarily context-sensitive redesign. Design is also presented as not antithetical to scientific expertise, nor to democratic local governance.

## 7.1 What's in a name?

When speaking of design, many things come to mind, and many of those things seem unrelated to rural development. However, if we understand design as more than art, as more than the creation of something esthetically pleasing or intellectually challenging, we can come closer to an understanding of design as potential driver of rural development.

In the previous chapter, we spoke of policy integration, of spatial planning as a site and form of policy integration, and we introduced design perspectives as highly relevant for spatial planning, because in the knowledge of and manipulation of space, policies can be integrated and made compatible with space. Design can work on several issues at the same time, and create new qualities in space. It can make it possible to work towards common goals in space, and the space itself can embody them. Design can represent sustainability and it can enable other actions towards more sustainability (e.g. learning sites, specially designed residential or commercial zone designs, new forms of multi-functional land use).

Indeed, more land uses are usually possible in a place, than competing or discussing actors realize, if the space is properly designed. Many land use conflicts do not have to be conflicts if they are integrated in a design that gives them a proper place, mitigating negative effects, maybe even harnessing synergies of their co-presence.

A planning perspective, in our view, entails an image of the place, and the presence of that image in decision making makes it easier to recombine interests, assets and problems. A design perspective continuously entertains the possibility to manipulate these images of space, and further down the line, physical space itself. Land consolidation can be part of rural design, it can be a form of rural design, albeit a rudimentary one, mostly focused on agricultural productivity, and only manipulating a few elements and structures in space: parcels, maybe roads and ditches. Rural design can go much further however, and can extend to a reconfiguration of villages, landscapes, regions. When speaking of community design, there is usually the implication of a more radical embedding in governance, of a comprehensive design for a community by a variety of stakeholders, in a more or less participatory form of governance, with an implied large measure of local autonomy.

Before going further into the discussion of rural and community design for rural development, we need to introduce a few more concepts. These concepts can be useful in the mapping and understanding of governance paths in general. They deepen the understanding of what an 'actor' is in governance, and how the main configurations in governance are entwined.

We distinguish between practice, naming practice, perspective, profession and discipline. Usually, these distinctions are not made, and in different communications, the meaning of 'the designer' (landscape architect, architect, urban designer) is a different combination of elements of the list just mentioned:

- A practice is the practice of designing, of manipulating space. An architect can design a house, and the design is the practice.
- A naming practice is the practice of giving names, e.g. names of professions, disciplines, departments, schools. Calling something a school of architecture is a naming practice, and so is calling someone an architect. It is a convention to call someone with a professional certification an architect, someone else not. In each community, naming practices are different, and the practice is never entirely coupled with a name. Non-architects can design a house; sometimes the person will be called architect afterwards, sometimes not.
- A profession is a group of people carrying out a similar practice, e.g. a design practice, and who enforce the coupling of practice, name and group: an architect is supposed to be a member of the professional association, is supposed to have a diploma, is supposed to do certain things, in order to bear the name. A profession will try to present these couplings as natural – while they are not.
- A perspective is a conceptual structure which allows for a way of seeing and thinking, related to a practice and its concept. A design perspective allows to look at space as something that can be manipulated, in order to pursue other goals – beauty, practicality, sustainability, profit, practicality for a certain user, or for more users.
- A discipline is a group of people and a conceptual structure which reflect on practices, e.g. on design, planning, rural development.

From these distinctions, we can immediately derive a few things with regards to planning and design. We can see now that planning or design is not merely a matter of planners and designers. If people coordinate the organization of space, they are doing the practice of planning; if they manipulate space in order to solve problems in the planning effort, they are doing design. Design can be carried out by individuals, and by groups. In governance, design perspectives can be useful, to explore options of policy, to investigate scenario's, investigate the effects of policies on each other, without this ever leading to actual designs (we can speak of research by design). Design is also possible without embedding in planning; if there is no balancing of interests, no embedding in governance, only e.g. the pursuit of beauty by a single donor, one cannot speak of design as planning and one cannot consider it truly part of a rural development strategy.

With regards to rural development in general, we can say that the people choosing the label of 'rural development specialist', the organizations focusing on 'rural development' and the theories and practices of rural development are not one and the same thing, and that people, organizations, perspectives, disciplines without the label, being part of different naming practices, can still be very important for rural development. Hence our broad perspective, and our inclusion of rural development approaches which sometimes are not seen as or do not see themselves under the heading 'rural development'.

The distinctions made, render the 'actor' a more complicated being. It is possible that design actors, e.g. are not present in governance, but design perspectives are,

---

**Example 7.1. Minnesota Design Team: rural development 'light'.**

The Minnesota Design Team (MDT) is a volunteer group established in 1983 as a group of students, teachers and professionals as the Governor's Design Team, placed under the umbrella of the Minnesota Planning Agency, an agency for regional planning which disappeared in subsequent political shifts to the right. The team did not disappear, however, and under the new name Minnesota Design Team, it has been hosted since 1992 by the American Institute of Architects (AIA). Links with several universities also persisted, as well as with a substantial network of pro-community design civil servants at several levels of government.

The volunteers in MDT are students and professionals in landscape architecture, architecture, planning, geography, sociology, community development helping smaller, mostly rural communities to develop shared visions for their future, with a focus on spatial change, on creating more attractive neighborhoods and downtowns, working on economic, social and economic sustainability. Since 1983, MDT visited and helped well over 100 communities in Minnesota, some of them visited twice.

MDT does not embrace a cookie-cutter approach to community design, and does not emphasize design in the narrow sense in each and every case. Sometimes, the result of a team visit will be a detailed streetscaping of a downtown, sometimes design guidelines, in other cases a sketch for a comprehensive plan, and elsewhere a set of policy recommendation accompanied with a few sketches, depending on the place and the process. The combination of specialisms is different per community assisted.

The process is as follows: thanks to a history of projects, a good network, and strong communication channels in the state, the MDT is known to many communities. If one is interested in assistance, one can apply for a visit. The application is discussed, and if there is an initial interest, a self-study follows in the community, mapping assets, economic, ecological, social, cultural, providing basic statistics, but also discussing the rationale for inviting MDT and the political landscape. This allows MDT to get an idea of the real support behind the application, thus possibly behind the result, and the political cleavages and cultural coalitions. If one disgruntled local community leader invites, MDT will get immediately embroiled in local controversy, and the resulting plan will not likely be supported. A visit by a small delegation follows, and if the impression is positive, a date is fixed for a team visit, a long weekend of 3 days, where 12-18 team members come over. The community

---

with farmers, economic development associations, heritage groups, etc. This means that perspectives can create similarities and differences between actors, that they can enable or disable narrative or discursive migration: the movement of stories and ideas between actors. Convincing someone is easier when there is a shared or overlapping perspective; overlap can mean the sharing of certain narratives of concepts, not others.

is heavily involved in the organization, enabling a rapid learning process, a series of short presentations by various stakeholders (also conducive to social learning in the community), then a community event where community identity, assets, values, threats and opportunities are discussed.

After that, the focus moves to discussing appropriate principles within the team, and then to sketching and writing within sub-teams associated with focus points for the community. The final evening, another community event is organized where MDT presents the results and a public discussion can ensue. After the main visit, follow-up visits are scheduled, where questions can be asked in two directions. The MDT network can further assist, with more volunteering and more formal professional assistance, when more substantial planning, design or policy work is undertaken.

MDT never tries to impose an approach on a community and is not per se a lobby group for more state-led planning and design. It does recognize a lack of capacity in many rural communities, and offers a flexible and cheap alternative to blanket rules or heavy planning and development administrations per community. Many towns do not have specialists, do not have a budget even for comprehensive plans, do not know how to apply for support to get to a plan. MDT realizes that a real local demand for their advice is essential. If there is no awareness that a coordinated effort towards visioning is useful and necessary, then MDT will be perceived as a bunch of nosy intruders, and their work will be perceived as an extra burden on already difficult local governance.

When called in, and with all the attention to sense of place, local politics and local assets, MDT does have an agenda: it believes in context-sensitive planning and design, in asset-based work, in development as redevelopment, in public space, in community organization, in environmental quality and compact development in and around downtowns, with a variety of housing types accommodating for a variety of people and lifestyles, and fitting different neighborhood characters. Certainly not all recommendations made were followed, but in many cases, an MDT visit did set local governance on a different path.

### Further reading

Mehrhoff, A. (1999). Community design: a team approach to dynamic community systems. Thousand Oaks, CA, USA: Sage.

It is possible that an actor represents an organization with goal A, but silently also identifies with a professional group with goal B (think of the engineer in various governmental organizations). Actors have layered identities and loyalties, and even within the same identity ('the public works guy'), there can be several overlapping, but also partly contradictory perspectives. Around the governance table there can be a 'scientist', representing some discipline (e.g. rural development), but in practice, she also represents a routinized practice ('best practice') where there is little space for scientific reflection on that practice ('this is how we experts do it').

How these different aspects of the actor play out depends, again, on the set of co-evolutions we call the governance paths. Distinguishing these aspects also allows for a better grasp of the co-evolving configurations. We can bring back the earlier introduced concept of the role. Actors have an actual role, and a desired role, and except in rare cases, these two do not coincide. The difference propels and motivates actors to be successful in governance, to achieve not only particular goals in particular projects, but also a better position in governance. One shouldn't think only of power and control here; the desired role could also be that of a trusted adviser, of a broker, of a critical voice, of a voice for the environment, for the poor and oppressed.

For us interesting here, is the implications of this difference actual/desired role for the evolution of practices and perspectives in governance, and the impact on the articulation of visions for community development. If an actor sees its role somewhere else, then he will try to make this future role part of a future community, part of a vision for such future. As we know, power/knowledge can never be extricated from each other, and a future influence is also a future influence of perspective. The understanding of practices is hoped to be different, so these practices will be different (even if not directly prescribed by the dreaming and ambitious actor). Other actors, their perspectives, are placed in different roles than now, around the reinvented own role. Theories might be invoked in this dreaming and strategizing, or not.

## Further reading

Arendt, R.G. (1999). Growing greener: putting conservation into local plans and ordinances. Washington, DC, USA: Island Press.

Meeus, J.H.A., Wijermans, M.P. and Vroom, M.J. (1990). Agricultural landscapes in Europe and their transformation. Landscape and Urban Planning, 18(3), 289-352.

Ryan, R.L. (2002). Preserving rural character in New England: local residents' perceptions of alternative residential development. Landscape and Urban Planning, 61(1), 19-35.

Thompson, I.H. (2000). Ecology, community and delight: sources of values in landscape architecture. Abingdon, UK: Taylor & Francis.

Thorbeck, D. (2013). Rural design: a new design discipline. London, UK: Routledge.

Van Assche, K., Beunen, R., Duineveld, M. and De Jong, H. (2013). Co-evolutions of planning and design: risks and benefits of design perspectives in planning systems. Planning Theory, 12(2), 177-198.

## 7.2 Ordering principles and structures

Coming back to planning and design, we can refer back now to another concept introduced earlier: *first ordering structure*. Actors involved in planning-as-design will tend to see their influence and identity in the future in different forms: their impact on rules, on other roles, on the type of knowledge used in plans, the values and goals embedded in them, preferably reflecting their own or what they see as a fair balance of several. If we see design as more than throwing diverse elements in space, as representative of wishes of different actors, but rather, as an attempt to create a space based on existing qualities, and accommodating different wishes and uses in a harmonious manner, then the concept of spatial structure becomes important.

In a modernist perspective, there is such a thing as an essential spatial structure in a certain space, and designing is working with that structure, transforming it into an objectively better one, in which land uses could be optimized. The early land consolidation versions described, can be seen as modernist versions: there is one correct way to organize the parcels, to optimize agricultural production. A trained eye could recognize the existing structure, and recognize the potential for a better one. The essential expertise was then that of recognition of structure and potential structure, based on the knowledge of a universal language of space. Other people do not have access to that language; learning it would require long training as an architect, landscape architect. The correct of interpretation of space was that of a design professional.

Nowadays, few designers and few government actors employing them, still believe in this modernist version of space and design. There are many interpretations of space, and new spaces can be designed using different design perspectives. Space can be used to tell different stories, it can embody different values and resonate with different histories and social identities. Essential and correct spatial structures do not exist. Rural development cannot try to grasp this structure, and then realize it. The 'optimal' organization of the countryside only exists as a product of the wishes, values, desires of a community at a given point in time. What is appreciated changes, the economic and other uses of space in a community fluctuate, and how they relate in space has to be re-evaluated all the time. We can say that spatial planning and design, if part of governance, of rural development is an ongoing conversation in a community as to the organization of space, a conversation in which the images of current self, and future self are confronted and recombined all the time. Reflection on the present and desirable identity of the community, on good development, is linked to spatial images, of now and later, and consensus is sought to a level that allows for coordination, for design.

*Spatial structure* makes a comeback in such post-modern and governance-embedded version of design. If we want to reorganize space to create qualities and solve problems, and ideas and values are changing all the time in the community, we need something to anchor decision-making in space, stable elements that prevent extreme swings in the community to do damage that cannot be undone by later decisions, stable elements that can be the carrier of a resilient vision for future development. Besides laws and rules as stabilizing elements (we spoke of these), spatial structures can also anchor decision-making in space. They can embody path-dependencies, inspired by the qualities of the existing landscape. Spatial structures can give order to many other policies, functional order (how things work), visual order (what they look like). Spatial structures can therefore be anchors in physical and policy landscapes. They can be catalysts of policy integration: the structures themselves can fulfill several functions (recreation, residential, cleaning water, air, connectivity for animals), and they enable the integration of functions and policies around them, they structure the whole.

Many possible structures are possible in a landscape. Some can be combined, others not. But there can only be one first ordering structure, the result of a first ordering principle. If water functionality is most important, then water expertise offers the first ordering principles, leading to a water structure as first ordering structure, and the rest will fit in, following water-related principles, and, where there is conceptual space left, following other rules. The structure reflects principles, part of a perspective, part of a form of knowledge, which becomes privileged in the design exercise. Structures are therefore always a matter of debate, of contention, even if all are aware they are necessary. All actors are aware that the chosen structures, and certainly the first ordering structure, will determine their own importance in the future, the importance of their perspective, expertise, the importance of the institutions they most closely associate with. If suddenly 'innovation' rises on the political agenda, and management schools produce innovation specialists which suddenly get carte blanche by governmental and other actors very afraid of lack of innovation, the ecological structure that previously dominated planning for the future, might disappear to the background, replaced by a zoning for innovation parks, all close to highways, industries, universities.

If space becomes designed space, structured space, then governance discussions and conflicts over space become discussions over spatial structure, over the stable and powerful elements, shaping future roles and rules. The more science-intensive a government or a governance situation is, the more this can turn into a competition between scientific disciplines and their perspective on what space is, how it works, and on what is important for the community. Agricultural engineers can push a zoning based on soil quality, hydrologists organize communities around water structures, ecologists around ecological networks, infrastructural engineers and some economists see the future as clusters around highways, ports, maybe company headquarters, and resource rich zones.

**Example 7.2. Community planning for climate change adaptation in West-Timor Indonesia.**

Toineke village in West-Timor, Indonesia – as so many villages located along the equator – increasingly faces precursors of climate change: the dry seasons are getting longer, leaving the village suffering under prolonged droughts; the rainy season brings heavy rains and floods, destroying planted fields, drowning livestock and damaging houses. The increasing irregularity of the weather endangers agriculture and so livelihood security. The local population has developed a number of strategies to cope with and adapt to these changes. As the local livelihood system is highly dependent on the natural environment, the ability and innovativeness to develop such strategies are of immediate importance. These include: (1) re-active, short-term coping strategies for dealing with the direct consequences, like the collection of fruits and roots in the forest, the production and selling of building material from the forest as alternative income strategy; (2) future-oriented, anticipating coping strategies, preparing temporarily for the consequences, such as the elevation of houses or the moving of livestock; and (3) long-term, proactive adaptation strategies, such as moving houses further up the hill, seeking employment in the nearby town, but also the terrassing of the land to use flood water for irrigation.

These strategies of short-term coping and long-term adaptation are thought of, tested and developed by local individuals and – if proven useful – are passed on to neighbours, family members and friends. In terms of community planning, especially the locally found long-term adaptation strategies are of interest: first, moving house, animals and cultivated land; second, raising the house and third, protecting cultivated land by fencing. The prerequisite for moving house, anmials and cultivated land is access to higher ground in the village. However, most villagers do not have access to higher ground for construction, so they concentrate on securing higher land for cultivation or ask owners to permit them to cultivate their land for them and share the harvest. Success in these cases depends on social capital such as family relationships and personal networks. To raise the houses, local construction materials (wooden pillars) or home-made cement blocks are used depending on income. Furthermore, fencing the vegetable gardens is intended to protect the cultivated areas from floodwater, sediments and branches carried by the floods.

**Further reading**

Hornidge, A.-K. and Scholtes, F. (2011). Climate change and everyday life in Toineke Village, West Timor – uncertainties, knoweldge and adaptation. Sociologus, 61(2), 151-175.

Scholtes, F. and Hornidge, A.-K. (2010). Waiting for the water to come? – Poverty reduction in times of climate change. Bonn, Germany: Care International Germany-Luxembourg e.V. and Center for Development Research (ZEF).

If design becomes community design, more firmly embedded in governance, and more thoroughly discussed among a variety of actors, then actors ought to be aware of this.

In more participatory governance, local knowledge can improve the anchoring of structures in the landscape, and can prove a healthy corrective for disciplinary perspectives on good structures. It can also make designers and scientists alike more aware of the specific conflicts locally and of the specific combinations of land uses, structures and associated forms of expertise, which might make more sense here. First ordering structures ought to be thoroughly debated in a community, and their rigidity and flexibility ought to be honestly discussed. Rural development by design might be necessary and positive in many cases, but there is always the risk of introducing hard path dependencies, rigidities that make adaptation in the future tough. Reflection on the hardness of structures, on the openness for other ordering principles to be combined later, for other forms of expertise to step in later, seems highly commendable. A structure of irrigation canals might solve many problems, but also blocks many development paths, so the decision on this first structure ought not to come from the irrigation engineers, but from the community at large.

## Further reading

Arendt, R.G. (1999). Growing greener: putting conservation into local plans and ordinances. Washington, DC, USA: Island Press.

Beatley, T. (1999). Green urbanism: learning from European cities. Washington, DC, USA: Island Press.

De Jong, H. (2013) Groot Apeldoorns landschapskookboek. Wageningen, the Netherlands: Blauwdruk.

Getzels, J. and Thurow, C. (eds.). (1979). Rural and small town planning. Chicago, IL, USA: Planners Press.

Meeus, J.H.A., Wijermans, M.P. and Vroom, M.J. (1990). Agricultural landscapes in Europe and their transformation. Landscape and Urban Planning, 18(3), 289-352.

## 7.3 Towards community design

We argue that design as a rural development strategy makes most sense when it is community design. Yet, there are many examples where only governmental actors and their expertise were included. We can think of socialist irrigation and land reclamation schemes, but also large scale rural restructuring based on development plans drawn up by more capitalist national governments, or suggested by international organizations (such as World Bank or one of the development banks).

Community design, for many design specialists, is not very attractive. It sounds too much like 'design by committee', a watering down of strong principles in endless

Figure 7.1. Fish art in Revelstoke, British Columbia. A community design project capitalized on the identity of place by interpreting and revealing the rich underwater landscape in the nearby river. Photo: Monica Gruzmacher. © ZEF/University of Bonn, Germany.

discussions, a preference for tacky esthetics, and a loss of structure, in favor of a mish mash of principles and elements. Design in governance is understood as tough for these reasons. It is a lot of hassle, a lot of headaches, for us, designers, who know 'best'. We would say that design can be prevalent as perspective in governance, without leading to design by committee. What could better community design look like in practical terms? We list a few possibilities. It all depends on the process architecture of spatial governance, and the relation with other aspects of governance.

- Design perspectives can be cultivated each step of the planning process: this can include the use of sketches and draft plans, but also more elementary the systematic reflection on spatial intervention as a way to solve problems, and to investigate the effects of policies on each other, in different spatial configurations. ('If we decide this, we could plan it like that, and that would mean these effects for this and that.') So, instead of policy evaluation, design can be useful to assess versions of policy integration. Instead of checking what this policy would mean in isolation (e.g. cost-benefit analysis of a new train), one could think what the effects would be in combination with other measures, other policies, in the frame of a design, a new space (e.g. cost-benefit analysis of a new train if also the planning around new stations is taken into account, the effects on the environment, etc.).

- A comprehensive design can frame the community's decisions on many other domains of policies. A regional landscape structure can frame a governance process which is otherwise highly participatory. All is possible as long as the structure remains untouched.
- Smaller scale designs are the result of attempts at policy integration for smaller spaces, in a participatory manner.
- A design specialist is hired to follow the governance process, to embed a design perspective more structurally in the decision-making. Quick research by design becomes part and parcel of the exploration of policy options and options for policy integration.
- A specialist is hired, follows a participatory process, and produces a design as final result. She can convince the actors that this is what they wanted.
- A specialist is hired, and produces the design itself in a more participatory process.
- No specialist is hired, and actors in governance produce a design themselves.
- No specialist is hired, and the community at large creates a design, in an extremely democratic form of consultation, where all can send in their ideas. All meet and come to a consensus, or one is voted in.
- The community chooses among a few options produced by specialists, after listening to other actors in governance.
- The community delegates full authority to local government, who has the specialist in house, to create a comprehensive plan. A few essential actors are quietly consulted.

It might be clear from this list that it could be much longer, and that there are as many possible versions of community design as there are variations of governance. The never ending debates on the best form of public consultation, and of participatory governance, testify to this. Perfect planning and perfect governance do not exist; there are always different perspectives and models, and different ways to organize each model and perspective in practice. In the case of design, there is an additional complication: ideas never translate immediately into designs. One idea can lead to different designs (e.g. a carefully constructed consensus) and one design can lead to different ideas. People can agree on something until they see the design, or they can disagree until they see what kind of nice neighborhood could be created under an ideology they officially despise. Landscape architects can have a final plan already in mind, then listen to many arguments, and finally present what they had in mind as the result of involvement in governance. Many might recognize what they wanted in the design; they might see in what came about outside governance as an attractive and workable consensus among many interests in the community.

Community design as rural development strategy highlights the importance of *narratives* of the future and how they can be materialized in space. Those narratives are based on narratives of identity and history. Who we want to be is materialized in a future space, a space that takes into account, who we are now. The community we envision has a certain appearance, a certain physical structure, and we can work towards that structure by means of design. The design has to be context-sensitive, as the community identifies with its place, with certain elements, structures, activities in place. Certain elements make sense as part of narratives of self, and thus require a place in plans for the future. Heritage, nature, certain activities can be seen as defining, and expected to be framing for future development. In more simple terms: we can define community design also as the articulation of a spatially cohesive vision of the future, a vision that embodies a story about who we are and want to be, an expression of future identity rooted in present identity and physical space.

Some limitations of community design can easily be seen here: a spatial design can be rigid, it can only imperfectly express how the community sees itself, and it cannot solve all community issues or create all the desired qualities. Changing space does not completely change the community, and redesigning places cannot solve all the issues in these places. Modernist designs made with the best intentions created neighborhoods plagued by social and economic problems, and neighborhoods that work very well, can go down quickly, for reasons that have nothing to do with design. And, while more than

Figure 7.2. Art in the river polder. Kalken, Belgium. Community design is not restricted to artistic perspectives, but art can play a role. One can think of small scale town design, of public art, ambitious architecture, but also, as here, landscape art and land art, reminding us that art is, in essence, a way to shift people's perspective, on landscape, history, the community, on themselves. Photo: Kristof Van Assche. © ZEF/University of Bonn, Germany.

is assumed by many actors is possible within a place, and design can reduce conflicts between users, design cannot make every combination of uses and users possible. Conflict and tensions can remain.

One solution might be what we call *flexible policy integration*: which form of policy integration is strived for, is not defined a priori. It is decided in the governance process. Which form of design, how it is embedded in governance, is decided per case. Some projects might be long term (e.g. involving the creation of project offices, as temporary organizations), others might be short term, small scale, and more dependent on professional designers. Sometimes, a blue print approach might be preferable, e.g. when there is strong agreement on one spatial structure that can guide development later, while in other cases, there might be no overt design, but only design guidelines, differing per zone, and more and less stringent dependent on the spatial context. Sometimes, participation can be more radical than on other occasions. One can even consider spending the money and relinquishing authority temporarily to get a famous designer, if there is a real consensus on this strategy, and if there is a reason to say that the name and the quality of the work will contribute to the development of the area.

Flexible policy integration also means that it remains possible not to design, that there are ways to consider other development approaches when necessary. Visions for the future evolve, rural development efforts change all the time, as new problems and opportunities show up. It is possible that a comprehensive design guides many other policies for a while, but specific issues can require a different approach. Some places can be designed further in detail later, in the frame of the general vision, but for other places a different package of policies can be conceived, e.g. new local bylaws, investment in environmental quality, or, more flexibility in permitting when more local autonomy is considered essential to reduce conflict.

Flexible policy integration means that design cannot be generically imposed and its procedures cannot be prescribed in detail in local/regional laws. These laws should however allow for design, and pre-define procedures and forms of design, which can easily be started when the need arises (e.g. by allowing for conservation design in certain areas, for cases when sustainability issues become important in a governance situation). It also means that the expertise cannot always be in the house, for rural local governments. That means that, when it is decided to rely on design, it should be somewhere else: at a regional government, with a regional university (cf our extension discussion), or with non governmental organizations (such as design teams, which could be sent at low cost). Flexible policy integration further means that resources are likely not structurally available. Which means they ought to be somewhere else: one can think of grants given by higher level governments, subsidies (when explicitly applied for) or grants from specific departments (one can think of a department of natural resources giving grants to local governments opting for conservation design).

## Further reading

Botes, L. and Van Rensburg, D. (2000). Community participation in development: nine plagues and twelve commandments. Community Development Journal, 35(1), 41-58.

Brett, E.A. (2003). Participation and accountability in development management. Journal of Development Studies, 40(2), 1-29.

Hornidge, A.-K. and Kurfürst, S. (2011). Conceptualizing public space in Hanoi and Singapore: the power of state visions. Internationales Asienforum, 42(3-4), 345-369.

Lozano, E.E. (1990). Community design and the culture of cities: the crossroad and the wall. Cambridge, UK: Cambridge University Press.

Mansuri, G. and Rao, V. (2004). Community-based and-driven development: a critical review. The World Bank Research Observer, 19(1), 1-39.

Mathbor, G.M. (2008). Understanding community participation. In: Mathbor, G.M. (ed.), Effective community participation in coastal development. Chicago, IL, USA: Lyceum Books, pp. 7-24.

Mehrhoff, A. (1999). Community design: a team approach to dynamic community systems. Thousand Oaks, CA, USA: Sage.

Michener, V.J. (1998). The participatory approach: contradiction and co-option in Burkina Faso. World Development, 26(12), 2105-2118.

Sanoff, H. (2000). Community participation methods in design and planning. New York, NY, USA: John Wiley & Sons.

Thorbeck, D. (2013). Rural design: a new design discipline. Abingdon, UK: Routledge.

Van Assche, K., Beunen, R., Duineveld, M. and De Jong, H. (2013). Co-evolutions of planning and design: risks and benefits of design perspectives in planning systems. Planning Theory, 12(2), 177-198.

## 7.4 New benefits of design spotted: resilience and brand value

If we assume a democratic environment of some sort, in principle nothing has to be designed. Besides the already mentioned benefits of design, i.e. working on several issues and creating new qualities, two other things might be missed then: design can increase resilience and it can support branding. The first element might sound funny, as we already know that design can increase rigidity, when it is imposing a spatial structure that makes many activities hard to accommodate, that makes it hard to adapt to new uses and new requirements. Design however can increase resilience when it offers structures and qualities which allow for reinvention in different directions. If design imposes a structure which cannot be repurposed easily, e.g. a mono-functional agricultural landscape tied to one irrigation infrastructure defining everything else, then it hampers resilience. The negative aspect here is double: the imposition of a structure that cannot accommodate many uses, and the erasure of elements and structure which could be of future value. A post-consolidation landscape might be attractive for corn farmers for a while, but if all old landscape structures, heritage elements, and local products and traditions are gone, if the diversity in inhabitants is gone, then reinvention is harder because there are fewer starting points for reinvention. Places forgotten by consolidation design might be better off, and even better off might be areas where the community decided actively on the preservation of this and that, in such and such structure, in other words, decided on a design. Preservation by design is keeping the options open for later, while maintaining more different qualities now, in a multi-functional landscape that is not optimized for one activity.

**Example 7.3. Conservation design for rural and urban places.**

Conservation design is an approach to the development of communities that is radically asset-based and design-oriented. Initiated by Randall Arendt, an American landscape architect with European experience, conservation design is quite critical about the evolution of US planning and landscape architecture, with landscape architecture relegated to private spaces and planning relegated to local bureaucrats handing out permits and variances. Also the so-called cluster zoning, an approach in which residential or commercial clusters with higher density are fit into a green frame (resulting in the same average density as written in the zoning plan) is criticized, after observation that the green frame is in practice the combination of leftover spaces, where building is tougher, not the optimal framing for high quality neighborhoods. Similarly, Arendt dismisses traditional PUD's (planned unit development), where developers are given more leeway with zoning rules, often higher densities, when offering public spaces and amenities, after observation that usually the dense areas are built, sold, and for a variety of reasons, the amenities and public spaces do not materialize.

Conservation design proposes to start with a thorough mapping of assets, in which are to be included minimally: (1) wetlands and their buffers, (2) floodways and floodplains, (3) groundwater resources and their recharge areas, (4) moderate and steep slopes, (5) woodlands, (6) productive farmland, (7) significant wildlife habitats, (8) historic, archaeological and cultural features, and (9) scenic views. Mapping these features, ideally not by a single designers but in several steps by several community members (with a designer), is a good starting point, as it creates awareness of what is valuable, what could be used as building blocks, as framing devices, and what could form an obstacle. It helps to make the plan more site-specific. Not all elements have to be preserved, and will show up in the final plan, but an awareness of their existence makes it easier to draft several alternative green structures or networks, which can then structure the distribution of built up areas, and the nature of these clusters.

The overall density can be the same as under a 'normal' subdivision, following standard surveying practices, but with more green space (including agricultural remnants) and higher density residential in selected places in the green frame. The frame, a design, not a sum of elements, can be kept private, part of the building lots, but protected by a covenant (an

Resilience by design can be increased when there is a thorough understanding of the functioning of the landscape, the ecological processes and the way elements relate and reproduce. Landscape architect Paul Roncken speaks of 'the landscape machine', a telling metaphor, indicating the power of landscapes, integrated systems of elements and processes, that can do things. They can be partly redesigned, sometimes fixed. If the functioning of landscapes is well understood, we can work with the elements and

agreement between developer and home buyers). Preferably, it is placed under a conservation easement, written in the title, stating that it cannot be developed. That easement can be held and monitored by local governments, land trusts or conservation organizations. The building lots are thus smaller, keeping a large percentage in communal (community association) or community (municipal) ownership, and the design approach also entails a reasoning with masses, not lot lines: in stead of thinking in terms of lot lines, seeing this as the design and the result, one has to think in terms of masses, how they fit the green frame and the overall design and how they together create neighborhood character. The location of homes on lots is thus essential (e.g. following a stream, a street, a view shed, a forest edge, or clustering below the top of a hill, around a lake) as is the site-specific dimensioning, thus density: higher here, lower there, more massive here, slender there. An urban villa with 6 condo's can be easily located in certain rural villages, with less impact than a small new standard subdivision. Rural character can be better preserved, in many cases, with higher densities in a more rural frame, than with spread out development ('rural sprawl').

The approach calls for access to the whole design by all residents. The possibility to experience the whole place allows people to recognize the quality, and the difference with traditional approaches. This entails not only communal ownership and conservation easements, but also careful design of streets, trails and open spaces, finding a balance between access and privacy. When confronted with the possible critique that this is more expensive, complicated and more regulated, Arendt answered me that developers can make just as much money with this approach (true), that it is in fact less regulated, since one conservation design ordinance can replace a number of different rule sets (true, in fact a rule saying one has to produce this type of design is all needed), and he admits that indeed it takes more time than traditional subdivision, since careful study and design is needed, and if you make it more participatory, this is even more the case.

### Further reading

Arendt, R. (1999). Growing greener. Putting conservation into local plans and ordinances. Washington, DC, USA: Island Press.

processes, to achieve things. The landscape machine can be harnessed to clean water, protect species, buffer soil and other contamination, make people healthier, combine more activities close to each other, improve the esthetics of and well being in residential environments. Knowledge of the existing landscape has to be understood as more than knowledge of elements and structures. Its dynamic dimension, the sum of integrated processes (flows of water, formation and erosion of soils, interaction between plants and water, plants and soil, etc.), helps it to rebound from shocks, and from ever changing human demands. Good design then starts from an understanding of the functioning of landscapes, and a careful manipulation of its elements to accommodate new human demands, maintaining the functionality. This way of thinking is related to the 'ecosystems services' approach to nature conservation (ecosystems provide services to the community, therefore add value), but is more open to the possibility of design, and to the investigation of co-existence of man and nature. Both ecosystems services and landscape machine perspectives instill a cautious approach to existing landscape structures, including an appreciation of traditional uses.

Figure 7.3. Place branding and high art in Rothsay, Minnesota, USA, Prairie Chicken capital of the World. Prairie chickens are now rare birds of the American plains, formerly widely hunted, now attracting mostly eco-tourists. Photo: Kristof Van Assche. © ZEF/University of Bonn, Germany.

Rural development

One way of thinking about the valuation of tradition, in terms of the physical landscape and in terms of the economic and other activities is that of *place branding*. The core idea is that a place, the image of a place, and the products and activities there can create value for each other. If a place is attractive, the products made there, the houses there, will increase in value, and when a product, or a basket of products, is appreciated and known widely, the place itself will become more attractive, to live, to retire, to visit. Rural landscapes can be protected better when they are perceived as intricately linked with products and activities creating value. Both place and product need to be promoted together then, and the quality of both place and product need to be safeguarded, to retain their specificity (difference with mainstream products and places) and to protect and reinforce their linkage. Ideally, the product recalls the place and the place recalls the product; they are part of the same web of associations we can call place brand. Place brands cannot be entirely created; they work best when rooted in a real locale and really local products and traditions.

Design can protect and reinforce the spatial structures and qualities that make up the place image. This form of design has to be highly context-sensitive, with context being the physical landscape, the local aspects of the economy, and the narratives of place and product that can be used to promote them, but also used to build on them by design. Residential development can be allowed only in ways that improve a certain landscape character, polluting activities can be slowly extinguished, production zones can be allowed but in certain places, and certain categories, which fit the general development strategy, tied to a certain place brand. Sometimes, when the brand is already strong, it will not require much policy support and design, as initiatives tend to organize themselves along certain lines, and as local resistance will block damaging activities easily. When the place brand is not strong yet, policy support, active design, might be more needed.

## Further reading

Arendt, R.G. (1999). Growing greener: putting conservation into local plans and ordinances. Wasgington, DC, USA: Island Press.

Talen, E. (1999). Sense of community and neighbourhood form: an assessment of the social doctrine of new urbanism. Urban Studies, 36(8), 1361-1379.

Van Assche, K. and Lo, M.C. (2011). Planning, preservation and place branding: a tale of sharing assets and narratives. Place Branding and Public Diplomacy, 7(2), 116-126.

## 7.5 Community design and knowledge

Community and rural design can thus offer many benefits as a rural development approach. It is very suitable to produce a spatial structure that gives space to many activities, and preserves certain elements and qualities deemed important for the community, close to community identity. Preserving spatial structures and elements can be combined with creating new ones, into a spatial frame that can express what a community is and wants to be, and create conditions for the coexistence of humans and nature, and for many different human activities often considered harmful to each other.

Design, as a far reaching form of policy integration, can solve several problems at the same time, and create new qualities. It can enhance resilience and create value by supporting and co-creating place brands. A subtle understanding of landscapes, including the underlying processes, a fine appreciation of existing structures, natural and man-made, are important qualities of such design.

Community and rural design as rural development strategy are compatible with most models of governance, and most development approaches, even when they do not explicitly consider it as a possibility. It can be a form of policy integration which weaves together the threads in the implementation of many development perspectives. One can imagine design for sustainability, for livelihoods in a place, for innovation. Development perspectives focusing on institutional change and macro-policies do not contradict design approaches, give more space to them when nested development policies (see above) are promoted: projects within enhanced policy frames. Community design rests on participation, but participation committed to strong spatial policy integration, open for different combinations of expertise and local knowledge per design, and open for the specialized knowledge of designers. How that specialized design knowledge is integrated in the governance process, how it relates to local design opinions, local opinions in general, and to other expert knowledge, will determine which expertise comes in, is incorporated, and can possibly structure the design. If designers are important actors, their influence will probably prevent that the expertise of one scientific discipline turns into the first ordering structure in the community design. A good thing, since that is likely to undermine resilience.

Community design can best avoid rigidity (as main issue with design for rural development) when it is an ongoing conversation, on the future of the community, on the good design, and on the importance and role of design itself in specific cases. Such conversational character of design will be enhanced when the institutional structure of governance itself enables flexible policy integration, when design expertise and resources can be mobilized when and where necessary, when one role of design in governance is not prescribed and codified in law.

## Further reading

Mansuri, G. and Rao, V. (2004). Community-based and-driven development: a critical review. The World Bank Research Observer, 19(1), 1-39.

Sanoff, H. (2000). Community participation methods in design and planning. New York, NY, USA: John Wiley & Sons.

Shutt, C. (2006). Power in aid relationships: a personal view. IDS Bulletin, 37(6): 79-86.

# 8. Rural development: institutional reform

## Abstract

In this chapter, we investigate the potential for rural development of institutional reform strategies. We refer to political, legal and market reform, and possible combinations of these. The rule of law emerges again as an important yet contested concept, and so does the concept of property rights, as coupling between the economic and legal systems. We discuss scales and institutions, and nest development strategies, with institutional reform as framing approach for other interventions. Institutional reform can have many meanings and forms and is likely to be part of any development strategy, and the linkages with ideology and hotly contested ideological topics are complex.

## 8.1 Different sorts of rules

Institutional reform and development are almost synonymous. If communities want to move in a certain direction, this is very likely to bring changes to the rules. This is the case for local governments, and it holds true for regional and national governments. And the rules can be legal, political, economic, educational, scientific, and religious. As institutions we consider all rules that coordinate interactions and transactions in society, to include laws, policies, and plans. Earlier, we distinguished formal, informal and dead institutions, with dead institutions as officially sanctioned rules that remained or became paper rules. Dead institutions can be revived. Let us first take a closer look at some other basic concepts we have been working with in previous chapters, and redefine them based on the insights gained there.

*Policies* are temporary conceptual structures coordinating power/knowledge. They are tools to coordinate actors in governance and outside governance, and change all the time in effect because of confrontations and combinations with other power/knowledge configurations. Policies are born in governance, are enacted by actors enmeshed in power relations, relying on other institutions and on knowledge. Policies can be focused on problems, on topics, on creating qualities. They can be ad hoc, carefully deliberated, reactionary or visionary.

*Plans* can be spatial plans, but also economic plans, health plans and so forth. They are policies which coordinate or further integrate a variety of other policies and have a goal or set of goals defined in time. Plans can be designs, when they consciously manipulate space. Plans can be merely combinations of policies and laws, or they can articulate a new vision for the future, which transcends the policies integrated in it. Plans rely on other plans, policies, laws for their implementation, and, to a high degree, on informal institutions, with actors allowing to be planned, and incorporating them in their strategic calculations.

*Laws* are institutions which are expected to be more binding for action. In a constitutional democracy, all are bound by the law, including governmental actors. The stronger binding power is achieved by increasing rigidity and creating more exclusive links with political actors: only the legislative branch of government has the right to codify decisions into law, whereas the executive has the right to make policies and plans (within confines set by law). Laws are harder to make and harder to change than policies and plans. Their greater binding power is potentially more oppressive and deserves greater caution, while they also require more cautious change because they are the rules that are expected to stabilize expectations. Laws are the rules expected to be stable, and the ones best to include in strategizing and coordination with others.

Speaking of rural development by institutional reform, many people refer to changing laws. Speaking of economic, political, legal reform, they are still speaking of laws, laws pertaining to economic transactions, to political interaction, to the professions and organizations somehow involved with law. Confusion abounds therefore, as 'legal reform' refers to changing laws (on whatever), changing laws on the legal systems, and changing other things on the legal systems (a policy to raise salaries of notaries, to mentioned something).

For us, legal reform is the change of the legal system, not just a new law on this or that, but a new way for law to function a new way to relate to politics, economy, religion and the other functional domains.
- Legal reform will be different depending on the governance system, which implies a certain role of law in government, and depending on the general development approach.
- Economic reform is the reform of the institutional frame governing economic transactions, including laws, policies and plans.
- Political reform we see as the transformation of the actor/institution and power/ knowledge configurations which are recognized under formal institutions. A change in governance under formal institutions.

Collectively binding decisions are taken in politics, sometimes by means of law, but not in law. Institutional reform in that sense is always political, as development is per definition a matter of politics, of how the community wants to see it itself in the future.

## 8.2 Economic reform

What we find unfortunate is that, under economic reform, there is often a very narrow reference to macro-scale reform in a modernist vein, towards minimal regulation of markets, under the umbrella of neo-classical economics. By which we mean to say that the entire scope of economic reform is often not considered for development purposes. A well functioning economy is understood as a very free capitalism, with little room for policy and planning, little room for the articulation of development visions. The question where we want to go as a community finds little space, because the ideal development path is thought to emerge from markets evolving rationally in the direction of what people want and who is doing that most efficiently, and the same is true for politics. Economic reform, or market reform, has often been prescribed by international organizations (IMF, World Bank, European Development Bank). This strategy is very strongly linked to the neo-liberal governance model but not entirely restricted to this.

The package of policies that is prescribed under economic reform varies, even for the neo-classical economists. It usually includes low national debt levels, low inflation rates, a balance between import and export, easy registration of firms, low taxation, wage moderation, strong property rights and contract law. Certainly, more technical descriptions can be given. Policies envisioning collective goals are seen as introducing inefficiencies in the markets, since markets will bring about collective goals by offering

**Example 8.1. Water rights, American evolution and general options.**

Who owns water? Who has use rights? US history offers a variety of answers, which can be instructive for other places.

Colonization started in the north eastern states, and there, so called riparian rights developed, where owners of land adjoining or incorporating streams, rivers, wetlands, had the rights to use water and change its quality, yet limited by the reasonable expectations of other users downstream. Courts had to settle disputes, and balancing the rights of upstream and downstream was tough, caused long and acrimonious litigation. Since the middle of the 20th century, several federal acts, such as the clean water act, but also the wetland protection act and others, reduced the influence of riparian rights and local courts. Power moved to the federal level after struggles and disasters at the local and state level, and new expertise on pollution, ecology, hydrology, came into policy. Federal government opened local branches at county level, the soil and water conservation districts, while pollution control agencies are in charge of quality control.

In the western states, more sparsely populated in the time of early legislation, and dryer, the early practice was to come and claim land (before many formal institutions existed) and before ownership of land was formally regulated, water was already claimed in spot A and piped to spot B, where it could be made useful. This precedent created a strong path dependence not broken yet. Even now, so-called senior claims supersede most other claims; who comes first owns the water. By now, all water has been claimed a while ago, and forms of markets are created, where developers, water suppliers and others can buy registered water rights. Older rights are more secure and more expensive. Federal legislation still applies though, so old claims are not entirely secure. Markets are also restricted in other ways; in many states, agricultural water (for irrigation) cannot be sold far away. Prices can peak locally without the option for distant farmers to bring water. Such localization of water markets seems a form of strategic suffering, where farmers in drought-stricken areas are sacrificed by the agro lobby to maintain the status quo. It is feared that opening the market would also reopen the larger discussion on water rights, and question the generous irrigation rights of farmers in areas where both urban residents and natural areas are suffering – California is the prime example.

The US example shows the classic institutional options visible elsewhere: water rights can go to the owner or claimant of the land, the owner or claimant of the water, to a government

products and services (creating environments?) which people want. Markets with clear and simple and cheap rules (low transaction costs), with fair rules and enforcement of rules, will become fluid and transparent: they will react fast to changes in supply and demand, and they will provide all the necessary information for adaptation quickly. In transparent markets, prices 'correctly' express the balance between supply and demand. The more is treated as a product, which can be bought and sold (the

agency, to a body consisting of governmental and non-governmental actors. Water rights and water management can be separated, or they can be in the same hands. Quantitative and qualitative rights and obligations can be articulated, and management for quality and quantity can be in the same or different hands. Forms of riparian rights (you use what's on your land) can be combined with forms of communal ownership (governments as only sellers of water). Water can be free then for all, if water is seen as a natural or human right. Taxes elsewhere can make this possible. If water is seen as a scarce resource, and also used by non-humans, then pricing, by government or in some form of market, will look more attractive. Water reform is notoriously difficult. Since water moves freely, and water is needed for so many purposes, water governance will be rigid, highly marked by path dependence and interdependence. Handing water governance over to a completely free market undermines the possibility to envision many other public goods. On the other hand, complete government control over water makes it almost impossible to adapt to very local needs and circumstances (One can think of arid areas dependent on government-controlled irrigation system). Two concepts came up in a variety of contexts, that could help find middle ground, and enable coordination of water policy and other policies: watershed management, in which not departmental, bureaucratic, boundaries but natural units of water flow guide policy making, for water, agriculture, planning, nature conservation, etc. (towards a more efficient and natural policy integration). Secondly, water user associations, where governmental and other actors decide on water management; in such more participatory water governance, the interdependency between actors can become more visible and more manageable. (Water user associations are old. We can refer to the Dutch system of water boards, dating back to the 10th century, where farmers and others together decided on new dykes, new reclamation projects, in what was in essence the kernel of local governance).

### Further reading

Platt, R. (2004). Land use and society. Geography, law and public policy. Washington, DC, USA: Island Press.

Gunawansa, A. and Bhullar, L. (eds.) (2013). Water governance. An evaluation of alternative architectures. Cheltenham, UK: Edward Elgar.

stronger commodification), the larger the domain of the market becomes, the more activities it covers, and the easier it will be for markets to bring about collective goods, to further the type of development that is desired. If people do not want to pay for a clean environment, then we should either not pursue it, or assume that the market is not efficient yet here; we could e.g. consider then breaking up monopolies, if present, of companies affecting the environment, or one could consider the commodification of environmental services, where clean water, air, soil, are priced and competition can ensure a fair pricing. Usually, 'development' for neo-liberal market reform is simply seen as increasing national income, without reference to any substantive goal.

This *absence of substantive goals* we see as the essential element of many market reform recipes for rural development. Simply opening up 'the market' is supposed to unleash the forces of economic development. The multitude of economic transactions that is then supposed to take place is expected to lift all ships, to generate a distribution of benefits for all. We also note a further assumption behind neo-liberal market reform: the existence of one market, in one ideal form, which is as free as possible, with law mostly focusing on property rights, making transactions easy and secure. Politics should stay out of the economy and should not use law to interfere. Competition, supply and demand, is all that is necessary. There is little talk of infrastructure, investment in education, environment, science, safety, health, as part of a good business environment. And there is little talk of different forms of markets, different relations between economy, law, and politics.

We argue for an understanding of markets as embedded in communities, with various links possible to law, economics and science. Market reform might work as a strategy. There might be obstacles to economic transactions, obstacles to well functioning credit markets, lacking incentives to trade, to produce for trade, if selling and buying is difficult, if prices are unclear and unfair. The type of reform that might indeed improve incentives for various players to invest, learn, work and cooperate, will hinge on the form of differentiation in the community, and, again, its evolutionary path. What might be lacking for a form of market to function might be just as well more rules than less rules. New institutions can improve trust in the quality of products, in contracts, in property, can improve infrastructure, provide workers with skills, can avoid conflict rather than sending them to the courts, can give more people the capacity to buy and to decide on how things will be commodified. Politics and law can shape markets in various ways, and the other way around. Collective goods, as seen in politics, codified in law, policies, plans, do not restrict or disturb markets necessarily; they can just as well restructure them, changing the calculations of players without crowding them out. Governments and institutions can just as well create and stabilize demand, and they can limit and restructure supply (of land, houses, water, trained doctors, etc.).

## 8.2.1 Rule of law

These different perspectives on market reform are translated into different perspectives on the *rule of law*. For neo-liberal versions of market reform, the rule of law is simply a legal basis for economic transaction, and a protection of the players. The rule of law means the presence and the systematic enforcement of these laws. Institutional economists of recent generations expand the notion (and we are on their side), understanding the rule of law as the stabilizing and enabling function of the entire legal framework. If other laws are not enforced or selectively enforced, if corruption is possible, then in the long run all kind of interactions, including all kind of economic transactions, can be affected. Your subcontractor might not do his job, or might be replaced by the niece of the president. Your factory might suddenly burn down and the insurance firm doesn't exist anymore. Your dead workers are not dead for regional government, and their salaries still have to be paid.

One can expand the notion further, and say that the rule of law includes the fair access to all aspect of law, including law-making. This means that there ought to be democratic access to the creation of laws, that in all likelihood people can express their interests, as individuals and as groups, in the creation of new laws, expressing common goals, maybe a vision for development. And not only by (not) buying and selling things. This can mean that certain transactions (selling nuclear waste, animals, weapons) might be made difficult, that taxes on certain things might be high, that subsidies on other things might be provided, that certain places can be privileged (downtowns e.g.) in attracting business, etc. Sharing power through participation and/or representation becomes part of the rule of law then. This entails a much tighter coupling between politics, law and economy.

We would argue that the rule of law understood in this last, broader sense, still allows for economic actors to do their calculations and find motivation. As long as there is stabilization of expectations among actors, as long as rules are there, known, clear and enforced. Economic actors and other citizens still have the option to signal their disagreement with policies through voting and participating in governance in other ways. All three versions of rule of law can stabilize the expectations of actors, increase the trust that makes transactions possible, enable calculations for shorter and longer term. Rule of law makes in that sense development easier, investment, learning, capacity building. In the most narrow sense, this is restricted to economic actors, but in the broader sense, government can induce other actors to do so, or can do it itself. Planning becomes possible then, and policy integration for rural development strategies becomes more possible. We mentioned earlier the weakest link: in absence of the rule of law, there is likely to be some weak link in the development process. Slowly achieved results can be quickly undermined by corruption, by passivity, by theft.

In the broadest definition of rule of law, each community has its own version, as each is marked by a specific differentiation of the function systems. Which brings us back to governance paths: in these paths, economy, law and politics are linked in a specific pattern, and this establishes what we can call a community rule of law. As communities are never entirely independent, dependent on others and embedded in larger scales, there will always be a sharing of rules, of frames. We can bring back to mind our discussions on models of democracy, and on development approaches. Each governance model has a different notion of rule of law, a different influence of law on politics, politics on law, of politics on economy and economy on politics, and different procedures of decision-making on changing the laws and the scope of laws.

We mentioned there that each empirical, real world, community can be described as a *hybrid of governance models*, showing traces of older eras, older internal and external conflicts. This hybridity brings about a better fit with certain general development approaches; a specific actor/institution configuration, and a power/knowledge configuration, will work better with certain development approaches, or a certain hybrid of development approaches, and once carried out, the approach will be in some manner institutionalized. In other words, it will reshape actor/institution configurations again. Governance paths are marked by a rule of law, which predisposes them to a development approach, which will reshape rule of law, through its institutionalization. What law can do, how it stabilizes expectations, how it structures the calculations of economic (and other) actors, hinges on the nature of governance, and the ways governance relies on laws in its self-transformation. We refer back to the anchoring nature of laws as special institutions, one aspect of this anchoring being the slowing down of self-transformation of governance (today socialism, tomorrow tribalism!), and one effect the opening up of longer time horizons for economic actors.

## 8.2.2 Property rights

The different versions of rule of law can be moved in different directions according to the existing rules of self-transformation. More simply: governance can decide to modify the rule of law, this modification being restricted by law. Rural development can be improving the rule of law, within governance, subjected to the ruling configurations of governance, and restricted by law.

Property rights are central in effort. For economic reform to work, to contribute to development the rule of law even in its minimum version entails clarification and enforcement of some form of property rights. If people know what they own, what ownership means, how it can be transferred, then buying, selling, and investing becomes easier. If markets are not overly volatile, then property rights also contribute to the stabilization of a financial sector and thus access to capital for many players, and greater ease of investment (since assets can be collateral, and the investment in case of failure can easily be taken over by the bank). Intellectual property rights contribute to innovation, maintain the motivation to innovate, by promising protection of the results.

Property is not a monolithic concept. In neo-liberal versions of development theory, the chain of assumptions is often that property rights were absent in a community, and should now be created, that it is one thing, an absolute control over the owned object. *Commodification* should go hand in hand with privatization: ownership of land, resources, and production should be as little as possible in government hands, since government is per definition inefficient, other forms of ownership, including collective ownership, are seen as inefficient. Private ownership over maximum resources would unleash the forces of motivation inspired by ownership, and of competition over price and quality.

Without ignoring the powers of motivation and competition, and the need for some form of ownership, this liberal democratic reasoning seems largely a fiction. One reason being that collective ownership in various forms (cooperative, community, state) can work well for resource exploitation and production, another reason that property rights are never complete and always evolve. In the USA, property rights in the past extended to other people, to slaves, wives and children, and the Civil War started formally over infringement on Southern property rights (taking away property by changing property rights). More realistic, we believe, is to say that property rights are *use rights*, bundles of use rights and obligations. You can buy a stick and use it as a cane, but not to beat people with. You can buy land, grow wheat, but not weed, pump water up, but not so much that your neighbor's land becomes useless. In the case of land, zoning can restrict use, say which uses are possible, and planning more broadly, can guide the development of areas, the combinations of uses possible and desirable there. Common uses can be carried out on private land, without buying, through easements; a new sewer system might cross private land, a new road, a trail, and some landscape elements can be protected. Planning brings a wide variety of modifications of possible uses, of property rights.

Property rights *couple* law, politics and economy: politics, in governance, can redefine property rights slowly, within the checks and balances of the governance system, and the existing package of property rights shapes and limits the intervention of government in the economy. Politics enacts property rights law to enable economic development, and to guide and stabilize itself in its interventions in the economy: From the perspective of the economic system, the essential political intervention is the definition of property rights, since before any economic transaction takes place, before there is question of development and investment, it needs to be clear what you own and what it means. In the neo-liberal ideology, absolute ownership requires no continuous redefinition, it is always the same, simple and clear, and so there is no need for a discussion on the role of governance in shaping property rights. Government should simply protect an object that is clear and simple.

**Example 8.2. Coffee in Colombia: institutional transformations (with thanks to Monica Gruezmacher).**

Coffee production in Colombia dates back to 1730, when it was still a Spanish colony. First exports took place around 1835, while ca. 1850, production expanded towards the western and central parts of the country. Coffee cultivation then reached what is now known as the coffee region (Eje cafetero), consisting of four departments (Quindio, Risaralda, Caldas and parts of Antioquia), in the foothills of the northwestern Andes. The development of railroads in the late 19th and early 20th century, and infrastructure development on the Cauca and Magdalena rivers, helped the rise of the coffee business, while the coffee growers themselves lobbied for these improvements.

In 1927, the Federation of Coffee Growers (Federacion Nacional de Cafeteros) was created and in 1938 it established the Coffee Research Institute (Cenicafe), while the 1947 founding of the Colombian merchant fleet was closely associated with coffee exports to New York. Revenues from coffee exports helped create the National Coffee Fund which was initially used to buy export quality coffee from growers and offer them credit opportunities; nowadays its main focus is to buffer volatility of international prices. In this way the Federation teamed up with the Colombian government to promote quality improvement, pest research, marketing, export controls and quotas and try to provide a secure income for coffee growers in the country. A large scale marketing campaign in the 1980's made Juan Valdez, the man and his donkey, a household image in the USA (although the character had been created in 1959). In 1982 cooperative efforts with Cenicafe resulted in the discovery of a new coffee variety (var. Colombia) resistant to rust desease. Since the 1980's, Colombian coffee became synonymous in the USA with high quality (Arabica, shade grown) coffee, a remarkable result of cooperation between government and the professional association, involving various forms of regulation, government and cooperative investment. In the 1990's, world prices for coffee plummeted and the Colombian model suffered. As a response to this crisis the sector increased its dependance on subsidies from the Federation and the government until 2002 when the National Coffee Fund was not able to buffer the volatility of international prices anymore. Critics noticed that although a more cooperative model was indeed beneficial for a sector with many small farms (over 500,000 families owning on average 5 ha of coffee in 2014), the sector had become too reliant on government subsidies, too close to government, and too dominated by an internal elite. Exported coffee requires acredition by the Federation and its network of organizations. When the Colombian markets opened in the 1990's under more neo-liberal governments, the Federation showed itself flexible and adopted several strategies: a terroir approach (guarantee of origin, e.g. visible in the 1995 special coffee program), even stricter quality controls and the establishment of a coffee chain, Juan Valdez, an answer to new but feared rival Starbucks.

Talking to coffee growers in Quindio, we heard about the success stories, but also noticed a lot of critique: farmers found the sector over-regulated, with a de facto export monopoly for the Federation. More growers operate independently, even start to roast, and sell to American and European roasters looking for unique flavours and terroir but direct export that bypasses the Federation is close to impossible. The coalition between Federation and government is often felt as suffocating, and many farmers perceive that the Federation elite is willing to adapt but only when it suits their interests. What started as cooperative, is not perceived as such anymore. The combination of price shocks in the past, pests and earthquakes, shrank production and acreage, and it is still smaller now than in the 1970's. Many plantations have been turned into banana territory, and bringing coffee back requires a long term vision that is hard in a volatile economic and political environment (coffee trees take ca 7 years to become productive). Tourism in some places offered a way out, and in the coffee region, coffee tourism has been actively promoted, infrastructure developed, as yet mostly for Colombian visitors. The more independent growers hope to benefit from tourism in a second way: they hope educating Colombians with regards to coffee (special preparations ei cappuccino, expresso, etc. only recently appreciated within the country) will grow their domestic market. The independent growers can export to the cities, where coffee produced by independent growers is now popular, so this market is essential for them.

Both government (Federation) and independents assert that improving product knowledge among more players would be helpful: teaching Colombians how to distinguish quality, how to make good coffee at home can develop the local market, tourism, and it can make quality control a more natural and bottom-up process. In the coffee region, many farms now offer tours, historical shows, and coffee classes, including brewing and tasting, while, following the example of wine, competitions, shows and tastings are promoted, and professional courses for coffee taster (catador) are offered at local community colleges. As of now, most top quality coffee is exported, so few Colombians are familiar with their own best coffee, but more and more people argue that some should stay there, for reasons of national pride and enjoyment, but also to teach Colombians how to recognize quality.

In recent years, production has gone up, and it seems that the combination of a slightly more flexible Federation, active independent growers, and still strong foreign interest in specialty coffees, offer a window of opportunity for a reinvention of the sector.

### Further reading

Bates, R. (1999). Open economy politics: the political economy of the world coffee trade. Princeton, NJ, USA: Princeton University Press.

Figure 8.1. Tulip fields in the Netherlands. The tulip came to Holland from Turkey via Vienna and Flanders, but the Dutch were the first to turn the bulb from mountainous areas into a lowland power house and an icon of their country. Expertise in cultivation, in marketing, transportation and auctioning, a history of professional association, government and university extension and investment all add up to an added value high enough to continue the activity, despite labor costs and very high land prices in the densely populated and wealthy coastal regions, luring farmers away from farming. Photo: Monica Gruzmacher. © ZEF/University of Bonn, Germany.

If we see it as not so clear and simple, as evolving, with bundles of use rights shifting in governance all the time, responding to internal and external change (e.g. slavery is not acceptable anymore), then a more tight link with governance becomes visible, and the shifting of property rights can then be understood as reflective of a shifting balance between private and collective goods and shifts in the priorities of collective goods. Common goals, as visible e.g. in rural development visions, will become more or less important vs. private goals (protected in property rights) so, the power of policies and plans to impose common goals will change over time. Besides resistance which can be politically mobilized and captured, and reenter governance, there will be resistance translated into legal action, referring to infringed property rights. Certain common goals will become more important than others, more allowed to redefine property rights (and other rights) than others. 'The national interest' as overriding policy goal, overriding public good, will be reinterpreted continuously, and so will national security, the environment, safety, health, well-being, quality of life, prosperity, social justice, etc.

The more goals are embraced in governance, and the more comprehensive a rural development vision is, the more various property rights will be affected, the bigger the economic effects will be. In a neo-liberal perspective, this will be seen as negative impact. We would say that the effects can go in every direction. There can be economic costs, offset by collective goods (say, public health), there can be little collective tangible benefit, only rhetorical grandstanding (for political benefit) about collective goods. And it is very well possible that policies aiming at common goals also create new private benefits, new products, places with new qualities, new resources available, new brands with a new value.

Market reform can thus focus on facilitating economic transactions, in a minimalist version of the rule of law, and it can try to do this without relying on the fiction of autonomous markets. If we stretch up the understanding of rule of law (which seems warranted by observation of development trajectories), market reform can become more context-sensitive, that is, sensitive to the context of a specific market itself, result of a history of interactions with government and law, and sensitive to the context of governance and society at large. Signals for market reform can come from within the market itself, and from society at large; they can come about through economic shocks and ruptures, and through governance. Market reform can thus be part and parcel of more comprehensive development strategies, not only recipes to liberate markets and then avoid any substantive statement on what and where we want to be as a community in the future. Market reform in this sense is compatible with rural development strategies of different sorts. We come back to this.

The proponents of very free markets did have a point, we believe, in criticizing central steering of the economy by governance, of extremely comprehensive planning, of linking spatial and economic planning. They did have a point saying that societies are too complex for allow such steering and prediction, that comprehensive economic planning creates problems in terms of complex logistics (government actors deciding on what to make, how, how to organize the logistics of production, where parts come from, etc., and of distribution, where products are going). Private property and pricing mechanisms do drive efficiency, create motivation (to own, to produce, to accumulate, to trade). Pursuing only collective goods in daily life, without possibilities to improve your own situation, does not seem to fit the human condition. Some form of private property, some form of property rights, some form of the rule of law, all those do seem necessary to capture the creative energies of communities, while stabilizing them, and allowing for long term visions, for individuals and for the community itself. Which form makes most sense, will emerge in governance paths. Before trying any market reform, a deep understanding of these paths is required: what are the existing (informal) property rights, the existing (informal) economic actors, actual form of rule of law (formal + informal).

Understanding these things can help to formulate visions for market reform that can render economic transactions easier, encourage investment, without breaking abruptly with the current mechanisms, without relinquishing the option of pursuing collective goods through market reform (including property rights effects). In the other direction, actors in governance, deciding in politics on market reform, ought at least intend to understand the logic of the local economy: what is driving development, what is motivating, what will be the effects of new policies on the autonomy and motivation of economic actors? Consultants can be useful, a presence of business experience in governance, in administration, but also a capacity to distinguish business rhetoric (e.g. asking for complete autonomy, economic freedom) from business practice. In practice, business can adapt to many things, exploit many governance systems, as long as governance can often a stable and reliable frame for their calculations and strategies. Co-evolution is a keyword again: if business actors are used to interacting with certain government actors, if they are used to work within a policy frame aiming at individual freedoms plus public goods, they can adapt and often thrive. New niches can be found for profit, in and thanks to the new policy frame, and negotiations can take place with political actors, so the new policies can make it easier for private parties to benefit from the pursuit of collective goods as well. What this looks like, will be different per case. A perfect balance does not exist, and public scrutiny in and outside governance is always necessary; corruption thrives in the dark.

Market reform has not surprisingly a very mixed track record, depending on the quality of the preceding context analysis. We discuss the supposed rationality of markets and the relation between market rationality, optimization and the two main configurations discussed earlier (actor/institution and power/knowledge). It is argued that, besides adaptation to existing patterns of differentiation, willingness to embrace combinations of market reform in broader policy packages is key to its success. Property rights are and will be a recurring theme.

## Further reading

Acemoglu, D. and Robinson, J. (2012). Why nations fail. The origins of power, prosperity and poverty. New York, NY, USA: Crown Business.

Bergh, S. (2004). Democratic decentralisation and local participation: a review of recent research. Development in Practice, 14, 780-90.

Beunen, R., Van Assche, K. and Duineveld, M. (eds.). (2015). Evolutionary governance theory: theory & applications. Heidelberg, Germany: Springer.

Gerber, T.P. and Hout, M. (1998). More shock than therapy: market transition, employment, and income in Russia, 1991-1995. American Journal of Sociology, 104(1), 1-50.

Jacobs, H.M. (ed.). (1998). Who owns America?: social conflict over property rights. Madison, WI, USA: University of Wisconsin Press.

Ostrom, E. (2009). Understanding institutional diversity. Princeton, NJ, USA: Princeton University Press.

Platt, R. (2004). Land use and society. Geography, law and public policy. Washington, DC, USA: Island Press.

Van Assche, K., Duineveld, M., Beunen, R. and Teampau, P. (2011). Delineating locals: transformations of knowledge/power and the governance of the Danube Delta. Journal of Environmental Policy & Planning, 13(1), 1-21.

Webster, C.J. and Lai, L.W.C. (2003). Property rights, planning and markets: managing spontaneous cities. Cheltenham, UK: Edward Elgar Publishing.

World Bank (1997). World Development Report: the state in a changing world. Oxford, UK: Oxford University Press.

## 8.3 Political and legal reform: means and ends

Now we investigate the importance of political and legal reform as a route to rural development. We take a closer look at the various roles of laws, policies and plans in society, and in relation to 'development'. Indeed, many market reformers would also ask for some measure of political and legal reform, to take away obstacles for market formation, yet also in the other models of governance, there are many hopes for some forms of legal and political reform, in different combinations, with various goals, including redistribution, fairness, environmental quality, education, health and so forth. Political and legal reform, it is assumed, can create the conditions for other development initiatives to work.

In other perspectives, these reforms are enough by themselves. In our view, different packages of reform can work in different contexts, and reconstruction of governance paths, of both the internal and external environments of governance, of its dependencies, and the two configurations is a sine qua non for the evaluation of appropriate package of measures. Also the time and spatial scales issue comes back here: one needs to secure that the time scales required by reform and for reform are possible to construct, maintain and coordinate within the given context, and one needs to take care that the reform is implemented at the appropriate scale. Taking an evolutionary perspective, we argue that the impact of policies will differ according to the governance path, its dependencies and configurations. Property rights appear in different lights depending on the governance model espoused.

In the neo-liberal idea of market reform, legal reform, as the minimum version of rule of law, can be disconnected from political reform. We know what 'the market' is, and we know what the legal minimum conditions are, and these conditions can be achieved under any political condition. We would beg to differ, and refer to the different forms markets can take, the different ways they can be structured by politics and law, in specific co-evolutions. Also for the political reform side, such a modernist approach

**Example 8.3. Good governance and development according to Machiavelli.**

Niccolo Machiavelli (1469-1527) was a Florentine diplomat, spy, policy advisor, politician and writer, now often regarded as the father of modern political theory and a main proponent of the form of democracy we called civic republicanism. Machiavelli became most famous and notorious with one little book, The Prince, offering advice to aspiring autocrats on how to obtain and maintain power. However, it is clear from all of Machiavelli's other works that he preferred democratic forms of government, based on his conviction that one person cannot embody all of the skills, knowledge, and flexibility necessary to face ever changing circumstances of governance.

Perfect laws and policies for Machiavelli are perfectly adapted institutions, adapted to internal and external circumstances. Development can never be the approximation of a final state, in economic, cultural or institutional terms; things can work, for a while, and then they don't fit circumstances anymore, will deteriorate. The state, but also the community forming the state, has to reinvent itself every so often. It has to go back to its roots, and re-imagine those roots. In periods of crisis and turmoil, transitional regimes might be helpful which do not adhere to any commendable principles, but do the job. Development therefore is always uncertain evolution, and governing is the art of adaptation, including the skill of risk management.

Good governance for Machiavelli differs from most recipes found in recent literature. Some of the things he recommended a prince, an authoritarian leader, he would also recommend to elected leadership. Some of the more controversial principles, in brief:

Leadership is important. Good governance and good decisions can per definition not be derived from rules, from laws and policies, and policies cannot be simply derived from laws or public opinion. Judgment is essential, and leadership requires strong judgment in many situations, including the capacity to find and learn from the appropriate advisors in a given situation.

Leaders cannot always stick to the rules they make and apply to others. The common good, as development potential, or in a negative form, as a crisis requiring action, can make it impossible to follow certain legal or moral principles otherwise necessary. Dirty work can be necessary, and can be followed by a transition in leadership or by a cover up.

Which brings us to the idea of transparency: entirely transparent governance is impossible and destabilizing. Extreme transparency shrinks the room to maneuver for actors, within the community, or in dealing with external actors. Such space is necessary, because other actors do not necessarily stick to the rules the community is envisioning, because necessity might require to break rules, and, last but not least, because the community is never entirely cohesive and consistent in its wishes, and never completely aware of the strategic situation.

People want contradictory things, and want things without facing or understanding the consequences and requirements. Transparency is important for fighting corruption, but has limits. Those limits cannot be pre-defined by laws, but have to be assessed and managed.

The same logically applies to public participation. For Machiavelli, active citizenship is the essence of democracy, with people ideally being well informed, debating issues in everyday life, and participating as individuals, as members of organizations, as party members. A diversified and critical form of active citizenship can curtail the ever present powers of corruption, and can increase the quality of judgment of the leadership, its adaptive capacity. Yet, with this, leadership needs to maintain spaces of autonomous judgment. It has to be remembered here that leadership is a role for Machiavelli, a force requiring a counterforce of scrutiny and participation. Power by representation can never be fully replaced by participation.

Conflict is a positive in this game of force and counterforce. Checks and balances are there to create stability, to avoid corruption, but also to enable, to tease out conflicts. Conflicts are productive when they show the actual diversity in positions in the community, the diversity in ideas, the real differences, but also overlaps, and learning potential. Conflict makes a diversity visible that can be interpreted as a source of adaptation options, and it can lead to learning, to the finding of new options in argument and negotiation. Conflict becomes destructive when it undermines checks and balances, stabilizing institutions, and the rules to peacefully change the rules.

The discussion of these more controversial features of his theory immediately show how they are interwoven with many things not so often disputed, and often seen in isolation. Checks and balances are recommended in most versions of good governance, a form of rule of law, participation, and transparency. Machiavelli shows how none of these exists in one perfect version, how too much of them becomes unhealthy, and how, most elementary, active citizens and a strong state are both necessary, and necessarily existing in a state of tension. The point is to make these tensions productive. Appropriate development strategies can not be determined in advance, can only come out of this interplay, and can only work when they are adapted to internal and external environments. 'Development' for Machiavelli becomes more powerful when a vision is more persuasive, and one of the key features of a good leader is such persuasive power, not only as a good speaker, but also as an astute observer of factions and histories, creative and capable of forging community by forging stories that inspire.

### Further reading

Mansfield, H. (1996). Machiavelli's virtue. Chicago, IL, USA: University of Chicago Press.

exists, whereby 'the democracy' is furthered somewhere else, that democracy usually being a version of liberal democracy, which is then understood as the only model of democracy. We would beg to differ, and mention again our previous discussions on the different models of democracy and governance, and the preferential ties with certain development models. A third misunderstanding, we believe, is the idea that formal institutions, once enacted, do the job. What is on paper, becomes reality. 'Good laws', supposed to bring the benefits of capitalism and/or democracy, are enough. If we believe these three myths, then a new law with a few simple rules can quickly create a new political and economic environment, which immediately will move the community forwards on the best possible development path.

If we drop the ideas of one ideal democracy, one ideal market, and simple connection by means of minimal law, and consider the co-evolutions of political, economic and legal systems, of formal and informal institutions, political and legal reform will likely still be an important part of development strategies. Entirely relying on existing institutions, on existing political and legal structures, in formulating development visions, rarely works. If communities want to move in a different direction, it is likely that some rules and some decision-making rules and procedures have to change. How to move forward can best be decided when looking at the pattern of existing formal and informal institutions, as they together structure interactions, and as formal change will more likely succeed if it takes into account reigning informality.

What to do concretely? One recommendation is not to look immediately for concrete reform measures that could be copied from somewhere else. This applies to substantive policies, and to policies changing procedures and rules (the actual legal/political reform). Best practices are to be scrutinized carefully, to figure out if they were actually so good in their original context, and then to see if they might fit in the receiving context. That extends to the functioning of legal/political structures, and to the practices of reform of those structures. New institutions, and new ways to make institutions can be inspired by foreign examples, but their compatibility has to be studied. The effects will be different per community, and the less aware one is in a community of the actual functioning of governance (broader than government, including informal institutions, understanding power relations.) the less predictable these effects of governance innovation becomes. In other words: the more a community believes in simple myths regarding the steering by government (or its irrelevance), regarding the universal power of laws (or their powerlessness), the more it will stay caught in these myths, and will not be able to anticipate the effects of new policies or new decision-making structures. Reflexivity, once more, is of the essence, for researchers, but all the more so for communities trying to figure out new paths. Understanding their current path and functioning is essential.

Let us try to get more in detail now, and see how we can understand institutional reform in a way that is more compatible with the thinking of evolving governance.

First of all, we can hark back to a few previous distinctions: policies, plans and laws, and formal/informal/dead institutions. With regard to the latter: political/legal reform per definition is a change in formal institutions. What is possible there, hinges on the configurations of governance (who will push this, accept this, who understands the implications?). What deserves special attention is the pattern of informal institutions, since, as we know, this also includes the rules governing the interpretation and implementation of formal rules. If there is a tradition to ignore all laws enacted by a previous government, and governments change every two years, any new law will have questionable effects, and probably many of the previous laws were made in full awareness of this situation, have a strategic nature that does not make them very applicable even when politics changes. If certain groups are marginalized in governance, and they are so beaten into submission that they don't even try anymore, and don't trust new initiatives coming from the governing coalition of actors, new laws probably won't work, and the same is true for new formal decision-making structures. Other sorts of initiatives might be needed, including education, sustained outreach activities, maybe even legal action against the current coalition.

The best forms of institutions to use cannot be decided upon too fast, for the same reasons as discussed above. In some communities, plans will work better, in others, policies, while elsewhere laws are the best tools to effectuate change. In most real-world communities, a combination of policies, plans and laws will be the way to go. Which types of plans to use for which topics and goals will again depend on the governance configurations. The different models of democracy discussed, and the different development approaches, all entail a different idea regarding the combination of policies, laws, plans. For liberal democratic market reformers, laws are enough. Other policies will be regarded as secondary, and plans as suspicious. In a sustainability/resilience perspective, there might be a tendency to rely on strong environmental laws plus highly comprehensive plans, where environmental expertise forms the backbone and the first ordering principle. In a livelihoods perspective, local planning plus national policies might be the way forward.

It should be noted that plans and laws are not necessarily opposed to each other (as often claimed in the more neo-liberal literature). It is useful to distinguish a few possible relations between laws and plans, useful when thinking of policy reform in a specific case. We can distinguish between law's roles in upholding, enabling and codifying plans. Laws can codify plans, in the sense that the plan, result of a policy integration effort in governance, can acquire the status of law itself, which can then increase the impact of the plan (but also its rigidity). Law can uphold plans, meaning that the right to make plans, plans of a certain type, plans including certain measures, can be defined and circumscribed by law. Some communities and countries have a maximalist planning tradition, meaning that there is an assumption that all can be planned, until there is protest, while others can be called minimalist (such as the USA), where the right to plan anything emerged precariously in a context of localism, legalism, and individualism. If individual property rights are seen as absolute, if government intervention is seen as suspicious and wasteful in general, and if intervention is understood only in legal terms, then doing planning will have to be carefully upheld by legislation, and the case for plans as embodying collective goods will be a tough one. Thirdly, laws can enable plans, as the fate of plans is partly determined by the legal tools for implementation. The implementation process cannot be reduced to the operation of enabling however; in the different steps of the process, the three functions, enabling, upholding and codifying are probably entwined.

The desirable mix of policies, plans, laws, will thus be defined by the *starting point*, the governance systems, but it should also be sensitive to the *destination*, the goals that are envisioned. Thinking of rural development, a development policy will likely produce a package of policies, plans, laws, representing a basket of collective goods. Policy and legal reform do not only envision economic growth, but also various other goals, some of which can be intermediate goals for economic development (e.g. more inclusive governance) but others can be goals in and by themselves. We come back to the perils of the neo-liberal formulas for the market, the good democracy, and the minimum rule of law. If we take this at face value, we do not only ignore how governance really works, how function systems co-evolve, but we also ignore the possibility to strive for and combine several public goods. In some cases, new institutions are needed, as in new rules, in other cases more drastic change might be required, a rethinking of the structure of the legal system, its role, and the process of governance. If we forget this possibility, we also forget the possibility to carefully design packages of policies, forms of policy integration, possibilities of synergies, and possibilities of long term improvement. Both the starting point, the governance situation, and the destination, the package of goals, need to inspire the search for an appropriate package, and a choice of policy forms which could work best.

Planning does not have to be understood as introducing rigidity, and neither does design. Planning can be more or less comprehensive, can envision short, middle and long term goals, can be more or less technocratic, and can be more or less embedded in governance. It is possible to rely on planning for a while (e.g. earlier in a development path, or in crisis, or when there is a strong belief in a necessary restructuring or missing infrastructure). Later, less integrated policies can take over. What seems trickier, as we mentioned before, is the reduction of plans to numeric targets, the problem being that the numbers tend to veil what is really happening and what is really possible, by drawing the attention to themselves, as opposed to the whole governance situation and community context. Planning requires a cultivated sensitivity to several contexts (see above), so it can become clear what is more and what less conducive to planning, which structures could be more stable, what can vary more easily, which policies can be more easily integrated in plans. Numbers can sometimes represent an integration of several goals, and a measure of the success of the integrated policies. In many cases, they do not say much, and can also actively cause trouble, by inspiring strategies to cheat (cook the books, dilute quality) and by eroding the actual productive assets (abused to get to the numbers quickly).

A very precise answer as to what can be planned and what not (where other policy tools should be used, and where government should be absent), cannot be answered without reference to the contexts of community and governance, the technical aspects of the issue, and the community ideology. We know that each of the models of democracy, and each development perspective brings its own preferences as to which policy mix and policy intensity is preferable. Now we would like to add that a keen understanding of governance, the contexts and issues, can help to take some distance from the reigning ideologies, to see whether maybe the ideology creates some of the issues, makes it more difficult to articulate development visions that are adapted and appropriate. Governance analysis does have a critical aspect therefore. Without prescribing which governance model, development perspective has to be taken, it can help communities to reflect, and this sometimes will create a distance with beliefs held.

The same precise answer has to be given regarding the absence of precise answers in goal setting, the substantive side of development policy. Nobody can tell a community, large or small, what is important to them, what they should strive for. However, it is possible, as analyst, as observer and as community member, to point out that some goals might be hard to get to, that striving for some goals can create serious problems, that some goals are harder to integrate, and that the governance forms existing and embraced, are more adapted to this set of goals than to another one. Outside observers and community actors therefore require a critical distance, in order to figure out the sort of policy package that might bring the envisioned future closer. One should be very cautious with prescriptions regarding goal setting and later assessment, as e.g. offered by many inspired by new public management, and rather emphasize the continuous conversation on goals, means and ends in governance. Maybe a plan produced something else than expected, but people love it; maybe a policy was highly inefficient in terms of achieving goal A, but it produced a variety of positive side effects which contributed to the transformation of the community. This, too, is adaptive governance.

If we bring up goals, collective goods, and institutional reform, we have to re-introduce the concept of good governance. While previous paragraphs discussed goals and their integration, good governance can be considered an overarching goal of institutional reform. Good governance, it was said, is largely depending on context, on governance paths, but one can also delineate a few properties independent of context. Good governance can be effective and efficient governance (achieving its goals, without wasting resources), it can be well informed governance (including the right kind of knowledge) and governance that is transparent and fair, that relies on, produces and enforces institutions which are just and maintain a just situation. These meta-principles can stand, even if their actual content will differ per case, per governance model and development perspective. What is just, will be seen differently, what is transparent can be discussed, which expertise, is certainly dependent on the path of governance and the dominant ideologies.


## Further reading

Benda-Beckmann, F. (1989). Scape goat and magic charm. law in development theory and practice. Journal of Legal Pluralism, 28, 129-48.

Beunen, R., Van Assche, K. and Duineveld, M. (2013). Performing failure in conservation policy. The implementation of European Union directives in the Netherlands. Land Use Policy, 31, 280-288.

Beunen, R., Van Assche, K. and Duineveld, M. (eds.). (2015). Evolutionary governance theory: theory & applications. Heidelberg, Germany: Springer.

Przeworski, A. (ed.). (2000). Democracy and development: political institutions and well-being in the world, 1950-1990 (Vol. 3). Cambridge, UK: Cambridge University Press.

Schetter, C. (ed.). (2013). Local politics in Afghanistan: a century of intervention in social order. New York, NY, USA: Columbia University Press.

Sen, A. (2006). What is the role of legal and judicial reform in the development process? The World Bank Legal Review, 2(1), 21-42.

Weingast, B.R. (1995). The economic role of political institutions: market-preserving federalism and economic development. Journal of Law, Economics, & Organization, 11(1), 1-31.


## 8.4 Institutional reform: transparency and opacity

'Good governance' is also understood as the absence of corruption. Good institutional structures and processes make corruption difficult. In a Machiavellian vein, we would argue that reflection, adaptation, discussion, scrutiny remain necessary. The structure itself will not prevent corruption forever. Corruption we cannot define as simply the breaking of rules going unpunished because of bribes, services, connections. Many rules are broken, ignored, selectively interpreted, and often connections, money, favors are involved. We can say that this is often not very helpful to achieve governance goals, but it cannot always be deemed problematic. In some cases what looks like corruption for one, is helpful or even necessary to keep governance going, to keep administration doing its work. Many cases of 'corruption' we would call informal institutions at work, in places where the formal institutions do not work very well. What we would call corruption are cases where institutions are undermined systematically for private or factional gain, with negative consequences for the reproduction of governance and the implementation through administration.

We come back to the concept of the formal/informal configuration of institutions, and link it with the concepts of *transparency* and *opacity*. Often, there has been an assumption that transparency is always good, and that informality is always bad, partly because it introduces opacity, partly because it deviates form the formal rules. We would argue that in the assessment of governance, and the contemplation of institutional reform, one should not look at the functioning of formal or informal institutions in isolation. Rather, one ought to assess the functioning of the combination of formal and informal rules, understanding that they are part of one and the same thing, that they are two co-evolving sides of the formal/informal configuration. What is informal, hinges on what emerged as formal, while what is formal, became that and has effects in a context of informality. Formal and informal are intricately linked, and function as a whole. Assessing an institutional configuration should mean assessing three issues.

Does the present configuration:
1. ... perform well, deliver goods, do what the community wants?
2. ... contribute to the stabilization of expectations in a differentiated society, maintain the value of specialization and separation of powers?
3. ... maintain real options to transform institutions without disrupting stability? Are there effective rules to change the rules?

After answering these questions (another approach to the good governance question), one can start to evaluate which path of institutional reform might make the most sense. Formality is per definition visible, while informality is not always invisible. The alternative rules might be known to few, might be perceived as risky, but one can also think of cases where all know how to bend the rule, which rules are routinely ignored, etc. Transparency and opacity are relative notions, with many shades. Pure visibility does not exist for informal institutions, and a full grasp of the formal/informal configuration is impossible. One can never be sure how rules will be used, ignored, broken, how will be chosen between alternatives. Power/knowledge configurations are always in motion, and never completely transparent. Informality cannot be avoided (governance cannot work by formal rules alone) and opacity cannot be avoided (actors in governance cannot be completely transparent to each other, and to the community at large). Because of partial opacity, formal and informal can coexist, and their interactions are not fully visible, so there will always be unpredictable effects in governance: new formal institutions will trigger new informal ones, or unexpected effects because of unforeseen interplay between formal and informal further down the line (in the implementation process). Unexpected effects can include new problems, steering issues, but also, as already illustrated, unexpected benefits, and possibilities for adaptation to changing internal and external environments.

Opacity might also be necessary for other reasons: leadership needs it. Leaders, in whatever form of governance (including highly participatory versions) cannot be completely open

Figure 8.2. Visioning session in Afghanistan. Conflicts put pressure on governance, and also the most sensitive participatory development exercise will not be neutrally perceived. Conflicts can reshuffle landscapes of actors and institutions, and alter existing actors, their allegiances, their sense of belonging and (ethnic, cultural, political) identity. 'The community' can never be taken for granted. Photo: Bernd Kuzmits. © ZEF/University of Bonn, Germany.

about their strategy. For Machiavelli, the reason for this is that the community is never consistent, and that, even if all agree, public desires are partly inconsistent. People want something, but not what it looks like in this case; they want something, but cannot accept what is needed to get there. The community also is rarely aware of the complexity of governance itself, the power relations there, the configurations to deal with, and is rarely aware of the necessities brought by the strategic situation (dealing with internal and external environments). For these reasons, because of the benefits of opacity and the risks of transparency, one cannot strive for exclusion of opacity, but only management of transparency & opacity in governance. This applies to the daily affairs, and it certainly applies to any attempt at transformation in governance, since institutional reform will always affect power/knowledge relations, create winners and losers.

Governance always starts from an understanding of 'the situation', an understanding partly produced within the governance system, partly by observations of the outside world. Situations can be defined as landscapes of necessity, risk and opportunity, requiring decisions which have to consider formal/informal configurations. Changing governance, institutional reform, has to consider the same configurations, in two ways:

assessing their effects on everyday decision-making, and assessing their resistance and response to reform attempts, to change. When thinking of institutional reform, one has to consider formal/informal configurations undesirable when they do not deliver the goods, when they undermine the stability and differentiation of society, or when they reduce transformation options and hence adaptive capacity. Opacity renders the mapping of the configuration harder. It can be considered harmful when it contributes to either of these problems. Certain forms of opacity in formal/informal configurations become harmful for communities first and foremost when transformation options are restricted.

If opacity is generally high, if there is no way for actors in governance to figure out which rules will apply when, whom to deal with, and what is actually happening, then the development and stabilization of new coordination mechanisms becomes very hard. Then institutional reform, as an attempt to reconfigure both formal and informal institutions, starting from context-sensitive formal changes, becomes very hard. If opacity is the delineated area of silence where negotiations can take place, or the delineated area where the formal rules stop, or can be adapted, or the assumption that self-organization in sub-games will take place, then it is still possible to maintain forms of productive competition, checks and balances and sites in governance to envision common goods.

It also possible however, that opacity creates too much *uncertainty* for actors to maintain certain interactions with others, and develop long term perspectives for themselves and the community in those interactions. Such form of opacity should be considered harmful for communities. In those situations, people often fall back on the family, on older social identities (clans, tribes), on short term perspectives, while hiding assets. Elites can reinforce their positions through this negative form of opacity, but in many cases one simply deals with coping strategies of much less fortunate people. These short term coping strategies, by elites and commoners alike, further increase the difficulties for democratic institutional reform, because silence about the past, present and desirable futures becomes useful and important for many. Silence becomes an asset.

If we assume that development visions, and thereby governance for development, require some form of policy integration, the question of opacity becomes more complicated. If we are not sure what the real effects of some formal institutions are (if the interplay with informality is opaque), how can we even start to think of policy integration, e.g. in planning? Comprehensive plans, comprehensive development visions, as plans, can indeed be comprehensively used and abused, as they have many effects that are unpredictable, many possible interactions between the supposedly integrated policies, and many effects on power/knowledge configurations. We would go so far as to recommend not planning until a sustained reflection can take place in governance on transparency and opacity in the formal/informal configuration. Without such a preparatory phase, policy integration is bound to be fictitious, and there is unlikely to be any insight at all into the development effects of the plan.

Institutional reform should always aim at *good governance*, whatever the perspective and substance chosen. We knew that the formulation of an appropriate version of good governance has to start from a profound knowledge of governance paths, the configurations present. We can add now that institutional reform has to pay special attention (special, since important and often ignored) to the assessment of the formal/informal configuration. What can be changed by means of institutional reform, and what ought to be changed, has to be inspired by such assessment. What should be improved, what can be improved, towards a new development path, revolves around the effects of that configuration. The most important aspect of the assessment is probably the question whether the ruling configuration impedes self-transformation. If this is the case, the problem is serious. Institutional reform, towards whatever desirable future, becomes very difficult then, and one can see the horizon opening towards authoritarian, unjust, violent and chaotic governance.

In the assessment of formal/informal configurations, towards institutional reform, the balance between transparency and opacity becomes relevant. Good governance cannot be understood as striving for complete transparency. Complete transparency is not the absence of corruption. It is practically and theoretically impossible and it would create serious obstacles for governance. Both opacity and transparency will always be present in governance; both have positive and negative effects. Governance has an aspect of managing opacity and transparency, managing what is seen, so that negative effects are minimized and positive effects are maximized. Good governance will continuously assess the formal/informal configuration in terms of the patterns and effects of transparency and opacity. This can inspire reform options, taking into account the problems of current configurations and its susceptibility for reform. What remains invisible in governance does so in the interplay of formal and informal rules. It has positive and negative effects on governance, but will need to be understood, made visible as far as possible, when discussing transformation options.

Even with all these precautions, even with good understanding of governance paths, contexts, and a nuanced idea of what good governance could be for a given community, and which package of institutions could chart the course, one cannot expect everything from institutional reform. There is no such thing as a perfect institutional framework, there are only frameworks which satisfy less or more what people want at a certain point in time and space, and frameworks that are more or less adapted to external environments. Even such good institutional configurations do not bring development in and by themselves. There is no perfect frame, and no frame works itself. People are needed, expertise, actions, resources, continuous dialogue in governance, assessment of policies, continuous public scrutiny, and an investment to make checks and balances do their work. Development, however conceived, requires action and reflection. Yet, ... institutional frames have effects, deserve close attention, and can be redesigned to a certain extent.

## Further reading

Aidt, T.S. (2009). Corruption, institutions, and economic development. Oxford Review of Economic Policy, 25(2), 271-291.

Bardhan, P. (1997). Corruption and development: a review of issues. Journal of economic literature, 1320-1346.

Casson, M.C., Della Giusta, M. and Kambhampati, U.S. (2010). Formal and informal institutions and development. World Development, 38(2), 137-141.

Helmke, G. and Levitsky, S. (eds.). (2006). Informal institutions and democracy: lessons from Latin America. Baltimore, MD, USA: Johns Hopkins University Press.

Kolstad, I. and Wiig, A. (2009). Is transparency the key to reducing corruption in resource-rich countries? World Development, 37(3), 521-532.

Theobald, R. (1990). Corruption, development and underdevelopment. Durham, NC, USA: Duke University Press.

Van Assche, K., Beunen, R. and Duineveld, M. (2014). Formal/informal dialectics and the self-transformation of spatial planning systems: an exploration. Administration & Society, 46(6), 654-683.

Van Assche, K., Shtaltovna, A. and Hornidge, A.-K. (2013). Visible and invisible informalities and institutional transformation. Lessons from transition countries: Georgia, Romania, Uzbekistan. In: Hayoz, N. and Giordano, C. (eds.) Informality in Eastern Europe. Frankfurt, Germany: Peter Lang, pp. 89-118.

Wang, H. and Rosenau, J.N. (2001). Transparency international and corruption as an issue of global governance. Global Governance, 7(1), 25-49.

## 8.5 Nested strategies and framing strategies

Institutional reform can take place at different levels. It can contain or frame other change processes. It can accommodate and combine with other development approaches.

As we know, almost all development approaches discussed, require some kind of institutional reform. The other perspectives are generally more substantive, have an idea regarding the direction of development that should be targeted. We also know that governance is almost always *multi-level* governance; what happens in a place is almost certainly tied to binding decisions taken at different levels or scales of governance. Scales or levels can be more or less tightly linked, meaning that they can ignore the other scales more or less easily, and governance can be more or less cohesive over scales, meaning that there is a perspective on governance that is visibly at work at the different scales; they can be clearly part of one design, and also share substantive foci, or not. The power can also be distributed in different manners, from very centralized to very localized, over some cases where regional governance is most important. The importance of each level can depend on the topic; some topics or domains of policy can be decentralized, while other topics remain or became under central control. The different distinctions we just made can be really observable, or they can exist more on paper. There can be a formal distribution of powers, and an informal one. Relations between levels can be amicable, cooperative, and it can be conflicting, full of tensions and elaborate negotiations. In other words, multi-level governance can be a harmonious family with parents, younger and older kids, and it can be a dysfunctional family, where all varieties of trauma can be found. As with families, levels of governance can divorce, and sometimes they get rid of each other. Divorce can be peaceful, or rather horrible.

These different relations between the levels of governance have implications for the possibilities of institutional reform and for the possible coexistence of different development strategies at different levels, or at the same level in different communities. We already talked briefly about *nested governance*, and here we can add that nested development approaches are possible, institutional reform usually being one of them. The most obvious case is national level macro reform, political, legal or economic, and other approaches existing at smaller scales. If these smaller units don't like the national level too much, they might tend to ignore the signals coming from there, and develop different initiatives.

What is nested might be similar or dissimilar development approaches. Dissimilar development approaches are more likely to clash, but they can also offer alternative paths, coexisting, each with the possibility of being tried and tested. Similar nesting can mean institutional reform in institutional reform, institutional reform maybe aiming in the same direction. Dissimilar nesting can refer to project approaches within institutional reform, or institutional reform and at lower levels sustainability, or livelihoods, or innovation work. The more autonomy different levels have, the more likely to find nested and dissimilar approaches to rural development.

We would like to distinguish nesting and *framing* as mechanisms relating different levels and approaches. One approach frames another one if one becomes the precondition of the other one, giving direction. Framing can be spatial, temporal and conceptual. One spatial scale can force another one to accept some of its points and premises. Or, a first step in a policy procedure can be obliged to take one approach, after which some more diversity can develop. Conceptual framing can refer to a mandatory starting point in the reasoning, after which diversity can develop. Nesting will entail stronger framing if the levels are more integrated; in more autonomous relations between levels, the framing will tend to be subtler, and will less likely extend to all three aspects of framing.

These new distinctions relating to multi-level governance are pertinent for the student of institutional reform. Whatever reform strategy is opted for, it will be more closely linked to one level than to others. Usually, it is considered from the point of view of one level. In communitarian governance, often in livelihoods approaches, this can be the local level, while e.g. in liberal democratic reform in the modernist tradition, the national level will be the main place to tinker with institutions. Considering the other levels becomes important then, the degree of coupling and autonomy, the friction. This holds true when there is the expectation of national policies working through the different levels, but it is also highly recommended when devising local reforms, where other levels can sometimes easily undo the result of painstaking reform work, e.g. in participatory fashion.

## Further reading

Beunen, R., Van Assche, K. and Duineveld, M. (eds.) (2015). Evolutionary governance theory: theory & applications. Heidelberg, Germany: Springer.

Global Water Partnership Technical Advisory Committee (2000). Integrated water resources management. Stockholm, Sweden: Global Water Partnership.

Hajer, M.A. and Wagenaar, H. (eds.) (2003). Deliberative policy analysis: understanding governance in the network society. Cambridge, UK: Cambridge University Press.

Rogers, P. and Hall, A.W. (2003). Effective water governance. Stockholm, Sweden: Global Water Partnership.

Van Assche, K. and Djanibekov, N. (2012). Spatial planning as policy integration: the need for an evolutionary perspective. Lessons from Uzbekistan. Land Use Policy, 29(1), 179-186.

## 8.6 Institutional reform and knowledge and expertise

Institutional reform is reform of governance: it is working on institutions, therefore on actor/institution configurations, and, because of co-evolution, on power/knowledge configurations. Everything what was said about governance evolutions in earlier chapters, can and will occur if we look at the whole landscape of institutional reform options. Institutional reform changes informal institutions, affects the map of and relations between actors. It will affect power relations and the presence/absence and impact or non impact of knowledge in governance. It will influence the relevance and weight of different sorts of knowledge in policy-making and the resulting policy, and in the case of plans, it will decide on the formula of knowledge integration (on the back of policy integration). In some cases, institutional reform can alter the first ordering principle of planning, and the *first ordering structure*.

Institutional reform is reform of governance: it will be shaped by and reshape the pattern of dependencies in the governance path. This, in turn, will redefine the position of different types of knowledge. If a plan is successful, the next plan is more likely to be successful since actors are used to coordination using this institution, and the forms of knowledge and knowledge integration marking the first plan will be more likely accepted. A goal dependency has been redefined, and this structured knowledge in governance differently. If economic actors were routinely given more access to governance, and reform restricts that access, the influence of economic expertise on policy is likely to decrease. A path dependence has been altered. If politicians were dependent on scientists to legitimize their policies and on economic actors to fund their campaigns, and institutional reform changes this, then scientific knowledge might become less important in policy but also more independent of policy (and maybe more innovative). An interdependence was changed, and consequently the role of a kind of knowledge.

These principles remain true for all kinds of institutional reform. Both the procedure and the substance will change however depending on the governance system and development approach. Some development approaches will push directly for a kind of knowledge to be inserted in governance through reform, others will push for a certain reform, which creates new spaces for certain kinds of knowledge (sustainability approaches an example of the first, direct relation, livelihoods approaches more an example of the second, indirect relation).

One way institutional reform can have a longer lasting effect on the role of knowledge in governance, and on the power/knowledge configurations, is by changing the *knowledge infrastructure*. We understand this to be the conditions that make the creation, survival

Figure 8.3. Signage in an ice fishing village on Lake Mille Lacs, Minnesota, USA. These villages on frozen lakes can be miles from shore, and show complex forms of organization which rely purely on informal institutions. Attempts to formalize, to use modest institutional reform have been dodged locally by the main actors to emerge in their history, the owners of fishing resorts. Photo: Kristof Van Assche. © ZEF/University of Bonn, Germany.

and distribution of a sort of knowledge possible. Depending on the type of knowledge, the infrastructure will be different. Survival of local knowledge, for example, might be predicated only on the existence of a social group and the persistence of storytelling in that group. In contrast, for some sorts of scientific expertise, e.g. in agriculture, knowledge infrastructure can include field stations, libraries, schools, universities, research institutes, etc. Minimizing the role of a particular expertise in governance does not necessarily undermine the knowledge infrastructure, if there are reasons to keep it intact, e.g. to make money, or to raise professionals. But if it is the case that expertise persisted only because of a privileged position in governance, then a marginalization in governance can erase the knowledge infrastructure, and a return of the expertise will be less likely – at least a return as such. There may be good reasons to abandon expertise, but we would argue that the reasoning needs to be very solid, as lost expertise, even it does not appear useful at a given time, can later play a role in the ongoing adaptation of evolving governance.

We would argue that the *reflexivity* we spoke of earlier, as a sustained reflection with all actors in governance, can prove useful here as well: reflecting on the knowledge effects of institutional reform can help to delineate more carefully which knowledge might be missing to have to reform achieve its goals. It can help to understand better which valuable knowledge might be marginalized or forgotten in the institutional reorganization, with risks for other public goods, or risks in the longer run. And it might help to understand the effects on power relations between actors, and thus between their forms of knowledge.

Along with James C. Scott and William Easterly, we would like to warn for institutional reforms that are either ignorant of their knowledge assumptions and effects or assume they can have a complete overview of all these effects, and think they can steer them. ongoing observation, conversation, and looking for a balance between total steering of knowledge (and society) and total individual freedom (and no knowledge used for collective goals) seems commendable. For virtually all of the development approaches presented this remains possible, and the case-specific combination of perspectives, can also serve this purpose of finding a unique middle ground for each community and each governance path. A related warning (wag the finger) concerns technocratic perspectives, in which useful expertise is expected to be defined by the experts in science and administration themselves, independent of politics, law, economy. Technocrats tend to define expert solutions without participation, without citizens asking. If institutional reform is allowed to emanate from technocrats, then it is de-politicized. If reform for development is shaped by technocrats, the future of a community will be shaped with no input from the community itself. Both politically and scientifically this is problematic: the desires of the community are not translated into policy and scientists project pseudo-objective ideas as absolute and absolutely useful truths. De-politicization in development policies undermine the self-transformation and adaptation of communities. It will likely hit the wall of reality at some point, because it does not take into account the working of the other functional domains, and because it ignores the governance paths it emerged in. The results can then either be that there is little effect, given little compatibility with the actual governance path, or an effect that is highly conservative, the result of silent assumptions present in the governance configuration and in the pseudo-science.

## Further reading

Andrews, M. (2013). The limits of institutional reform in development: changing rules for realistic solutions. Cambridge, UK: Cambridge University Press.

Buntaine, M.T., Buch, B.P. and Parks, B.C. (2013). Why the 'results agenda' produces few results: an evaluation of the longrun institutional development impacts of World Bank environmental projects. Vasa, 1-38.

Easterly, W. (2013). The tyranny of experts. Economists, dictators and the forgotten rights of the poor. New York, NY, USA: Basic Books.

Hornidge, A.-K. (2007). Re-inventing society: state concepts of knowledge in Germany and Singapore. Sojourn. Journal of Social Issues in Southeast Asia, 22(2), 202-29.

Pierson, P. (2000). The limits of design: explaining institutional origins and change. Governance, 13(4), 475-499.

Rivera, W.M., Qamar, M.K. and Van Crowder, L. (2002). Agricultural and rural extension worldwide: options for institutional reform in the developing countries.

Swatuk, L.A. (2005). Political challenges to implementing IWRM in Southern Africa. Physics and Chemistry of the Earth, 30(11), 872-880.

# 9. Rural development: environmental and resource governance

## Abstract

In this chapter, we focus on environmental policy and natural resource governance as routes to rural development. We single out these forms of policy because they represent important currents in the literature and are associated with several disciplines oriented toward implementation and real-world influence: ecology, forestry, hydrology, geography, environmental science more broadly. Despite being a relatively narrow policy and science domain, these fields have produced influential rural development schemes and perspectives, which we treat here as one rural development model.

## 9.1 Resources as assets

A key element of this approach to rural development is that development is thought to revolve around environmental quality and environmental assets (natural resources). The path taken can go in very different directions:
- some perspectives focus on the resources, their maximum exploitation;
- others on the sustainable use and development of resources; and
- yet others mostly on sustainability or environmental quality itself.

In all versions, governance is then expected to be organized around the resources and environmental qualities. In most versions of the exploitation narratives, and the sustainability narrative, expert knowledge dominates. In the case of exploitation engineering, geology, hydrology, forestry, in the case of sustainability goals ecology, environmental science more broadly. The sustainable development version can have a mix of these forms of expertise and can be more open to local knowledge too, through more participatory governance, or through the study and later inclusion of local knowledge. Rising policy themes and narratives as sustainability, resilience, climate change have contributed to the prominence of environmental science in development policy and practice.

The link between environment and development is made in positive and negative ways: a good environmental quality and resource governance can contribute to development directly, and it can indirectly stimulate it by taking obstacles away. Poor environmental quality can harm community health, safety and well-being, poor resource governance can cause political instability, inequality, can undermine incentives to act, and the functioning of the legal and political system as such.

## 9.2 Rural development by maximum resource exploitation

The countryside for environmental & resource governance perspectives is not essentially an agricultural area. It is also not an area with diverse uses. It is just an area where resources are located. Governance is control over resources. If the land is owned by the federal or national government, the lobby will be with that level of government to allow for exploitation or to privatize the land. If the land is owned by lower level governments, the lobby will be easier probably. If the land is owned by many, then the way property rights are organized will influence what is possible – are mineral rights part of the title, or do they belong to government who can sell them to other parties? Ownership of land and resources are not always coupled, but even when this is the case, there is usually the issue of access to the resources (over land owned by others). The willingness to sell land and/or mineral rights, if in private hands, will make a big difference for exploitation,

**Example 9.1. Foraging and sustainability.**

Foraging is finding food in the wild. Which is of course not very special when you are a member of an Amazonian tribe, but it is special when one is used to frozen meals and restaurants. Foraging as a movement is essentially North American, one of the responses against the dominance of industrial scale food production and processing. Arguments pro can be that wild foods are healthier, cheaper, tastier, and that the activity of foraging brings one closer to nature, and engenders a deeper awareness of the provenance of our foods, the issues with existing food options, and the possibility of alternatives, of social-economic change. Some focus on the search for medicinal plants, rendering foraging a part of alternative medicine.

Urban foraging is looking for wild foods in cities, which can be fun, but which also begs the question what 'wild' is in North America. New York City's parks department often complains about foragers taking things they just planted. Foragers in the Pacific Northwest are testing the limits of park wardens, but also of property owners. Another possible critique is that this protest against unsustainable agriculture is not necessarily very sustainable itself, for the simple reason of potential over-harvesting. (Especially when there is a market pressure, e.g. from restaurants looking to source truly wild ingredients.) The health benefits can also quickly disappear when risks are not recognized, and, more elementary, when the right species is not recognized.

Foraging thus places heavy demands on expertise: where to go, when, what to pick, how, what to leave (for regeneration), but also, after collection, how to process and preserve. The appeal of the wild, in a romantic, Thoreau-style of individual exploration, can best be tempered therefore in a social circle. Some form of organization seems commendable, so social learning can be fostered, knowledge can be shared, and some form of coordination can be initiated, to reduce risk and avoid over-harvesting. In some places, this is happening already.

**Further reading**

Lerner, R. (2013). Dandelion hunter: foraging the urban wilderness. Portland, OR, USA: National Book Network.

but this willingness reflects often a general attitude towards development and resources. We come back to this.

In this version of the perspective, what will drive development is in the first place the exploitation of resources, be it mining, forestry, oil or other things. If the community is sympathetic to this, either because of poverty or because of held beliefs and values, then it will be easier for companies to come in and start restructuring the local economy. If that economy is weak, if the community is small, if it is divided, then the impact of the resource actors will be strong. We can expect to see then a simplification of land use,

### Example 9.2. Certification as private governance?

One of the obstacles towards more sustainable production of anything is that consumers often cannot tell the difference between what is produced sustainably and what not. This, in turn, is tied to the more elementary lack of information regarding the provenance of many things. Sometimes, as with fish, even the identity is unclear: about half of the fish in American supermarkets appears to be mis-labeled. And customers do not notice. If consumers do not know what they eat, where it comes from and how it is produced or harvested, and they do not care, then there will be little economic and political incentive for sustainable production. Another obstacle is that producers, when not explicitly forced by law, have little reason to make their own life difficult and aim at sustainability, thus restricting themselves in many ways. Certification tries to address both problems: it offers the consumer more clarity regarding the product, and a less guilty conscience, and it offers the producer a way to distinguish himself, and a reason to ask and explain higher prices. If wild caught North Sea sole is actually wild caught North Sea sole – and not farmed Chinese flounder, that might be a reason to pay a bit more. And it might help to establish and protect brand value for producers.

It is never simple. With the distrust by environmentally aware customers in both producers and governments (perceived to be in league, too friendly to each other, or at least uninformed), the idea of third party certification gained traction in the 1990's. It was thought that independent organizations (NGOs) could more easily establish criteria for sustainable production and monitor their implementation. The resulting certificate was then thought to communicate clearly, more clearly than the simple assertion by producers, and more than the price or presentation, a measure of respect for planet and people. Yet the non-governmental nature of third party certifiers attracted controversy, with the certifying organizations being blamed for being more than one (competing certifications came into existence), for being not government (and imposing uniform rules), for adhering to one version of sustainability (not another one), for allegedly pursuing their own interests. Other critics focused on the potentially undermining effects of third party certification for democratic and equitable governance: it can be interpreted as private governance becoming entrenched and blocking a path towards inclusive, local decision-making on sustainability and economic development. In this critique, certifying NGOs are not much different from businesses, as they are not subjected to political checks and balances. Industries themselves, meanwhile, came up with their own certification methods, some more sincere than others.

The certifying NGOs also encountered problems in tracking and checking, and unfortunately, some of the products most in need of some sort of certification proved hardest to certify. In forestry, the FSC (Forest Stewardship Council) proved quite effective in monitoring and certifying softwood production, and the derived pulp and particle products (paper, particle board, etc.). In a Scandinavian country, what is called chain of custody certification is realistic: one can follow with relative ease the path from pine tree to paper. Yet tropical hardwoods, including many threatened species, are almost impossible to certify, because very few plantations exist, and logging operations in the forest are scattered over huge areas, with ownership of land often entirely unclear.

In addition, one has to mention that, even with best intentions, becoming certified might be a daunting task for many producers, especially in poorer countries, where preparing the certification process might be nigh impossible (preparing documents, studies, bringing in people, using the right machines, etc.). Following all the rules of operation, but also the application process itself (auditing), can be forbidding. This triggered a critique that the poorest and most poorly governed countries, where hit and run strategies and unsustainable management are rampant, have the greatest difficulties in integrating into a certification economy, offering a possibly sustainable path to economic development. Those blessed with global connections, expertise, resources, can more easily benefit. Large businesses can more easily move towards certification than small producers.

One could argue that certification by itself is not enough in poor conditions, and that capacity building, infrastructure development, and investment aid are necessary to prevent that certification systems increase inequality. In our terms, one can say that a livelihoods perspective might be useful. One can further argue that certification requires so much from governance as such that it makes most sense as part of a concerted effort towards improving governance (we touched briefly on the intersections with land tenure, education, infrastructure development). If more of the poorest are to benefit, alternative forms of organization have to be envisioned, and some of the certification programs more sensitive to the social aspects of sustainability (e.g. Fair Trade), encourage formation of cooperative and extension structures.

Because of the diversity of certifications, umbrella programs emerged, which recognized certain existing standards, and included them under their label. In forestry, the afore mentioned FSC and the PEFC are the main umbrella programs. PEFC, e.g. recognizes three North American certification standards, while FSC includes five. Rainforest Alliance certifies many different products.

### Further reading

Old, G. (2014). Constructing private governance: the rise and evolution of forest, coffee and fisheries certification. New Haven, CT, USA: Yale University Press.

with resource extraction, derived businesses, waste of the industry, services for workers there, will tend to dominate the landscape. In the short term, this will not look like a simplification, since the spatial structure will likely become more scattered. It will stop following the logic of previous land uses, policies and their integration, but will start following the logic of resource extraction. We can say that the technicalities and commercial needs of the extraction companies will produce the *first ordering principle* of space, with all other things finding a place in the cracks, in the gaps, or not finding a place. The resulting space is ordered, and there is a form of policy integration, but not in the literal sense; rather, what produces unity is the logic of the industry, and the coordination within the larger extraction companies and between those companies and associated businesses (subcontractors, service providers, developers, etc.). Policy integration takes place outside community governance, without plans in most cases, and relying on interactions between a small set of economic actors.

What has been described is not a law of nature. It does not necessarily or automatically take place. Governance paths can never be entirely predicted, and some starting points are not so susceptible for the scenario we outlined just above. Yet, there is a high degree of likelihood that some of these things will occur, because of positive feedback loops in governance. In terms of the governance paths, we can say that new actors with resources, with powerful connections already, will be able to make new connections at the local level easily, so they themselves can become an actor in local governance. Once they are an actor, the resources and the relations will combine into a stronger and stronger position, and a stronger influence on the forms of expertise that play a role in governance, and in the new institutions. Over time the new resource actors can shape both power/knowledge and actor/institution configurations. They can help to introduce new actors in their network to local governance, they can marginalize others, and can acquire an influence on rule-making that more firmly embeds their perspective and their expertise in local governance. Policies will become more and more friendly, and the development perspective becomes more and more one of resource development.

More and more locals will become dependent on the industry network; some will leave, and newcomers will tend to be closer to the network. Both, participation and representation support now the industry perspective dominance. This further reinforces the governance configurations in a certain position, and makes it less likely that different expertise is allowed to make a difference in governance. Schools can become influenced by the perspective of these actors; vocational education will become focused on the industries, and carry its ideology and development vision. As a consequence, vocational education will become more attractive compared to more intellectual pursuits with the best jobs being industry jobs. If this goes on for a while, questioning the industry driven development narrative becomes tough. Because of the governance configurations, but also because the perspective will become naturalized. It can be shared and embedded in the community to such an extent that this becomes reality. It is forgotten that this

Figure 9.1. Abandoned farm in Alberta, Canada. Most communities in the Canadian west disappeared after a generation. People tried, it didn't work, or for a while, because of draught, infertile soil, cold, better opportunities in mining, oil, trade, in the cities. And they moved on. Rather than altogether condemning this, one can explore how such dynamics can refine our ideas of sustainability. Photo: Monica Gruzmacher. © ZEF/University of Bonn, Germany.

reality has been created, is contingent on a governance path, and can still be remade. The way people see their roles, and the way they look at the map of possible roles, fits into the narratives of development that are naturalized in this manner. Leaving becomes the only alternative, until the economic cycle brings us to the next bust.

As long as the boom phase lasts, the performance of success, the emphasizing how good this is, adds another layer of resistance to possible questioning (and adaptation) of the governance path. The economic success is ascribed to the current governance configuration ('We are doing well') and there is no consideration of alternative governance configurations that could also exploit resources but do it differently, e.g. by reinvesting more in collective goods, by planning more, configurations that could combine exploitation with other land uses and economic activities in a long term vision. Usually, these things are not considered when resource industries take over local (and regional) governance. Planning is seen as government interference, as obstacles to development, and policy integration is not considered necessary. What slowly develops, is a one industry community and a governance situation completely *symbiotic* with the industry. It also institutionalizes further short term perspectives. This might work well for a while if the community strongly supports the industry. But, because of the *feed-back loops* described in the governance path, it creates a configuration that is highly rigid. Adaptation to changing environments becomes harder and harder. This takes place in the *boom* phase of industry. After a crash, reinvention on a different basis is harder, since actors, institutions, power, knowledge are stuck in a situation where they lost the tools to understand alternative futures and tools to get there.

After a crash, resource towns that follow this scenario are therefore likely in trouble. People stay and become impoverished. Or they leave and the place becomes a ghost town. Quite peculiar, we think, is that even after a series of crippling crashes, social memory often sticks with the discourses produced in the boom period. Development is often understood as going back to the boom days of rapid resource exploitation. Bring back the mine! Few seem to question the governance path taken in those years, and the effects on adaptive capacity, on resilience. This observation has consequences for governance after busts. It represents a limit to radical participation and a limit to local autonomy. New development visions will likely be unrealistic and problematic if they are only local products, after such a governance path and traumatic history. Multi-level governance in those cases is highly desirable, and at the local level, a package of measures that can slowly introduce different perspectives, increase adaptive capacity and cultivate reflexivity.

## Further reading

Grimble, R. and Wellard, K. (1997). Stakeholder methodologies in natural resource management: a review of principles, contexts, experiences and opportunities. Agricultural Systems, 55(2), 173-193.

Holling, C.S. and Meffe, G.K. (1996). Command and control and the pathology of natural resource management. Conservation Biology, 10(2), 328-337.

Sterner, T. and Coria, J. (2013). Policy instruments for environmental and natural resource management. Abingdon, UK: Routledge.

## 9.3 Rural development by focusing on environmental quality

This perspective on rural development is a rarity. When it occurs, it is often focusing on a negative link between environmental quality and development: the environmental quality is so low, the problems so severe, that development options are very restricted. The nature of the problems can inspire different combinations of policies to fix them. And different combinations of expertise. Deforestation calls for forestry, geology, hydrology, engineering. Water pollution calls for toxicology, hydrology, ecology. And so forth.

The situation described just before, a resource or industry community which landed after a bust, with various side effects of the industry that created an unhealthy, unattractive, dysfunctional landscape, can be a typical case where it sometimes does appear. One can

---

**Example 9.3. Bulb nature and the productive nature of conflict.**

In the Dutch so-called 'Bulb Region', the area north of the Hague, close to the North Sea, the national government was thinking about a new city in the 1990's, in an as yet rural area. The local municipalities did not agree, and neither did the tourism business, nor the flower growers. This is the area of the famous Dutch tulip fields, and that fame was used in the resistance against the proposed city, quickly dubbed 'Bulb City'. A local flower auctioneer showed himself a brilliant networker and organizer, and a regional alliance against the city was formed, under his lead. The alliance included governmental and non-governmental organizations, and in the years of resistance, the tulips became the core of two new discursive objects, mobilized in the governance conflicts: bulb nature and bulb heritage.

Studies were carried out, showing a specific combination of birds liked the flower fields, and these were presented as 'bulb birds'. More studies then showed these bulb birds were not doing well, as was bulb nature in general; good reasons not to build the city. The tulips and other flowers were simultaneously highlighted as central to the local/regional identity, as heritage, and events, publications and studies followed revolving around this heritage under threat. The province, i.e. regional government, first didn't take sides, later reverted to the side of the new regional alliance, who was de facto becoming more important in regional governance. The pact signed between partners in the alliance was translated into formal policy documents at the local, municipal, level. In the end, the national government withdrew, and the plans for Bulb City were shelved. One can debate the merit of the idea of Bulb City, but one can say, we believe, that the conflict was productive in several ways: it reinvigorated regional governance and checks and balances, it created the new discursive objects of bulb nature and heritage, and it inspired a set of new policies aiming to grasp, protect, and carefully manage natural and cultural assets. More people became more aware of what was valuable in the area, even if those values were partly produced in the governance process. New policies were less likely to assume a blank slate and simply obeying local governments and citizens. Some landscape objects and structures were protected as heritage or nature, and new nature has been created. Existing actors created a new actor (the coalition), new institutions, new knowledge, and were able to shift power/knowledge configurations.

**Further reading**

Duineveld, M. and Van Assche, K. (2011). The power of tulips. Constructing nature and heritage in a contested landscape. Journal of Environmental Policy & Planning, 13(2), 79-98.

---

**Example 9.4. Mining and land use conflicts: knowledge and power.**

Mining takes place usually in more rural and natural areas, because it needs a lot of space, since it causes a variety of problems in more densely populated areas, and simply because it follows the minerals and ores. Also in rural areas, there are classic issues. Farming, fishing, hunting can be made difficult, because of the site itself but also because the activities interrupt networks and flows. Movement of people and animals can be restricted, people might have to resettle. In general, and especially when there is a strong presence of indigenous people, problems arise with changing place identity and (the perception of) disrespect of traditions. Often national governments prefer to work with large international mining companies, because they seem easier to regulate, to tax, to work with, and because they reliably promise quick employment gains and export revenues. This tendency does pose problems, for fair competition, for local and regional governance.

Mining can bring a variety of benefits to communities, especially when there is local investment and employment, but issues always remain. When larger mining companies come in, usually in consultation with national governments, issues of local governance arise, of self-determination, including property rights and access to resources. Existing economies can be disrupted and lose viability, even when otherwise sustainable. Cultural rights, local knowledge, traditional practices, can be lost or rendered difficult to maintain. Communal lands, communal access to other lands, various informal property rights, lose value in the face of hardening property lines and disputes involving governments and companies relying on formal institutions.

Conflict mitigation strategies exist, and many revolve around communication: showing mines to locals, and explaining them how the environment and their traditions are respected as much as possible, surveys regarding community values, needs and desires, partnerships between companies and local schools, providing capacity building benefits for the community but also an additional channel of communication (not by indoctrination but by explanation and discussion, not only in classrooms but also at school board meetings, community events at the school, parent-teachers association). Liaison groups can be formed, to channel

speak of a clean-up phase, where the negative effects of previous governance paths have to be undone by a focus on solving environmental problems. For a while, higher degrees of policy integration and planning can be observed, and new expertise enters governance. Usually, higher level actors take over more power in the community (or, more rarely, a dramatic political swing at the local level). Usually, there is local resistance and nostalgia for the boom days. When it happens, it is usually in social-democratic communities, or in social democratic phases (e.g. the USA during depression). If new people come in, and the clean up does create new assets and benefits, and opens the minds for alternative feedback in two directions. Public meetings can be organized, including representatives of the local community, government and companies.

These strategies can all be helpful, but 'communication' can not resolve all problems, when power differentials are the heart of the matter. Often, local communities cannot exert an influence on large corporations in league with national governments. Or, on corporations simply left alone by government. A functioning multi-level governance, and some form of participatory decision-making on mining operations seems necessary. If this proves impossible, then at least one ought to consider compensation programs for local communities (in which participation is also recommendable).

Gavin Hilson proposes that such compensation programs consist of at least the following elements: (1) a thorough research report showing community groups in details the company's compensation procedures, relevant stakeholders, and, if applicable strategy and details of community relocation; (2) direct compensation to individuals for any natural and economic resources impacted by mining; (3) in the event of relocation, provision for housing, wells, medical facilities and roads; (4) direct funding for re-skilling and employment programs; (5) issuance of a mandate to hire locally, and a commitment to training. One can add many things and devise many versions – including contributions to pension funds, utilization of local services, cultural life, scholarships to universities, partnerships with local small scale miners and subcontractors.

We would add that mining companies either ignoring local governance or taking it over, reduces in the longer run the resilience of the local communities. Further, that local communities cannot be left to their own devices when dealing with mining corporations. Thirdly, that national involvement cannot be restricted to issuing new laws and regulation, but has to include monitoring, and active participation in local/regional governance and planning.

### Further reading

Hilson, G. (2002). An overview of land use conflict in mining communities. Land Use Policy, 19, 65-73.

narratives of the future, then a swing back to more de-centralization does not mean a return to the old rigid governance configurations.

To our knowledge, maintaining such a development focus on environmental qualities is difficult. Except for cases where there is a special coalition, or a special consensus on environmental quality and its value. One can imagine a small community of retirees in a beautiful landscape they want to preserve, a cohesive town of environmental enthusiasts in the green margin of a large country that is not so environmentally friendly, an area with small villages that is continuing agriculture but surviving on tourism, and realizing that they are dependent on a high quality landscape.

## Further reading

Beer, A. and Higgins, C. (2004). Environmental planning for site development: a manual for sustainable local planning and design. London, UK: Routledge.

Laurian, L. (2004). Public participation in environmental decision making: Findings from communities facing toxic waste cleanup. Journal of the American Planning Association, 70(1), 53-65.

McLaughlin, P. and Dietz, T. (2008). Structure, agency and environment: toward an integrated perspective on vulnerability. Global Environmental Change, 18(1), 99-111.

Meyer, P.B. and Lyons, T.S. (2000). Lessons from private sector brownfield redevelopers: Planning public support for urban regeneration. Journal of the American Planning Association, 66(1), 46-57.

Morton, J.F. (2007). The impact of climate change on smallholder and subsistence agriculture. Proceedings of the Natural Academy of Sciences of the USA, 104(50), 19680-19685.

Scholtes, F. and Hornidge, A.-K. (2009). Warten bis das Wasser kommt – Armutsbekämpfung in Zeiten des Klimawandels. Bonn, Germany: Care Deutschland-Luxemburg e.V. and the Center for Development Research (ZEF).

Selin, S. and Chevez, D. (1995). Developing a collaborative model for environmental planning and management. Environmental Management, 19(2), 189-195.

Simonds, J.O. and Starke, B.W. (2006). Landscape architecture: a manual of land planning and design. New York, NY, USA: McGraw-Hill.

## 9.4. Rural development as sustainable development

A third version of this perspective tries to avoid cleaning up later, by preserving assets, qualities, in the environment, and by organizing the industry and its impact in such a way that damage can be minimized and a post-extraction future remains possible. Sustainability in this perspective will emphasize environmental sustainability. We would add that aiming at social and economic sustainability too is necessary for the environmental goals (the meaning of the 'sustainable development' slogan). Poor people, people in unstable communities or in violent situations, and people with few options will not care so much about environmental goals in and of themselves. If environmental qualities and wise resource use are part of a vision and narrative of the future that is persuasive, that creates more options for more people, then sustainable development can be a reality.

Using resources while protecting environmental qualities is more than a balancing of these two things, as we know by now. It requires tinkering with governance, maintaining and aiming at a more diverse economy, maintaining and creating a diversity of expertise

Figure 9.2. Rural pollution. Algae in an eutrophied lake in Alberta, Canada, surrounded by agricultural land. A rural development strategy revolving around environmental policy can start from existing assets but also from existing problems which need to be addressed. Usually this happens only when other assets are undermined, when other profitable activities are jeopardized and when simply moving and restarting elsewhere is not an option. Photo: Monica Gruzmacher. © ZEF/University of Bonn, Germany.

and an openness to local knowledge, supporting media and a broadly conceived education, keeping an eye on checks and balances and, a product of all these efforts, maintaining and enhancing the flexibility of governance. A variety of perspectives on the present situation, including the role and impact of industry actors, ought to be present around the table, and a variety of development visions ought to be part of the conversation. As we noticed in the previous sections, once a particular governance system is established, it is difficult to reverse it or change completely. Once expertise is forgotten, especially when the actors promoting it are gone (even if it survives tenuously in administration), it is difficult to nurture it again. Once rules are in place that are compatible with only one form of economy or land use, bringing back diversity is tougher. If we can avoid naturalization of and domination by one perspective and one type of expertise; and if we can organize governance as the continuous confrontation and deliberation of alternative visions and expertise; then resilience will be enhanced.

If ecological and social sustainability forms the focus of the adopted development perspective, we would therefore recommend cultivating difference and maintaining diversity, even at an initial cost. A long term perspective is needed, since we already know that the resource future is limited. Policy integration and planning will be necessary, since in the resource exploitation era, several activities and land uses will have to coexist. Planning as design can be recommended. The costs of sustainable development are real, but they are the costs of a more resilient community and of a likely better future, a smaller chance of turning into a ghost town or deserted area. Coming very close to the cleavages between the models of democracy discussed, to traditional ideological cleavages, this cost requires *redistribution*. Either resource income or income more broadly can be redistributed. The different governance models each espouse different ideas on redistribution, with liberal democracy being the most negative and socialism the most positive.

Redistribution also hinges on the form of property rights in place, and this again links back to a certain relationship between the functional domains of law, politics, etc., or, in other words, to a governance model and a governance path. If companies can do whatever they want with resources, taxing them later will be harder; if property rights are modified and shaped more clearly by policies and plans, then it can be easier to work together with companies on sustainable development visions (whereby also their expertise can be harnessed) and it can be easier to tax them (and possibly the community) in order to generate revenues to be cautious, for remedial measures, and to support activities that represent alternative development paths, or elements of a mix that can lead to a more sustainable future. Agriculture can be supported, as can education, natural and cultural heritage policies, and start-ups. One can think of a

Figure 9.3. Fruit trees on a former coffee plantation in western Colombia. Photo: Monica Gruzmacher. © ZEF/ University of Bonn, Germany.

Rural development

combination with innovation policies. Redistribution can also take place by supporting ongoing participatory planning exercises, bringing in expertise for that, for community design. Another element can be the simple virtue of saving, for reinvestment later, to meet unknown needs carry out future solutions to sustainability.

## Further reading

Berkes, F., Folke, C. and Colding, J. (eds.). (2000). Linking social and ecological systems: management practices and social mechanisms for building resilience. Cambridge, UK: Cambridge University Press.

Berkes, F. (1989). Common property resources: ecology and community-based sustainable development. Princeton, NJ, USA: Belhaven Press.

Campbell, L.M. and Vainio-Mattila, A. (2003). Participatory development and community-based conservation: opportunities missed for lessons learned? Human Ecology, 31(3), 417-437.

Grimble, R. and Wellard, K. (1997). Stakeholder methodologies in natural resource management: a review of principles, contexts, experiences and opportunities. Agricultural Systems, 55(2), 173-193.

Hornidge, A.-K., Oberkircher, L., Tischbein, B., Schorcht, G., Bhaduri, A., Awan, U.K. and Manschadi, A.M. (2011). Reconceptualising water management in Khorezm, Uzbekistan. Natural Resources Forum, 35(4), 251-268.

Kellert, S.R., Mehta, J.N., Ebbin, S.A. and Lichtenfeld, L.L. (2000). Community natural resource management: promise, rhetoric, and reality. Society & Natural Resources, 13(8), 705-715.

O'Brien, K., Hayward, B. and Berkes, F. (2009). Rethinking social contracts: building resilience in a changing climate. Ecology and Society, 14(2), 12.

Sterner, T. and Coria, J. (2013). Policy instruments for environmental and natural resource management. Abingdon, UK: Routledge.

Turner, T. (2004). Landscape planning and environmental impact design. Abingdon, UK: Routledge.

## 9.5 Expertise, local knowledge and the nature of resources and qualities

Earlier in the book, we presented natural resources as objects that do not exist in nature. Of course, there are things in the forest and under the ground and in the water, but they become a resource *after* they are recognized as such in a community, by people who attribute value to particular things rather than others, who delineate objects in nature in a specific way, and who use individual things in different ways. Gold would have no value if people did not attribute value to it, neither does oil, which is only useful because people organized themselves around its use in machines. Natural resources are scarce by nature, driving their value up, but changes in outlook in society can drive value down. The extraction and processing of resources is subjected to expert knowledge of various sorts, drawing on local knowledge only initially, if at all; but, in terms of the level of appreciation for a resource, local knowledge is essential. If people start to hate cars, then oil will lose value.

**Example 9.5. Sustainable communities and vanishing towns.**

Large scale quantitative historical research in Canada showed that most towns there disappeared after less than 20 years of existence. Post offices, a good indicator of community life, disappeared that fast. The American midwest had its population peak in the 1920's. Often, the towns were tied to one natural resource, and it got depleted, or prices plummeted. Or, settlers tried agriculture, but conditions proved too hard. Or, one hoped for a railroad that never showed up. Or, one hoped for a status as regional market town but another railroad town took that role. A local industry collapsed. Land speculators came, bought, surveyed, sold a story, sold the land, disappeared, and only a few people ever settled. A gold rush brought settlers, for many it never worked out, they stayed and tried to build a town.

These stories are thus very common. Community sustainability, we believe, has to be understood against that background. Often, a ghost town is seen as a failure, a failure maybe for the settlers, but also for the larger community, the country maybe, that left them to die. A moral duty is implied for all actors, including academic observers, engaged scholars, and for people in politics and administration; a duty to keep the community alive. We would say this is not a very fair and very helpful perspective. Communities come and go. Some towns cannot stay alive, or they could if they transform drastically, but they are not willing to do this. We would argue that the moral duty is vis-a-vis the people, not the community. Investing in a community should come after analysis, not before, and, especially after self-analysis. Academics, politicians and civil servants can help in this process, for sure.

Sustainability has to be understood differently. Academics cannot impose a definition and cannot prescribe that each and every ghost town has to be revived. Which elements of social, ecological and economic sustainability are emphasized, at which scale, is a matter of politics, not science. If we don't pay attention, sustainability becomes another excuse for modernist technocratic control, or another utopian vision referring to a non-existing unity in the social-ecological system. All of this easily leads to new forms of authoritarianism.

**Further reading**

Gunder, M. and Hillier, J. (2009). Planning in ten words or less. A Lacanian entanglement with spatial planning. Aldershot, UK: Ashgate.

The example of oil also illustrates how the economics of resources is shaped by values that do not fluctuate freely. Changes in appreciation do not always affect values much, since resources can be a necessity for a community to survive. And they do not translate into governance easily, because they can create strong dependencies. Oil is not only used by cars, but it and its components are part and parcel of modern life (e.g. as plastics). This adds to the influence on governance that resource industries often have (e.g. in the vein

Figure 9.4. A combination of coffee and banana cultivation near Armenia, Colombia. The combo is classic, yet when coffee prices drop, banana takes the upper hand. Photo: Kristof Van Assche. © ZEF/University of Bonn, Germany.

of the previous sections). What is called resource dependency refers to other rigidities in governance, beyond the effects on power/knowledge, etc. described above. It refers to the influence the use of the resource has on the functioning of the community, and the effects when the use would abruptly stop. These effects will show up in governance, but are not restricted to the governance arena.

The *resource dependencies* are harder to transform in governance when more is coordinated around their use, when the interdependencies in the community are far-reaching and revolve around a shared resource. The path dependencies instilled by resource dependence can vary, and can stem from physical infrastructures (say, road systems designed for automobiles, low density neighborhoods for automobiles), knowledge infrastructures (one can forget how to build a train), institutional infrastructures (the actor/institution configuration being affected). Economic or other necessity, we believe, almost never exists: if governance is not completely monopolized by an actor/institution configuration that stays in power because of the resource, then there

Figure 9.5. Borjomi mineral water, Borjomi, Georgia, coming from an aquifer 1,200-1,400 m below the surface, mineralized by volcanic activity. Water can be a source of development in a literal sense, when mineral water becomes the driver. Tourism is often entwined with the marketing success of such places and waters, and especially the 19th century spa tourism, or elegant, high class, health tourism, which spread across Europe quickly, from much older (Roman) roots. Borjomi saw Russian elite tourism in the 19th century, a spa, an appreciation of its salty waters which the communists picked up and never went away. Photo: Kristof Van Assche. © ZEF/University of Bonn, Germany.

are always alternatives. There are always costs too, and governance, with its stabilizing effects, can help economic actors and their buyers to modify their calculations regarding what is normal, what is cheap, and what deserves reflection. The oil crisis in 73' hit so hard because apparently there had been little reflection on what would happen if prices would rise, and the panic that ensued became the core of the problem. If there are alternative modes of transportation in an area – and this can be maintained during cheap oil periods – then the community will be more resilient after an oil shock; people will find their way, will be able to organize their lives more easily, will freak out less, and do less unpredictable things on the stock market. As indicated before, this approach requires investment, reflexivity, long term perspectives and the co-existence of different futures in governance.

In this line of reasoning, enhancing resilience entails the *co-existence of different sorts of expertise* in governance. Giving too much prominence, and creating too deep entanglement of exploitation expertise in governance, creates the problems mentioned before. The same however holds true for giving a hegemonic place to environmental expertise. In a clean-up situation as described, or in a freak-out situation, such as a country worrying about climate change, there can be a tendency to give environmental expertise suddenly a central place in governance. This can cause the neglect of checks and balances, a sudden shift in the balance between representation and participation. Other actors and other forms of expertise do not have the chance to respond adequately, and the arguments for the roles of their expertise might not be heard. This can lead to a de-politicization, in the sense discussed earlier: administration experts take over from politics, and within administration, one expert perspective starts to dominate decision-making. Local knowledge and other expert knowledge are forgotten and cannot be coupled with different voices in the community, and therefore the continuous adaptation of power/knowledge configurations to changing communities will become difficult. In the climate change example, but also in the case of environmental protection, this has been observed often. Good intentions lead to privileging expertise which then undermines governance, renders it more authoritarian, while the adaptive capacity so important for climate change governance is undermined exactly by this reduction in voices and perspectives.

Looking at the three quite different versions of the environmental quality & resource governance perspective on rural development, we can say that these versions are likely to occur under very different conditions. Maximizing policies often come up in a boom, in places that are very young, or in a tenuous economic condition, with not too many alternatives immediately visible. Focusing on environmental qualities will be a special case, when there is a serious clean-up to do, e.g. one caused by the previous scenario. Sustainable development is also still rare in practice, since few communities systematically and seriously reflect on the long term effects of their use of resources and space. As a model, however, it seems to be the most solid of the three versions, indeed the most commendable. Given the continuing dependence of communities on fossil fuels and other scarce natural resources, it makes a lot of sense to move toward sustainable development.

Sustainability has been introduced as a guiding concept in several other development and rural development approaches: people speak of sustainable transitions management, working towards sustainable communities, community sustainability design, and high tech agriculture for sustainable futures. In general, the maximum exploitation perspective fits well with liberal democracy, and with modernist development approaches, e.g. market reform. The two others require more government action and citizen action. They fit well with the other governance models and can in many ways be combined with other development and rural development perspectives. For the other versions, some institutional reform is likely required, in a maximalist interpretation of the rule of law. One can imagine a role for community design, land use planning, and also of extension, in the more recent manifestations. Learning will have to be part of the equation, with governmental and non-governmental actors, and learning towards sustainability governance will require an increased level of reflexivity, since many things, many aspects of governance have to be reconsidered, in their sustainability effects. Sustainable development will require multi-level government and thus does not entirely fit with a communitarian governance model. It will require this because adaptations at several scales are required and need coordination, and also because resource-dependent communities or former addicts, do need to re-learn how to envision different possible futures. Entirely local democracy cannot work there, and new forms of social learning can enable a reorientation of governance. Extension can help there, in showing alternatives, coordinating learning process, but checks and balances associated with higher level governance can be necessary too. The community cannot always be understood as the local community, and common goods are not only found at the local level.

## Further reading

Adger, W.N., Dessai, S., Goulden, M., Hulme, M., Lorenzoni, I., Nelson, D.R. and Wreford, A. (2009). Are there social limits to adaptation to climate change? Climatic Change, 93(3-4), 335-354.

Batterbury, S.P. Fernando, J.L. (2006). Rescaling governance and the impacts of political and environmental decentralization: an introduction. World Development, 34(11), 1851-1863.

Hornidge, A.-K. and Scholtes, F. (2011). Climate change and everyday life in Toineke Village, West Timor – uncertainties, knoweldge and adaptation. Sociologus, 61(2), 151-175.

Mollinga, P., (2010). Boundary work and the complexity of natural resource management. Crop Science, 50, 1-9.

Paulson, S. and Gezon, L.L. (eds.) (2004). Political ecology across spaces, scales, and social groups. New Brunswick, NJ, USA: Rutgers University Press.

Vaccaro, I. and Norman, K. (2008). Social sciences and landscape analysis: opportunities for the improvement of conservation policy design. Journal of Environmental Management, 88(2), 360-371.

Zimmerer, K. (2006). Globalization & new geographies of conservation. Chicago, IL, USA: University of Chicago Press.

# 10. Rural development: transition management and innovation

*There is nothing more difficult to take on, more perilous to conduct or more uncertain to succeed than to take the lead in the introduction of a new order of things*

Niccolo Machiavelli, 1513

## Abstract

In this chapter, we investigate two more recent approaches to rural development: transition management and innovation policy. Both originate in the west and do not uniquely focus on rural areas, but both have a growing impact worldwide, including on rural areas. Both can be associated with Western fears for growing competition from each other and from developing countries. A need for innovation is perceived, and a need for linking up various innovations for increased impact can be seen as a need for transition, requiring transition management. This chapter explicitly links with the section above on transition management and innovation policy as a general development approach. In this case, the rural version can be seen as a subspecies of the general perspective. Whereas other rural development models only indirectly relate to one development approach, and often link with several ones, the transition/innovation perspective in rural areas is mostly a straightforward application of the general perspective. What has been said about that general perspective will not be repeated. Transition management and innovation policy share in many cases a social engineering assumption, where transition management tends to go farther in pushing that assumption, by aiming at more ambitious socio-economic transformations, on the basis of interlinked and managed innovations.

## 10.1. Rural development as high tech agriculture

As in the general development approach, the rural version of this perspective tends to focus on technological innovation, versus social innovation. Within the sciences, agricultural engineering, and biotechnology are privileged conversation partners for governments embracing this approach. The technology can appear on the field, e.g. under the guise of precision agriculture, or in the processing phase, in the plant. There

---

**Example 10.1. 'Follow the innovation': a participatory innovation development approach.**

Agricultural research generates findings that offer the potential for improving the existing situation of farmers. Yet, many innovative ideas and technologies generated through research are not implemented or adopted, because most innovations do not address the real-life complexities faced by farmers. Scientific research carried out in agricultural projects often takes place in isolation from the intended users of the innovations. To overcome the lack of fit between scientifically generated innovations and the local reality, participatory innovation development approaches in which local and scientific knowledge interacts systematically offer much potential.

Innovations produced by research projects without interaction with and adaptation to real-life situations are difficult to feed into local and national systems of policymaking as well as into development projects. In order to overcome this challenge, the 'Economic and Ecological Restructuring of Land and Water in the Khorezm Region of Uzbekistan' project of the Center for Development Research (ZEF) at the University of Bonn, Germany, in collaboration with United Nations Educational Scientific and Cultural Organisation (UNESCO) and Urgench State University, Uzbekistan, devised in 2008 a participatory and transdisciplinary approach to innovation development. The project called it the 'Follow-the-Innovation' (FTI) approach. The process had the twofold objective of: (1) testing, adapting and thus validating four selected scientific innovations in real-life settings of rural Khorezm; and (2) drawing lessons for the use of this approach in future innovation development projects and outscaling in Uzbekistan and in other parts of Central Asia.

The FTI component envisaged the creation of inter- and transdisciplinary research teams around innovation 'packages' developed by the project and regarded as 'plausible promises' to resolve some of the problems of sustainable land and water management in Khorezm, Uzbekistan. Four such teams of scientists were formed. In a workshop series involving international resource persons, these teams were trained, supported in work planning, and provided with relevant tools, methods and skills for stakeholder interaction and joint experimentation. Between the workshops, all FTI teams were supported and accompanied by a fulltime FTI facilitator. Some stakeholders who became involved in FTI implementation joined all or some of the subsequent workshops, allowing the learning process to become

---

can be coordination of innovations in the production and processing chain, taken care of by government actors, industry actors, or in an interplay between government, science and industry. Because of the complexity of coordination, and in many cases the capital intensive nature of these innovations, the farmers are usually not the initiators anymore. For the large scale, high tech agriculture and processing, it is more appropriate to see innovation as emerging and coordinated mostly within agro-industrial complexes, groups of interdependent companies in control of large chunks of the chain.

very focused and lead directly to planning of next steps. The FTI process was continuously monitored, documented, critically discussed and adjusted accordingly by all partners.

In the end, none of the four teams could follow the FTI process to the full extent as originally planned. Project-related factors, stakeholder constraints and wider policy developments such as the land reconsolidation continued to interfere, forcing teams to improvise and/or look for shortcuts. For example, several key stakeholders could not make the step to join the FTI team in experimenting with the new salinity measurement approach. However, one key stakeholder finally did join and is now convinced to have found a way to put the approach into practice in Uzbekistan. The trees that are part of the agroforestry work are still too small to allow final conclusions to be drawn; the design of the experiments with farmers had to be adapted and the number of farmers involved is still limited. But the work is progressing and farmers' interest in agroforestry is growing, as evident from the number of requests for work in this area received by the project.

Results of the process in moving the innovations forward towards adaptation and acceptance by stakeholders have thus been mixed so far. Some FTI teams have made considerable progress; others have a longer way to go. This depended, among other things, on the complexity of the innovation chosen and the strength and dynamics of the FTI teams.

In all cases, though, the FTI activities have increased the understanding among staff involved in a wide variety of aspects of real-life confronting local stakeholders and affecting the potential and effectiveness of relevant innovations. This will certainly influence the staff members' future work in their respective fields.

### Further reading

Hornidge, A.-K., Ul-Hassan, M. and Mollinga, P.P. (2011). Transdisciplinary innovation research in Uzbekistan – 1 year of 'Following The Innovation'. Development in Practice, 21(6), 825-838.

Ul-Hassan, M., Hornidge, A.-K., Van Veldhuizen, L., Akramkhanov, A., Rudenko, I. and Djanibekov, N. (2011). Follow the Innovation: participatory testing and adaptation of agricultural innovations in Uzbekistan – guidelines for researchers and practitioners. Bonn, Germany: Center for Development Research.

Much has been said about the future of the countryside in technological innovation, but most of that seems to rely on the same premises:
- rural areas have primarily an agricultural future;
- agriculture businesses in the future are large and high tech;
- these firms are not autonomous but mostly controlled by processing and financing actors;
- who also delineate and promote useful innovations; while
- government and its research institutes pay for some of the r&d and infrastructure.

This future is then presented as necessary (a modernist assumption). In most narratives institutional reform is good but not enough; government needs to stay involved in the innovation process and its coordination. Other land uses, other industries, other farm types, or autonomous firms combining farming and other activities are not part of the picture, while governance is almost entirely absent from the analysis. The countryside is almost understood as a machine that has to be optimized by the experts, without participation of local actors, or, worse, without even considering whether this is what a community wants and whether this is the best option for the physical context and governance path. This is what Easterly called the 'tyranny of the experts'. A presumed common good, innovation, is captured by a few experts (and the economic interests behind them) and the overriding importance of this common good is allowed to undermine governance.

Luckily, it's not always so bad in practice. In reality, there are some limits to this approach which prevent it from full application. Land ownership can be fragmented, preventing the large scale. Financing might be tough, with the same effect. Local governments and communities can be diverse, well-informed and active (in the spirit of civic republicanism), preventing the takeover over all land by a few owners, and the reduction of economic, ecological and social diversity. The legal strength of local government and local plans will be crucial, since large companies can afford lawyers to challenge any restriction that comes with plans and policies aiming at more diverse futures. Another limit on the power of the agro-industrial complex, in the last few decades, are the supermarkets (large retail chains). Their power over food production has increased so much (because of their purchasing power and control over the market) that not only small farmers can be pressured by them, but just as well the large corporate complexes: shunning systematically their products can hurt them as well. Practices perceived as unethical, products perceived as unhealthy or unattractive can be punished in that marketplace, while positive preferences for more local, small scale, organic products can shift the focus in their direction.

Yet, the prevalent discourses on rural transitions and agricultural tech innovation should not blind us from the positives of innovation itself. Even the form of agriculture promoted by the agro-industrial complex can be appropriate in some cases. The

**Example 10.2. 'Innovation' and 'innovation systems'.**

While the term 'national innovation system' was originally coined by Christopher Freeman in the late 1980's with regard to Japanese institutional networks linking public and private sector activities for technology development, the idea of assessing the innovative capacities of societies rather than merely their current economic situation, increasingly also enters development discourse. As such, in 2010, UNESCO published its UNESCO Science Report 2010 as well as its World Social Science Report 2010 drawing the attention to knowledge production in the developing and developed world. It here becomes obvious that even when applying Science, Technology and Innovation (STI) indicators originally developed by the OECD for OECD countries, knowledge production in the developing world is growing and increasingly gains the attention of developing countries' governments. The term 'innovation' in these debates captures more than merely a technology-focused definition and instead encompasses social, institutional, financial and technological innovations. These different types of innovations are no longer developed merely in the ivory towers of academia but increasingly in 'real-life' situations together with 'local stakeholders' or the 'problem owners'.

**Further reading**

Freeman, C. (1987). Technology policy and economic performance: lessons from Japan. London, UK: Frances Pinter.

United Nations Educational, Scientific and Cultural Organisation (UNESCO) (2010a). UNESCO Science Report 2010. Paris, France: UNESCO.

United Nations Educational, Scientific and Cultural Organisation (UNESCO) (2010b). World Social Science Report 2010. Paris, France: UNESCO.

starting point makes all the difference: cutting down rainforest to introduce palm oil plantations in high tech fashion is more problematic than replacing one form of large scale corporate agriculture with another form (as in parts of North America and Europe). As the proponents of high tech agriculture often repeat: their approach can lead to less wasted resources, less fertilizer and pesticides used, less labor, and a generally more controlled environment that makes it easier to check inputs, outputs, waste, the well-being of animals and the quality of the product.

Many forms of agriculture become less and less recognizable as agriculture, more part of an industry. This is problematic for those who stick to ideas of the countryside as a rural idyll, with agriculture taking place only in that context. But one could argue that it makes it possible to intensify production in some areas so others can remain more idyllic, and it can be argued that tech innovation can make some forms of high tech agriculture (think stables, greenhouses) more compatible with other land uses. In other words: they can be done anywhere, including in other economic zones, making planning more flexible, and taking away a burden from rural areas. High tech agriculture can become more urban, and this can have advantages for both urban and rural (close to products e.g. for urban, less stress on rural water systems). This scenario does obliterate the images that make the countryside attractive, and that some want to see associated with agricultural products.

## Further reading

Bindraban, P.S. and Rabbinge, R. (2011). European food and agricultural strategy for 21[th] century. International Journal of Agricultural Resources, Governance and Ecology, 9(1), 80-101.

Douthwaite, B. (2002). Enabling innovation: a practical guide to understanding and fostering technological change. London, UK: Zed Books Limited.

Pretty, J., Sutherland, W.J., Ashby, J., Auburn, J., Baulcombe, D. and Bell, M. (2010). The top 100 questions of importance to the future of global agriculture. International Journal of Agricultural Sustainability, 8(4), 219-236.

## 10.2 Organic high tech?

The same tech innovation, we believe, can be used in other forms of agriculture, and in different ownership situations. Then, the fit with other development approaches changes and it can become part of more comprehensive development strategies. One can say that a decoupling of innovation thinking and the modernist corporate recipe sketched can render more recombinations possible with elements of other approaches. Systematically reflecting in governance on innovation will not necessarily lead to technological breakthroughs, but those are not necessarily of the essence in rural development. One can think of linking systematically with tech innovation circles in governance, at local or regional level, but one can also reflect on innovation present and absent in more diverse forms. Social innovation, new ways of organizing people, resources and knowledge to work on problems and towards common goods, can be just as relevant.

If ownership is not so concentrated, and if governance includes a variety of stakeholders, representing a variety of different perspectives and economic activities, then there can be a more profound reflection on the need for tech innovation and the utility locally of new technologies. If reflection on tech innovation becomes embedded in governance like this, it also becomes easier to harness the combined powers of social and tech innovation, through coordination in governance. If such coordination occurs, an innovation approach can become more deeply rooted in the community, can affect actor/institution configurations and this can increase the resistance against subsumption under the standard corporate approach. Cooperation can lead to planning which guides development, which protects landscape structures and hydrological systems, heritage, and a diversity in economic activities. It can lead to new commons and to cooperative forms of ownership, processing, promoting. The resistance can take the form of active resistance, but it can also simply mean that more alternative visions for the future are present in governance and the community at large.

---

**Example 10.3. Singapore and UNESCO's evolving policy approaches to creative industries (with thanks to Catherine Reynolds).**

In Singapore, creative industries were long a neglected field of government investment in comparison to other areas of knowledge, in particluar technological expertise. This was rooted in a strict governance focus on economic growth. Gradually, Singapore's government began to take a different approach, however, recognizing the economic potential of creative industries and channeling increasing resources to them. Even if the country is still hesitant to promote, for examle, fine arts for their own sake, and Singapore's constitution still lacks a guarantee to the right of free speech; the country has made strides towards fostering culture and the arts. Over time, the governance strategy shifted to incorporate creative industries in the hopes that cultural articfacts and can be applied to, form the basis of, or enrich other economic sectors and contribute to their profit and growth.

The overall approach of UNESCO can be seen as following an opposite, complementary trajectory. Initially UNESCO set out to foster only cultural activities not related to profit earning. A clear distinction between market-based activities and arts/culture was seen as protecting creative endeavors from being co-opted and thus corrupted as a means to profit-oriented ends. UNESCO's stance has since been revised and begun to loosen, to highlight synergies between cultural and economic wealth. UNESCO, like Singapore, now also promotes what it calls 'cultural industries'.

These transitions in Singapore's national policy and UNESCO's global policy frameworks have led to a shifting institutional landscape. Early on, Singapore's policies were so disparate to UNESCO's that in 1985 the country decided to leave UNESCO in protest, following a precedent set by the USA and the UK. Starting in 2000, however, Singapore began to send representatives to high level UNESCO meetings on policies related to cultural knowledge. UNESCO, for its part, also increasingly opened its doors to Singapore, although the country remained a non-member.

**Further reading**

Hornidge, A.-K. (2011). 'Creative industries' – economic program and boundary concept. Journal of Southeast Asian Studies, 42(2), 253-279.

---

If there is an awareness that alternative paths are possible, that there are assets and qualities that can be linked and built upon, then routine modernization can often be avoided, governance itself can stay intact, and a more diverse economy and community can be maintained. We refer back here to a point made earlier: once land use and governance are optimized for one activity, then other visions disappear from the horizon, are hard to bring back, and then the physical, social and economic landscapes will be so damaged and/or simplified that reinvention becomes harder. In such one-industry rigid governance systems, the boom years will also make the reflection disappear on other assets in the community, on the value of diversity, ecology, heritage, other activities, while negative effects of the reigning industry will not be observed. Only later it will be seen that much has been lost, and much damage has been done.

High tech innovation can be part of the solution, is not only part of the problem. As said, there are situations where full-fledged intensive agriculture is very appropriate. There are other cases where tech innovation can fit into strategies towards different futures. An example: if agriculture is still seen as central to the future of the community, but sustainability, health and local control are concerns, then organic agriculture can be a way forward. Organic agriculture works well with a sustainability perspective on rural development, and it can be part of many different physical landscapes, can be combined with other land uses and economic activities in the community. The scale can be large or small, crops can be diverse, landscape elements in between can be preserved, and there are possibly synergies with tourism, residential use, small businesses (in a networked environment).

Organic agriculture, we believe, can be more easily part of an economic mix in a post-industrial society, where urban/rural divides are blurry, and internet and other connectivities make a variety of economic activities possible in the village. In pre-industrial societies it can be useful as a re-labeling of existing forms of agriculture, adding value, and making it possible to maintain more local control ('Oh, what we are doing is organic?'). In such cases, a pure maintenance of tradition is not likely to work. A new reflection on tradition, and the adding of new expertise (e.g. in marketing) will be necessary, and this can best happen in governance, possibly with semi-autonomous circles focusing on the activity (chambers of commerce, organic agriculture clubs, innovation circles, etc.). Maintaining traditional uses, knowledge and landscapes (leading to a product now seen as organic) takes effort, since there will be various pressures for change. And this effort in many cases is to take place in governance, by coordination of actors and integration of policies. And on top of maintenance there is adaptation, modification, and the coupling with new expertise.

We dwell here on the potential of high tech innovation in such context, in such strategy to show how it can be un-bundled, and how elements can be made useful elsewhere. In our story of organic agriculture in a diverse landscape, high tech innovation could

Figure 10.1. Modernity and traditional lifestyles exist parallel to each other. Here a photo of a shepherd and his animals on the pasture in front of a power station in Uzbekistan. Photo: Anna-Katharina Hornidge. © ZEF/ University of Bonn, Germany.

reduce labor (hence costs) of some farms (think weeding), protect crops (biological pest control), improve efficiency (precision agriculture), further reduce impacts on the environment (minimal water use), and it could even make the return of heirloom varieties more feasible (by tailoring specific protection strategies for these vulnerable varieties). In combination with social innovation, one could think of shared labor arrangements (weeding, harvesting), and even a local return of commons, of shared use and shared resource spaces. Once more, generic solutions do not exist, but reflection on innovation and tech innovation in (sub-)governance can engender flexible adaptation, also of organic agriculture. Once a community of organic farmers is in place, once they are used to coordination, to informal governance, and to regular feedback to formal governance structures, a positive path dependence can occur, where innovation can more easily be spurred, and the benefits can more easily be reaped.

## Further reading

Ammann, K. (2009). Why farming with high tech methods should integrate elements of organic agriculture. New Biotechnology, 25(6), 378-388.

Hall, A. (2007). Challenges to strengthening agriculture innovation systems: where do we go from here? Maastricht, the Netherlands: United Nations University, UNU_MERIT.

Röling, N. (2009). Conceptual and methodological developments in innovation. In: Sanginha, P. C., Waters-Bayer, A., Kaaria, S., Njuki, J. and Wettasinha C. (eds.), Innovation Africa. Enriching farmers' livelihoods. London, UK: Earthscan, pp. 9-34.

Röling, N. (2005). Gateway to the global garden: beta/gamma science for dealing with ecological rationality. In: Pretty, J. (ed.), The Earthscan reader in sustainable agriculture. London, UK: Earthscan.

## 10.3 Innovation for diverse ruralities?

These remarks already point the way to the use of innovation strategies to produce more diverse ruralities, development visions not relying on one sort of agriculture and not on agriculture necessarily. We believe it is necessary to take a step back again, improve our theoretical understanding, and then come back. First, we briefly discuss the relations between innovation, place and policies. Then we will distinguish innovation networks and governance networks, and return to the issue of innovation for diverse rural futures.

### 10.3.1 Innovation and place

As often in this book, the literature is vast and does not offer clear guidelines. That is not a problem. We can distill some principles which can help to discern the potential of different sorts of institutions to spur and manage innovation and its effects.

Spatial planning in and by itself seems to have little innovation on innovation in a place. Planning can create problems for innovation though, if it steers towards mono-functional land use, enables erosion of historically multi-use environments. It can also create obstacles by introducing rigidity, by restricting activities too much, and conceiving land uses and activities entirely in old categories ('commercial', 'residential'). Starting a high tech company in a rural garage is entirely illegal in many countries. Planning can also, with the best intentions, create another problem: redevelopment, usually to solve various socio-economic ailments, tends to drive up prices, which can clean up poor people (in the eyes of elites). It also makes it harder to use space for different purposes (cf financial risk), and it drives out many creative and innovative types – often poor, at least for a while. Spatial planning can be used however as a strategy in conjunction with other strategies, and after a broader discussion on innovation in the community. In the early years of Silicon Valley, the absence of planning was very helpful, and the low prices; old school buildings in suburban to rural environments were repurposed as labs, or for small businesses, while garages, attics, sidewalks were used for meetings, markets, exchanges.

Below the scale of this book, we want to briefly mention *architecture*. While planning and design of larger areas rarely spurs innovation without flanking measures, there seems a more direct effect of the smaller spaces of architecture. Some similarities between scales can be seen however: rigidity is to be avoided. Spaces that allow for flexible uses and for flexible reorganization tend to foster creativity. Another aspect often mentioned is the potential for random meetings, leading to unexpected exchanges of ideas, unexpected networks. In spatial terms, this can refer to larger buildings with rather open floor plans or movable walls, or to smaller buildings open to a flow of diverse people (coffeehouse?)

Figure 10.2. A restored coffee pickers house in Colombia's western coffee region. After coffee prices went down in the late 1980's, regional governments, together with the well organized coffee sector, aimed to stay afloat by investing in innovation in the sector itself, but also by broadening it and making it part of a tourism development strategy. Photo: Monica Gruzmacher. © ZEF/University of Bonn, Germany.

*Clustering effects*, often discussed regarding innovation parks, industrial concentrations, commercial strips even, are not imaginary, but cannot be simply engineered or predicted. The small building with an intense flow of diverse people can receive this flow because of its position in a cluster, or a tight network of similar buildings. Synergies are possible, in terms of efficiencies, and in terms of innovative potential, but they do not take place automatically after clustering, by creating new clusters or renaming places as clusters.

In Silicon Valley, the model of innovation, clustering effects are important (Steve Jobs thanked 'the Valley' on his deathbed) but proximity or design are not the explanation. As we mentioned before, Silicon Valley has to be understood as the success of a specific network structure in which roles crystallized (e.g. venture capitalists) and where combining and moving between these roles is deemed acceptable. Informal institutions and new actors co-evolved, and made an enviable but highly contingent balance of competition and collaboration possible, a balance which spurred innovation and made it possible to implement, scale up and market them at breakneck speed.

Since 'innovation' is not one thing (even if some policy and scientific discourses want to make us believe it) the internal complexity and diversity of innovation means that

**Example 10.4. Knowledge hubs along the Straits of Malacca.**

World history has known areas of relative isolation and areas of high intensity of cultural interaction. The Mediterranean Sea, the Silk Road or the Straits of Malacca can be cited as such crucial contact zones. Within these areas, centres sprung up that served as interfaces between cultures and societies. These 'hubs' emerged at various points throughout the contact zones, rose to prominence and submerged into oblivion due to a variety of natural calamities or political fortunes.

Until the end of the 19th century, when sailing vessels were replaced by steamships, maritime trade in the Indian Ocean completely depended on the monsoons with the impossibility to cross the entire Indian Ocean in a single monsoon. Consequently with increasing international trade conducted, the trade routes were divided into sections or stages and port cities and trading centres acted as intermediaries and therewith rose to their glory. Entrepot trade meant that goods were assembled at strategically located ports and then reloaded and transported to other minor ports. Supply and trading routes were closely guarded secrets. Therefore 'commercial' as well as 'maritime intelligence', i.e. local knowledge on products, wind, currents, sea routes and access to harbours turned out to be valuable cultural capital. Trade was enabled and accelerated by commercial and maritime knowledge.

The rise of each of these knowledge hubs in the Straits was determined by the ability to establish an efficient, strong and stable government which secured trade as the main income-generating source. This ability did not merely determine the rise and fall of the ancient empires in the Straits of Malacca region, i.e. Srivijaya and Majapahit, but furthermore the rise and fall of trading centers such as Malacca, Aceh, Johor, Georgetown/Pinang and later Singapore which – through trade – also emerged as regional knowledge hubs. Strong coalitions between the ruling aristocracy or bureaucracy and the long-distance traders, two powerful (local or colonial) strategic groups, secured access to local products and markets as well as the arrival of trading ships in a certain, not any, port in the Straits. These coalitions were often further strengthened by religious conversions and marriage between traders and the local aristocracy, as outlined above. Once a trading center had established itself as main hub in the region, established and enforced institutions regulated trade. These institutions were responsible for assuring that trade interactions were conducted in a smooth manner and consequently that the trading center was able to compete with the services offered in other centers along the Straits. Economic and cultural prosperity served as a means to justify the existing power structures. In the case of Singapore the connection between trade and knowledge has now moved to a new stage of development, namely to trade of knowledge as well as the explicit construction of Singapore as a knowledge society by its government.

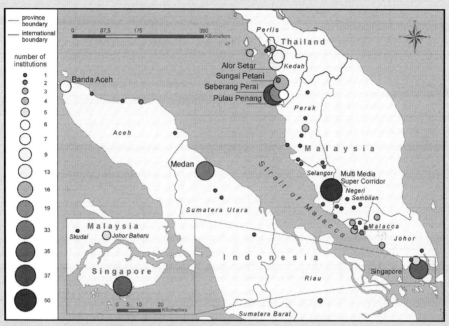

Figure 10.3. Knowledge hubs along the Straits of Malakka in South-east Asia (Evers and Hornidge, 2007).

Actions taken do not merely focus on knowledge exchange but furthermore these actions are accelerated, legitimised and marketed by the matching semantics and terminology, subsumed in Singapore under the terms 'knowledge-based economy' as well as 'creative society'. Production of new scientific knowledge and the sale of knowledge based products and patents, especially in bio-medical technology, have moved Singapore onto the rank of a global knowledge hub.

### Further reading

Evers, H.-D. and Hornidge, A.-K. (2007). Knowledge hubs along the Straits of Malacca. Asia Europe Journal, 5(3), 417-433.

Hornidge, A.-K. (2010). An uncertain future – Singapore's search for a new focal point of collective identity and its drive towards 'knowledge society'. Asian Journal of Social Sciences, 38(5), 785-818.

Hornidge, A.-K. (2011). 'Creative industries' – economic program and boundary concept. Journal of Southeast Asian Studies, 42(2), 253-279.

the resources, networks and policies that can enhance one sort of innovation, are not necessarily useful for others. It becomes easier to see this when we take a distance from the mythologies of innovation as tech innovation, as susceptible to steering, of tech innovation as the main driver of economic success. Then we see that the innovations that made a difference in society are sometimes technical, sometimes organizational, sometimes cultural, that they are sometimes to be ascribed to individuals, sometimes not, that they were sometimes recognized as innovation, sometimes not. And that commercial success derived from a new scientific or even technical insight could happen much later, in unexpected places. Agricultural innovation is not the same as food processing innovation is not the same as innovation in the bundling of activities in rural areas and the creation of place brands.

## 10.3.2 Innovation and policy

Innovation policies can work. But often this is only seen afterwards, often it is not fully understood what exactly worked, and also the positives might be in unexpected places. The unpredictability does not have to detract from the value of reflecting in governance on innovation; it does mean that basing policy on predictable innovation is not a good idea. The ability even in the short term to figure out what really is an innovation and which innovation will have more economic effects ('picking winners') is not a good idea either. The focus on short-term and specificity can easily erode the broader innovation base, where various experiments (in technical, social, scientific, economic sense) are going on all the time, and can build on each other in ways not always observed. Picking winners can jeopardize long-term innovative capacity, because the short term specific focus is in fact an optimization for circumstances that will change, and that are not entirely understood. In other words, it is not even an optimization.

The *innovation base* in other words, remains important. Investment in research and education, in infrastructure, in media, debate, in flexible institutions allowing for experiment of the various sorts listed, all make sense. If many experiments take place now, if there is space and autonomy to think, to tinker, to discuss and compare, to find investors, to adapt rules and regulations, the innovation base can be secured. Investors can still pick winners, but that is less risky than government focusing its resources and adapting institutions to those supposed winners. In the same line should be mentioned so called boundary-spanning organizations and boundary objects, organizations and objects which can bridge boundaries between disciplines, between government, science and industry. Such objects and organizations can speed up innovation and amplify its effects, but they can also erode the innovation base, undermine existing scientific and educational infrastructure, and they can increase transaction costs and make innovation more sluggish (by creating new procedures, bureaucracies, grant systems, control mechanisms, by forcing research and education in directions picked by industry).

Governments guessing the next big thing will therefore not only be wrong in most cases, but the institutionalization of that guessing will likely subsidize and entrench certain firms and ideas, certain tracks of innovation. Power/knowledge configurations will be altered, with less input from a variety of actors, more obstacles for adaptation and self-transformation. It will also make the economic playing field less level, by giving some corporate actors benefits and forgetting the rest of the business world. This approach thus hampers innovation directly. It makes it harder for alternative understandings to merge and assert themselves. Indirectly, it has a negative influence by closing off the market, by handing it over to already established players. Silicon Valley is far away, indeed.

As we know now, innovation is highly unpredictable. What is actually new, what is new and important, what is new and profitable, what is new and creates jobs: all these things are hard to see in the moment. And all these things are different. For the understanding of innovation and the possibilities of policy, this awareness of difference is very valuable, because it can warn against overly simplistic steering ideas. It can also help in structuring discussions on innovation potential and policy in governance. The aspects of innovation mentioned are also highly dependent on the differentiation in society, on the way economic, legal, scientific and political contexts are linked. A different version of property rights creates different economic calculations, different potential profits of innovation. A different relation between politics and science, alters the autonomy of science, and can push innovation in one very applied direction, while forgetting fundamental science, creative innovation, synergetic innovation, and applications and profits much further down the line. Nuclear energy became possible because of Einstein, because of German mathematicians in the 19th century, because of Leibniz and Newton in the 17th century. Nobody knew the innovation trail. American government gave a last concerted push during World War II, but by then all the pieces were already in place.

Based on the ideas put forward in these last paragraphs, we make a distinction between innovation networks and governance networks.

*Innovation networks* we see here as explicitly more than organizations labeling themselves as innovation networks (platforms, institutes, councils...). We see them as networks that shape and transform local/regional economies. The use of the word innovation, the declared interest in innovation can vary, the participation of governmental actors will be different per case, the speed of change, the intensity of knowledge use and production, the composition. All these can and will vary. Our concept of innovation network is broader than what one usually finds in the literature, where these networks are often understood as consciously designed, composed by government, to push innovation in a certain economic sector or on a topic. Our concept is related to the network ideas of

Stephan Fuchs and Bruno Latour, who see innovations with impact as the product of various interacting networks (economic, scientific, legal, political).

*Governance networks* we already know, as the systems of connected actors which contribute to the making of collectively binding decisions for a community.

Governance and innovation networks are not the same. Innovation policy emanates from governance networks, not from innovation networks. Governance networks do not steer innovation networks, and they are often not completely aware of their existence. Innovation cannot be easily tied to place, to time, cannot be easily steered. A careful analysis of both innovation networks and governance networks can help to see what the overlap is between these two networks, their form of coupling, their mutual influence. It can help to see whether current innovation patterns rely on governmental actors and/or institutions. There is always an innovation patterns and an innovation

---

**Example 10.5. 'Knowledge for development'.**

In 1996, the World Bank President, James Wolfensohn, rebranded the bank from a 'lending bank' into 'the knowledge bank'. The underlying idea of 'knowledge' being a key element of successful development cooperation and poverty alleviation was detailed out and culminated in 1999 in the publishing of the World Bank report entitled 'Knowledge for Development'. Envisioning a future saturated with knowledge and knowledge application, the report states: 'Knowledge is like light. Weightless and intangible, it can easily travel the world, enlighten the lives of people everywhere' (World Bank, 1999: 1). With this report, the notion of 'knowledge' as a driver of development, and a topic of debate for centuries, reached the summit of global (donor-driven) development discourses. From there it globally triggered further development interventions framed around the issue of 'knowledge for development'. The report focuses, as explicitly stated on page 1, on two sorts of knowledge and two types of problems, perceived as 'critical to developing countries' by the bank. These are 'knowledge about technology', also referred to as 'technical knowledge' or 'know-how', as well as 'knowledge about attributes', such as 'the quality of a product, the diligence of a worker or the creditworthiness of a firm'; and incomplete knowledge about attributes, referred to as 'information problems' (World Bank, 1999: 1). As such, the report adopts a technology focused as well as highly applied definition of knowledge, based on the clearly stated assumption (World Bank, 1999: 1) that the employment of these two types of knowledge as well as their delivery by international institutions and developing-country governments to places of need will further enable the donor organizations' activities, projects and programs in bringing about 'development'. The report consequently adopts a

network, since power/knowledge configurations are always changing. This double mapping can also help see whether the perceived problem, threats and opportunities are best captured in terms of a new and needed innovation discourse and, if so, whether this leads naturally to a high tech focus. The mapping can further help to discern whether a new innovation narrative is susceptible to materialization by means of policy. If the innovation network wants new innovation forms and has a new narrative about the sort needed and the way to get there, will it reshape itself, tighten the link with governance networks, and do things together in way that is recognizable as 'innovation policy'? All these questions together, based on the network mapping, can be more simply seen as the question about the actual influence of governance on innovation in a certain place.

The double network mapping can help to see which forms of local/regional innovation can be desirable, appropriate and realistic. They can be linked to the image an area has of itself, of the future. They are part and parcel of general development narratives,

conceptualization of 'knowledge' that at that time and until the present day also forms the core of envisioned future societies, replacing the development stage of the 'modern society', namely of 'knowledge societies'.

Earlier research underlining the crucial role of indigenous, traditional and local tacit knowledge for the development of communities, basically standing in opposition to the 'expert knowledge' focused development paradigm of the 1950's to 1970's, were acknowledged in the report (Chapters 2 and 10). The focus on 'knowledge about technology' and 'knowledge about attributes', both types of knowledge relatively more in the possession of industrialized countries, until today generally the countries of origin of these technologies, nevertheless renewed the former focus on 'expert knowledge' from the North. Past experiences with sustainability issues involved in large scale technology transfer, were incorporated in a strong focus on institutional and system-level capacity building (getting the policy frameworks right), knowledge communication strategies and the diffusion and out scaling of technologies and their 'social attributes'.

### Further reading

Hornidge, A.-K. (2012). 'Knowledge' in development discourse: a critical review. In: Hornidge, A.-K. and Antweiler, C. (eds.) Environmental uncertainty and local knowledge Southeast Asia as a laboratory of global ecological change. Bielefeld, Germany: Transcript, pp. 21-54.

World Bank (1999). World Development Report, Knowledge for Development. New York, NY, USA: Oxford University Press.

and should be. Innovation drives development, indeed, but development has to be understood as framed in and by governance, as a narrative about the future of the community in which certain forms of innovation become more sensible and valuable. Analysis of the governance paths also delineates more clearly which forms of innovation, of governance for innovation and innovation in governance, are more realistic and appropriate.

In the search for locally adapted innovation forms, the policy question ought to be asked all the time but without ever assuming that policies are the best answer or that policies can always be implemented. The innovation network in Silicon Valley relied initially much on military sub-contractors, but besides that, the impact of governmental policies, including innovation policies, was minimal. In the case of the Valley, one can say that place branding (as self-branding) was more influential than innovation policy or policy in general.

In the search for locally embedded innovations, we believe that iterative processes can be very helpful, a regular revisiting of the question in governance, and a regular attempt at *linking* the governance and innovation networks. We would suggest that the what question and the how question are alternative over and over again, within the two networks, and that the insights are shared between networks. The what question is the search for suitable innovation forms, while the how question includes but transcends the question of policy intervention (e.g. innovation policy). If the answer to the how question is a recurring demand for policy intervention, if the innovation networks actually believes that policies can bring the community closer to a desirable innovation or innovation pattern, then this can still not be presented as an argument for 'innovation policy'. Wish and reality are not the same, and a critical distance with at least some players in the networks, is very helpful. If such distance is not there, then at least the consultant or scientific analyst can cultivate it.

### 10.3.3 Back to diverse ruralities

These previous paragraphs helped to develop our understanding of innovation in place and of innovation policy. What does it mean for the use of innovation or transition policy towards more diverse ruralities, towards rural futures not restricted to (high or low tech) agriculture. The organic agriculture examples already illustrated how innovation networks and governance networks can be different but coupled and how such coupling can benefit community development.

We believe we are in a better position now to see that innovation & transition approaches to rural development can work best when simple mythologies of steering innovation are abandoned. An innovation focus can be helpful, when there is an understanding of the limits of steering, and an understanding of the coexistence of the two networks.

And when the possibilities of social innovation are considered, in conjunction with scientific and technical innovation. Social innovation places us more firmly in the governance context, and if consultations with the innovation network are frequent, one can imagine the governance arena as a place where not only the value of this or that innovation is discussed, the need to support it with resources, infrastructures, rules, but also the possibilities to couple social and other forms of innovation. Social innovation can help to amplify the impact of technical innovation, but it can also spark scientific innovation, economic innovation (more likely), and it can contribute to the safeguarding of the innovation base.

Governance is also the place to further buttress this innovation base, the best guarantee for success in the long run (economic success, adaptive success). Such broad understanding and organization of innovation for development, we believe, is more promising for most cases than a narrow focus on institutionally reinforced high tech futures. Certainly in rural areas. In exceptional cases (comparable to the clean-up scenario for environmentally-focused development), in crisis situations closely associated with innovation gaps that can be filled by strong coordination and a shared focus in governance, the narrow definition could be helpful. Then again, before deciding on this, before seeing the gap and trying to fill it this way, it is helpful to take a step back and reflect in the way we proposed in this section.

In rural areas, innovation networks can include the corporate research stations far away, but also local businesses, farmers, chambers of commerce, community associations, active citizens, journalists, and teachers. Some of those are part of governance networks, but others are not. As long as governance is not stuck in a hegemonic high tech agriculture governance path (comparable to the extractive industries monopoly), an innovation focus in rural governance can more easily maintain an open definition of innovation, and structuring the linkage with innovation networks can help to maintain a diverse input of signals regarding innovation present, absent, and possible. One can imagine also that governance networks can assist in structuring the innovation network, without trying to take it over, without trying to merge the two directly. Discussions on innovation and its economic implications can best be held at a distance from power for a while, should follow their own logic.

In such an approach, the possibly mutually enriching social and economic innovations can pertain to different economic sectors and activities. Also in an economic environment dominated by highly specialized agriculture, there can be economic synergies between different forms of agriculture (and one type of innovation could be the reinvention of mixed farms). There can certainly be synergies between farm and non-farm activities, at the farm level (broadening the economic base of farms) and at the level of the community. In a high tech world, an attractive rural environment can also attract new residents doing their business over the internet, or retirees, or tourists. Maintaining an attractive environment, as has been said, can increase resilience. Innovation tracks can keep that in mind, and can partly follow from such a broad approach. An environmental design approach can be coupled with an innovation track focusing on better internet, better signage, and promotion of home office business.

If the rural area in question in scarcely populated, it will be tough. If there is little civic engagement, it will be tough. We can refer to the traditional North American townships, small rural communities, with a core little town serving a group of scattered farms. There, it could and can be seen very clearly that self-organization and local participatory democracy can be very powerful, can generate development visions and harness innovation. But it can also be seen that this requires very strong civic engagement, with farmers serving on several councils and committees, and willing to learn continuously on a variety of topics, for the sake of good governance – administrator-experts are rare. It is also clear that in complex modern times, with too much knowledge to digest and too many powerful actors at other levels, it can only exist in the frame of multi-level governance. Without embedding in other governance levels, and without very active citizenship and social learning, such townships (and any other small rural community elsewhere in the world) will be very vulnerable for large corporate actors pushing their economic vision and innovation agenda. Then, chances are that innovation paths are decided somewhere else, become decoupled from governance paths, and lead to mono-functional countrysides.

Certainly, our recipe is not sufficient. Coupling and structuring networks, social learning and civic engagement or active citizenship (partly an agenda of civic republicanism) does not always produce a diverse, economically and otherwise sustainable rural community. There are no simple answers. We can refer however back to the previous chapters, where different rural development approaches can provide more form and substance which can be helpful and tailored to individual communities. Such art of combining and crafting strategies ought to be inspired (yes, we repeat and underline) by a serious study of governance paths, its configurations and dependencies.

## Further reading

Christensen, C. (2013). The innovator's dilemma: when new technologies cause great firms to fail. Cambridge, UK: Harvard Business Review Press.

Gijsbers, G.W. (2009). Agricultural innovation in Asia – drivers, paradigms and performance. ERIM Ph.D. Series in Research in Management, 156. Rotterdam, the Netherlands: ERIM.

Rhoades, R.E. and Booth., R.H. (1982). Farmer-back-to-farmer: a model for generating acceptable agricultural technology. Agricultural Administration, 11, 127-137.

Richards, P. (1985). Indigenous agricultural revolution: ecology and food-production in West Africa. London, UK: Hutchinson.

## 10.4 Innovation, governance and expertise

*Governance cannot force innovation.* This is true for urban and rural areas. Rural areas used to be more at a disadvantage in terms of innovation approaches to development, because of problematic connectivity, less access to resources and to knowledge. This can still be the case here and there, but many rural areas are not rural in this sense anymore. The 20th century path towards more mono-functional rural areas does not have to be followed anymore. The way out is the way of governance, of adaptive governance, and, we believe, in rural areas the way of very active citizenship.

We already discussed which innovation approach can make most sense towards diverse ruralities, and we noted that mono-functional, large-scale, high-tech futures can be appropriate for some places. In the last case, there is probably a preference for or simply a dominance of neo-liberal policies, giving free hand to large corporations, whereas the former probably works best in civic republicanism. The reasoning followed above also indicates that a rural innovation approach can best work in a participatory fashion, with attention to the crafting of livelihoods, with care for sustainability effects. Depending on the emphasis, on the approach most present in the framing policies, one can speak of an innovation model in participatory fashion, a sustainability model with innovation accents, or another hybrid. We would like to remind the reader that both the type of policy espoused and the effects can be linked to the path of governance and the desired model of governance.

With regards to knowledge and expertise, the version of the innovation model we presented tends to be open to local knowledge and various sorts of expertise alike. It tends not to privilege technical knowledge (e.g. agricultural engineering), unless, in the dialectics between the innovation and governance networks, it becomes clear that such technological innovation is an essential element of the community vision, or is already becoming so important that it requires a new development vision in which there is place for it. What is not very important in our proposed model of innovation for development is the supposed expertise of innovation or transition experts, especially when they give clear and simple prescriptions for innovation. Just as any other simple development formula, this should be regarded as snake oil, or, in a more lenient assessment, as another book promising you the 'seven steps to get rich'.

A final remark, linking to the next chapter, is that local/regional innovation policy is often partly a *branding operation*: saying that this is an innovative place, saying it out loud, turning it into a slogan, and hoping that the slogan creates an innovative reality, that it becomes performative. Innovation policy, in other words, is often partly a place branding strategy. It can also work, and such performative effects we would ascribe to the same structure of coupled innovation and governance networks we discussed earlier. Less often discussed, but also holding a promise, is the use of place branding to stimulate innovation and give it a local form. Place branding can be the articulation of a vision for the future, as incapsulated in the brand, and the coordinated policies to make the brand more visible, and develop it in terms of local qualities and activities, can stir innovation. Place branding in this sense will likely require spatial planning and design, where the brand image, the image of the place, and the kind of innovation that fits in, are defined together. Also here, social innovation and other forms of innovation can create synergies.

## Further reading

Chambers, R., Pacey, A. and Thrupp, L.A. (1989). Farmers first/farmer innovation and agricultural research. London, UK: Intermediate Technology Publications.

Chambers, R. and Jiggins, J. (1986). Agricultural research for resource-poor farmers: a parsimonious paradigm. IDS Discussion Paper 220. Brighton, UK: IDS.

Douthwaite, B., De Haan, Nicoline C., Manyong, V. and Keatinge, D. (2001). Blending 'hard' and 'soft' science: the 'follow-the-technology' approach to catalyzing and evaluating technology change. Ecology and Society, 5(2), 13.

Freeman, C. and Soete, L. (2009). Developing science, technology and innovation indicators: what we can learn from the past. Research Policy, 38(4), 583-589.

Hall, A. and Nahdy, S. (1999). New methods and old institutions: the 'systems context' of farmer participatory research in national agricultural research systems. The case of Uganda. Network Paper, 93. London, UK: ODI Agricultural Research & Extension Network.

Hornidge, A.-K., Ul-Hassan, M. and Mollinga, P.P. (2011). Transdisciplinary innovation research in Uzbekistan – 1 year of 'following the innovation'. Development in Practice, 21(6), 825-838.

Outshoorn, N. and Pinch, T. (eds.) (2003). How users matter: the co-construction of users and technology. Cambridge, MI, USA: MIT Press.

# 11. Rural development: local, local, local

## Abstract

In this chapter, we discuss the tangle of discourses on rural development we would describe as 'local, local, local', a call for localism in many versions, for self-reliance, local food, local business, local democracy, local tourism, for self-organization and for diversity and design. We revisit the concept of place branding in this perspective. Whereas the innovation perspective on development is not always easy to pinpoint in its rural form, and not always easy to localize, to tie to place, this perspective is in essence local and rural. Yet the essence is not much more than that, a call for localism in a globalized world. For that reason, the focus on localism can integrate many elements of the other rural development approaches, and different versions can sprout from several general development perspectives. Though other perspectives may tie in as contributing elements, however, the call for the local is the defining element of this perspective, the one offering the framing of policies.

## 11.1 Nostalgic and other versions of localism

A call for the local is often a call for a return to the local, tinged with nostalgia. The past evoked in localism is usually a construct of the present, not an accurate historical reconstruction. What is longed for, the past and the rurality that are desired, are responses to situations now. That can be a current situation where traces of the past have been erased (e.g. by a long history of modernist policies, say rough land consolidation), or where a globalized agricultural innovation discourse has created yet another corn town, after losing other crops, other activities, old landscape elements and a formerly vibrant downtown. There can be nostalgia for older forms of local democracy and self-organization, lost in either very bureaucratic or very neo-liberal regimes. Nostalgia emerges for a local social and cultural identity that is fading, along with the physical landscape, rituals, dress, dishes, and products that substantiate it. Disaffection with features of the present rural economy and society generates images of the past that can then guide collective desires and, consequently, governance.

In its different manifestations, the balance between an orientation on the past and on the future differs. New localism can include innovation discourses. If it is more about survival of old rural communities, a resilience of livelihoods can be invoked. If there is an accent on rural local futures at higher levels of decision-making, institutional reform may be a central element of development policy, reform which, in turn, can focus on preserving the past or on building a new future. Nostalgia can be productive, where it inspires to preserve, to rebuild, to reconnect, to rethink old communities in a new context, to adapt and reinvent where necessary and preserve where possible. And nostalgia can be dangerous, when the desire for a lost 'perfect' world blinds us for the opportunities of the present, for the problems in the past, and for the evolving nature of communities and their governance. Nothing stays the same.

What is often blamed for the ailments of rural communities is modernity itself, the structure of nation-states, their bureaucracies, reliance on science, erasure of local identities in favor of national citizenship, its forgetfulness of traditions and local knowledge in favor of science and whatever is useful in a globalized economy. That economy is also blamed for environmental pollution, unhealthy and tasteless food, animal abuse, the loss of family farms, and the homogeneity of contemporary landscapes, contemporary food and life as such. It can also be blamed for a perceived loss of spirituality, and a lost connection with the natural world.

While many of these problems are a bitter reality, and while many connections exist among them, it is problematic to create one big enemy, one boogeyman out of this cluster of issues, which then explains everything and has to be fought or resisted. Often, the boogeyman is modernity itself; for other nostalgics it is liberal democracy (neo-liberalism) which is understood as the dominant form of capitalist democracy, promoted by the USA and rolled out over the rest of the world. What is problematic in this analysis? Isn't it possible to choose one's ideology? Indeed, no question about it. We refer back to our sections on models of democracies, and on the intricate connections with development approaches. But that reference is also a warning for creating overly monolithic concepts, too big and too harshly delineated concepts of which too much explanation is expected. We also bring up again the evolutionary character of governance, and the achievements of modernity: economic growth, science, a separation of powers, checks and balances (less oppression), the differentiation of law, politics, science, education and religion (so, e.g. religion doesn't define science and politicians are not judges), and a higher degree of freedom in the reinvention of self and community (so a past identity doesn't define your present and future completely). In other words, rejecting modernity as a whole does not make much sense, and it is impossible, while understanding all the problems as resulting from one bad thing does not make much sense either. It veils the diversity in forms of democracy and capitalism, it veils the options for self-transformation in governance. Anti-modernism is not a viable ideology. It does not explain much and it does not inspire any realistic practical advice.

Figure 11.1. 'Please close the door behind you. This helps the bakery maintain an even temperature for our bread makings process'. Teaching the customers in a village near Bellingham, Washington, USA. The bakery is a cooperative, focusing on organic, local products and small scale community development, by offering youth an opportunity to learn the trade. Photo: Monica Gruzmacher. © ZEF/University of Bonn, Germany.

**Example 11.1. Terroir and local products.**

Terroir is basically the idea that place makes a difference. It is best known from the world of wine making, where French (and other European) winemakers traditionally opposed the practice in new wine countries (USA, Australia, Chile, New Zealand, etc.) to use the grape variety (Merlot, Cabernet Sauvignon...) as the main marker of a wine's identity. For the French, terroir is everything, not simply the grape. Grapes and wines taste different according to the place of production: climate, soil, micro-climate, exposition, drainage, methods and times of pruning, picking, blending, pressing, fermenting, barreling make a difference. Emphasizing the notion of terroir means emphasizing the importance of this blend of characteristics that make a place unique, a product unique, and tie the product to the place. The terroir system in France is highly regulated and institutionalized, following a systems of AOC's (Appellation d'Origine Controlee), where wine regions are divided in subregions (AOC's, e.g. Bordeaux including Pomerol), and subregions in AOC and non-AOC lands. In the Bordeaux area, one can own vineyards which do not fall under one of the subregions, and in a subregion, one can be blessed with the AOC label (thus higher prices, but also production criteria), or not. In the USA and elsewhere, terroir is invoked more and more frequently now, with wines named first after a place (Napa Valley in California, Mendoza in Argentina), while in Europe, the influence of American and international markets and tastes brought about the production of new wines based on one grape (versus a blend) or the re-labeling of existing wines now under the grape variety name. Especially for wine makers not covered under the more prestigious denominations (so outside AOC in France, outside similar boundaries in other European countries), referring to the grape, maybe also the country, provides an easier marketing strategy.

Localism fits well into the governance model of communitarianism, and the reflections on nostalgia and anti-modernism apply to a large degree to the whole communitarian tradition. There, a similar balancing act between past and future can be observed, and a forgetting of the double nature of old small-town life, the caress of familiarity and mutual support and the suffocation of local control, tradition and suspicion of everything new and unfamiliar. Closer inspection of our other governance models allows us to see however, that localism can also work under neo-liberalism (allowing for greater local diversity in a larger small government frame), in a civil society model (if not dominated by a few large corporate players) and, most notably, under civic republicanism. We believe that especially this last governance model offers a way to rethink localism, in a more future-oriented way, and a way that can overcome the traditionalist bias.

If localism can be truly participatory, and emphasize educated, active and critical citizens that never entirely identify with one faction or one sort of group, then there are

There are, of course, other agricultural products with a similarly long history of appreciation, of local identity and excellence. The wine history helps however to understand similar discussions there. In order to distinguish oneself, to move out of the market of bulk products, and into different price ranges and production and distribution channels, more and more agricultural products try strategies of specification, by branding according to variety and/or terroir. Coffee becomes Arabica coffee becomes Colombian Arabica and then Bourbon Arabica from Quindo, Valderosa Estate. Coffee drinkers around the world are becoming more discerning, and this helps the evolution. Chocolate might be following a similar path. One can observe often a combination of rediscovery of local quality and product quality, of tradition, and an invention of tradition.

Over-emphasizing terroir is excluding many potential competitors, and especially new arrivals on the market. The new wine countries often complained that the French insistence on terroir was simply a trick to keep them out. On the other hand, it cannot be denied that Riesling grapes can produce the most diverse wines, depending on place and production method. It is a never ending discussion. But, we would insist, the level of the discussion will be higher, and the quality of judgment, when more players have a better understanding of the place, the production, and the product. A generation ago, nobody in North America (outside the Italian immigrant communities) knew what espresso is. (Other terroir products, as of now: maple syrup, cheese, spirits, beers, etc.).

**Further reading**

Trubek, A. (2008). The taste of place: a cultural journey into terroir. Berkeley, CA, USA: University of California Press.

definitely more openings towards other development models and rural development perspectives. One can think of rural innovation approaches in the line of our previous chapter, of sustainability perspectives, or, under more tenuous circumstances, livelihood approaches. Since local autonomy is emphasized, policy integration at the local level becomes more feasible, and land consolidation and other forms of spatial planning can be considered more easily. In a civic-republican community, rural localism will be well-informed, and this can enhance the quality of institutional reform, and the adaptive capacity of governance. Another useful point of civic republicanism for localism is precisely that tradition should be respected but transformed, that laws can never be rigid. Tradition can never be allowed to create rigid governance and unchangeable laws. Good laws are adaptive laws, responding to changing internal and external environments. Tradition guides community values, but those values change. Existing governance, existing identities, and existing traditions (visible in informal institutions, underpinning many formal institutions such as laws) should always be observed and understood as the starting point of any action and decision in governance, but governance itself, and broader community change, change that starting point.

If, e.g. a community is proud of an almost forgotten vegetable, then simply returning to the crop in the old production and marketing method is not a good idea, while simply forgetting the crop can also be criticized. From the civic republican perspective on localism just proposed, one could derive that a new marketing campaign is needed, that promoting the beautiful village can promote the vegetable that a new and hardier variety might be profitable, leading to calls for extension activity. That new variety might become the claim to fame a generation later. Another example: a local dish might be almost forgotten, and a tourist entrepreneur can see its value. One ingredient is also almost forgotten, inspiring another entrepreneur to fill the niche. The two business women team up with local government to start a place branding campaign in which both the ingredient (another vegetable) and the dish figure prominently. One of the business women decides to take the dish to the provincial capital, in a new restaurant, and five years later decides to move there. One person left the community, but contributed first, and a more adaptive spirit of localism is still alive.

## Further reading

Blair, H. (2000). Participation and accountability at the periphery: democratic local governance in six countries. World Development, 28(1), 21-39.

Cox, K.R. and Mair, A. (1988). Locality and community in the politics of local economic development. Annals of the Association of American Geographers, 78(2), 307-325.

Cox, K.R. (ed.) (1997). Spaces of globalization: reasserting the power of the local. London, UK: Guilford Press.

Feagan, R. (2007). The place of food: mapping out the 'local' in local food systems. Progress in Human Geography, 31(1), 23-42.

Hinrichs, C.C. (2003). The practice and politics of food system localization. Journal of Rural Studies, 19(1), 33-45.

Johnson, C. (2001). Local democracy, democratic decentralisation and rural development: theories, challenges and options for policy. Development Policy Review, 19(4), 521-532.

Lane, M.B. and Corbett, T. (2005). The tyranny of localism: indigenous participation in community-based environmental management. Journal of Environmental Policy and Planning, 7(2), 141-159.

Mander, J. (ed.) (2014). The case against the global economy: and for a turn towards localization. Abingdon, UK: Routledge.

Mohan, G. and Stokke, K. (2000). Participatory development and empowerment: the dangers of localism. Third World Quarterly, 21(2), 247-268.

Ranger, T. and Vaughan, O. (eds.) (1993). Legitimacy and the state in twentieth-century Africa. London, UK: Macmillan Press.

Spear, T. (2003). Neo-traditionalism and the limits of invention in British colonial Africa. The Journal of African History, 44, 3-27.

Swyngedouw, E. (2000). Authoritarian governance, power, and the politics of rescaling. Environment and Planning D, 18(1), 63-76.

## 11.2 Place branding, community design and narratives

In the quest for new localism, in a modern and globalized society, we want to touch on the possibilities of place branding (introduced earlier) and, in particular, the potential of combined planning/branding strategies. Place branding policies can be a way to integrate other policies, while focusing on and valuing features of the local physical and social landscape. A combination of place branding and planning can make planning more sensitive for the economic implications of planning (negative and positive), while planning can make place branding more sensitive for the governance embeddings of any activity touching place identity, and for the potential of spatial intervention and landscape preservation for tradition-based innovation. Stories, or *narratives*, will be essential in the formation of such combined planning/branding strategies, which can give a new content to localism. We explain.

Planning strategies will hinge on the value that is attached in local narratives to an image of place. If not embedded in local understandings of place, its value, planning will have little effect – another case of formal institutions and their informal substrates. Planning strategies will rely on the planning tools available – they have to take the existing actor/institution configuration as a starting point. And they will have to rely on the informal rules of implementation and enforcement of the planning tools. Places with strong planning traditions will have less problems in making and implementing new plans, as actors got used to coordination by planning, and the community will more likely trust that plans can reflect and further community narratives. But even in places with weaker planning traditions, we believe it is possible to come up with planning strategies that are respectful of the local landscape and culture, and are economically sustainable, if there is already a strong place identity. Place identities are not concepts with clear and simple definitions; they are evolving narratives about the past, present and future of a place, stories containing associations with images, sounds and smells.

We need to go deeper into place branding theory now, and clarify that place identities exist, but can also be created. They are always created, in the sense that they do not exist in nature, are social constructions, but we are saying here that a conscious, deliberate creation is possible to a certain extent. Place branding can help, place branding embedded in governance and linked to spatial planning, can help more. It can make the creation of new images and narratives more context-sensitive, more rooted in existing images and stories, and it can make them more tangible and influential by the power of planning – and community design. A strong place identity can easily create value and attract demand, and therefore realign the incentive structures for local actors. It can underpin place branding efforts, so more and more people can become invested in maintaining and improving places and landscapes, since these underpin the image driving and safeguarding economic value. Place branding is also marketing, and in that regard, we can say that it is better to sell existing and appreciated assets than to repackage scarce assets based on a narrative that is not shared in the community. A valuable place brand encourages local cooperation, long-term strategies, sustainable use. It can also encourage comprehensive planning and respect for the landscape (an important part of the matrix enabling quality maintenance and ease of reinvention at later stages).

Spatial planning, and especially community design, can contribute to the discovery and the creation of a place identity that produces economic value. A new place identity can sometimes be synthesized out of the voices and valuations one finds in a community; this scenario can be realistic when there is not strong place identity, when it is not promoted and when place branding is firmly rooted in governance (and not, e.g. simply in the hands of an external consultant). People in a community are often not aware of

Figure 11.2. Landscape near San Gemigniano, Tuscany, Italy. Tuscany was a powerful place brand before place branding was invented, relying on product quality, old trade, early tourism, self-promotion through the arts and literature, and relying not on grand planning and marketing schemes but on informal arrangements and later selectively and erratically applied formal policies. We believe it worked because of a deep awareness with all actors that the main asset was and is Tuscany itself. All are aware of the virtuous circle that brought prosperity, the perceived links between product quality, quality of life, and the appearance of the landscapes and towns of Tuscany. Photo: Thor Hendriks. © Thor Hendriks.

Rural development

the value which might be assigned to their surroundings or traditions. Place branding offers the possibility to combine certain features and activities under a shared theme, a common denominator, which can serve as the starting point for brand construction. Brand construction can recombine assets and starts from the recognition of existing assets, but it is important to see, we believe, that brands, as new unifying images and narratives, create new assets: features and elements of a community that had little value, can acquire value when place identity and place brand (the complex associations with products) create a new interpretive frame. New features and elements can be added which make sense in that frame. If Tuscany is a gastronomic paradise, then Tuscan tomatoes must be superior; if Tuscan tomatoes are superior, then Tuscan zucchini cannot be too bad either – so why not pay more? Of course, this is commodification in the sense described earlier, and for some ideologies and development discourses, this will not be palatable.

We believe that planning or community design and place branding can find their synergies by capitalizing on existing place narratives, narratives which structure place identities and highlight certain things as assets. Figuring out what these narratives are, and how they define assets, is then important for both planning and place branding. It offers both professionals and other actors embracing the perspective the opportunity to work towards a shared narrative on the present that can coordinate decision-making on the future.

If we want local development strategies that look for synergy between design and place branding, we will have to look for a narrative for the future that is site-specific, and not driven by planning formulas, development formulas or branding formulas that will lead to uniformity. The development plan can be partly a design then, a design which builds on existing narratives and associated assets, and provides a new framing narrative. The choices in the plan ought to be inspired by that narrative, and because of its importance, that narrative itself ought to come up in governance, after deliberation of alternatives. We emphasise that we are far here from marketing slogans or simple repetitions of existing routines. Understanding and mapping of existing narratives in a small, rural community is not only important for planning, design and branding professionals potentially involved, but for all actors in governance.

If such sensitive mapping and reflection takes place, it will be easier to identify a mix of existing and desirable assets that will make sense for both local residents and for potential visitors, new residents, investors and future buyers of products associated with the place. If there is no persuasive link between narrative and assets, between place and assets, between current and proposed narratives, then the branding/planning hybrid will not work as a development vision. In places like Tuscany, with already strong place identities, place brands and a familiarity with value creation by means of planning (design) and branding, one can say that planning, identity creation and value

**Example 11.2. Place branding as policy integration.**

Place branding has often been dismissed as a purely neo-liberal exercise, where places are reduced to products, to be sold, adapted to markets, at the expense of local values and democracy. We would present a slightly different picture. Place branding came up in the early 2000's as a concept referring to a bundle of strategies at several scales, from the very local to the national. Simon Anholt wrote the most influential books. Nation branding can help economic competitiveness, but also diplomatic efforts, and it can provide an internal focus of reflection on long range strategy. Regional development and local development are similarly served by a reflection on what is unique, valuable in the area, in terms of physical qualities, heritage, skill sets, industries, networks, and how this matches the images circulating abroad. Both these existing images and the local ideas can embody value, can be starting points of policy-making. Positive internal images can start policy coordination to build on these assets, while positive external images can have the same effect. The perception of value in the environment and/or the perception of value internally can spark the creation of value. In that sense, both can become performative, can have reality effects.

Place branding can be the catalyst and the place for policy integration towards rural development. If place branding becomes a way to structure development efforts, it cannot be separated from governance, from economic development, infrastructure policy, from planning and design. Such integration can make the brand more grounded, more close to community values and identity, and it can give it more impact, implementation power, while, conversely, the brand constructed will less likely be a constraint on the future development. Brands represent value, and if brands are tied to qualities of a place and a community, that economic value can help to protect these qualities and stabilize the community. But if brands are narrowly defined yet imposed on a variety of policies, if they are shaped solely by external consultants steeped in marketing expertise, then they will be an obstacle to reinvention in a different direction. Tuscany can sell olive oil and hotel beds and jewelry because of Tuscany, and these things help to preserve the Tuscan landscape, but the brand tied to history, landscape, food, beauty, has been a hindrance to attempts at high-tech diversification.

creation proceeded in a dialectical process. Step by step, they reshaped each other. In other places, this did not happen yet. Sometimes, it will be very tough, when conflicts and divisions are acute, when few assets can be conceived, from whatever narrative, when existing narratives offer few opportunities for development new, more productive ones, more able to support community visions and designs. Yet, in such situations, any development vision, from any approach, would fall on barren, infertile soil. When the proposed new localism, localism by branding and design, does work, it can create a simultaneous strengthening of existing qualities and creation of new qualities, a gradual

Place branding has therefore to be considered as an ongoing conversation and an ongoing reconstruction of brand, its content, its representation, and its impact on policy integration. If a brand is only for tourism promotion, it can be more specific and stable, but it does not utilize the full potential of place branding, the spillover effects to other activities, current, and possible. On the other hand, if the brand is present everywhere, and is expected to guide development in general, it cannot have the same specificity. It is always a balancing act, and many motto's for regions and cities are disappointingly bland and similar. We believe this is the result of several entwined misunderstandings: first of all a narrowing of place branding to slogans and mottos. While there is no need to rely much on those devices, and can communicate and reinforce a brand through actions, through coordinated action in governance, leading to a new and related activities, to a recognizable approach in spatial development, heritage preservation, in community organizing. After which this unity can be named and renamed. Secondly, there is the usual tendency to copy success stories and best practices, while this does not work (cf the rest of this book) and while this approach is inherently inconsistent with place branding, looking for unique characteristics and selling points.

Coming back to the critique of place branding as neo-liberalism, we can add that what is sold and what is protected does not have to be the same: what is protected can help to sell other things, what is sold can help to sell other things, and if nothing has to be sold in a literal sense, if simply making qualities visible is enough to stabilize the financial base (by attracting new residents, tourists, etc.), then that is fine too. Place branding, in our view, is simply a reminder to think of what is unique, of how that could be valued, developed, be associated with economic value, a reminder that policy integration is possible towards that end. It represents an economically inspired path towards context-sensitive development strategy.

**Further reading**

Govers, R. and Go, F. (2009). Place branding: glocal, virtual and physical identities, constructed, imagined and experienced. London, UK: Palgrave Macmillan.

improvement of a physical and socio-economic frame that makes it easier to stabilise value of existing products and activities and spin off new ones.

When it does work, governance itself starts to revolve more and more around narrative. It becomes storytelling. We can see this as something unique to this approach to rural development, but we can also say that in this case it just becomes more visible that development is always storytelling. Futures can never be entirely predicted and never be entirely steered. Governance, with its configurations can think up certain futures and bring them closer, and what makes plans, laws, policies, development visions, more persuasive is their narrative nature, and the fit with existing narratives, stories people and communities tell themselves to make sense of the world.

The knowledge and expertise that will be more influential in development visions, e.g. in this new branded localism, can come from different places, and will be framed by the story. As mentioned before, localism as such is open to very hybrid development strategies, and can include elements of most of the strategies discussed before. In the case of the branded and modern localism proposed, the nature of the story, the nature of the images, the nature of the assets found, will determine which methods will be used, and which knowledge will be foregrounded. One can imagine sustainability narratives and environmental expertise, or a new agricultural focus, in organic fashion, and new extension initiatives. And one can imagine a re-examination of history and heritage, and a livelihoods approach inclusive of tourist development.

## Further reading

Govers, R. and Go, F. (2009). Place branding: glocal, virtual and physical identities, constructed, imagined and experienced. London, UK: Palgrave Macmillan

Hobart, M. (1995). As I lay laughing – Encountering global knowledge in Bali. In: Fardon, R. (ed.), Counterworks. Managing the diversity of knowledge. London, UK: Routledge, pp. 49-72.

Hornidge, A.-K. (2011). 'Creative industries' – Economic program and boundary concept. Journal of Southeast Asian Studies, 42(2), 253-279.

Nygren, A. (1999). Local knowledge in the environment-development discourse. Critique of Anthropology, 19(3), 267-288.

Sillitoe, P. and Marzano, M. (2009). Future of indigenous knowledge research in development. Futures, 41, 13-23.

Sillitoe, P. (1998). What, know natives? Local knowledge in development. Social Anthropology, 6(2), 203-220.

# III Combining and concluding

In this part, we reconnect the different parts of the book and work towards practical and theoretical conclusions. We know by now that simple recipes for rural development do not exist and that anyone (including ourselves) espousing the like should be treated with some suspicion. What we present is a framework for understanding development strategies as embedded in governance, as well as a framework for analyzing a specific community, its governance path, its ideology, and its issues. Analysis using these frameworks can help a range of actors recombine elements of the different development and rural development approaches discussed in this book and then craft a strategy suitable for a given community.

# 12. Bringing the pieces together

*Politics have no relation to morals*

Niccolo Machiavelli, 1509

## Abstract

In this chapter, we return to the models of democracy presented in the first chapters and link them more systematically with different approaches to development and rural development. We work towards an open methodology for the analysis of communities and their governance path, and of ways to think about combining elements of rural development approaches, and of linking governance models, development perspectives and rural development approaches. In some cases, the links between the governance model and the approaches to development and rural development are so tight that they cannot be easily separated and recombined; in other cases, the couplings are looser, such that more opportunities for recombining and reaping the benefits of several approaches exist.

## 12.1 Looking back

Evolutions in governance always take place in various framings; they are more likely to happen in this direction than in that direction, depending on patterns of differentiation, dependencies, power/knowledge and actor/institution configurations. If a certain model of democracy is already recognizable in current governance, and if the dominant discourses in that community still find that model desirable, then there is little chance of imposing a shift of governance towards another model, regardless of the expertise or force applied. If, on the other hand, there is a growing awareness among various actors that change is needed and existing configurations make it possible to move in a different directions, many entrenched dependencies can be overcome. Nothing in our analyses amounts to the idea of determinism. Nevertheless, various dependencies and configurations do shape the likelihood that certain policies will emerge in certain places, that they will be interpreted in a certain manner, and that they will have certain effects. They also shape the niches for various forms of expertise in these processes of policy formulation, enactment and implementation.

Our conceptual frame can help us to quickly discern a few recurring issues in many proposals for rural development, projects, visions, and integrated policies. We know now how to quickly make a first assessment of any vision that comes up. First of all there is the need to scrutinize any proposal for social engineering assumptions: what can be steered and how? We must then evaluate the assumed level of policy integration. Many forms of development projects and policies, as well as environmental policies with development aims, assume high levels of policy integration (and therefore expertise integration), which are either entirely unfeasible or threaten to undermine both the democratic quality of governance and the advantages of specialization and differentiated expertise in governance. They can be unfeasible by relying on levels and types of coordination that are impossible to achieve, within given configurations, or by assuming straight, clear and strong impacts of policies, laws and plans that are much more nuanced and unpredictable in reality. Furthermore, many approaches and projects assume levels of transparency in society at large and governance systems in particular that do not exist in reality. Partly this is related to a blurry vision of informality. Ideal scenarios are often conflated with reality, as recognized already by Machiavelli; this is an issue in both policy making and science aimed at influencing in policy. On the other hand, we can see that the simplification of society to market and the reduction of development to market development ignores many real complexities of society and environment.

So, the proposed theoretical frame can help to make quick assessments of a plan or policy for rural development. For people in a community or observers and analysts of a community it can be necessary to get a deeper insight in the nature of the community and its issues, and the possible ways forward, to come to new policy proposals.

We propose a two-part method: first analysis, then crafting of a strategy.

Who is doing the analyzing and the crafting already depends on the (first) analysis, on the nature of the community and the issues. In a very communitarian environment, in a highly participatory version, the analyzing and crafting will likely be all local, while in a neo-liberal environment with low participation levels, there can be analysis and crafting (of, e.g. an institutional reform proposal) by hired consultants and national-level administrations.

The reader will have to make up her mind, when looking at a community, which role she is willing to play and can play: is she an insider trying to push governance in a certain pre-conceived direction, as an activist convinced a priori of the value of this or that approach? Or, an insider who wants to broker a new pact between other players, so the community can move forward? An outside observer with an agenda, or without an agenda? A consultant wishing to sell services? A scientist wishing to understand what happened in a community and how it is trying to move forward? For all these roles, and others, the conceptual tools offered in this book can be useful, but, we argue, it is important to reflect on the role assumed.

## 12.2 Analysis: path and context

For the analytic part of the strategy, we can be relatively short. We refer back to the first chapters, and draw the attention to additional concepts introduced step-wise in later chapters, building on the initial frame. Analysis for rural development is in our view first of all governance research and analysis. This can be further distinguished in path analysis and context analysis (or, context mapping and path mapping).

*Context analysis* can extend to physical landscapes, economic landscapes and political/legal landscapes. It can extend to the natural resources relevant for the evolution of governance, the historical landscape, the economic structure and issues, and the institutions of higher-level units and communities (in multi-level governance). As we know, context is in principle infinite, so the analyst has to draw boundaries. These boundaries come up, become visible in the analysis. One has to start somewhere, and the somewhere is the community itself. Some assumptions are safe: if there is a higher level authority with influence on rural development in the community, some sketch of its influence will be part of the context mapping. If the community is highly dependent on a natural resource, some mapping of the physical landscape has to be part of the context mapping. Even in those two simple examples, however, it is still clear that the context mapping starts from the community. What is a relevant context for a community becomes visible by analyzing the community, and drawing circles from there, not by starting with a comprehensive mapping exercise, leading to an encyclopedia with many facts and few insights.

*Path analysis* is the analysis of the co-evolution in communities, drawing on the concepts of configurations discussed in detail above: actor/institution, formal/informal institutions, power/knowledge configurations. It can pay special attention to rigidities in the evolution of governance, by paying attention to path dependency, interdependency, and goal dependency. Path analysis can go back far in time, or not. If at the starting point of initial analysis there is a configuration that apparently structures much of what comes later, then an understanding of how this configuration came about might lend insight into how it could possibly be changed. Many other concepts introduced earlier can be useful, depending on the nature of the path and the nature of the mapping exercise (e.g. your role and goals as the one doing the mapping). We will not list all of these concepts again; the reader can consult the previous chapters to see them in context, as part of the overall reasoning, and she can consult the Glossary at the end.

Governance extends beyond government actors, and this makes the mapping exercise more complex but also more interesting. The 'actors' change over time, and they can be found in unexpected places. A land owner might not be visible in government but can have much influence; a group can be silent, but this silence can be strategic, intended to push policy in a certain direction. Actor/institution configurations link actors and institutions, and the institutions there include informal ones. This creates an interesting complexity too: actors can play one role on the front stage of governance, another role on the back stage. They can officially espouse one vision, but hold differing opinions in practice. They can adhere to a policy for one official reason, but de facto stick to it for very different reasons. The coalition in power can present a plan supposedly for the common good, for their ideological vision of the common good, but in fact it can be a response to a perceived threat to their power. Or, it can be both. A new plan can be presented as a product of the brain of a talented designer, who presents an elaborate explanation of the design, but the main structure can really reflect the power struggle between three actors, or the struggle between three sorts of expertise, each associated with an actor.

The mapping and analysis of governance evolutions is therefore not a simple matter, and it cannot be simply tied to this or that discipline. Which *methods* are most useful in a given case, and which kind of information or disciplinary knowledge is useful, all of this will differ. Governance analysis can therefore be team-work, and it can be inter-disciplinary. From the general method of governance paths mapping, we need to derive methods that can be useful for specific cases. We speak of detailed methods, or ancillary methods, fitting in the frame of the general path mapping approach. The combination of detailed method hinges on the case, but also on the ambition and speed of the analysis: do we need a quick preparation for a council meeting, is this a preparation for a new comprehensive visioning exercise which can take a few years, or is it a student research project of three months? It crucially depends on the role assumed: who is doing it, in which role, for which purpose? This being said, and with a casual reference to research methods books for more information, we can list a few detailed methods for path analysis.

*Participant observation* can be very valuable for understanding governance configurations. relying on documents or formal interviews alone will not necessarily reveal much on power/knowledge configurations. Participation, spending more time, gaining trust, participating possibly in different roles (cf our remarks on positionality) can bring an insider's perspective, as well as the testing of different perspectives. Participation, especially over time and when deeply embedded, will necessarily influence the observation. Long term observation holds the promise of observing more complex patterns and configurations, and it holds the risk of becoming too involved, losing critical distance. Distrust of older modernist methods, e.g. relying on a few statistical parameters supposed to grasp the 'key characteristics' of a community, brought the even older participation observation method to the fore again.

*Interviews and surveys* can be useful. Surveys serve to link governance with community, i.e. to grasp community perceptions of governance, issues and the ways governance has tackled these issues – of plans, laws and policies. Interviews can be structured or open, using a detective method, following leads, finding clues and building on previous interviews and insights in the reconstruction of networks, power relations and informal institutions and their relation to formality.

*Document analysis* is a key element of path analysis. Documents can include minutes of council meetings, versions of policies and plans, press releases from government, internal memos and assessments, but also documents produced by other organizations involved in governance: alternative plans emerging from neighborhood associations, visions and policies of the chamber of commerce, minutes of an environmental council long shunned by local government, etc. Again, which documents become relevant will transpire in the course of the path mapping. Actors can also be found to be relevant, implying the importance of documents revealing their nature and strategies.

What can be done with the documents? In addition to offering facts, documents can form the basis for *rhetorical analysis*. Texts are true in a situation where they convince a relevant group of people that convincing rules have been applied in a convincing way; therefore, it becomes interesting to study the different ways people tried to convince each other. Different techniques of persuasion cannot be separated from different concepts of truth, of text, of science. Rhetorical analysis of policy-related documents can be the analysis of ways to persuade, leading to an understanding of how persuasion relates to governance configurations and evolutions. Which arguments were apparently persuasive? Which type of knowledge was invoked? Which methods were used? To which authorities (including specific actors) do the documents refer? What was apparently naturalized, and therefore very convincing? What went without saying or was not questioned, prefaced by phrases like 'We all know ...'?

Rhetorical analysis can lead into *discourse analysis*. Discourse analysis tries to distinguish different discourses, different perspectives, conceptual structures that are tied with a certain version of reality, of past, present and future, on the community, its problems and futures. Some discourses are clear narratives, stories, traces and elements of which can be easily spotted with various actors in documents, while others are conceptual structures, providing perspectives which cannot be so easily found, as they might lie deeper under what is communicated visibly. Discourses can be more and less comprehensive (covering more or less of the world), they can evolve slower or faster, and they can form discursive coalitions, which can lead to a merger into one more influential perspective, or into one absorbing another one. Actors can be closely tied to one discourse, or not. Coalitions between actors can be easier because discourses are overlapping or show affinities. Discourses exert power, because a perspective on reality always highlights aspects and hides others, highlights certain relations and larger concepts, hides or undermines others. Controlling discourse is controlling reality, and therefore power. We refer to the passages on power/knowledge configurations.

If documents go back farther in time, the classical historical method of analysis deserves attention. The *historical method* fits well the Sherlock Holmes metaphor in the path mapping methodology. It is the analysis of historical documents in light of their authenticity, influences, authorship, causality and genre. In post-modernism, universal claims of truth are met with suspicion, so the historical context of anything becomes more important. A truth is a truth in a time and space and group. The historical antecedents of behavior, structure, organization, knowledge, become more important. The classic methodology to find historical documents, check their authenticity, connect them chronologically and causally, finds application in other disciplines than history proper. For governance path analysis, going back farther in time, historical method can help, e.g. to establish the lineage of documents in reality, as opposed to what it claims to be. A plan A can refer openly to plan B as its precedent, and it can refer to plan C as its larger context, but historical, rhetorical and context mapping together can point out that the actual antecedents are 1 and 2, associated with actors not acknowledged now, that the reference to C is largely rhetorical, and without much substance.

A special and more theoretically refined version of the classic historical method is Michel Foucault's duet of methods: *genealogy* and *archaeology*. Genealogy is the search for the background of a concept, i.e. its predecessors, looking in a wide variety of contexts (e.g. not only the predecessors with the same name or in the same organization). Rural development approaches have a lineage that extends beyond concepts and theories and practices labeled 'rural development'. Genealogy uses a wide variety of historical documents. A search for the predecessors of a concept then often leads to deconstructions and reconstructions of older frames of concepts, and older concepts of knowledge. What counted as expertise in governance 200 years ago would not count as such now. Uncovering clearly ideological roots of certain expert concepts opens the

Figure 12.1. Traditional knowledge in new categories to enable linking with other forms of knowledge. Plant lore collected and organized by family in a research laboratory of the University of Brunei Darussalam in the middle of primary rain forest. Photo: Anna-Katharina Hornidge. © ZEF/University of Bonn, Germany.

door to reassessing their role in governance. Archaeology is not limited to the series of transformations of a single concept. Rather, it looks for the backgrounds of a concept while digging deeper on the spot. The picture of the backgrounds on the spot is more important than the migrations of a concept – necessarily implying the reconstruction of some other backgrounds. Governance of a place uncovered through archaeology will lead to different actors, institution, contexts and expertise than following the concept of municipal governance back in time (genealogy) and then linking with the evolution of a particular community.

Moving away from the documents and the observation of governance sites, we can go out in the community for more open *fieldwork*. Fieldwork can be broadly understood as all the document collecting, interviewing and data gathering that takes place on site. We can also refer to it as the combination of all sorts of observation in site. What should be observed? This depends on the path analysis and context analysis together. One can always start with exploratory observation, to get an idea of the community. Later, themes can emerge, sites and topics and groups. One can observe people, their activities in a place, but also the organization of space, the surrounding landscape, the use of natural resources.

*Observation* can lead to *sketching, mapping*, to *map collecting, map analysis*. Again, what is to be sketched, mapped, collected, analyzed, and how, will come up in the analysis itself. Environmental quality can emerge as an important theme, so mapping can focus on that, and the same holds true for map collection and analysis. Often, much information is already avaiable, many maps, GIS (geographical information systems) files and so forth. GIS can assist in further analyzing spatial data. Observation can lead to other data collection, to counting, looking for existing statistics and possibly producing new ones. As with maps and as with context in general, statistics knows no boundaries. Just as context is limitless and mapping can go on forever, counting never stops. And just as with context and maps, what is relevant does not emerge from encyclopedic exercises, but in an investigation, and through the use of a conceptual framework.

The last paragraph brought out, too, that potentially any sort of knowledge, associated with any disciplines, can become relevant for path analysis. If environmental issues prove important, then ecological expertise or environmental engineering expertise can be helpful to fully assess governance paths (showing, e.g. issues in a different light, problems in places, qualities in places, showing alternative analyses, alternative decision-paths, showing more clearly the patterns of inclusion/exclusion/selective interpretation of scientific knowledge). That does not mean our reader needs to be a universal specialist. It points again at the potential for teamwork and at the need to cultivate reflexivity and a pragmatic approach. It also holds a more simple methodological point: that the net for interviews and document collection might have to be cast wider than expected. One can include an ecologist in the research team, but sometimes it might be enough to interview an ecologist, or maybe to discuss a more technical issue or document with her, to refine your interpretation.

## Further reading

Al-Kodmany, K. (2002). Visualization tools and methods in community planning: from freehand sketches to virtual reality. Journal of Planning Literature, 17(2), 189-211.

Burgess, R.G. (2002). In the field: an introduction to field research. London, UK: Routledge.

Bryman, A. (2003). Research methods and organization studies. London, UK: Routledge.

Burrell, G. (1988). Modernism, post modernism and organizational analysis: the contribution of Michel Foucault. Organization Studies, 9(2), 221-235.

Chambers, R. (1994). The origins and practice of participatory rural appraisal. World Development, 22(7), 953-969.

DeWalt, K.M. and DeWalt, B.R. (2010). Participant observation: a guide for fieldworkers. New York: Rowman Altamira.

Escobar, A. (1985). Discourse and power in development: Michel Foucault and the relevance of his work to the Third World. Alternatives, 10, 377-400.

Flyvbjerg, B. (1998). Rationality and power: democracy in practice. Chicago, IL, USA: University of Chicago press.

Flyvbjerg, B. (2001). Making social science matter: why social inquiry fails and how it can succeed again. Cambridge, UK: Cambridge University Press.

Forester, J. (ed.) (1993). The argumentative turn in policy analysis and planning. Durham, NC, USA: Duke University Press.

Foucault, M. (2012). The archaeology of knowledge. New York, NY, USA: Random House LLC.

Gill, J. and Johnson, P. (2010). Research methods for managers. Thousand Oaks, CA, USA: Sage.

Grbich, C. (2012). Qualitative data analysis: an introduction. Thousand Oaks, CA, USA: Sage.

Jacobs, K. (2006). Discourse analysis and its utility for urban policy research. Urban Policy and Research, 24(1), 39-52.

Jason, L.A., Keys, C.B., Suarez-Balcazar, Y.E., Taylor, R.R. and Davis, M.I. (2004). Participatory community research: theories and methods in action. Washington, DC, USA: American Psychological Association.

Martin, A. and Sherington, J. (1997). Participatory research methods – implementation, effectiveness and institutional context. Agricultural Systems, 55(2), 195-216.

McNabb, D.E. (2013). Research methods in public administration and nonprofit management: Quantitative and qualitative approaches. Armonk, NY, USA: ME Sharpe.

Mikkelsen, B. (1995). Methods for development work and research: a guide for practitioners. London, UK: Sage Publications.

Miller, G.J. and Yang, K. (eds.) (2007). Handbook of research methods in public administration. Boca Raton, FL, USA: CRC press.

Patton, C., Sawicki, D. and Clark, J. (2012). Basic methods of policy analysis and planning. Chicago, IL, USA: Pearson.

Rose, G. (1997). Situating knowledges: positionality, reflexivities and other tactics. Progress in Human Geography, 21(3), 305-320.

Shafer, R.J. and Bennett, D.H. (1969). A guide to historical method. Homewood, IL, USA: Dorsey Press.

Yanow, D. (ed.) (2000). Conducting interpretive policy analysis. London, UK: Sage.

## 12.3 Crafting a strategy: concepts of combining

The problem remains of how to craft a rural development strategy for a community, small or large. As said, we would recommend first an analysis of the sort described above. The analysis and the strategy depend on the role you are assuming (reader), and on the type of development strategy or vision one is thinking of: how comprehensive, how participatory, how long-term, etc.? This last question will probably be answered differently before and after the analysis.

As we have stressed above, there are no simple recipes or formulas. The models of governance, development and rural development perspectives discussed here may claim to each be the best, but that in fact each recipe has stronger and weaker sides, and an individual community can probably combine ingredients from several recipes. We tried to offer a conceptual framework that can help different actors to take another look at the existing situation in a community and the path that led to it, before evaluating what the issues are and how they can be addressed.

This is also the reason why we did not go very deep into the analysis of 'typical' rural issues one might find discussed at great length in many other handbooks: shrinking populations, lack of services, lack of jobs, etc. These are indeed important problems one will meet in many rural areas across the world, and we touched on them in the introductory chapters and here and there later, but, these issues will look different from the different perspectives discussed in this book. Situations become problems from certain perspectives, and the suggested solutions will also emerge in those perspectives. What is seen as 'lack of services' in Holland, will look very comfortable indeed in Western Canada. What looks like a dangerous dependence on one industry in Germany, will look utterly normal in the USA. What is a serious population decline in a Belgian village will be looked with a shrug in Australia or the USA, where they are used to ghost towns with a short life span. We tried not to take position, except where we believed our own normative assumptions were touched upon.

These normative assumptions were introduced in our analytic chapters, where they could be presented in the context of arguments. We can distill the most important ones now:
- Nothing is rural in essence: some development issues are more common in sparsely populated areas, some are more common in predominantly agricultural areas, but calling this rural does not help the analysis.
- Problems and solutions are only problems and solutions in a given context: in a given perspective and for a given community using (consciously or not) that perspective.
- There is no single recipe for rural development. Perspectives explicitly stating they possess such a recipe, ought to be distrusted.
- The more simple the miracle formula, the more deserving of suspicion.
- Democratic forms of governance preferable over authoritarian ones: they are more adaptive, respect the personal freedom of decision-making and can create better circumstances for more people.
- Adaptivity is a key concept of good governance for development: visions have to be adapted to the context and path, and they will have to be adapted along the way.
- Adaptive governance enhances resilience, the capacity to bounce back.
- Cultivating difference, in voices, in local knowledge and expertise, can help lead to better solutions and adaptations, as well as create more qualities and assets.
- Good institutions are essential; they can stabilize expectation and simultaneously enhance adaptation.
- Good institutions are configurations of formal and informal institutions (institutions with local grounding) that are not entirely opaque, that are functional (do their job), and maintain adaptive capacity.

Situations that looked like problems from this perspective were the ones addressed in this book. The reader does not have to agree with this basis, of course. Coming back to the crafting of strategy, our normative assumptions already introduced some rigidity or restriction in the combination of elements from the different perspectives we dealt with. If, for a community somewhere in Africa, short term development ideas are needed, and any form of democracy seems a long shot, there are more options for combining perspectives, and for quickly implementing (imposing) them, e.g. through rapid construction of infrastructure, bypassing local democracy, rapid imposition of food crop cultivation (to deal with hunger vs. export), rapid state organized exploitation of resources and massive reinvestment in industrialization (as in China and the USSR).

These quick examples reflect real-world situations, so we cannot mix up wishful thinking and reality too much, and assume a starting point where our basic assumptions are respected. The reader is of course entitled to her own assumptions, and, in many cases, one will find that the path and context analysis show that some assumptions are untenable. For situations like that, we do want to share that wisdom might be found in considering long term and short term effects of the resulting development strategy. In the words of Machiavelli, 'extraordinary measures' (i.e. weakly democratic or undemocratic measures) might be necessary in some cases, when democratic institutions do not work, or are causing more damage to common goods (e.g. election of dictators, local enthusiasm for projects leading to local environmental destruction) but the problem is that short term easily becomes long term, that the extraordinary measures do not erase themselves after a while, do not re-introduce rules to change the rules (think of power/knowledge configurations). Short-term coping strategies can easily undermine long-term adaptive capacity and development; this is true for the coping strategies of authoritarian leaders and well-meaning elites, but it is equally true for locals simply trying to survive by resorting to informal institutions which undermine the rule of law and make it harder to revert back to a more stable and transparent institutional configuration later.

With and without the normative assumptions held in these chapters it remains possible to combine features and elements of several perspectives. The democratic governance models discussed, the general development and rural development models are approaches we found influential – some more in practice, others in theory. For the rural development approaches, these are perspectives we found to be influential in rural areas, irrespective of the label used for it (think of the difference between perspective, practice and naming practice encountered earlier). All communities in practice are some hybrid of governance models, some hybrid of development approaches and some hybrid of rural development approaches. The conceptual frame of evolving governance offered in this book, in combination with these different typologies of governance and development, can help to better understand where a community stands, i.e. which governance model and development approach are dominant. Often, a community is

Figure 12.2. Signage near Bellingham, Washington, USA. Place branding as part of governance, as an aspect of community visioning. The regional community has a strong interest in local agriculture, in local/regional food systems, and the locals in the village, arrivals often from Seattle, refashioned local agriculture and local governance. Photo: Monica Gruzmacher. © ZEF/University of Bonn, Germany.

not explicitly aware of its own governance path and configuration, of the specificity of its form of democracy, of the development approach implicitly taken, and of and the dependencies introduced by series' of decisions. One role of the active analyst can be to encourage and cultivate reflexivity in the community, as well as to increase awareness of past and present and options for moving forward.

The interpretation of the community in terms of the governance path and context, and in terms of the typologies of governance and development perspective, can be useful in understanding why certain features of development strategies are more easily introduced than others and why certain ones can be more easily combined than others.

We can say now that these limits on crafting a strategy to use all the conceptual and practical resources available, has two main sources:
- The rigidity of the governance paths, its combination of path dependence, goal dependence, and interdependence.
- The different nature of links between the governance models, development and rural development perspectives.

The first source of combinatory restrictions we dealt with in sufficient detail above. The other one deserves more explanation, and this explanation is only possible now, a, having introduced a landscape of rural development perspectives. We introduce the concept of couplings to describe the possibilities to combine perspectives in the crafting of a rural community development strategy. We distinguish:

- couplings within a typology (of governance models, development perspectives, or rural development perspectives);
- couplings between typologies (between a governance model and (rural) development perspectives);
- couplings within a governance level (e.g. at the municipal governance or neighborhood level);
- couplings between governance levels (in multi-level governance).

Any of these can be *tight coupling*, *loose coupling*, or *short circuit*. Short circuit couplings are nearly impossible, are bound to create problems somewhere in the governance system. Loose couplings are combinations which are possible but in no way necessary. Tight couplings have an element of necessity: one can be a logical consequence of the other, or one can be the specification (or sub-species) of another. A highly centralized national level bureaucracy (in e.g. a socialist system) is probably short circuiting with highly participatory local governance aiming at piecing together livelihoods. Somewhere in the governance system, it will produce inconsistencies and conflict. A national level liberal democratic system is loosely coupled to local initiatives aiming at sustainability and national level institutional reform aiming at sustainable development (sustainability and development). In the following paragraphs, we bring back the different typologies, and will discuss more and less likely combinations emerging from the different types of couplings. We cannot be comprehensive, part of this exercise will be carried out in the context of a particular path analysis. Before going into this, it can be useful to draw further distinctions in what we loosely called 'combining'.

Combining elements of perspectives and models in concrete policies can have different forms. We distinguish nesting, framing, mixing, specifying and specializing. Forms of coupling determine which forms of combining are possible:

- Nesting we discussed earlier: one level contains another, one approach contains another at a lower level. Nesting can be similar and dissimilar.
- Framing we also met before: one approach becomes the precondition of the other one, giving direction. Framing can be spatial, temporal or conceptual.
- Mixing is any combination of dissimilar elements (associated with different approaches) in any given policy or governance arrangement.
- Specifying is the relation between two policies where one is the subspecies of the other, a tightly coupled form of framing where the next step, the lower level, or the conceptual detailing is an application, a further articulation of the principles in the first policy in the second one.

- Specializing is the application of an approach on a limited domain, and the application of another one next door. At the same governance level, different approaches are combined, yet strictly delimited to one topic or policy domain.

**Example 12.1. Apples, old and new, in new lifestyles.**

According to most accounts, apples (*Pomus domesticus*) originate in Central Asia, where wild trees (e.g. *Pomus sieversii*) can still be found. Kazakhstan promotes itself as the place of origin, but the highest diversity can be found in Eastern Turkey. Winter apples, stored at low temperature, helped many farmers in Europe and Asia to survive for millennia. About 7,500 varieties of apples are known today.

This number masks big swings in popularity and diversity. Most of the varieties are rarely encountered and many are on the verge of extinction. While new varieties are still being bred, for changing tastes and industry requirements, many others were sifted out because they did not do well on the more profitable miniature trees dominating the current landscape, or because they do not fit into current ideas about apples. Many old varieties were created for winter eating and selected on preservation potential. Some of those, and many others, were most suitable for use in a variety of dishes, e.g. meat stews that are uncommon now, while others were designed for use in cidre (apple wine) or calvados (a spirit distilled from cidre). Others were most suitable for desserts, more sweet and easily dissolved while cooking. The idea of the apple now is more of a fruit eaten separately (bigger, juicier, crispier), and the preferred flavor has shifted to the acidic and the simple, since the 20$^{th}$ century worldwide

Figure 12.3. Old, mostly forgotten, varieties of apples and pears, with written reminders of their names, and a visual reminder of their diversity. A farmer's market in Beervelde, Belgium. Photo: Kristof Van Assche. © ZEF/University of Bonn, Germany.

Loose couplings generally allow for the most freedom in combining and in combination forms. Tight coupling makes certain combinations much more likely, sometimes necessary, and pushes for similar nesting, strong framing or specifying. Short circuit

success of Granny Smith, a variety stemming from a chance seedling spotted by Maria Anna Smith in her Australian compost heap in 1868.

Colonists brought apples to North America in the 17th century, and by the 18th century, American varieties had developed (with and without help from humans). Thomas Jefferson was an early enthusiast. He grew a number of varieties at his estate in Monticello, and looked down on European apples ('They have no apples here to compare with our Newtown Pippin', he wrote from Paris). The 19th century was an era of experimentation and expansion, leading to many new varieties, but, in a familiar tale, the 20th century brought distributors, processing plants, investors, scientists, who were not interested in variety, tradition, and saw only 'inconsistency' and obstacles for easy production and maximal profits. Small apples and small orchards and big trees and complex flavors disappeared. Very few varieties reached supermarkets. Color became a selection criterium: Jonagold, Red Delicious and others were developed for more red, as American consumers believed red to be a sign of tastier and healthier apples (the 'blush').

In Europe and North America, a recent movement tries now to preserve more apples, by celebrating diversity in taste and in uses. It requires a dissemination of, again, product and processing knowledge. Rare apple tasting festivals are organized (mostly in the USA), and community organizations and governments team up to preserve or bring back orchards with tall trees (or just trees, in a more densely built environment), while food writers rediscover old varieties and their potential. Cidre is making a comeback in many countries (it was never forgotten in France and the UK). In the USA, John Bunker (founder of Fedco trees) played an important role in this revival attempt; he hung posters in many communities inquiring about rare varieties ('Wanted', they said), and author Rowan Jacobsen claims Bunker alone saved more than 80 varieties.

Scientists do notice the budding movement, and many new varieties are created which are close to forgotten apples. New distribution channels play a role too: farmers markets, bio-stores, delicatessen shops, restaurants might be outlets for new varieties that would not make it to supermarkets. (Cornell's apple breeding program still exists, and its head stated that ca. 130 new varieties have been created in the last six years).

**Further reading**

Jacobsen, R. (2014). Apples of uncommon character: 123 heirlooms, modern classics and little known wonders. London, UK: Bloomsbury.

couplings create conflict somewhere but they are prevalent, too: actors in governance or the community at large is not aware of the internal inconsistencies of an ideology, or of a practical compromise in policy. They can be aware of an inconsistency, but think it can be solved by means of specializing, or that it can be safely deferred to the long term (think public revenue consequences of inconsistent policies). Finally, they can be aware of the short-circuit nature of a coupling and use the predicted conflict strategically.

The analysis of path and context will teach us how de facto things were combined in the history of the community, and what the effects were. This can tell us more about the combinatory possibilities of models and approaches in general, and in the specific path one is interested in. The path analysis, underpinned by insights in combinatory potential, can reveal how rigid the dependencies in a community are, where the room for flexibility is, what can be predicted regarding preferences for and impacts of new attempts at policy integration, eg. in a rural development vision. The shifting combinations of elements one can discern in a governance path can reflect pragmatic accommodations between actors, who had to come to some agreement, shifting contexts and configurations. They can reflect deeper divisions in the community, between factions and discourses, but also, a more complicated matter, internal contradictions and tensions within the governing ideology, within the narrative and discursive coalition shaping the images of present and future.

## Further reading

Bobrow, D.B. and Dryzek, J.S. (1987). Policy analysis by design. Pittsburgh, PA, USA: University of Pittsburgh Press.

Fischer, F. and Miller, G.J. (eds.). (2006). Handbook of public policy analysis: theory, politics, and methods. Boca Raton, FL, USA: CRC Press.

Folke, C., Hahn, T., Olsson, P. and Norberg, J. (2005). Adaptive governance of social-ecological systems. Annual Review Environmental Resources, 30, 441-473.

Hajer, M.A. and Wagenaar, H. (eds.) (2003). Deliberative policy analysis: understanding governance in the network society. Cambridge, UK: Cambridge University Press.

Miller, H.T. (2002). Postmodern public policy. Albany, NY, USA: Suny Press.

Nelson, N. and Wright, S. (1995). Power and participatory development: theory and practice. London, UK: Intermediate Technology Publications Ltd. (ITP).

Ostrom, E. (2005). Understanding institutional diversity. Princeton, NJ, USA: Princeton University Press.

Sanoff, H. (2000). Community participation methods in design and planning. New York, NY, USA: John Wiley & Sons.

Sharp, L. and Richardson, T. (2001). Reflections on Foucauldian discourse analysis in planning and environmental policy research. Journal of Environmental Policy and Planning, 3(3), 193-209.

Walzer, N. (ed.) (1996). Community strategic visioning programs. Portsmouth, NH, USA: Greenwood Publishing Group.

Yanow, D. (ed.). (2000). Conducting interpretive policy analysis. London, UK: Sage.

## 12.4 Crafting a strategy: assessing combinations

### 12.4.1 Couplings between models of governance

We distinguished five democratic governance models: liberal democracy, civic republicanism, civil society, communitarianism and socialism/communism. We know that each real-life community, certainly every nation-state, is a hybrid of several of those models. Elements of non-democratic models of governance can also be mixed in, e.g. a streak of authoritarianism, oligarchy, or theocracy. And a state clearly designed after this or that model can be descended into chaos, called a failed state. Nation-states can also be more or less centralized. Communism lends itself to high centralization, for example, but even liberal democracies are able to demonstrate strong centralizing tendencies despite small governance and minimal regulations. Even in centralized governance systems, formal institutions and government actors will not entirely define governance; indeed, multi-level governance will remain a practical necessity. In multi-level governance, the layers can be very autonomous, or not, there can be a strong local autonomy, or not. The couplings between levels can vary strongly, with the possibility to maintain the larger scale as an empty shell, keeping up the appearance of unity for external or other purposes. Some levels of governance can be more marked by formal institutions, whereas elsewhere, informality plays a greater role. This can be a matter of rules and plans touching physical or economic reality at the smaller scale, and it can be a matter of mid-level plans touching different political or economic realities at a higher level.

Couplings between the governance models are complex, as the history of hybrids and the eternal discussions in political theory testify. Some hybrids (with loose couplings) are very common, such as social democracies existing in Europe and other places, which can be seen as mixes of socialism and other models, usually liberal democracy, civil society or civic republicanism. The USA started out as mostly civic republican in design, strongly civil society in practice, and evolved towards a dominance of liberal democracy, with a social-democratic phase before World War II. The older phases left traces in the current neo-liberal high tide. The system of strong checks and balances can be considered a leftover of civic republican design, helpful in keeping the system adaptive in some cases, while creating a gridlock in others.

Communitarianism and to a certain extent civic republicanism seem designed for the smaller scale, and can be nested at lower levels of liberal democratic and civil society regimes (even nested within authoritarian or failed states). Communism can de facto rely on communitarianism at the lower level, as it can rely on older social identities to make the state machine work. Communitarianism or civic republicanism can not be tightly coupled with liberal democracy at the same level, it seems. Civil society models can coexist with virtually anything, and can easily acquire the character of either elite rule (oligarchy), or organized resistance or activism against a regime deemed oppressive or flawed.

If the formal institutions do not work well, then there can be much space for other forms of organization to work at lower levels. A state such as Tajikistan can be regarded as de facto a combination of smaller political entities, with governance models varying from theocracy via oligarchy to communitarianism and civic republicanism. If these units can coexist at the same level without much friction, there is no need to speak of short circuit couplings. When development ambitions increase and coordination becomes more important and intense, then the inconsistencies in governance can become more acutely felt, leading to a short circuited coupling.

Within the level of a nation-state, specialized policies can be associated with a coexistence of governance forms. Environmental governance can be more social-democratic, while heritage policy is civic republican and economic policy is neo-liberal and oligarchic in organization. These cleavages will become more problematic when coordination is needed, or when a highly controversial topic arises which forces a decision on the hierarchy of the models: what do we really want as a community, what is most important to us? The options for coexistence depend on the buffering options between the policy domains: one can think of big school budgets (rather social democratic) easily set aside by neo-liberal governments with enough resources, and governed in a social-democratic manner. One can think of constitutions or silent agreements separating spheres of influence, with old elites taking care of foreign and military policy, new elites (differently organized) managing economic policy and local governments, and a forum for debate and coordination.

Much more can be said. The reader will find a vast literature spanning diverse disciplines. We would recommend looking beyond political science for inspiration, e.g. in institutional economics, comparative history, political geography, political anthropology and, last but not least, political philosophy. More pragmatically, the community studied will provide valuable clues and guidance as to which governance models left traces, are combined, and when this leads to tensions or incoherence.

## 12.4.2 Couplings between governance models and development perspectives

More complexity ensues at the next step. Liberal democracy, civic republicanism, communitarianism, civil society and socialism link up differently with the development perspectives discussed. We list them again:
- modernist models of development (including community development, structural adjustment);
- structuralist economics/industrial policy/science policy;
- dependency theory;

- livelihoods approach/asset-based development;
- sustainability/resilience perspectives;
- innovation/transition management;
- participatory development/resource management;
- institutions;
- post-colonial/post-development approaches.

*Modernist models* of development can be found, interestingly enough, at the opposite sides of the political spectrum, in neo-liberal environments and under communism. We know that communism had a clear and not so simple idea on the perfect society, while liberal democracy had a clear and simple idea, visible e.g. in their recipes for post-socialist transition and for development in Africa's poorest nations. These policies include institutional reform, at the national level most of the time. Minimum versions of the rule of law fall under this category, too (see the discussion on the rule of law). Community development approaches relying on a clear recipe presumed to bring the best result (e.g. build social capital and connect it with economic assets in a manner perfectly fitting those economic assets) are also modernist in nature; these find a receptive ear in communitarian conditions or under civic republicanism (at least for a while). Whenever checks and balances and participation are strong, modernist approaches tend not to hold long, as their redesign of power/knowledge configurations meets strong opposition. Furthermore, in such an arena, no encompassing formula will be entirely persuasive; there are always different perspectives and expertise immediately present and protected.

*Structuralist economics*, dependency theory and the like usually target national level governance, but one can derive and find versions apt for local/regional governance. Historical power relations between regions can be found wanting if one region is perceived as dominant and as imposing an economic model that benefits itself and keeps other regions dependent. In this case, different policies can be advocated for for the region under discussion, policies that can guide away from the historical dominance of one region. In extreme cases, one can speak of internal colonies, in other cases, of internal margins, and internal enclaves. When ethnic or religious boundaries coincide with the boundaries of these enclaves, etc., tensiosn can easily rise, as governance conflicts become identity conflicts. Regional development policy can have the character of structuralist economics and dependency theory, and the search for regional identity and regional economic niches and niche strategies (differing views on rights to import/export to other regions and other countries) can sometimes be understood like this. These perspectives seem less useful for the very local level. At the regional and national levels, they can combine with virtually all models, however. Even in the USSR, regional strategies were developed (partly out of ideology, partly out of necessity) that resembled those of dependency theory and structuralist economics. Differences between the models are revealed in discussions of the path envisioned towards the objectives outlined, e.g. the level of participation foreseen and the level of influence desired from administration experts and local governments, as well as checks and balances in place.

*Livelihoods approaches* and asset-based development tend to focus on piecing together livelihoods at local and sometimes regional scales, with a strong interest in existing assets of various sorts, and the links between social and ecological systems. We already know that what is an asset and an acceptable livelihood depend on the perspective taken, and on the path of governance taken. 'Poverty reduction' has to be seen in this light. There is no absolute measure for poverty, nor for an acceptable livelihood (as not leading or keeping people into poverty). Livelihoods approaches sometimes seem to write off the possibility of a functioning nation-state at a higher level. This might be more or less justified, depending on the case, but it brings to attention at least the requirement to think in terms of multi-level governance; livelihoods, even in remote places, are not disconnected from larger scales and the governance there. In the fashion of nested policies, livelihoods perspectives can work with neo-liberal governance models. If the pragmatic character of searching for livelihoods in a social and political landscape is in the focus of attention, civil society models at the local level can work well, especially when dealing with the balance between different factions or other social units tied to the use of different resources or different places in the environment. In tough environments that are very isolated, a livelihoods approach can also fit seamlessly with communitarianism, stressing interdependence and the need to rely on a variety of overlapping social networks. In this case, however, projecting European or American social network ideas, without a clear understanding of social structures elsewhere, can give a thoroughly distorted view of interdependence and its policy implications. If sustainability is the focus of a livelihoods approach in an unstable ecological environment, then civic republicanism can be an attractive model, with its strong checks and balances and, most importantly, a cultivation of participation in different guises, as well as a high intensity of public scrutiny and debate of policies and their implications.

*Innovation/transition management* came up in social-democratic states with modernist tendencies, believing in the myth of social engineering for scientific/technical innovation and economic success. Yet, a focus on concerted innovation can be fruitful for a development perspective, and, as the management and geography literature shows, there are plenty of ways to find interpretations and versions for the local and regional level (innovative regions, creative cities, high-tech regions, etc.) Distinguishing between branding, aspirations and realities remains important. In lighter versions, versions in which government is not trying to tie scientific, economic and political actors to a magic formula, but where discussion and coordination and the possibility of policy integration for innovation are always options, innovation policy can work with several governance models, except, we would argue, where communities are considered in isolation. Innovation policy can be a transitory policy for a period where the community believes it somehow lags behind the rest; in this case, cultivation of awareness of the quality of the existing governance situation, as well as of the innovation forms and potential already present there, seems highly recommendable. Innovation policy in a civic republican version and environment could be useful here by fostering a continuous discussion of which relevant innovations are present and absent in a particular community, thereby heightening the awareness of the linkages between innovation networks and governance networks, and of the actual innovation base and what might be missing there. As with 'development', 'innovation' means nothing without being grounded in a perspective, and it has no relevance except for that given to it by particular communities. As with development, innovation always takes place, and the observation of what has already happened is just as relevant as the reflection on what should happen. In civil society models, innovation policy is tricky, as the 'actors' defining good innovation policy have an interest, too, and the innovation policy can likely reinforce the actor/knowledge position in place, and thus in the long run undermine innovation and adaptation.

*Participatory development/resource management* emphasizes the line of power through participation. This sometimes takes place at the expense of the line of representation, or at the expense of checks and balances, but not necessarily. In many cases, participatory development comes up after previous approaches did not work or were no longer compatible with changing notions of democracy in the community, small or large. This could mean, e.g. that a socialist system had been moving to a social democratic system

Figure 12.4. Learning English as gateway to innovation and progress? An advertisement of an English language school in Nepal. Photo: Anna-Katharina Hornidge. © ZEF/University of Bonn, Germany.

to a more civil society system, and what people wanted and found democratic, was not reflected in the political structures and institutions (yet). It is also possible that a more centralized social democracy had been transitioning to a more decentralized version, with more elements of civic republicanism at the local level; calls for change can be framed in terms of increased 'participation' in this scenario. Or, one can imagine a situation in a rather poor country where national governments imposed imported modernist development recipes on very diverse local communities and the strategy backfired; this could lead the government to be extra wary of being deaf to calls for more participation, in this case meaning more local adaptation of development perspectives and more inclusion of local knowledge.

Participation does not work well under highly centralized systems (possible in any of the government models, even at the local level), and with systems where representation is the only channel to bring perspectives and knowledge into governance (not entirely overlapping with the previous category). In calls for more participation, what is resented can be more the expert knowledge routinely incorporated into policies, or more direct political exclusion of voices and opinions, when the system of representation (e.g. in a party structure) does not allow many choices for voters. We already discussed the dangers of extreme participation, as well as the value of differentiation and representation; we can add here that the risks will appear differently in different governance models. In social democracies, it can undermine the expert-driven routines that actually work and have wide support (not always visible in participatory governance arenas). In liberal democracies, it can undermine a carefully thought out balance between local and regional governments, protecting the autonomy of communities marked by different political cultures, ethnic cleavages and business environments.

*Institutions* and *institutional reform* can also play a role in different governance systems. Socialism can be less compatible when there is a strong belief that the existing institutional structure is perfect and that substance of policies (e.g. their expert character) should precede their coordinative role. Yet there are versions of socialism, and they are/were not all blind to the need for continuous attention to the modes of coordination needed to implement policy. Soviet history can be seen as a long struggle with institutional reform, where the limits of the ideology were felt in practice, and many institutional experiments failed and had to be replaced. In neo-liberal circles, one can perceive something similar: if there is the belief that neo-liberalism is one concrete formula and it is already in place, then thinking about institutions as a path to development makes no sense, but if there is an idea that neo-liberalism (liberal democracy) is a perspective in which government has minimum tasks, but nevertheless tasks, then there can still be a continuous deliberation on the best institutional structure to fulfill them. Neo-liberalism can also be compatible with local governments pursuing different strategies, and formulating more comprehensive development visions, a different type of institutions, not usually associated with the basic policy frames of neo-liberalism. We refer again to the discussions of versions of the rule of law and the possibility to plan. For neo-liberalism, plans are much more than institutions, they are excessive government intervention, imposing too much substantive policy and too many rules on too many actors (with the form that rules take and their substance of course not really separable). For socialism, plans are institutions, including others, integrating others. Institutional reform is at the core of public debate in civic republicanism; the important distinction is between rules that can change fast and ones that guarantee stability. Rules for self-transformation become essential and, within those, treatment should differ with regrd to institutions evolving slowly or rapidly. For civil society models, the patterning of influence of different players and organizations on governance deserves scrutiny; if one wants to stick to a civil society model, the access to governance, and the transparency of governance assessment and deliberation of all claims coming to them, can be a target for institutional reform.

*Post-colonial/post-development* approaches, we claimed, are not necessarily opposed to development policy, as understood in this book. We refer to the discussion above on their positive contributions to development theory & practice. We can say here that they are, to an extent, compatible with all governance models, as long as they allow for and enable

Figure 12.5. Lady selling lemons on an Uzbek market. The success of institutional reform depends on many things, one thing often neglected being the actual and potential roles of small entrepreneurs to move, transform, exchange products. This, in turn, connects to the larger question of permissible roles in society, to the rights and opportunities of women, of vulnerable religious and cultural groups. Photo: Anna-Katharina Hornidge. © ZEF/University of Bonn, Germany.

critical reflection on the path chosen, the provenance of concepts and perspectives, the power relations they might propagate, and the suitability for the community. Exposing hidden assumptions and dominance can be productive in the sense that it frees up more possible path, and in the sense that elements of formerly imposed strategies can now be consciously appropriated and modified. Such critical reflection can also show new ways to organize participation, to include local knowledge. The most difficult relation will exist with liberal democracy and socialism in their modernist versions; these will be exposed as ideologies like any other, with both oppressive and liberating effects.

### 12.4.3 Couplings between development perspectives

After briefly discussing the possible relations between development perspectives and governance models, we naturally come to the question of which development perspectives can be more easily combined. We will not systematically discuss all possible relations, since we believe that the reader has the conceptual tools to do this exercise herself. A few examples and principles might still be useful.

*Principle 1*: The type of hybrid between governance models, can be linked with the hybridity in development approaches. Example: Civic republicanism at local level, in a largely liberal democratic national frame, can lead to modernist institutional reform being subtly undermined by fierce local discussions and a comprehensive local development strategy based on socialist principles.

*Principle 2*: Think of levels of governance and domains of policy, and then think of the combinations modes we presented: nesting, framing, etc. (see above). The more autonomous governance levels are and the more domains are buffered, the more combinations of development approaches can coexist. Example: An elite controls the natural resources in an area, but keeps its hands of all communities outside the extraction sphere. At the national level, a civil society model can lead to maximum exploitation models for the resource towns, and a mixed bag of semi-theocracies and neo-liberal towns elsewhere, each choosing different development approaches.

*Principle 3*: In hybrid governance systems (all), perfect consistency between development perspectives does not exist. For reasons of political compromise, and because collective memory and desire are fickle and inconsistent. Example: A socialist village in France can pay for services and projects because of tourism, and because of a place branding campaign inviting both tourists and tourism entrepreneurs. The business people are given exemptions from various plans and rules, depending on the revenue and employment effects of their business. After a while, the business people redefine local socialism but nobody wants to see a difference with the past or some possible incoherence in the development perspective.

*Principle 4*: Conflicts can tell something about uneasy coexistence of development approaches, and coexisting development approaches can generate conflict. What creates the conflict is not always the conceptual incompatibility, however, but often changes in actor/institution configurations and power/knowledge relations. Example: At city council meetings, a few councillors leave the room, doors slamming. They complain about lack of environmental awareness. The new policies causing the ire of the councillors were not ostensibly less green than the previous ones, but claim a green sensibility for the other parties, who hitherto had relegated this to the now angry faction.

*Principle 5*: Compatibility of development approaches has to be considered in terms of formal/informal institutional configurations. Perspectives might be incompatible on paper, but practical accommodations relying on informal institutions might have evolved. Conversely, a combination (through nesting, framing, etc.) of different development perspectives might look good on paper, but ignore a reality of informal coordination following different principles. Example: Socialism in the USSR survived the 1920's thanks to Lenin's new economic policy, allowing for small-scale private entrepreneurship. This fed the hungry population, and created enough taxable revenue to speed up industrialization by government investment.

## 12.4.4 Couplings between development and rural development perspectives

Development perspectives and rural development perspectives are not necessarily different. This we know by now. The rural development perspectives outlined earlier are simply approaches which are prevalent in either theory or practice of development in rural areas. Since the world is not a place of logical consistency, we cannot expect that what happens in rural areas is always a result of specification of general development policies, nor the result of bottom-up, specifically rural approaches that are then fitted in general policies and ideas, which are possibly altered by this input. There are top-down and bottom-up movements in theory and in practice, and there is an incredible variety of experiments combining them. One can also speak of a combination of *induction* and *deduction*: deduction occurs when rural development principles are derived from more general development principles, and induction is the specification and transformation of general principles by means of typically rural local observation and experimentation.

What makes the combination of induction and deduction logical and natural is that many rural issues are not per definition rural, just as many places are not per definition rural. Multiple definitions of rurality coexist. What makes something a problem or an asset, or simply a characteristic, entirely depends on the perspective on governance and development embraced. For all these reasons, a rural development perspective does not have to differ from a general development perspective, while it cannot necessarily be derived from it either. There can be loose, tight and short circuit couplings. They can be combined in the various forms of nesting, framing, etc. discussed earlier, depending on the coupling and the specific governance path. A bit more explanation.

*Innovation* and *transition management*, as we mentioned, entirely lacked a rural focus in the beginning. When it acquired a rural version, based on high tech agriculture

**Example 12.2. Wageningen University and rural development (at home and abroad).**

In 1876, the Dutch state took over the local Agricultural College in Wageningen, a small town in the center of the Netherlands. A year later, the government established the first research station in Wageningen, to support the college, and to create stronger ties with agriculture in practice. The next decades saw new research stations popping up in the different agricultural regions of the country, as well as a fisheries institute, botanical gardens, and a dairy institute. In 1904, the Agriculture College became a Higher Agriculture College, ratified as higher education at university level in 1918, while the network of research institutes grew, becoming more internationally oriented after World War II. In 1986, the Agriculture College was renamed Wageningen University, and, in 1997, Wageningen University and Research Centre was formed, a merger of the University and the research institutes (DLO). Internal mergers of (parts of) institutes continue into the present.

Wageningen University was very influential in the Netherlands and abroad, and has to be understood as part of a larger agro-food cluster in the Netherlands which dominated rural development. Initially, industry involvement was relatively small, but links with farmers associations were there (later LTO) from the start. Government extension services were centralized (later called DLV) and also linked to the Wageningen cluster of research institutes. National government was the central player for a long time, and the post-war period was marked by what was called the 'Iron Triangle', a tight cooperation between farmers associations, national administration (mostly the Ministry of Agriculture, renamed a few times later) and a group of politicians/agriculture specialists in parliament (tied to the Christian parties). The Iron Triangle promoted an 'OVO triangle' approach to rural development: research, extension and education. Wageningen was the place were all three could feed off each other. Government, at different times, provided production subsidies and extension, and promoted and focused scientific research, while farmers associations had an influence on research and policy, and researchers could suggest new practices to farmers and government. Banks and insurance companies originally tied to the farmers associations became more autonomous, but also grew significantly, which allowed them to play an important role in the further development of capital-intensive agriculture (yet on their own terms).

As Dutch agro-food companies grew bigger, partly because of the nurturing environment of the Iron Triangle, they became increasingly influential in the Wageningen cluster and in their dealings with government, and farmers associations lost influence by comparison. Extension

and agri-business clusters and chains, it was largely a specification of the general development model, without looking at a range of specifically rural issues. The same rhetoric was used and the same procedures were proposed as what was perceived to be responsible for Silicon Valley. Rural innovation and transition management thus started reasoning from a very limited understanding of rurality, one much influenced by a mix

services were downsized, as were many of the agricultural and food research institutes, believed to be less essential because of development of private R&D. The remaining, smaller research institutes were supposed to operate more freely and sustain themselves in 'the market', that market being one of mostly other Dutch government actors, European subsidies and contract research for private business. Creation of spin-off companies and patenting revenue were not facilitated through policy (in contrast to the Silicon Valley approach). When the government began to adopt national innovation policies referring to a concept of the 'Golden Triangle' in 2010, they were highlighting the close cooperation between industry, government and research institutes, modeled after what they saw as the successful example of Dutch agriculture, forgetting the original form of that model (more farmers' influence, more research autonomy, but also more government steering of rural areas).

The influence of this web of organizations and this perspective on development was amplified through a series of other government investments and policies: physical infrastructure, trade infrastructure, access to cheap fodder (soy) via Rotterdam harbor, cheap heating for greenhouses (Dutch gas), and intensive land consolidation schemes, first restricted to agricultural land use, later becoming wholesale restructuring efforts of rural areas (accommodating a variety of land uses).

The Dutch model in a different sense, that is, the combination of highly educated farmers, capital intensive and expertise intensive mechanized agriculture, involving high levels of 'science transfer' became one of the drivers of the so-called 'Green Revolution' (ca 1940-1970), where hunger in the Global South was addressed through modernization of agriculture. Wageningen and the Dutch agro sector were and are very active in the FAO (United Nations Food and Agriulture Organization), and the CGIAR (Consultative Group on International Agricultural Research), a group of government and non-government actors who came together in 1971 to establish a series of specialized agricultural research institutes across the world.

### Further reading

Rosenboom. J. and Rutten, H. (1999). Financing agricultural R&D in the Netherlands. The changing role of government. In: Alston, J., Pardey, P. and Smith, V.H. (eds.), Paying for agricultural productivity. Baltimore, MD, USA: Johns Hopkins University Press/IFPRI.

of neo-liberal and social-democratic attitudes. Because the general development model generated its own critique, leading to additional concepts such as social innovation, we propose an alternative version of the rural innovation model, based on a broader understanding of rurality, of community goals and values, and of linked innovation and governance networks. This version of rural innovation can be combined with elements of potentially all general development approaches, but within a development vision organized around innovation, with innovation as the enabler of adaptation.

*Extension models* also transformed, broadening to include more forms of learning and teaching, and to comprise more participatory and comprehensive versions. Several versions existed early on, initiated by different combinations of actors, but the focus was mostly on the teaching of agricultural expertise. Local knowledge was not in the picture, and learning for other economic activities, and for common goals defined by the community, did not become a focus of extension forms until much later. If we see rural extension models as essentially aiming at individual and social learning for development, then they look like an essential component of almost all the development approaches that go beyond macro-economic prescriptions and elementary institutional reform. As soon as common goals and socio-economic change are considered more in detail, and more susceptible to steering and organization, extension seems to be a natural part of the policy package and development process. If serious changes are required of communities, and these will not simply be imposed by higher authorities, then learning could become of the essence. Sustainability perspectives on development, livelihoods approaches, more broadly understood innovation approaches (as defined above) in most cases come up where serious issues are perceived, and where serious modification of governance and behavior might be necessary. Extension in all its variations, including in participatory versions, can be essential there, the secondary principle and goal, after sustainability, or innovation, or livelihoods. Innovation approaches broadly understood can come closest to making extension its organizing principle: learning for innovation for adaptation.

*Institutional reform* for rural development can simply be a specification of a broader recipe for institutional reform, or even more simply the application of the broader reform in rural areas. It can also be disconnected from modernist and/or neo-liberal models and become inclusive of various community goals. In rural areas, these goals can reflect many issues and qualities seen as rural. A broader understanding of institutional reform entails a broader understanding of the rule of law, which can incorporate principles of redistribution, reinvestment, social justice, sustainability, etc., reflecting, again, a set of specific community goals that can be tied to a rural situation. Institutional reform in this broad sense will become, like extension, a natural part of many rural development strategies derived from other general development models. Sustainability perspectives will likely require institutional reform (which can be underpinned, preceded and accompanied by social learning processes). Innovation

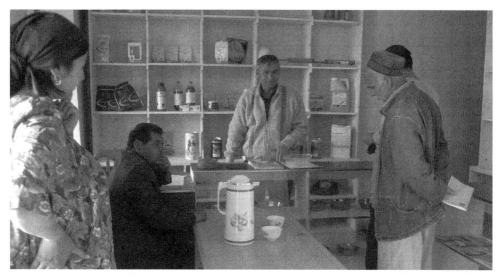

Figure 12.6. Agricultural extension in Tajikistan. Extension projects supported by foreign governments, NGOs, universities, aiming at real impact learned to rely on local trainers, instructors more familiar with the local cultural and political context and, importantly, remnants of older systems of state extension (in this case Soviet) and social learning more broadly. A seed shop founded with the assistance of MerciCorps in rural Tajikistan. Photo: Anna-Katharina Hornidge. © ZEF/University of Bonn, Germany.

and transition management can preserve existing structures and institutions, but can also go further, slowly restructuring governance based on a central goal of adaptive innovation. Dependency theory or even post-development approaches can inspire first of all institutional reform, to break open older constricting modes of development, after which new and locally supported development perspectives can crystallize, which lead to a new round of institutional reform.

*Environmental* and *natural resource management* come up more easily under rural conditions because of the space available. We discussed maximum extraction, maximum protection sustainable development versions, and these link differently to the general development models treated. Maximum extraction is often linked with a neo-liberal approach of minimal government and minimal institutional reform, but that is not an exclusive link. Communism saw it as its duty, in its modernist development approach, to maximize extraction, equating it with economic development and deeming it the best way to develop the infrastructure for true communist society. Under civic republicanism, or civil society models, institutional reform perspectives, or even participatory resource management approaches, can lead to de facto maximum extraction policies. Sustainable development versions of the model are still more rare in practice, but abound in theory. In this theoretical world, sustainable resource development can be the core of rural development strategies based on several of the general development approaches, from dependency theory to livelihoods approaches to (more obviously) sustainability perspectives. Up till now, the practiced versions of sustainable rural development approaches do not seem to treat sustainable development as the key principle for the restructuring of governance. The approach seems concerned foremost with limits to exploitation and protection of a minimal environmental quality. However, it does not have to stay this way.

*Land consolidation* and *land use planning* came up as rural development strategies for similar reasons: space. Rural areas have more space for land consolidation and land use planning, as well as less vested interests in many cases. However, this connection, too, hinges on governance models and development approaches. In neo-liberal contexts, the idea persists that rural areas require less planning than urban areas and that land consolidation will be delivered by the market, provided the latter is fluid enough (following institutional reform). Traditionally, land consolidation and land use planning were not very participatory, not looking beyond agriculture for livelihoods analysis, and placed innovation in the increased efficiency of larger and redesigned land holdings (maybe offering a frame for other forms of innovation later). We observed that land use planning and consolidation can offer frames for the implementation of other general development approaches, sometimes by becoming more participatory, sometimes by governance looking at more different goals for rural 'improvement'. One can think of sustainability goals (ecological structures in reorganized landscapes), but also of livelihoods or assets-based approaches (looking for optimization of more land uses, allowing for a more diverse rural economy).

Figure 12.7. An image of Holland: road infrastructure, water infrastructure, highly organized farmland, all close to each other, a proximity caused by and causing high levels of coordination between actors, and, in the 20th century, a formalized and centralized spatial planning system. Photo: Monica Gruzmacher. © ZEF/University of Bonn, Germany.

*Rural* and *community design* can be understood in line with this broader version of land consolidation/land use planning. It works well in development approaches where high levels of policy integration are accepted and desired, and where a variety of goals is embodied in the policies to be integrated. This can mean a variety of land uses that each have to find a place, or a variety of activities and infrastructure to be supported. This approach will almost certainly require institutional reform, and its results will be, beyond a design, a set of new accompanying institutions enabling its implementation. It can work well with a livelihoods approach or sustainability approach or innovation perspective, all development approaches where the actual situation, as well as its assets, infrastructures and networks, have to be studied, and form the basis of new spatial and policy frameworks. Community design can be participatory, i.e. part of participatory governance, yet it will require expert knowledge of different sorts, scientific and design-wise.

*Local, local, local* seems the essence of communitarianism, and the associated development approaches (see above), but the recent calls for rural localism transcend this ideological heritage. Localism cannot be extreme in a connected and globalized world and, in its recent versions, it relies on larger networks of connections and resources, rather than ignoring them. Rural localism can be the embodiment of a livelihoods approach, of a participatory development model, a resilience model, or a combination of those. It can be more or less green, more or less informal (versus institutional reform-based), more or less open to innovation (possibly leading into local innovation perspectives). For the new rural localism, useless or inefficient traces of suboptimal agriculture (in a modernist innovation view) can be assets, to be connected with others, possibly in a design, or else in informal cooperation forms, or a new governance structure.

## 12.4.5 Couplings between rural development perspectives

Innovation models, extension models, land consolidation and land use planning, rural and community design, institutional reform, rural localism, and environmental and natural resource management can be combined in many ways. Once more, inspiration will have to come from path and context analysis, and from the linkages between governance models, development perspectives, and rural development perspectives, as discussed in the previous paragraphs. The rural development approaches can exist in very different forms, with each form establishing different connections with general development and governance models. The principles we presented for inspiration in combining development perspectives largely apply here, too, to the combinatory possibilities of rural development approaches.

When crafting rural development strategies, in whatever role, we would recommend never to forget the path and context analysis, and the lessons these can hold for the combining of policies and perspectives towards rural development. Seeing what was possible in a given community in the past, not only which governance paths, but which mechanisms of framing, nesting, mixing, specifying and specializing were at play, can offer valuable inspiration for rethinking combinations in an attempt to shift the path in a different direction. This local observation can combine with community comparisons, to learn about other paths or combinatory strategies, and to see how hard or soft the different sorts of couplings are. The knowledge and expertise needed to create a rural development strategy, to possibly effect a shift in the governance path, will likely be different from the knowledge and expertise guiding the more routine reproduction of the adjusted governance system. However, this distinction cannot be rigid, as keeping more than the routine expertise available can be necessary for future adaptation, to guide self-transformations in new directions. In other words, for the crafting of the next rural development strategy.

## Further reading[1]

Allen, C.R. and Gunderson, L.H. (2011). Pathology and failure in the design and implementation of adaptive management. Journal of Environmental Management, 92(5), 1379-1384.

Chossudovsky, M. (2003). The globalization of poverty and the new world order. Shanty Bay, Canada: Global Outlook.

Cleaver, F. (2012). Development through bricolage: rethinking institutions for natural resource management. Abingdon, UK: Routledge.

Green, M. (2010). Making development agents: participation as boundary object in international development. Journal of Development Studies, 46(7), 1240-1263.

Hornidge, A.-K. (2007). Knowledge society. Vision & social construction of reality in Germany & Singapore. Münster, Germany: Lit-Verlag.

Hornidge, A.-K. (2011). 'Knowledge Society' as academic concept and stage of development – a conceptual and historical review. In: Menkhoff, T., Evers, H.-D., Chay, Y.W. and Eng, F. P. (eds.), Beyond the knowledge trap: developing asia's knowledge-based economies. London, UK: World Scientific, pp. 87-128.

Ledwith, M. (2011). Community development: a critical approach. Bristol, UK: Policy Press.

Mintzberg, H. (1987). Crafting strategy. Cambridge, MA, USA: Harvard Business School.

Radomski, P.J. and Van Assche, K. (2014). Lakeshore living: designing lake places and communities in the footprints of environmental writers. East Lansing, MI, USA: MSU Press.

Rappaport, J. (1995). Empowerment meets narrative: Listening to stories and creating settings. American Journal of Community Psychology, 23(5), 795-807.

Voß, J.P. and Bornemann, B. (2011). The politics of reflexive governance: challenges for designing adaptive management and transition management. Ecology and Society, 16(2), 9.

---

[1] Note: This chapter is about analyzing the development path of a community and then crafting a rural development strategy, and this is presented as a process of carefully selecting, adjusting and combining elements and aspects of the approaches and perspectives discussed earlier; for literature pertaining to this chapter, we also refer to these previous chapters.

# 13. Rural development, expertise and local knowledge

## Abstract

In this chapter we take a closer look at the links between expertise and development, and on the path from knowledge and narrative to policy inclusion and policy implementation. To understand the role of expertise in this path better, we introduce more concepts from narrative analysis and the sociology of knowledge. We here argue that the mutual influence of narratives of development as well as actual stages, categories and steps towards development on each other is often undecipherable. A given development or rural development perspective can lead to different stories, meaning very different versions of stories can coexist in one category, even if these stories had the same starting point.

## 13.1 Stories about the future

In a rural development strategy, there is always knowledge incorporated, and it will have effects on knowledge, on the inclusion/exclusion of expertise and local knowledge later in the policy process, and in the community at large. If e.g. extension is part of the strategy (or its core), then the knowledge effects on the community can be substantial. Social learning and individual learning can be reoriented. The degree of participation in the strategy, but also the interest of government actors in non-expert knowledge will affect the balance between expert knowledge and local knowledge. More generally, the selection of knowledge in and by a rural development strategy will hinge on everything we discussed in this book: governance paths and context, as well as couplings between governance models, development perspectives and rural development perspectives.

Knowledge is associated with actors or institutions; through mechanisms of participation and representation, it can become a central part of power/knowledge configurations, or rather remain in the margins. It can be a core part of a development strategy, or emerge later through the application of the strategy in a given community, bringing substance to the strategy. The following will likewise depend on the properties and of the given governance paths and (rural) development models:
- what is recognized as knowledge in the first place;
- what is recognized as expert knowledge;
- how to balance expert and local knowledge;
- what expert and local knowledge is considered relevant for development;
- how forms of knowledge are confronted and combined leading to policy;
- how implementation is understood and how this affects knowledge selection.

The combination of path properties and model properties will further determine the role and importance of a unifying narrative for the development of the community. In some institutional reform models, there is no space for such a narrative, in others there is; in some extension models, the narrative is simply to increase agricultural engineering expertise, in others, there is the possibility for communities to rethink themselves, craft a unique development narrative in a participatory fashion, and rethink learning in the community accordingly.

## 13.2 Narratives and development revisited

The concept of *narratives*, or stories, we can foreground more in this final chapter. The path and model properties together delineate the space for a narrative, and the openings for narrative rejuvenation. Community design, for example, can easily incorporate existing stories and can contribute to the creation of a new story for the community, what it is and how it could move forward. Policy integration can happen under a unifying narrative, while a narrative about the future can lead to a myriad of policies that are more easily integrated as a whole because they already fit a narrative. Narratives combine description with prescription: this is who we are; this is our place; this is what is important for us; this is how we move forward. Narratives can be provided by some of the models, while in other cases the substance has to come from elsewhere. They can already clearly exist in the community, or not, they can be clearly visible in the governance path, or not. The substance of the narrative can come from many places: if not from the development and governance models directly, they can be tied to an older community identity, but they can also come from stories far away, stories about different topics, places, times. We speak of discursive migration. Stories on pollution far away can inspire new stories on good rural development; an economic collapse far away, and the story explaining it, can alter the story your community tells about itself. Ideas in a specific discipline, e.g. expert ideas on public health, can influence the image a community has of itself and its future.

The stories of *self*, of *place* and of *history* tend to entangle, as communities and as individuals. An understanding of self is a story about self, and this is usually linked to a story about the past, with implications for the stories we create about a desired future. Another way of saying this is that social identity, place identity and image of history shape each other. And from this triangle usually emerges a view of the good and appropriate future, the core of a development vision, even if it is not understood as such. Which knowledge is useful in and for such a vision, hinges on the nature of the story itself. Narratives can guide policy integration, and policy integration can produce narratives. Summing up and integrating expertise for development can lead to narratives which help in this effort, while, conversely, existing narratives tend toward the selection of knowledge that makes sense in and for the narrative. If a community sees itself as green, its future as green, then green knowledge will be central. While it is also possible that various expertise is already present in governance, and slowly leads to a green narrative – 'look what we're doing already, we are the greenest community in this area. ' This little example also shows how narrative migration can always be at work; the recognition of something in the light of a narrative, can happen because these stories circulate already in wider circles.

Narratives of self can restructure narratives of place and of history, and then inspire policies and plans aiming at the future. Communities who rediscover or redefine themselves may look at their environment differently, for example, and then come up with a different way of organizing that environment. Individuals can find themselves in new places, become inspired by them and write about their experiences; the images of place they create can then catch on locally and inspire new ideas about what is valuable and how to manage it. We would say that narratives already present in the community, with values already implicitly or explicitly embedded in the community, have a better chance of leading to implementable policies than narratives that are entirely a product

Figure 13.1. Re-enacting old rural development as a new strategy. Retelling the story of the first greenhouses in Denmark. Photo: Monica Gruzmacher. © ZEF/University of Bonn, Germany.

of pragmatic accommodation or branding exercises in the policy sphere. We refer to our earlier paragraphs on place branding and narrative, as well as to our discussion of formal and informal institutions, which highlighted the advantage of formal structures being embedded in informal ones.

So, rural development is about *storytelling*, in different modes and to different extents, depending on the measure of condensation of possible futures into stories, the measure enabled and desirable in a given governance path and by the combination of governance models and development models chosen.

What makes things more complicated and simplifies them at the same time, is that all the governance models, development and rural development perspectives discussed earlier are *stories themselves*: stories about essential values, the right kind of democracy and the best ways to organize it, the best ways to articulate common futures and how to move in a desirable direction. All these are, in the end, stories people tell themselves and each other about how the world is and how it should be. Some of those stories are presented as expert knowledge ('political theory', 'public administration', 'planning', 'development', 'environmental science', 'development economics'), and many of these stories include forms of expert knowledge deriving from a variety of disciplines, but their basic structure is that of a narrative.

The narrative is ideological, in the sense that it says something about the good society. It is often hidden, silently structuring the reasoning of the experts and people listening to them. Expert clashes can be about cold facts, but, more often than not, they are a matter of clashing assumptions, of clashing underlying narratives about the world, communities and where they should go. The fights between experts to acquire influence in governance, to provide possibly the first ordering principle in the case of comprehensive development visions, are not just fights over the relative value of expertise A or B for 'practice', nor are they fights over power for its own sake, although this certainly plays a role. Foremost they are fights between narratives (underpinning the disciplines), and a fight over a new narrative for the future of the community.

Why does this make things more complicated and simple at the same time? Why does the narrative nature of development and governance models, and of expert and local knowledge change things? We would say it makes things more complicated for the analyst because it can blur the lines between the categories and typologies we introduced earlier (governance models, development and rural development perspectives). It explains why the couplings between these models and their combinatory properties are so complex but also fluid: they are stories that are continuously transformed by retelling and reinterpretation, by discursive migration, by new contexts for their telling, by new heroes and villains and dramas and climaxes that can be incorporated, and by new experiences of reality in the community or in communities far away. The narrative nature also explains in a new way the difference in linkage between certain models and perspectives, the preferential links and obstacles. The more clear exposition of policy and development as narrative shows new limits to steering: an integrating narrative can change during implementation; the elements integrated can acquire new meanings at any time; and a traumatic community experience can cause the questioning of broad development narratives and community identity stories themselves.

And the discovery of storytelling as the basis of our community organization sees new sites and modes of rejuvenation, as discursive migration and transformation can happen any time a story becomes more or less persuasive for a group, becomes more or less tied to a social identity, a place identity, an image of history. It introduces new flexibility in governance paths, one that asserts itself without warning, when suddenly old values and their stories seem less persuasive (so we suddenly need 'participation' e.g. and forget about its old forms). And it can be amenable to management and coordination, too: stories have to be persuasive, within governance circles and within the community. Pretending that something is not a story, but purely an expert notion, an absolute truth, can work for a while, but the expertise fairytale will not be convincing for long.

**Example 13.1. Slow food and farm-to-table.**

As many things described in this book, slow food is not new at all, but the label is new, and it became more recently packaged and presented as a comprehensive approach to rural development. Slow Food started as an essentially European (or Italian) resistance movement against American-styled food production and consumption, understood as industrial scale agriculture, processing, and marketing, in a chain spanning from huge capital and input intensive farms to fast food restaurants. Slow food draws attention to the slow and carefully savoring of food, to the cultivation of taste. Enjoying life, enjoying food and recognizing quality go hand in hand and the movement hopes that a broader dissemination of what we called product knowledge inspires changes in production, processing and marketing knowledge. Slow food often has traditionalist overtones, in the sense of conservation of landscape, culinary and intangible forms of heritage. Some argue that there is an implicit argument for old forms of economic and family life which are not tenable anymore.

The Slow Food movement started in Italy in 1986, triggered by protest against the opening of a McDonalds restaurant near the Spanish Steps in Rome, and slowly broadened its substantive and geographical scope. The movement became inclusive of more and more goals and people: they organized meetings across the world where products and producers could discuss, network, look for solutions to survive and thrive in a context dominated by big business. The emphasis shifted from slow food to natural, healthy, fair food, fair for producers and consumers alike, without leaving most of the profits and product definition with powerful middlemen (agri-food business). In 1989, a founding manifesto was signed in Paris. Delegates from 15 countries were present. Now (2014) almost 200 countries have national branches and hundreds of local branches exist (called convivia). The local branches are largely autonomous, and define which products, which traditions, which issues have to be addressed locally, and when coordination at larger scales is needed. They organize a variety of events, ranging from wine tastings, farmers markets, to food festivals, lobby meetings, and protests.

Carlo Petrini is the founder of the movement. He co-authored several of the books promoting Slow Food and developing the perspective, while he was also one of the main anchors for the larger events, such as the Salone del Gusto (Salon of Taste) in Turin, Italy, and one of the founders of Slow Food's own university, the University of Gastronomic Sciences (Pollenzo and Colorno, Italy).

Slow Food is related to the Farm-to-table movement, better known in North America. Farm to table is close in philosophy to Slow Food, but less organized and less ambitious. It emphasizes local production or short chains of production and consumption, and often organic production at smaller farms. As Slow Food, it perceives the weeding out of small farms across the world as a threat to the environment, to fair competition, to public health and to quality of life. As Slow Food, Farm-to-table sees a broader awareness of the issues as essential for change, and understands that awareness of the big issues needs to be combined with a cultivation of product knowledge. If people do not recognize the difference between

Figure 13.2. Slow food website. © Slowfood.com

a beet and a parsnip, or between a factory chicken and a local free-roaming specimen, or between a frozen burger made with leftover meats, versus a fresh one made with good cuts of well treated animals, then the argument for better food and a better food production system will carry little political weight.

Different from Slow Food, Farm-to-table usually does not accentuate tradition and heritage, reflecting a different context, less marked by long and locally different culinary histories (e.g. compared to Italy, where neighboring villages can fight for centuries over ownership of a rabbit ragout recipe). The literary and intellectual sources invoked are also different, with Farm-to-table people often referring to North American authors as Wendell Bery and Michael Pollan. Both movements share a concern about the loss of variety in dishes, in food products, but also in crops. Many heirloom varieties in fruits, vegetables, and many breeds in farm animals disappeared or are in the process, under pressure of the combined homogenizing demands of industrial agriculture, industrial processing, large scale distribution and retail (supermarkets).

Farm-to-table activism can locally emerge with farmers, but also via influential restaurants and chefs, while it can be promoted by NGOs, community associations, academics and journalists. It can become more institutionalized, when a community comes together around the idea, and embraces what is sometimes called community supported agriculture. Farm-to-table then becomes part of governance, resembling the situation of some of the more active local chapters of Slow Food in their Italian (or German, French) communities.

### Further reading

Petrini, C. (2013). Slow Food nation: why our food should be good, clean and fair. New York, NY, USA: Rizzoli.

Pollan, M. (2006). The omnivore's dilemma: a natural history of four meals. New York, NY, USA: Penguin.

Pretending that a perspective held by a governance actor, on a policy topic, is just a purely personal or group belief (without link to broader stories) is also risky. It makes things more rigid than necessary. Understanding the narrative underpinnings of actor stories, the complex layering of discourses underneath, can show more possibilities to persuade them, to find common ground, or simply to improve the quality of the discussion. Not seeing these narrative underpinnings reduces discussion in governance more easily to rigid and confrontational identity politics – 'You think this, I think that, because I am like this, you are like that'.

Viewing policy, development and rural development as story-telling does not diminish the importance of the categories and the conceptual frame we have taken pains to delineate in this book. The frame can now be understood as an interpretive tool to help reveal how certain stories tend to engender others or link more easily with each other. Stories might share values, heroes, or a notion of crisis, for example, or they may embrace conflicting values, concepts, or things that conflict under certain circumstances. A given development or rural development perspective can lead to different stories, meaning very different versions of stories can coexist in one category, even if these stories had the same starting point, e.g. heroes and villains, etc. Narrative dynamics can change all the stories coexisting in a governance system, altering the potential of the latter to be coupled with other systems and development perspectives. Grand narratives circulating on a vast scale, in space and throughout time, can affect what happens at smaller scales, furthering changing the dynamics of what can coexist there. The influence of a particular narrative (e.g. the grand narrative of modernism) is dependent on both affirmative retelling, which stabilizes the narrative, and criticism or rejection, which keeps the narrative alive.

## Further reading

Briggs, J. (2005). The use of indigenous knowledge in development: problems and challenges. Progress in Development Studies, 5(2), 99-114.

Ellis, F. and Biggs, S. (2001). Evolving themes in rural development 1950's-2000's. Development Policy Review, 19(4), 437-448.

Hansen, R.H. (2010). The narrative nature of place branding. Place Branding and Public Diplomacy, 6(4), 268-279.

Hornidge, A.-K. (2012). 'Knowledge' in development discourse: a critical review. In: Hornidge, A.-K. and Antweiler, C. (eds.), Environmental uncertainty and local knowledge Southeast Asia as a laboratory of global ecological change. Bielefeld, Germany: Transcript, pp. 21-54.

Sandercock, L. (2003). Out of the closet: the importance of stories and storytelling in planning practice. Planning Theory & Practice, 4(1), 11-28.

Throgmorton, J.A. (1996). Planning as persuasive storytelling: the rhetorical construction of Chicago's electric future. Chicago, IL, USA: University of Chicago Press.

Van Assche, K. (2007). Planning as/and/in context. Towards a new analysis of participatory planning. METU JFA, 27(1), 110-119.

Van Assche, K., Beunen. R. and Duineveld, M. (2014). Evolutionary governance theory. An introduction. Heidelberg, Germany: Springer.

## 13.3 Narratives and rurality

As we know, not all governance models in rural areas are explicitly or consciously rural, and not every development or even rural development perspective in rural areas sees itself as rural. More generally, not every rural area sees itself as rural, and if it does, this does not always entail a need to organize governance differently or to come up with specifically rural visions as outcomes of governance. If communities see themselves as rural, see their place as a rural place, and see their history as a rural history, then the futures they come up with will likely be seen as rural, too. Rural issues will look different from the different perspectives discussed, and the same is true for rurality itself, the qualities that make you call a place rural. They will look different from within each governance path. And we can understand these differing and changing images of rurality by understanding governance and development through the lens of narrative dynamics.

For the study of rural development, the images and stories of rurality that circulate in society at large are of particular interest. We mentioned in earlier chapters the positive and negative images of the countryside, of small rural towns. We can add the images and notions of 'nature', which play a key role in narratives making a strong distinction between the rural and the city. If the countryside is understood to be very different from the city, then rural narratives often come close to, and incorporate elements of images and stories of nature.

Stories of rurality, what is the real and the good countryside, can be important in the identity politics of the community, and easily serve to frame policies, plans, or even their absence (if planning, e.g. is seen as an activity imposed by 'the government', associated with cities, with concerns not their own). Rural narratives, and the distinctions they draw between what is rural and what is urban, can sway public opinion in favor of governance and development models that desire scenarios as different as possible from what is seen in the city. Or, they can lead to a rhetorical reinforcement of existing, older governance traditions and associated narratives. Narratives' rurality can be old, it can be new (new stories being constructed internally and externally), or it can pretend to be old, in the fashion of invented tradition, as in 'We've been doing this for years' – meaning e.g. three years. The gloss of tradition helps to naturalize what was contingent, what could have been different.

Nothing is rural in essence. Situations, places, histories and people are interpreted as rural within the frame of narratives and images of the rural. These rural narratives can be of local origin, but often they are versions of older and bigger stories of city vs countryside, civilization vs nature, virtue vs vice, work vs leisure, etc. Rural communities, as said, can identify themselves for long periods of time with one narrative, or they can embrace one quickly in a specific political, cultural or economic situation. Some rural narratives more easily find a place in one particular governance model or development perspective rather than another. They can be reasons to move towards such a governance model or development perspective, and in the other direction, the model and perspective (and the more complex hybrids one will find in practice) can lead to the easier adoption of a certain story of rurality. The rural story can also help to simplify the real complexity of rural governance, the intricate combinations of models and perspectives that often result from long governance paths.

Rural development perspectives tend to rely on rural development narratives mainly as a rhetorical device, rather than for shaping governance and the substance of resulting policies. The rhetoric of rural identity is often invoked selectively, while governance and development are guided by very different values and concerns unrelated to rural stories. The rhetoric of an agricultural community can be found in places that do not rely on agriculture, for example, or where agriculture is dominated by a powerful few and closely linked to urban economies. Likewise, the rhetoric of a natural place can often be observed in communities that are barely aware of the ecological qualities of their surroundings, or communities that mostly see the physical landscape as a place of exploitation for the profit of urban economies.

The rhetorical use of rural narratives is not to be seen in a negative light. People and communities use stories for many purposes, including entertainment, short term conflicts, identity politics contained to specific situations and roles (as in 'As a member of the heritage club, I am proud of our rural heritage'). For the student of rural development, however, it is important not to over-estimate which narratives actually had an impact on governance structures, power struggles and outcomes, as well as the models and perspectives chosen, on the combinations of policies which can be observed, on configurations in governance and on transformation options.

Rural narratives can embody both rigidity and flexibility in governance, and towards development. They represent rigidity if they simplify identity politics to such an extent that alternative interpretations of qualities, assets, problems and solutions cannot come to the surface easily in governance. Rural stories can make it hard to see that they are rural stories, and that other rural stories are possible, including more economically and culturally diverse and ecologically sustainable futures. Adaptation to changing circumstances then becomes hard, development options are narrowed down, and even harnessing existing qualities and assets becomes tough, since these will not be recognized as assets and qualities. A more positive sort of rigidity introduced by rural narratives is the stabilizing and coordinative power they can bring. Rural identities, inspired by rural narratives, can also remain flexible enough to observe economic and environmental opportunities and necessities, while maintaining policies and infrastructures, seen as appropriately rural, which can generate economic, ecological and other value. Forms of rural design and place branding can rely on rural narratives in this way. Stability offers risks, but also opportunities. It can be a value in and by itself, especially in a world where things change fast and many people long for authentic, local, healthy, traditional foods, activities, places. Such positive forms and effects of stability associated with rural images, however, can only contain the risks of rural rigidity when reflexivity is cultivated in governance, and, maybe, in the community at large (in the vein of civic republicanism).

Rural narratives represent flexibility, if, in an environment of reflexivity and adaptive governance, they are considered in their diversity, as possible resources for rejuvenation and transformation of governance, as a treasure trove of stories that can enable adaptation. This aspect of flexibility can partly be managed, when comprehensive visioning takes place (possible in several of the perspectives), and there is, as said, an overview of alternative rural narratives. Such an overview is gained to a large extent through an awareness of other rural communities and their strategies, making learning from other rural trajectories possible, as well as learning from the role and management of other rural narratives there. The flexibility is partly a matter of coincidence, too, of changing stories and interpretations internally and externally. This cannot be managed easily, and the effects can be both positive and negative. Communities live their lives in and through narratives, but they change them at the same time, and the narratives can lose their credibility and legitimacy for a variety of reasons.

## Further reading

Phillips, M. (1998). The restructuring of social imaginations in rural geography. Journal of Rural Studies, 14(2), 121-153.

Potter, C. and Tilzey, M. (2005). Agricultural policy discourses in the European post-Fordist transition: neoliberalism, neomercantilism and multifunctionality. Progress in Human Geography, 29(5), 581-600.

Radomski, P.J. and Van Assche, K. (2014). Lakeshore living: designing lake places and communities in the footprints of environmental writers. East Lansing, MI, USA: MSU Press.

## 13.4 Narratives and rural expertise

We come to a point where things can be condensed again, into principles.
- Principle 1: stories create something as fact, as actor, as good and bad guy, as problem, as drama, as success, and as solution. They create an image of knowledge, and of expertise as a sub-category of knowledge, with a different validity and utility. What that utility is, e.g. its relevance for governance, e.g. depends on yet other stories, on good governance and on the type of expertise, the expectations associated with it and the discipline it was produced in.
- Principle 2: rural stories create images, actors, issues, problems, solutions, knowledge and expertise understood as typically rural, as associated with a certain type of places, people, histories.
- Principle 3: rural stories and rural governance are two different things. The rural stories and the governance and development stories embedded in the models and perspectives discussed can associate in various ways, as we saw, but they have to be distinguished as different categories of stories if we want to understand rural governance and rural development options.
- Principle 4: rural expertise, then, expertise for rural development, does not exist outside these two categories of stories, i.e. governance/development stories, and stories of rurality.

This is not an easy escape for lazy book writers, and it is not a cynical deconstruction of rural development. It is not easy, because it forces the analyst of rural development, and the person interested in contributing something to rural development, to look much more closely at specific governance paths, in which various stories interact, with positive and negative effects, and space is left for particular stories that have transformative effects. It is not cynical, since the scope of potentially useful knowledge and expertise for rural development is much bigger now, if it is not a priori tied to a few pre-existing images of rurality, and a few theories of governance and development. Each community has its own path, can craft its own rural development strategy, and find the knowledge and expertise that are relevant in and for that vision.

## Further reading

Borrini-Feyerabend, G., Pimbert, M., Farvar, M.T., Kothari, A. and Renard, Y. (2007). Sharing power: learning-by-doing in co-management of natural resources throughout the world. London, UK: Earthscan.

Dessel, A., Rogge, M.E. and Garlington, S.B. (2006). Using intergroup dialogue to promote social justice and change. Social Work, 51(4), 303-315.

Hornidge, A.-K. and Antweiler, C. (Eds.). (2012). Environmental uncertainty and local knowledge. Southeast Asia as a laboratory of global ecological change. Bielefeld, Germany: Transcript Verlag.

Leeuwis, C. (2008). Communication for rural innovation: Rethinking agricultural extension. New York, NY, USA: John Wiley & Sons.

Murray, M. and Dunn, L. (1995). Capacity building for rural development in the United States. Journal of Rural Studies, 11(1), 89-97.

Roling, N.G. and Wagemakers, M.A.E. (eds.) (2000). Facilitating sustainable agriculture: participatory learning and adaptive management in times of environmental uncertainty. Cambridge, UK: Cambridge University Press.

## 13.5 Institutionalization and the capturing of new narratives and knowledge

Harking back to our recently exposed normative assumptions on good governance seems appropriate for these final paragraphs. Good governance for rural development is adaptive governance, adaptive to changing internal and external environments. Adaptation requires the presence in governance of different, truly different perspectives, we believe, and, in line with Machiavelli, we would argue that, in a sturdy system of checks and balances, this should be accompanied with confrontation and conflict. Conflict can be productive, when it does not undermine institutions, when differences between perspectives become crystal clear, their risks and benefits more clearly exposed. When conflict is not automatically translated into identity politics, then learning is possible, not only as in finding common ground or possibly consensus, but as in actual learning, changing one's position, interpretation, narrative, in the discussion. Cultivating difference in governance for us means incorporating different perspectives (associated with actors, or not) in governance, allowing them to show their differences, possibly conflict, and, thirdly, keeping perspectives at hand, keeping knowledge and expertise available for when the need arises.

An openness to include new perspectives accompanies the *cultivation of difference*. Administration can fulfill this task, higher level administration too, or hired private or academic consultants. And a clear and accessible historical track record of the community, where it was, how it evolved, which perspectives and associated knowledge marked and guided that evolution. Cultivating difference in perspectives, in these different aspects, we consider highly commendable, for whatever rural development strategy. It supports continuous *adaptation* of governance, and helps to optimally harness the expertise and skills of the community. That is also the reason why we so vehemently opposed any development or governance model proposing a universal formula for good governance or development, and an associated formula for the 'correct' expertise. It is in the cultivation of difference that new unifying perspectives can be found which might actually carry a community into the future. If unity is imposed too early, without understanding existing differences in perspectives (without understanding existing power/knowledge configurations), then this perspective, e.g. a new rural development narrative, will meet much resistance, and it will not optimally use the cognitive resources of the community.

Figure 13.3. A wine village in the Mosel valley, Germany. The Mosel was part of Roman Germany. An area marked by a milder climate, the viticulture brought by the Romans never faded, and local knowledge accumulated on the basis of the old more generic expertise. Local growers developed new grapes, new techniques, colonized the very steep shale and limestone slopes, and learned to capitalize on minute differences in soil, exposure (to the sun), steepness, age of the vines, and date of picking, to produce in the narrow and meandering valley a bewildering variety of quality wines from one grape variety, Riesling. Photo: Monica Gruzmacher. © ZEF/University of Bonn, Germany.

Not much of what was said in a normative manner, not many of our policy recommendations can have any effect if reflexivity is not cultivated as well. Reflexivity is a precondition for adaptive rural development. Any routine solutions have to be examined routinely, and even the most stable guiding narratives have be questioned now and then: Are they guiding us? Should they still be guiding us? So, we argue for reflexivity in rural development, a cultivation of reflexivity with both scientific and other actors. Reflexivity which is widespread can contribute to an increased awareness of existing paths, dependencies and configurations, and of the assumptions built in many tools and theories of rural development.

Adaptive governance and cultivating difference becomes more realistic when institutional experimentation is accepted, and structurally possible. Things can be tried out at smaller scales, for shorter periods of time, for delineated topics, or without much investment, or without hardening the configurations much (we refer to the paragraphs about combinatory options), and this can take place within more stable frames, i.e. more slowly evolving frames.

Institutional experimentation has to be harnessed and contained. It needs rules that change more slowly, and are more subjected to scrutiny and checks and balances, to stabilize expectations and enable coordination. It can be encouraged and contained if, in governance, there are several options for institutionalization of coordinative practices. Self-organization can be a driver of innovation in governance. There can be delineated spaces where self-organization is possible, and when it occurs outside these spheres, there can still be measured and open-minded responses possible. If the combination of formal and informal institutions (e.g. existing institutions and new forms of informal self-organization) works well, one does not have to do anything. If there are problems but also potential, or if there is more potential for synergy between formal and informal, one can adapt the formal institutions, but one can also, depending on the case, choose for light institutionalization, a not too deeply entrenched and invested institutionalization, and one can organize a reflection in governance on possible formalization modes of the informal initiative.

And, no, there are no rules for that. What is good and what works, is decided in and by the community itself. Advisors, such as possibly the readers of this book, can help, give insight in paths, show tools and alternatives. Simply thinking of the possibility of institutional experiment, of light institutionalization, of formal/informal configurations with benefits, and of diverse formalization modes can already help a community to avoid routine response that in the long run undermines adaptive development. It can reduce the chance of taking either no decision or too drastic decisions. It can help to find the balance between flexibility and rigidity that works for your community.

## Further reading

Cleaver, F. (2012). Development through bricolage: rethinking institutions for natural resource management. Abingdon, UK: Routledge.

Fischer, F. (2009). Democracy and expertise: reorienting policy inquiry. Oxford, UK: Oxford University Press.

Healy, K. (2001). Llamas, weavings and organic chocolate: multicultural grassroots development in the Andes and Amazon of Bolivia. Notre Dame, IN, USA: University of Notre Dame Press.

Hornidge, A.-K., Oberkircher, L. and Kudryavtseva, A. (2013). Boundary management and the discursive sphere – negotiating 'realities' in Khorezm, Uzbekistan. Geoforum, 45, 266-274.

Patton, C., Sawicki, D. and Clark, J. (2012). Basic methods of policy analysis and planning, 3 Edition. Chicago, IL, USA: Pearson.

Walzer, N. (ed.) (1996). Community strategic visioning programs. Portsmouth, NH, USA: Greenwood Publishing Group.

Winslade, J. and Monk, G. (2000). Narrative mediation: a new approach to conflict resolution. San Francisco, CA, USA: Jossey-Bass.

# Glossary

| | |
|---|---|
| Actors | Actors are participants in governance, formally or informally. Actors are ascriptions, the result of observation, and sometimes of formal recognition as actors. |
| Actor/institution configuration | The unity of actors and institutions in a governance path. Actors and institutions co-evolve and whatever happens on one side of the configuration affects the other side. New actors affect old actors and old institutions, etc. |
| Agency | Agency is considered to be an attribution made by an observer. Agency can be attributed to human beings, organizations, structures or objects. |
| Assets | An element or quality in a community that is of value. Assets are recognized in and by a community as an asset, and value is attributed. Something becomes an asset in a certain perspective, in a certain practical situation and discursive configuration. A large labor pool can be an asset, when one/they can conjure up activities, and it can be a highly destabilizing factor, when there are no jobs. |
| Autopoiesis | Autopoiesis means self-reproduction. The concept refers to the operational closure of systems which implies that both the elements and the structures of a system are the product of the evolution of that system. |
| Boundaries | All boundaries are conceptual boundaries that delineate objects, subjects and places. The process of delineation can start with the demarcation of a difference, and it can start with the crystallization of relations, which then become considered as interior, and delineated from the environment. |
| Buffering | The separation of potentially incompatible or conflicting institutions, to minimize their effects on each other. Buffering can extent to policy domains (governed in different manners, according to different principles) and many forms (from assigning resources, reducing the connectivity of rules, creating formal exceptions in the domains for cases associated with the other, formal institutions to specify boundaries of the buffered institutions, informal rules to selectively interpret or apply each of the others. |
| Capacity | The resources needed in a community to move towards common goals, to develop. Capacity building usually refers to human resources, where the building is teaching, educating, organizing, so they can be more active and effective in community governance, in administration, as entrepreneurs or in other roles deemed useful for development. As with assets and resources, capacity does not exist in nature, yet emerges in a certain perspective, an economic discourse, a development discourse, a governance model. |

| | |
|---|---|
| Co-evolution | The entwined evolution of two systems or entities, whereby changes in one affect changes in the other. Co-evolutions are usually co-evolutions in networks or systems, where not two by many entities evolve in dependence on each other, in dependence on the whole environment created by the network of interactions. |
| Combinatory mechanisms | Mechanisms to combine institutions, possibly of different provenance, possibly associated with different models of governance and different development models. Can include nesting, framing, mixing, specifying, specializing. |
| Commo-dification | Delineating something, attributing a value and simplifying its circulation. Places, things, products, animals, activities can be commodified. One expansion of markets is the expansion of commodification. Commodification can be seen as privatizing and monetizing, and undermining common goals and goods, but it can also be used as a tool towards achieving common goals. |
| Common goal | Goals for a community, shared goals which can potentially structure policies, plans, development visions. Common goals can be rooted in common goods, shared values and shared necessities. Common goods cannot be simply assumed to exist, and certainly not by one actor or an elite faction in governance. Common goals cannot be derived from common goods in a simple and linear manner; this requires deliberation (in an agreed-upon balance between participation and representation) and it can require a variety of expertise – e.g. when it comes to planning, branding, design, livelihoods assemblage, entrepreneurship. |
| Community | A group and a territory. An open concept which can veil very different realities per governance path. Governance can create the impression of community as some sort of social identity and unity, and it can result and represent such unity. |
| Contiguity | A conceptual or physical proximity which resorts effects. Contiguity can be causality, but it can also affect objects and people more unpredictably. Contiguity is a form of tight coupling. |
| Contingency | That what is possible but not necessary. What is contingent, could also be different. It is the product of a context, of a governance path, of circumstances. Governance paths are structured but contingent. The expertise included in a governance path is contingent. |
| Corruption | The undermining of institutions for private or group gain. Not all informal institutions can be called corruption. Corruption can ensue more easily when formal and informal institutions do not fit, or, more properly said, when the formal/informal institutional configuration does not perform well, shows internal inconsistencies allowing for easy deviation from agreed upon collective goals. |

| | |
|---|---|
| Coupling | The relation between two conceptual entities whereby one has effects on the other. Coupling occur between levels of governance, between governance models, between development perspectives, between governance models and development perspectives, between actors, between function systems. We distinguish loose coupling, tight coupling and short circuit coupling, where combinatory attempts cause inconsistencies or conflicts somewhere in the governance system or in the community at large. |
| Dead institutions | Dead institutions are written down institutions that were once considered formal. They have no effects currently because they are not considered a real coordination option. The fact that they are on the books makes it possible to revive them. Dead institutions are thus the product of modern societies, and relevant for governance evolutions, as they can hark back to former stages in the evolution. They do not revive old times, but they can bring back some lost coupling between actors, lost objects, or give existing objects a new meaning and impact, renders some forgotten subjects relevant, etc. |
| Democracy | Democracy is essentially about rules to change the rules, about transformation options. Democracy exists in different versions, and some of these versions do not recognize each other as democracies. There is no recipe for democracy, but a form of functional differentiation, where law and economy can follow their path, without politics steering directly, can safeguard the flexibility of democratic governance, can maintain transformation rules and a diversity of voices. |
| Dependency | Rigidity in the evolution of governance, in a governance path. We can distinguish path dependence, goal dependence and interdependence. Dependency does not imply determinism: there are always options open, there is always a measure of contingency and freedom. |
| Development | The evolution of governance, of the community and the effects of governance on the wellbeing of the community. Development can take place with or without development policies, plans, visions. Different disciplines, different political ideologies embrace or produce different recipes for development, including different roles for government and governance in the development process. |
| Development perspectives | Conceptual structures allowing for the formulation of desirable futures in a community. Development perspectives combine prescription and description, are rooted in theory and practice, in different ways and to different extents. Some development models are closely related with governance models, others not. Some are highly compatible with the local or regional production of development visions, with high levels of policy integration to guide governance, whereas others find the best possible future in minimal intervention, experiment, in minimal institutional requirements (e.g. a minimalist version of the rule of law). |

| | |
|---|---|
| Discourse | A structured set of concepts that enables access to a certain part or aspect of reality, while simultaneously veiling other parts or aspects. Discourses can also be conceptualized as historically contingent social practices that produce the criteria for their own transformation. They are self-referential in the sense that they construct the world by means of references to their own elements and in the sense that new structures are always grounded in prior ones. In that sense discourses evolve. |
| Discursive migration | The dissemination of concepts, images, narratives and narrative fragments to new contexts. Discursive migration can reinforce certain narratives, undermine others, can create the potential for new discursive coalitions in governance. |
| Discursive coalitions | A combination of discourses which becomes possible and has effects in governance. Discursive coalitions can be directly associated with coalitions of actors, or not. They can have a direct goal or implication of institutional reform, or not. Discursive coalitions can also be associated with one actor, and they can be associated with larger changes in the narrative frames of the community. |
| Elites | Relatively small groups with accumulated wealth or power. Wealth can generate power and vice versa. Elite rule is a situation when elites have privileged access to power, through participation or representation, through formal and informal institutions. Elite rule can be buffered from more participatory or generally democratic policy domains. Elite rule in opacity can foster corruption. |
| Evolution | A process of change in a system whereby both external forces and internal mechanisms create a path, and both structures and elements of the system change over time. What can evolve are biological systems, psychic systems, social systems, including organizations and networks of organizations. Governance systems are not social systems by themselves, but networks of co-evolving organizations, each a social system. |
| Expertise | Knowledge considered of special value for governance, suspected of more direct access to a reality relevant for the pursuit of collective goals, by means of analysis or prescriptions for action and intervention. |
| Extension | A development perspective which hinges about teaching and learning expertise useful for development. Over time, extension shifted emphasis from teaching to learning, from individual to social learning, from agricultural modernization goals, to participatory methods of goal setting. |

| Failed states | Nation-states which can be considered dead institutions: the constitutions is not implemented, the unity and cohesion in governance envisioned by the formal institutions cannot be observed in practice. Observation of a failed state, designation as such, hinges again on the perspective taken, the model of governance embraced, the level of cohesion expected from a nation-state. A failed state for one can be a successful example of decentralized governance. |
| --- | --- |
| Formal institutions | Formality in our perspective is the result of a choice or decision made again in each situation where there are several coordination options. In such a situation one coordination option carries the weight of general expectation that makes it formality. The distinction between formal and informal is thus a labelling that takes place with each and every decision. In modern states, formality is regularly associated with the state, with rules written down on paper, and with state organizations, but this is not necessarily always the case. |
| Formal/informal configuration | The unity of formal and informal institutions in a governance path. The configuration as a whole was certain effects, positive and negative, which ought to be assessed, rather than the effect of either formal or informal institutions separately. A configuration works when it delivers the goods, when it brings common goods as close as reasonably possible. |
| Framing institutions | The relation between institutions whereby one forms the precondition of the other. Framing can be conceptual, temporal and spatial. |
| Functional differentiation | The separation of functional domains-law, science, economy, education, religion and politics. Function differentiation tries to grasp the essence of change in Western societies, a process of systemic change leading into eighteenth century enlightenment and the level of functional differentiation we call modernity. Its empirical manifestations are likely to be diverse. Once domains start to separate, functional differentiation takes over from other forms of differentiation. It can replace hierarchical differentiation, based on a center-periphery relation and an ideal of overview and control by a political center. It can also replace segmentary differentiation, a catch phrase for many pre-modern societies structured along lines of clans, ethnic groups, extended families and tribes. For Luhmann functional differentiation entails the formation of function systems with a specific logic of reproduction. |

Function systems  Social systems that distinguish themselves by the specificity of their perspective. A function system reproduces itself by applying distinct code. Such logic is based on the unique application of unique procedures of observation, grounded in unique basic distinctions. Each function reconstructs the whole world internally, simplified according to the schemes grounded in that basic distinction. Law, economy, politics, religion, science and education are examples of function systems that each play a role in the reproduction of society as the encompassing social system.

Goal dependency  The influence of plans and policies embedding collective goals on the present, on the co-evolution of actors and institutions, power and knowledge. Plans are rarely fully implemented, but often have an impact on governance and on the realities governance affects.

Good governance  Is defined differently in different paths and models of governance. A few shared characteristics we would (normatively) present: the formal/informal configuration delivers the goods, works towards common goods; transformation options remain open; stabilization of expectations in a differentiated society.

Governance  The taking of collectively binding decisions in a community by a diversity of actors, inside and outside government, with formal roles and without formal roles. Governance relies on formal and informal institutions, on formal and informal roles.

Governance dimensions  We can describe each governance arrangement by means of a set of choice dimensions. Both the dimensions that are considered important as well as the alternative positions on these dimensions show recurring patterns. Certain dimensions and clusters of dimensions will be more common than others.

Governance model  Governance models represent and simplify different paths of governance evolution. They can be distinguished as different modes of structural coupling between the most important function systems: politics, law and economy. They can also be seen as different compositions of basic concepts such as, individuals, organizations, communities, government, citizens, rights and duties, participation and representation, law, markets, politics, private and public goods. Each model represent a different narrative on existing and ideal societies and their modes of organization. No model of governance is perfect, as in perfectly legitimate, efficient, and stable.

Governance path  The specific evolution of governance in a community. Governance paths have to be carefully reconstructed to be understood in their identity and their implications for possible futures.

Governance mechanism  Mechanisms is a broad concept that includes institutions (as coordination mechanisms), mechanisms of object and subject formation, and stratagems or individual actor's devices to influence governance.

Governance sites   Places and occasions of higher communicative density. They refer to times and places when and where decisions are taken or prepared, where within or between actors alternative courses of collective action are assessed.

History   History can give depth to objects and subjects, can harden their boundaries, intensify the process of object stabilization, and render them more a part of the natural order. Images or narrative of history can harden the identity of actors, which makes governance less flexible and adaptive. In a similar way images of history can harden spatial boundaries that are institutionalized in administrative and political structures, such as governments linked to a particular territory. History differs from evolution as history is what can be rewritten from many perspectives, while evolution is the presence of history in the structure and function of systems.

Hybrid   That which is not pure. Nothing is pure in reality. We distinguish governance models, development models, community identities, unifying narratives. All these are conceptual categories and none of these will be found exactly embodied in governance. Nevertheless, the concept of hybrid can still be useful, to designate specific combinations of contributions by different identities, narratives, models to a situation empirically observed. A designation as hybrid should not be the end but the starting point of analysis.

Identity   That what makes something into what it is. For people, identities are narratives, stories they tell about themselves and which others tell about them. Identities can be tied to roles. Identity can also be attributed to places, times, groups, and then we speak of spatial identity, social identity and image of history. These three shape each other in the history of a community, and in governance paths. Governance can thoroughly reshape social and spatial identities, while shifting identities in wider circles will have governance effects at some point. Subjects and objects are identities; governance, in the daily negotiation and accommodation, the play of power/knowledge in politics, and in the impact of and on broader narratives and discourses, affects the formation and transformation of these identities.

Implementation   What comes after policy making, the steps needed to create real world effects of policies, laws, plans. A process of continuous reinterpretation, of divergence and convergence, of adaptation to new power/knowledge configurations in new discursive environments, to new objects and subjects, and to new institutions.

Informal institutions   Alternative coordination mechanisms to formal institutions. Informal institutions sustain, modify, undermine, reinforce, and complement formal institutions. Formal and informal institutions adapt to each other in governance paths.

| | |
|---|---|
| Innovation | Something new and important. In innovation discourses often reduced to technical innovation, which is supposed to lead to economic success. Innovation is an ascription a posteriori, is highly unpredictable in nature and effects, is barely susceptible to management. Innovation however can be the focus of ongoing conversations in governance, where reflection is cultivated on what is new, which innovation might be useful, how innovations could be coordinated, to produce synergies. |
| Institutional experimentation | The habit of adapting governance regularly to changing internal and external environments by altering institutional arrangements, aiming at specific topics or policy domains, or rethinking more fundamental governance schemes. Institutional experimentation can work best when there is a deep understanding of existing forms of self-organization (as informality, as emerging adaptation) and of the combined effects of formal and informal institutions currently. Governance aspires to enable both stabilization of expectations, catalyzing many sorts of transactions and interactions, and the possibility to adapt. Institutional experimentation is pushing the boundary of what is possible in governance, and high levels of reflexivity are needed to discern what the effects on governance stability are. Experimental domains can be buffered (see combinatory mechanisms), investment can be limited, space and time can be delineated for experiment, and one can distinguish various formalization modes (of informality) and light institutionalization modes (of arrangements deserving testing). |
| Institutions | Institutions are rule of coordination between actors. Institutions can take the form of rules, laws, policies and plans, with institutions in each case referring and linking to others, and often containing others. Plans are tools for policy integration, and usually include a variety of other institutions, while they require and rely on yet others for their implementation, that is, their path of increasing influence on the community. |
| Interactions | In social systems theory: conversations, fleeting, short-lived social systems. in a more general sense: meetings with content or purpose, between actors in governance, or in the community at large. |
| Interdependency | The restriction on action for an actor imposed by the relations with others. Seen from above: a rigidity in a governance path caused by the specific set of relations between actors at one point in time. Interdependence can arise from specialization, resource distribution, knowledge distribution, power distribution, and from other sources. It can be codified in formal rules, in informal rules, and it can organically emerge. |
| Irritations | The effect of social systems on each other, whereby their reproduction is affected by the environment, often another system, but without fully understanding what happened. A cause might be attributed, or not. The cause might be located in the system causing the irritation, or not. |

| | |
|---|---|
| Landscape | The material world surrounding and pervading a community, the place for agriculture, nature, recreation, natural resource exploitation, community expansion. Seeing these surroundings as a landscapes attributes a unity and possibly qualities of that unity, and the potential to manage landscape and thus create new qualities. |
| Law | A formal institution designed to stabilize expectations and guide action in a more rigid manner than rules, policies and plans. Laws are the slowest evolving institutions, and guarantee both stability and adaptation in and by governance. |
| Localism | The idea that governance at the smallest scale is the best. Often associated with identity politics, with the idea that higher levels of governance are associated with different identities, and that the unique local character will never be fairly reflected or present in higher level governance. Localism can be unproductive, when this attitude generates rigidity in governance, by nostalgia, and a general habit of looking inward. And it can generate flexibility, by harnessing local knowledge, generating high participation levels, cultivating reflexivity, all together possibly leading to development visions and policy integration more broadly which captures, protects and reinforces local qualities and assets in a vision eminently adapted and adaptable. |
| Local knowledge | Knowledge in governance which is recognized as local and as knowledge (not as background noise, or opinions), and differentiated from expert knowledge. Local knowledge can include elements of scientific knowledge, present and past. The desirable balance between local knowledge and expert knowledge differs per governance path and per governance model and development perspective. |
| Mapping | Mapping in evolving governance is reconstructing, reconstructing of governance paths and governance contexts. Mapping is always selectivity and interpretation: paths are infinitely detailed and context extend without limits in time and space. |

| | |
|---|---|
| Metaphor | A metaphor is the presentation of something as something else. Metaphors enable perceiving new features of an object, a person, or a situation and a new connection between these features, a new unity of the object. We can speak of a transformation of the object, a redrawing of the boundaries. Once a metaphor is adopted and spreads in a community, it tends to be stretched up. The brain is a computer, the mind is a computer, the body is a computer, organizations are computers and society as a whole might be a computer. With the over-application of the metaphor, the underlying comparison become weaker and weaker, and the shift in perspective minimalizes. Few new features are discovered, and the fact of prevalence itself makes it less likely that a new application of the prevalent metaphor will open the eyes of many. Metaphors are devices that can link different discursive fields, and make the interpretive schemes of one field available and useful for the other one. |
| Metaphoric slide | the set of discursive changes induced by changes in metaphorical activity. Metaphors can have governance effect by producing new insights by connecting semantic fields. If metaphors are produced, used, changed, or connected with other metaphors, objects can form and disappear, boundaries can be redrawn, narratives can lose or gain persuasiveness, and new narratives can be crafted. |
| Mixing | Any combination of dissimilar elements (associated with different appraoches) in any given policy or governance arrangement. |
| Mobilities | The fact of moving and changing at the same time. People, things and concepts move, they change in the act of moving through different contexts and they change each other when traveling together. Migration and discursive migration are mobilities. The broad concept of mobilities enables a perspective on governance as a context of change, and embedded in contexts of change. Mobilities affect governance in pattern complex because their interweaving and partial invisibility. |
| Models of democracy | Conceptual structures offering a perspective on democracy. Models are a combination of prescription and description, of theory and practice. We distinguish five main models which emerged in the course of Western intellectual and political history: civic republicanism, socialism/communism, liberal democracy (neoliberalism), civil society, communitarianism. Empirical states and communities can be considered hybrids, however their functioning and evolution can often be better understood when tracing aspects and elements of different models, and their lineage. |
| Multi-level governance | Multi-level governance implies that several governance paths exist in a community. These paths can run parallel, they can entangle, and they can block each other. Evolutions in one path can affect the other paths, both positively and negatively, by inspiring conformity or by inspiring deviation. |

| | |
|---|---|
| Narrative | A narrative is a form of discourse that has a particular conceptual structure. This structure can render the discursive materials more real and more compelling by introducing temporal, spatial and emotional order. A narrative is a particular assemblage of concepts, subjects, objects and events. It articulates for example particular events and episodes, flights and climaxes, heroes and villains, criteria and values, foreground and background. |
| Nation-state | A product of the modern era, of a slow evolution towards centralization of power in the center of larger territories. Nation-states recreate community, can be more or less centralized, rely more or less on formal institutions, are marked by different patterns of differentiation between law, politics, economy, science. |
| Natural resource | An object in the material world delineated in and by a community and receiving an ascription of value by a community. Something becomes a natural resource when a community uses it and attributes value to it. The value can derive from direct use or from symbolic attribution, but also the direct use value is tinged with symbolism, while symbolic value can be converted into use value when exchange systems (currencies, markets) exist. |
| Nesting | The nesting of institutions is a combinatory mechanism for institutions with the same targets where one contains the other at a lower level. One approach contains another at a lower level. Nesting can be similar and dissimilar. |
| Object formation | Objects are the product of discursive evolutions. Object formation combines the techniques of reification, solidification and codification. Reification entails the recognition of the object as a unity, separated from its environment, more than a loose assemblage of parts. Solidification refers to the tightening of internal connections in the concept, an increasingly sharp delineation of the emerging discursive object. Codification is the simplification of the object boundaries. |
| Object stabilization | A specific phase of object stabilization. As techniques of object stabilization, we distinguish objectification, naturalization, and institutionalization. Objectification is the acknowledgment of the object as part of the objective truth, established by scientific means. Naturalization is the strengthening of discourse that the object is part of the order of things, part of nature. It is the process that veils contingency, blinds the awareness that things could have been different, that objects could have been constructed differently. Institutionalization is the codification of discourse, including its objects, in organizations and institutions, such as policies, laws, and plans. |
| Observers | Observers in social systems terms are systems which make distinctions, which lead to the attribution of meaning. |

| | |
|---|---|
| Open concepts | Seemingly vague concepts that play crucial roles in the reproduction of governance. One could think of concepts such as sustainability, resilience, quality, identity, creativity, or innovation. Open concepts rupture the local discursive structure with an emptiness that invites divergent reinterpretations. |
| Organizations | Organizations can refer to subject or actors or to a particular type of social system. An organization as social system reproduces itself by means of decisions. The structure of the decision-premises is the result of the history of the organization, the images of self and environment, of goals and priorities, strengths and weaknesses that evolved in its self-reproduction. Decisions are taken based on an image of self that is delineated, that is different from other companies, that includes certain departments, persons, roles, procedures, membership rules, promotion rules and measures for success and failure. |
| Participation | Direct contribution by actors to governance, direct as opposed to indirect, delegated. Individuals can participate, or they can be represented in a certain role or interests by others, who could be called actors. Making governance more participatory probably increases the number of actors, but not necessarily. A closer look at governance paths and formal/informal configurations is needed. |
| Path dependency | A rigidity in governance paths whereby the next step in governance evolution is restricted by the existing governance configuration, by the history of governance leading to that configuration. Path dependence can follow out of interdependence, but all features of governance can potentially constitute path dependencies, as well as the externalized results of governance in the past (such as physical infrastructures). |
| Performance | Performance is the embodiment and inhabiting of a role and a script. Performance taking place in a governance context can have rhetorical effects far beyond governance, because of the nature of governance, the potential for collectively binding decisions, and shifting actor/institution configurations and power/knowledge configurations. Performance of success and failure can harden a governance path, as the implied values, roles and power relations are sanctioned or rejected. |
| Performativity | The reality effects of policies and plans, partly the result of performance, partly the result of discursive configurations, and partly of the functioning of the configurations in governance itself. |
| Place branding | The representation of a place not merely as a commodity, but as a bundle of qualities and activities which can generate new commodities. Planning can reinforce or undermine place branding, and place branding can do the same with planning. Place branding outside governance embodies a strong neo-liberal challenge to participation, to the inclusion of diverse voices in the articulation of community futures. |

| | |
|---|---|
| Planning | The coordination of policies and practices affecting spatial organization. Planning does not need planners, and it does not necessarily rely on plans. A site of policy integration. |
| Policy | Temporary conceptual structures coordinating knowledge and power, in constant transmutation, because of the confrontations with other power/ knowledge configurations. Policies are both an outcome of as a tool for coordination between actors. |
| Policy integration | The integration of various policies into a new one, with the aim to find synergies, increase efficiency of governance and minimize a mutual undermining of policies and the associated collective goals. A minimum level of policy integration is policy coordination, whereby a set of policies is scrutinized for their mutual effects, and this assessment leads to informal rules for the implementation of each, in reference to the others. |
| Positionality | The influence of a position on what one can see and think. Positionality becomes more important a concept in post-structuralism, where the perspective one chooses, the discourses one inhabits, always structure reality. In governance, positionality can refer to the perspective associated with a role, and the perspective which was gradually shaped by a trajectory through governance and through the community, in governance practice and as an observer/analyst. Awareness of positionality is an aspect of reflexivity. |
| Post-structuralism | A constructivist epistemology. In post-structuralist fashion, we analyze governance as a meeting ground of different worlds. We do not deny the existence of reality, but something as soon as we observe, communicate, or reason we are within discourse. As soon as something is said, it is subject to the mechanics of discourse, to metaphorical sliding, to distortions by the seeping in of utopias and dystopias, to entanglements with power that cannot be fully grasped. |
| Power | In line with Foucault power is conceptualized as a set of immanent force relations that is present and working everywhere and in every direction. Power is neither good nor bad, it is not necessarily tied to individual or group action, desire, and intentionality. Rather, it is the web of forces at micro-level that make things at the same time possible and understandable and that allows for aggregations of power at higher levels of understanding and authority. |
| Power/knowledge configuration | The unity of power and knowledge in a given governance path. Power shapes knowledge and knowledge shapes power and none can be understood without reference to the other. Governance is possible because of power/ knowledge configurations, which make reality understandable and malleable at the same time, and it is the place for configurations to become dense and compete, because of possible impact on the community at large. |

Practice          That which is recognized as practice, in distinction with concept or thought.
                  Practice can refer to the implementation of policies, to policy making, to
                  the world of activity outside governance (usually a reference to the business
                  world) or to action itself.

Property rights   An object is delineated and then connected with a person or legal entity
                  obtaining rights over it. If something becomes something and then
                  property, it is also commodified, and property rights include some form of
                  transfer right (giving, selling, etc.). However, in essence, property is use, and
                  property rights are bundles of use rights, combined with obligations and
                  restrictions on use. Governance transforms property rights continuously.
                  A myth of absolute property rights makes this transformation harder, and
                  thus raises obstacles for adaptive governance. Property rights embody a
                  coupling between political, legal and economic systems.

Reflexivity       The habit and attitude to reflect on one's actions and thoughts, to look
                  for the grounding assumptions, the underlying discourses, the effects.
                  In governance, reflexivity can increase flexibility, decrease rigidity, in the
                  governance paths; a deeper understanding of past and present shows more
                  and more realistic transformation options. Reflexivity in governance can
                  foster common goods, but, it can also making individual or actor strategies
                  more complex and intricate.

Representation    The delegation of power by citizens to others, to represent their interests and
                  perspectives. Those representatives can further delegate to administrations,
                  who can then delegate to experts outside administration (in business, at
                  universities). Each governance path shows a changing balance between
                  representation and participation.

Resilience        The ability of communities to bounce back after shocks. Governance which
                  can adapt and enhance adaptivity in society can be called governance for
                  resilience. Resilience can best be safeguarded by maintaining a variety of
                  perspectives and forms of expertise in governance, and by maintaining the
                  checks and balance. Not by a specialized form of expertise on resilience or
                  sustainability, which can undermine the institutions enabling adaptation
                  in the long run.

Rule of law       A description of good governance. The existence, consistency, fairness,
                  efficiency, implementation of a set of legal rules. Minimalist and maximalist
                  interpretations exist, each connected with different governance and
                  development models. In maximalist versions, rule of law includes criteria
                  such as broad participation in governance, and more extensive notions of
                  fairness, allowing for substantial redistribution of wealth, towards agreed
                  upon common goals or goods.

| | |
|---|---|
| Rurality | That which is perceived as giving a place, a community, a rural character. Rurality derives from images and narratives of the rural, which can be associated with models of governance, development models, narratives of the urban, or not. Governance and development models can make rurality explicit, or not. They can strongly push in the direction of one narrative, or of one rural organization disconnected from a rural narrative. |
| Social system | A specialized perspective on the world, marked by a unique logic, a unique way of making distinctions, and a unique form of self-reference. A communicative process that shapes historically contingent social practices of discourse. Constituted by on-going processes of interpretation and reinterpretation of internal and external environments. Luhmann distinguished three categories of social systems: interactions, organizations and function systems. |
| Specifying | The relation between two policies where one is the subspecies of the others, a tightly coupled form of framing, where the next step, the lower level, or the conceptual detailing is an application, a further articulation of the principles in the first policy in the second one. |
| Specializing | The application of an approach on a limited domain, and the application of another one next door. At the same governance level, different approaches are combined, yet strictly delimited to one topic or policy domain. |
| Structural couplings | Specific mechanisms that decide the duration, quality, intensity and institutionalization of the link between different social systems. Due to these structural couplings, events and communications in one system act as irritations for another social system and set off new events and communications there. if a system presupposes certain features of its environment on an on-going basis and relies on them structurally. |
| Subject formation | In governance, both objects and subjects can emerge and transform. Governance alters discourse, and in discourse, object and subject transform together. Subjects exist outside governance, but the power relations and potential for power in governance, as well as the confrontation with other actors and other perspectives, creates more intense, faster, more directly politicized formation of subjects. Governance creates subjects and create more political subjects. |
| Transparency/ opacity | The balance between transparency and opacity in governance requires management. Extreme transparency is impossible and has negative effects, and the same is true for opacity. Governance is never entirely transparent, neither for the actors in governance nor for the rest of community, for governance itself, maximum insight in the formal/informal institutional configuration is important to avoid corruption and inefficiency. |

| | |
|---|---|
| Unifying narrative | A story a community tells about itself, which provide cohesiveness in the interpretation of itself. A unifying narrative for the present can engender one for the future, a development vision, and a development vision can derive directly from existing unifying (identity) narratives, or be the product of more extensive deliberation, and deliberate construction of a narrative about a shared future which can guide governance now. |
| Vision | A unifying narrative for the future of a community, capable of integrating interests and policies. A vision can be a plan, or a comprehensive policy, it can be detailed, or a sketch. |

# References

Abu-Lughod, L. (1992). Writing women's worlds: Bedouin stories. Berkeley, CA, USA: University of California Press.

Acemoglu, D. and Robinson, J. (2012). Why nations fail. The origins of power, prosperity and poverty. New York, NY, USA: Crown Business.

Acosta, A. (2012). The Buen Vivir – an opportunity to imagine another world. In: Heinrich Böll Stiftung (ed.) Inside a champion. An analysis of the Brazilian development model. Quito, Ecuador: HBS.

Adam, C. (1995). Review article: adjustment in Africa: reforms, results and the road ahead. World Economy, 18(5), 729-735.

Adger, W.N., Dessai, S., Goulden, M., Hulme, M., Lorenzoni, I., Nelson, D.R. and Wreford, A. (2009). Are there social limits to adaptation to climate change? Climatic Change, 93(3-4), 335-354.

Aidt, T.S. (2009). Corruption, institutions, and economic development. Oxford Review of Economic Policy, 25(2), 271-291.

Alff, H., Hornidge, A.-K. and Boedeker, J. (in press). The key to the border: boundary production and negotiation at Asia's crossroads. Political Geography.

Al-Kodmany, K. (2002). Visualization tools and methods in community planning: from freehand sketches to virtual reality. Journal of Planning Literature, 17(2), 189-211.

Allen, C.R. and Gunderson, L.H. (2011). Pathology and failure in the design and implementation of adaptive management. Journal of Environmental Management, 92(5), 1379-1384.

Allina-Pisano, J. (2008). Post Soviet Potemkin villages. Politics and property rights in the black earth. Cambridge, UK: Cambridge University Press.

Allmendinger, P. (2001). Planning in postmodern times. London, UK: Routledge.

Ammann, K. (2009). Why farming with high tech methods should integrate elements of organic agriculture. New Biotechnology, 25(6), 378-388.

Andrews, M. (2013). The limits of institutional reform in development: changing rules for realistic solutions. Cambridge, UK: Cambridge University Press.

Antweiler, C. and Hornidge, A.-K. (2012). Introduction. the nexus of agency, knowledge, and environmental change in Southeast Asia. In: Hornidge, A.-K. and Antweiler, C. (eds.), Environmental uncertainty and local knowledge Southeast Asia as a laboratory of global ecological change. Bielefeld, Germany: Transcript, pp. 7-20.

Arendt, R.G. (1999). Growing greener: putting conservation into local plans and ordinances. Wasgington, DC, USA: Island Press.

Aristotle (1954). Rhetoric. New York, NY, USA: Random House.

Aristotle and Jowett, B. (350 B.C.E./1856). Politics, Book 2.7. Available at: http://classics.mit.edu.

Aristotle and Lucas, D.W. (1972). Poetics (Repr. with corrections. ed.). Oxford, UK: Clarendon Press.

Armitage, D.R. (2010). Adaptive capacity and environmental governance. London, UK: Springer.

Asimakou, T. (2009). Innovation, knowledge and power in organizations. Abingdon, UK: Routledge.

Atack, I. (1999). Four criteria of development NGO legitimacy. World Development, 27(5), 855-864.

Austin, J.L. (1962). How to do things with words. London, UK: Clarendon Press.

Avid, A.P. (2007). Path dependence: a foundational concept for historical social science. Cliometrica, 1, 91-114.

Bal, M. (1985). Narratology: introduction to the theory of narrative. Toronto, Canada: University of Toronto Press.

Bal, M. (2002). Travelling concepts in the humanities: a rough guide. Toronto, Canada: University of Toronto Press.

Bardhan, P. (1997). Corruption and development: a review of issues. Journal of economic literature, 1320-1346.

Barker, E. (1995). The politics of Aristotle. Oxford, UK: Oxford University Press.

Barnes, T.J. and Duncan, J.S. (1992). Writing worlds: discourse, text and metaphor in the representation of landscape. London, UK: Routledge.

Barthes, R. (1957). Mythologies. Paris, France: Éditions du Seuil.

Bates, R. (1999). Open economy politics: the political economy of the world coffee trade. Princeton, NJ, USA: Princeton University Press.

Batterbury, S.P. and Fernando, J.L. (2006). Rescaling governance and the impacts of political and environmental decentralization: an introduction. World Development, 34(11), 1851-1863.

Beatley, T. (1999). Green urbanism: learning from European cities. Washington, DC, USA: Island Press.

Beer, A. and Higgins, C. (2004). Environmental planning for site development: a manual for sustainable local planning and design. London, UK: Routledge.

Benda-Beckmann, F. (1989). Scape goat and magic charm. law in development theory and practice. Journal of Legal Pluralism, 28, 129-48.

Benjaminsen, T.A. and Lund, C. (2002). Formalisation and informalisation of land and water rights in Africa: an introduction. European Journal of Development Studies, 14, 1-10.

Bergh, S. (2004). Democratic decentralisation and local participation: a review of recent research. Development in Practice, 14, 780-790.

Berkes, F. (1989). Common property resources: ecology and community-based sustainable development. Princeton, NJ, USA: Belhaven Press.

Berkes, F., Folke, C. and Colding, J. (eds.). (2000). Linking social and ecological systems: management practices and social mechanisms for building resilience. Cambridge, UK: Cambridge University Press.

Beunen, R. (2010). The governance of nature: how nature conservation ambitions have been dashed in planning practices. Wageningen, the Netherlands: Wageningen University.

Beunen, R. and Duineveld, M. (2010). Divergence and Convergence in policy meanings of european environmental policies: the case of the birds and habitats directives. International Planning Studies, 15(1), 321-333.

Beunen, R. and Hagens, J.E. (2009). The use of the concept of ecological networks in nature conservation policies and planning practices. Landscape Research, 34(5), 563-580.

Beunen, R. and Opdam, P. (2011). When landscape planning becomes landscape governance, what happens to the science? Landscape and Urban Planning, 100(4), 324-326.

Beunen, R. and Van Assche, K. (in press). Contested delineations: planning, law and the governance of protected areas. Environment and Planning, in press.

Beunen, R., Van Assche, K. and Duineveld, M. (2013). Performing failure in conservation policy. The implementation of European Union directives in the Netherlands. Land Use Policy, 31, 280-288.

Beunen, R., Van Assche, K. and Duineveld, M. (eds.) (2015). Evolutionary governance theory: theory & applications. Heidelberg, Germany: Springer.

Bialasiewicz, L., Campbell, D., Elden, S., Graham, S., Jeffrey, A. and Williams, A.J. (2007). Performing security: the imaginative geographies of current US strategy. Political Geography, 26(4), 405-422.

Bierschenk T. and De Sardan, J-P.O. (2002). Powers in the village: rural Benin between democratisation and decentralisation. Mainz, Germany: Institut für Ethnologie und Afrikastudien.

Bindraban, P.S. and Rabbinge, R. (2011). European food and agricultural strategy for 21th century. International Journal of Agricultural Resources, Governance and Ecology, 9(1), 80-101.

Bird, G. (2007). The IMF: a bird's eye view of its role and operations. Journal of Economic Surveys, 21(4), 683-745.

Blair, H. (2000). Participation and accountability at the periphery: democratic local governance in six countries. World Development, 28(1), 21-39.

Blomley, N. (2008). Enclosure, common right and the property of the the poor. Social and Legal Studies, 17(3), 311-331.

Bobrow, D.B. and Dryzek, J.S. (1987). Policy analysis by design. Pittsburgh, PA, USA: University of Pittsburgh Press.

Booth, D. (1985). Marxism and development sociology: Interpreting the impasse. World Development, 13, 761-787.

Borrini-Feyerabend, G., Pimbert, M., Farvar, M.T., Kothari, A. and Renard, Y. (2007). Sharing power: learning-by-doing in co-management of natural resources throughout the world. London, UK: Earthscan.

Botes, L. and Van Rensburg, D. (2000). Community participation in development: nine plagues and twelve commandments. Community Development Journal, 35(1), 41-58.

Bourdieu, P. (1991). Language and symbolic power. Cambridge, UK: Polity.

Brett, E.A. (2003). Participation and accountability in development management. Journal of Development Studies, 40(2), 1-29.

Briggs, J. (2005). The use of indigenous knowledge in development: problems and challenges. Progress in Development Studies, 5(2), 99-114.

Brunner, R.D. (2005). Adaptive governance: integrating science, policy, and decision making. New York, NY, USA: Columbia University Press.

Brunner, R.D. and Lynch, A.H. (2010). Adaptive governance and climate change. Boston, MA, USA: American Meteorological Society.

Bryant, L.R. (2011). The democracy of objects. London, UK: Open Humanities Press.

Bryman, A. (2003). Research methods and organization studies. London, UK: Routledge.

Bullard, R. (2007). Land consolidation and rural development. Papers in Land Management, vol. 10. Cambridge, UK: Anglia Ruskin University.

Buntaine, M.T., Buch, B.P. and Parks, B.C. (2013). Why the 'results agenda' produces few results: an evaluation of the longrun institutional development impacts of World Bank environmental projects. Vasa, 1-38.

Burawoy, M. (2001). Transition without transformation: Russia's involutionary road to capitalism. East European Politics and Societies, 15(2), 269-290.

Burgess, R.G. (2002). In the field: an introduction to field research. London, UK: Routledge.

Burrell, G. (1988). Modernism, post modernism and organizational analysis: the contribution of Michel Foucault. Organization Studies, 9(2), 221-235.

Butler, J. (1997). Excitable speech: a politics of the performative. New York, NY, USA: Routledge.

Callon, M. (1991). Techno-economic networks and irreversibility. In: Law, J. (ed.), A sociology of monsters: essays on power, technology and domination. London: Routledge, pp. 132-165.

Campbell, L.M. and Vainio-Mattila, A. (2003). Participatory development and community-based conservation: opportunities missed for lessons learned? Human Ecology, 31(3), 417-437.

Cardoso, F.H. (1977). The consumption of dependency theory in the United States. Latin American Research Review, 12, 7-24.

Casson, M.C., Della Giusta, M. and Kambhampati, U.S. (2010). Formal and informal institutions and development. World Development, 38(2), 137-141.

Chambers, R. (1994). The origins and practice of participatory rural appraisal. World Development, 22(7), 953-969.

Chambers, R. and Jiggins, J. (1986). Agricultural research for resource-poor farmers: a parsimonious paradigm. IDS Discussion Paper 220. Brighton, UK: IDS.

Chambers, R., Pacey, A. and Thrupp, L.A. (1989). Farmers first/farmer innovation and agricultural research. London, UK: Intermediate Technology Publications.

Chauveau, J.-P., Colin, J.-P., Jacob, J.-P., Delville, P.L. and P.-Y. Le Meur (2006). Changes in land access and governance in West Africa: markets, social mediations and public policies: results of the CLAIMS research project. London, UK: International Institute for Environment and Development.

Chossudovsky, M. (2003). The globalization of poverty and the new world order. Shanty Bay, Canada: Global Outlook.

Christensen, C. (2013). The innovator's dilemma: when new technologies cause great firms to fail. Cambridge, UK: Harvard Business Review Press.

Cleaver, F. (2012). Development through bricolage: rethinking institutions for natural resource management. Abingdon, UK: Routledge.

Cloke, P. (ed.). (2013). Rural land-use planning in developed nations. London, UK: Routledge.

Cooke, B. and Kothari, U. (eds.). (2001). Participation: the new tyranny? London, UK: Zed Books.

Cox, K.R. (ed.) (1997). Spaces of globalization: reasserting the power of the local. London, UK: Guilford Press.

Cox, K.R. and Mair, A. (1988). Locality and community in the politics of local economic development. Annals of the Association of American Geographers, 78(2), 307-325.

Czarniawska, B. (1998). A narrative approach to organization studies. Thousand Oaks, CA, USA: Sage.

Czarniawska-Joerges, B. (2008). A theory of organizing. Cheltenham, UK: Edward Elgar.

De Jong, H. (2013) Groot Apeldoorns landschapskookboek. Wageningen, the Netherlands: Blauwdruk.

De Soto, H. (2003). Mystery of capital: why capitalism triumphs in the West and fails everywhere else. London, UK: Basic books.

Deininger, K. and Binswanger, H. (2001). The evolution of the World Bank's land policy. In: De Janvry, A., Gordillo, G., Sadoulet, E. and Platteau, J. (eds.), Access to land, rural poverty and public action. Oxford, UK: Oxford University Press, pp. 407-440.

Deininger, K. and Feder, G. (2009). Land registration, governance, and development: Evidence and implications for policy. The World Bank Research Observer, 24(2), 233-266.

Delanty, G. (2003). Community. London: Routledge.

Deleuze, G. and Guattari, F. (1987). A thousand plateaus: capitalism and schizophrenia. London, UK: Continuum.

Deleuze, G. and Guattari, F. (1994). What is philosophy? New York, NY, USA: Columbia University Press.

Deleuze, G. and Howard, R. (2000). Proust and signs: the complete text. London, UK: Athlone.

Derrida, J. (1967). De la grammatologie. Paris, France: Editions de Minuit.

Derrida, J. (1972). La dissémination. Paris, France: Editions du Seuil.

Derrida, J. (1973). Speech and phenomena, and other essays on Husserl's theory of signs. Evanston, IL, USA: NorthWestern University Press.

Dessel, A., Rogge, M.E. and Garlington, S.B. (2006). Using intergroup dialogue to promote social justice and change. Social Work, 51(4), 303-315.

DeWalt, K.M. and DeWalt, B.R. (2010). Participant observation: a guide for fieldworkers. New York: Rowman Altamira.

Dill, K.E. (2009). How fantasy becomes reality: seeing through media influence. Oxford, UK: Oxford University Press.

Djanibekov, N., Hornidge, A.-K. and M. Ul Hassan (2012). From joint experimentation to laissez-faire: transdisciplinary innovation research for the institutional strengthening of a water user association in Khorezm, Uzbekistan. Journal of Agricultural Education and Extension, 18(4), 409-423.

Djanibekov, N., Van Assche, K., Bobojonov, I. and Lamers, J.P. (2012). Farm restructuring and land consolidation in Uzbekistan: new farms with old barriers. Europe-Asia Studies, 64(6), 1101-1126.

Domingo, I. and Beunen, R. (2013). Regional planning in the Catalan Pyrenees: strategies to deal with actors' expectations, perceived uncertainties and conflicts. European Planning Studies, 21(2), 187-203.

Dorosh, P.A. (1994). Structural adjustment, growth, and poverty in Madagascar. Ithaca, NY, USA: Cornell Food and Nutrition Policy Program.

Douthwaite, B. (2002). Enabling innovation: a practical guide to understanding and fostering technological change. London, UK: Zed Books Limited.

Douthwaite, B., De Haan, Nicoline C., Manyong, V. and Keatinge, D. (2001). Blending 'hard' and 'soft' science: the 'follow-the-technology' approach to catalyzing and evaluating technology change. Ecology and Society, 5(2), 13.

Dryzek, J. (2000). Deliberative democracy and beyond. Oxford, UK: Oxford University Press.

Duineveld, M. and Van Assche, K. (2011). The power of tulips. Constructing nature and heritage in a contested landscape. Journal of Environmental Policy & Planning, 13(2), 79-98.

Duineveld, M., Beunen, R., Van Assche, K., During, R. and Van Ark, R. (2009). The relationship between description and prescription in transition research. In: Poppe, K.J., Termeer, C. and Slingerland, M. (Eds.), Transitions towards sustainable agriculture and food chains in peri-urban areas. Wageningen, the Netherlands: Wageningen Academic Publishers, pp. 309-324.

Duineveld, M., Van Assche, K. and Beunen, R. (2013). Making things irreversible. Object stabilization in urban planning and design. Geoforum, 46, 16-24.

Easterly, W. (2006). The white man's burden: why the West's efforts to aid the rest have done so much ill and so little good. New York, NY, USA: Penguin Press.

Easterly, W. (2013). The tyranny of experts. Economists, dictators and the forgotten rights of the poor. New York, NY, USA: Basic Books.

Easthope, A. (1998). Bhabha, hybridity and identity. Textual Practice, 12(2), 341-348.

Eco, U. (1976). A theory of semiotics. Bloomington, IN, USA: Indiana University Press.

Eco, U. (2000). Kant and the platypus: essays on language and cognition. New York, NY, USA: Harcourt Brace.

Eggertsson, T. (1990). Economic behavior and institutions: principles of neo-institutional economics. Cambridge, UK: Cambridge University Press.

Eggertsson, T. (2005). Imperfect institutions: possibilities and limits of reform. Ann Arbor, MI, USA: University of Michigan Press.

Eichholz, M., Van Assche, K., Oberkircher, L. and Hornidge, A.K. (2013). Trading capitals? Bourdieu, land and water in rural Uzbekistan. Journal of Environmental Planning and Management, 56(6), 1-25.

Elias, N. and Scotson, J.L. (1994). The established and the outsiders: a sociological enquiry into community problems. London, UK: Sage.

Ellickson, R. (1991). Order without law. How neighbors settle disputes. Cambridge, MA, USA: Harvard University Press.

Elliot, A. and Du Gay, P. (eds.) (2009). Identity in a globalizing world. London, UK: Sage.

Ellis, F. and Biggs, S. (2001). Evolving themes in rural development 1950's-2000's. Development Policy Review, 19(4), 437-448.

Escobar, A. (1985). Discourse and power in development: Michel Foucault and the relevance of his work to the Third World. Alternatives, 10, 377-400.

Escobar, A. (1995). Encountering development: the making and unmaking of the Third World. Princeton, NJ, USA: Princeton University Press.

Espeland, W.N. and Stevens, M.L. (1998). Commensuration as a social process. Annual Review of Sociology, 24, 313-343.

Esteva, G. (1992). Development. In: Sachs, W. (ed.), The development dictionary: a guide to knowledge as power. London, UK: Zed, pp. 6-25.

Evers, H.-D. and Hornidge, A.-K. (2007). Knowledge hubs along the Straits of Malacca. Asia Europe Journal, 5(3), 417-433.

Evers, H.-D., Kaiser, M. and Müller, C. (2003). Entwicklung durch Wissen: eine neue Wissensarchitektur. Soziale Welt, 49-69.

Feagan, R. (2007). The place of food: mapping out the 'local' in local food systems. Progress in Human Geography, 31(1), 23-42.

Ferguson, J. (1994). The anti-politics machine: 'development', depoliticization, and bureaucratic power in Lesotho. Cambridge, UK: Cambridge University Press.

Fernández, E. (2014). Trust, religion, and cooperation in western agriculture, 1880-1930. The Economic History Review, 67, 678-698.

Fischer, F. (1990). Technocracy and the politics of expertise. Newbury Park, CA, USA: Sage Publications.

Fischer, F. (2000). Citizens, experts and the environment. The politics of local knowledge. Durham, NC, USA: Duke University Press.

Fischer, F. (2009). Democracy and expertise: reorienting policy inquiry. Oxford, UK: Oxford University Press.

Fischer, F. and Miller, G.J. (eds.). (2006). Handbook of public policy analysis: theory, politics, and methods. Boca Raton, FL, USA: CRC Press.

Flyvbjerg, B. (1998). Rationality and power: democracy in practice. Chicago, IL, USA: University of Chicago press.

Flyvbjerg, B. (2001). Making social science matter: why social inquiry fails and how it can succeed again. Cambridge, UK: Cambridge University Press.

Folke, C., Hahn, T., Olsson, P. and Norberg, J. (2005). Adaptive governance of social-ecological systems. Annual Review Environmental Resources, 30, 441-473.

Forester, J. (1999). The deliberative practitioner. Encouraging participatory planning processes. Cambridge, MI, USA: MIT Press.

Forester, J. (ed.) (1993). The argumentative turn in policy analysis and planning. Durham, NC, USA: Duke University Press.

Foucault, M. (1968). Les mots et les choses. Paris, France: Gallimard.

Foucault, M. (1972). The archaeology of knowledge & the discourse on language. New York, NY, USA: Pantheon Books.

Foucault, M. (1973). The order of things. New York, NY, USA: Random House.

Foucault, M. (1979). Discipline and punish: the birth of the prison. Harmondsworth, UK: Penguin Books.

Foucault, M. (1980). Power/knowledge: selected interviews and other writings, 1972-1977. New York, NY, USA: Pantheon Books.

Foucault, M. (1994). The subject and power. In: Faubion, J.D. (ed.), Power. Essential works of Foucault 1954-1984. Volume 3. New York, NY, USA: The New Press, pp. 239-297.

Foucault, M. (1994). Truth and juridical forms. In: Faubion, J.D. (ed.), Power. Essential works of Foucault 1954-1984. Volume 3. New York, NY, USA: The New Press, pp. 1-89.

Foucault, M. (1994). Truth and power. In: Faubion, J.D. (ed.), Power. Essential works of Foucault 1954-1984. Volume 3. New York, NY, USA: The New Press, pp. 111-133.

Foucault, M. (1998). The will to knowledge. The history of sexuality: 1. London, UK: Penguin Books.

Foucault, M. (2003). Society must be defended: lectures at the College de France, 1975-76. London, UK: Allen Lane The Penguin Press.

Foucault, M. (2006). History of madness. London, UK: Routledge.

Foucault, M. (2012). The archaeology of knowledge. New York, NY, USA: Random House LLC.

Franco, J.C. (2010). Contemporary discourses and contestations around pro-poor land policies and land governance. Journal of Agrarian Change, 10(1), 1-32.

Freeman, C. (1987). Technology policy and economic performance: lessons from Japan. London, UK: Frances Pinter.

Freeman, C. and Soete, L. (2009). Developing science, technology and innovation indicators: what we can learn from the past. Research Policy, 38(4), 583-589.

Fuchs, S. (2001). Against essentialism: a theory of culture and society. Cambridge, MI, USA: Harvard University Press.

Gabriel, Y. (2000). Storytelling in organizations. facts, fictions, and fantasies. Oxford, UK: Oxford University Press.

Gay, P. (1996). The enlightenment: the science of freedom (Vol. 2). New York, NY, USA: WW Norton & Company.

Gerber, T.P. and Hout, M. (1998). More shock than therapy: market transition, employment, and income in Russia, 1991-1995. American Journal of Sociology, 104(1), 1-50.

Gerke, S., Evers, H.-D. and Hornidge, A.-K. (eds.) (2008). The Straits of Malacca – knowledge and diversity. Münster, Germany: Lit Verlag.

Getzels, J. and Thurow, C. (eds.) (1979). Rural and small town planning. Chicago, IL, USA: Planners Press.

Gijsbers, G. W. (2009). Agricultural innovation in Asia – drivers, paradigms and performance. ERIM Ph.D. Series in Research in Management, 156. Rotterdam, the Netherlands: ERIM.

Gill, J. and Johnson, P. (2010). Research methods for managers. Thousand Oaks, CA, USA: Sage.

Global Water Partnership Technical Advisory Committee (2000). Integrated water resources management. Stockholm, Sweden: Global Water Partnership.

Goodin, R. (2008). Innovating democracy: democratic theory and practice after the deliberative turn. Oxford, UK: Oxford University Press.

Govers, R. and Go, F. (2009). Place branding: glocal, virtual and physical identities, constructed, imagined and experienced. London, UK: Palgrave Macmillan.

Grbich, C. (2012). Qualitative data analysis: an introduction. Thousand Oaks, CA, USA: Sage.

Green, M. (2010). Making development agents: participation as boundary object in international development. Journal of Development Studies, 46(7), 1240-1263.

Greif, A. (2006). Institutions and the path to the modern economy: lessons from medieval trade. Cambridge, UK: Cambridge University Press.

Grimble, R. and Wellard, K. (1997). Stakeholder methodologies in natural resource management: a review of principles, contexts, experiences and opportunities. Agricultural Systems, 55(2), 173-193.

Grindle, M.S. (2004). Good enough governance: poverty reduction and reform in developing countries. Governance, 17(4), 525-548.

Grindle, M.S. (2007). Good enough governance revisited. Development Policy Review, 25(5), 553-574.

Guha-Khasnobis, B., Kanbur, R. and Ostrom, E. (eds.) (2007). Linking the formal and informal economy. Concepts and policies. Oxford, UK: Oxford University Press.

Guinier, L. (1994). The tyranny of the majority: fundamental fairness in representative democracy. New York, NY, USA: Free Press.

Gunawansa, A. and Bhullar, L. (eds.) (2013). Water governance. An evaluation of alternative architectures. Cheltenham, UK: Edward Elgar.

Gunder, M. (2006). Sustainability. Planning's saving grace or road to perdition? Journal of Planning Education and Research, 26(2), 208-221.

Gunder, M. and Hillier, J. (2009). Planning in ten words or less. A Lacanian entanglement with spatial planning. Aldershot, UK: Ashgate.

Hacking, I. (1999). Making up people. In: Biagioli, M. (ed.), The science studies reader (XVIII). New York, NY, USA: Routledge.

Haggard, S. (2004). Institutions and growth in East Asia. Studies in Comparative International Development, 38, 53-81.

Hajer, M.A. (1995). The politics of environmental discourse: ecological modernization and the policy process. Oxford, UK: Clarendon.

Hajer, M.A. (2005). Rebuilding Ground Zero. The politics of performance. Planning Theory and Practice, 6, 445-464.

Hajer, M.A. (2006). The living institutions of the EU: analysing governance as performance. Perspectives on European Politics and Society, 7(1), 41-55.

Hajer, M.A. and Wagenaar, H. (eds.) (2003). Deliberative policy analysis: understanding governance in the network society. Cambridge, UK: Cambridge University Press.

Hall, A. (2007). Challenges to strengthening agriculture innovation systems: where do we go from here? Maastricht, the Netherlands: United Nations University, UNU_MERIT.

Hall, A. and Nahdy, S. (1999). New methods and old institutions: the 'systems context' of farmer participatory research in national agricultural research systems. The case of Uganda. Network Paper, 93. London, UK: ODI Agricultural Research & Extension Network.

Hansen, R.H. (2010). The narrative nature of place branding. Place Branding and Public Diplomacy, 6(4), 268-279.

Hayoz, N. and Giordano, C. (eds.) (2013). Informality in Eastern Europe: structures, political cultures and social practices (Interdisciplinary Studies on Central and Eastern Europe). Bern, Switzerland: Peter Lang.

Healey, P. (2006). Transforming governance: challenges of institutional adaptation and a new politics of space. European Planning Studies, 14(3), 299-319.

Healy, K. (2001). Llamas, weavings and organic chocolate: multicultural grassroots development in the Andes and Amazon of Bolivia. Notre Dame, IN, USA: University of Notre Dame Press.

Held, D. (1996). Models of democracy (2 ed.). Cambridge, UK: Polity.

Held, D. (2006). Models of democracy. Stanford, CA, USA: Stanford University Press.

Helmke, G. and Levitsky, S. (eds.). (2006). Informal institutions and democracy: lessons from Latin America. Baltimore, MD, USA: Johns Hopkins University Press.

Herodotus and Waterfield, R. (2008). The History of Herodotus, Book 3.80. Oxford, UK: Oxford University Press

Hilson, G. (2002). An overview of land use conflict in mining communities. Land Use Policy, 19, 65-73.

Hinrichs, C.C. (2003). The practice and politics of food system localization. Journal of Rural Studies, 19(1), 33-45.

Hitzler, R., Honer, A. and Maeder, C. (eds.) 1994. Expertenwissen. Die institutionalisierte Kompetenz zur Konstruktion von Wirklichkeit. Opladen, Germany: Westdeutscher Verlag.

Hobart, M. (1995). As I lay laughing – Encountering global knowledge in Bali. In: Fardon, R. (ed.), Counterworks. Managing the diversity of knowledge. London, UK: Routledge, pp. 49-72.

Hodgson, G.M. (2006). What are institutions? Journal of Economic Issues, 40(1), 1-25.

Hoffman, M., Lubell, M. and Hillis, V. (2014). Linking knowledge and action through mental models of sustainable agriculture. Proceedings of the National Academy of Sciences of the USA, 111(36), 13016-13021.

Holling, C.S. and Meffe, G.K. (1996). Command and control and the pathology of natural resource management. Conservation Biology, 10(2), 328-337.

Holmes, S. (1995). Passions and constraint: on the theory of liberal democracy. Chicago, IL, USA: University of Chicago Press.

Holtz, U. (2013). Die Millenniumsentwicklungsziele. In: Ihne, H. and Wilhelm, J. (eds.), Einführung in die Entwicklungspolitik. Berlin, Germany: LIT Verlag, pp. 41-65.

Hornidge, A.-K. (2004). When the younger generation takes over: Singaporean Chinese family businesses in Singapore in change. Internationales Asienforum, 35(1-2), 101-31.

Hornidge, A.-K. (2007). Knowledge society. Vision & social construction of reality in Germany & Singapore. Münster, Germany: Lit-Verlag.

Hornidge, A.-K. (2007). Re-inventing society: state concepts of knowledge in Germany and Singapore. Sojourn. Journal of Social Issues in Southeast Asia, 22(2), 202-29.

Hornidge, A.-K. (2010). An uncertain future – Singapore's search for a new focal point of collective identity and its drive towards 'knowledge society'. Asian Journal of Social Sciences, 38(5), 785-818.

Hornidge, A.-K. (2011). 'Creative industries' – Economic program and boundary concept. Journal of Southeast Asian Studies, 42(2), 253-279.

Hornidge, A.-K. (2011). 'Knowledge society' as academic concept and stage of development – a conceptual and historical review. In: Menkhoff, T., Evers, H.-D., Chay, Y.W. and Eng, F. P. (eds.), Beyond the knowledge trap: developing asia's knowledge-based economies. London, UK: World Scientific, pp. 87-128.

Hornidge, A.-K. (2012). 'Knowledge', 'knowledge society' & 'knowledge for development'. studying discourses of knowledge in an international context. In: Keller, R. and Truschkat, I. (eds.), Methodologie und Praxis der Wissenssoziologischen Diskursanalyse, Band 1: Interdisziplinäre Perspektiven. Wiesbaden, Germany: Springer Verlag, pp. 397-424.

Hornidge, A.-K. (2012). 'Knowledge' in development discourse: a critical review. In: Hornidge, A.-K. and Antweiler, C. (eds.), Environmental uncertainty and local knowledge Southeast Asia as a laboratory of global ecological change. Bielefeld, Germany: Transcript, pp. 21-54.

Hornidge, A.-K. (2012). Wissen-fokussierende Wirklichkeiten und ihre kommunikative Konstruktion. In: Keller, R., Knoblauch, H. and Reichertz, J. (eds.), Kommunikativer Konstruktivismus – Theoretische und empirische Konturen eines neuen wissenssoziologischen Ansatzes. Wiesbaden, Germany: Springer Verlag, pp. 205-232.

Hornidge, A.-K. (2014). Discourses of knowledge – normative, factual, hegemonic. Post-Doctoral Thesis, Bonn, Germany: University of Bonn.

Hornidge, A.-K. (2014). Wissensdiskurse: Normativ, Faktisch, Hegemonial. Soziale Welt, 65: 7-24.

Hornidge, A.-K. and Antweiler, C. (Eds.). (2012). Environmental uncertainty and local knowledge. Southeast Asia as a laboratory of global ecological change. Bielefeld, Germany: Transcript Verlag.

Hornidge, A.-K. and Kurfürst, S. (2011). Conceptualizing public space in Hanoi and Singapore: the power of state visions. Internationales Asienforum, 42(3-4), 345-369.

Hornidge, A.-K. and Scholtes, F. (2011). Climate change and everyday life in Toineke Village, West Timor – uncertainties, knowledge and adaptation. Sociologus, 61(2), 151-175.

Hornidge, A.-K. and Ul-Hassan, M. (2010). 'From 'plausible promises' to transdisciplinary innovation research in Uzbekistan – process outline and lessons learnt'. Rural Development News, 2, 53-63.

Rural development

Hornidge, A.-K., Oberkircher, L. and Kudryavtseva, A. (2013). Boundary management and the discursive sphere – negotiating 'realities' in Khorezm, Uzbekistan. Geoforum, 45, 266-274.

Hornidge, A.-K., Oberkircher, L., Tischbein, B., Schorcht, G., Bhaduri, A., Awan, U.K. and Manschadi, A.M. (2011). Reconceptualising water management in Khorezm, Uzbekistan. Natural Resources Forum, 35(4), 251-268.

Hornidge, A.-K., Ul-Hassan, M. and Mollinga, P.P. (2011). transdisciplinary innovation research in Uzbekistan – 1 year of 'following the innovation'. Development in Practice, 21(6), 825-838.

Hornidge, A.-K., Van Assche, K. and Shtaltovna, A. (in press). Uzbekistan – a region of world society (?) Variants of differentiation in agricultural resources governance. Soziale Systeme (Special Issue edited by Rudolf Stichweh).

Howarth, D. (2000). Discourse. Maidenhead, UK: Open University Press.

Hubbard, P. (2008). Here, there, everywhere: the ubiquitous geographies of heteronormativity. Geography Compass, 2(3), 640-658.

Humphrey, C. (1998). Marx went away, but Karl stayed behind. Ann Arbor, MI, USA: University of Michigan Press.

Huntington, S.P. (1971). The change to change: modernization, development, and politics. Comparative Politics, 3, 283-322.

Ismailbekova, A. (2013). Migration and patrilineal descent: the effects of spatial male mobility on social female mobility in rural Kyrgyzstan. Crossroads Asia Working Paper Series, 12.

Ison, R. and Russell, D. (eds.). (2000). Agricultural extension and rural development: breaking out of knowledge transfer traditions. Cambridge, UK. Cambridge University Press.

Jacobs, H.M. (ed.). (1998). Who owns America?: social conflict over property rights. Madison, WI, USA: University of Wisconsin Press.

Jacobs, J. (1961). Death and life of great American cities. Harmondsworth, UK: Penguin.

Jacobs, K. (2006). Discourse analysis and its utility for urban policy research. Urban Policy and Research, 24(1), 39-52.

Jacobsen, R. (2014). Apples of uncommon character: 123 heirlooms, modern classics and little known wonders. London, UK: Bloomsbury.

Jamali, H. (2013). The anxiety of development: megaprojects and the politics of place in Gwadar, Pakistan. Crossroads Asia Working Paper Series, 6.

Jason, L.A., Keys, C.B., Suarez-Balcazar, Y.E., Taylor, R.R. and Davis, M.I. (2004). Participatory community research: theories and methods in action. Washington, DC, USA: American Psychological Association.

Jeffares, S.R. (2007). Why public policy ideas catch on: empty signifiers and flourishing neighbourhoods. Birmingham, UK: University of Birmingham.

Johnson, C. (1987). Political institutions and economic performance: the government-business relationship in Japan, South Korea, and Taiwan. In: Deyo, F.C. (ed.), The political economy of the New Asian industrialism. Ithaca, NY, USA: Cornell University Press, pp. 136-164.

Johnson, C. (2001). Local democracy, democratic decentralisation and rural development: theories, challenges and options for policy. Development Policy Review, 19(4), 521-532.

Jung, L.S. (1988). Feminism and spatiality: ethics and the recovery of a hidden dimension. Journal of Feminist Studies in Religion, 4(1), 55-71.

Kelboro, G., Stellmacher, T. and Hoffmann, V. (2013). 'Conservationists' and 'local people' in biodiversity conservation: the case of Nech Sar National Park, Ethiopia. Ethiopian Journal of Social Sciences and Humanities, 9(1), 29-55.

Kellert, S.R., Mehta, J.N., Ebbin, S.A. and Lichtenfeld, L.L. (2000). Community natural resource management: promise, rhetoric, and reality. Society & Natural Resources, 13(8), 705-715.

Kiely, R. (1999). The last refuge of the noble savage? A critical assessment of post-development theory. European Journal of Development Research, 11(1), 30-55.

King, M. and Thornhill, C. (eds.) (2006). Luhmann on law and politics. Critical appraisals and applications. Oxford, UK: Hart.

King, M. and Thornhill, E. (2003). Niklas Luhmann's theory of politics and law. Basingstoke, UK: Palgrave Macmillan.

King, R. and Burton, S. (1983). Structural change in agriculture: the geography of land consolidation. Progress in Human Geography, 7(4), 471-501.

Kolstad, I. and Wiig, A. (2009). Is transparency the key to reducing corruption in resource-rich countries? World Development, 37(3), 521-532.

Kolstad, I. and Wiig, A. (2009). Is transparency the key to reducing corruption in resource-rich countries? World Development, 37(3), 521-532.

Kooij, H., Van Assche, K. and Lagendijk, A. (2013). Open concepts as crystallization points and enablers of discursive configurations: the case of the innovation campus in the Netherlands. European Planning Studies, 22, 84-100.

Kornai, J. and Rose-Ackerman, S. (eds.) (2004). Building a trustworthy state in post-socialist transition. New York, NY, USA: Palgrave.

Lacan, J. (1977). Écrits: a selection. London, UK: Tavistock Publications Limited.

Lacan, J. and Fink, B. (2006). Ecrits: the first complete edition in English. New York, NY, USA: W.W. Norton & Co.

Lachenmann, G. (1994). Systeme des Nichtwissens. Alltagsverstand und Expertenbewußtsein im Kulturvergleich. In: Hitzler, R., Honer, A. and Maeder, C. (eds.), Expertenwissen. Opladen, Germany: Westdeutscher Verlag, pp. 285-305.

Lakoff, G. and Johnson, M. (1980). Metaphors we live by. Chicago, IL, USA: University of Chicago Press.

Lane, M.B. and Corbett, T. (2005). The tyranny of localism: indigenous participation in community-based environmental management. Journal of Environmental Policy and Planning, 7(2), 141-159.

Larson, A.M., Cronkleton, P., Barry, D. and Pacheco, P. (2008). Tenure rights and beyond: community access to forest resources in Latin America. Bogor, Indonesia: Center for International Forestry Research.

Latour, B. (1987). Science in action. How to follow scientists and engineers through society. Cambridge, MI, USA: Harvard University Press.

Latour, B. (1999). Pandora's hope: essays on the reality of science studies. London, UK: Harvard University Press.

Latour, B. (2004). Politics of nature. How to bring the sciences into democracy. Cambridge, MI, USA: Harvard University Press.

Latour, B. and Woolgar, S. (1986). Laboratory life: the construction of scientific facts. Princeton, NJ, USA: Princeton University Press.

Laurian, L. (2004). Public participation in environmental decision making: findings from communities facing toxic waste cleanup. Journal of the American Planning Association, 70(1), 53-65.

Leach, M., Scoones, I. and Stirling, A. (2007). Pathways to sustainabilitiy: an overview of the STEPS Centre approach. STEPS Approach Paper. Brighton, UK: STEPS Centre.

Ledwith, M. (2011). Community development: a critical approach. Bristol, UK: Policy Press.

Lee, R.L.M. (2006). Reinventing modernity: reflexive modernization vs liquid modernity vs multiple modernities. European Journal of Social Theory, 9, 355-368.

Leeuwis, C. (2008). Communication for rural innovation: rethinking agricultural extension. New York, NY, USA: John Wiley & Sons.

Leman, J. (ed.) (2000). The dynamics of emerging ethnicities: immigrant and indigenous ethnogenesis in confrontation. Frankfurt, Germany: Peter Land.

Lerner, R. (2013). Dandelion hunter: foraging the urban wilderness. Portland, OR, USA: National Book Network.

Lévi-Strauss, C. (1968). Structural anthropology. London, UK: Allen Lane.

Leydesdorff, L., Dolfsma, W. and van der Panne, G. (2006). Measuring the knowledge base of an economy in terms of triple-helix relations among technology, organization, and territory'. Research Policy, 35(2), 181-199.

Ligrom, P., North, D. and Weingast, B. (1990). The role of institutions in the revival of trade: the law merchant, private judges and the champagine fairs. Economics and Politics, 2(1), 1-23.

Lister, S. (2009). Changing the rules? State-building and local government in Afghanistan. Journal of Development Studies, 45(6), 990-1009.

Loewe, M. (2012). Post 2015: how to reconcile the Millennium Development Goals (MDGs) and the Sustainable Development Goals (SDGs)? Briefing Paper 18/2012. Bonn, Germany: German Development Institute.

Lopes, C. (1999). Are structural adjustment programmes an adequate response to globalization? International Social Science Journal, 51(162), 511-519.

Lovell, S.T., Nathan, C.A., Olson, M.B., Ernesto Méndez, V., Kominami, H.C., Erickson, D.L. and Morris, W.B. (2010). Integrating agroecology and landscape multifunctionality in Vermont: an evolving framework to evaluate the design of agroecosystems. Agricultural Systems, 103(5), 327-341.

Lozano, E.E. (1990). Community design and the culture of cities: the crossroad and the wall. Cambridge, UK: Cambridge University Press.

Luhmann, N. (1988). Die Wirtschaft der Gesellschaft. Frankfurt am Main, Germany: Suhrkamp.

Luhmann, N. (1989). Ecological communication. Chicago, IL, USA: University of Chicago Press.

Luhmann, N. (1990). Political theory in the welfare state. Berlin, Germany: Mouton de Gruyter.

Luhmann, N. (1995). Social systems. Stanford, CA, USA: Stanford University Press.

Luhmann, N. (1997). Die Gesellschaft der Gesellschaft. Frankfurt: Suhrkamp.

Luhmann, N. (2000). Art as a social system. Stanford, CA, USA: Stanford University Press.

Luhmann, N. (2004). Law as a social system. Oxford, UK: Oxford University Press.

Luhmann, N. (2010). Introduction to systems theory. Cambridge, UK: Polity.

Luhmann, N. (2012). Theory of society, Volume 1. Cultural memory in the present. Stanford, CA, USA: Stanford University Press

Lund, C. (1998). Law, power and politics in Niger. Land struggles and the rural code. Hamburg, Germany: LIT Verlag.

Machiavelli, N. (1988). The prince. Cambridge, UK: Cambridge University Press.

MacKenzie, D., Muniesa, F. and Siu, L. (eds.) (2007). Do economists make markets?: on the performativity of economics. Princeton, NJ, USA: Princeton University Press.

Mahoney, J. (2000). Path dependence in historical sociology. Theory and Society, 29(4), 507-548.

Mander, J. (ed.) (2014). The case against the global economy: and for a turn towards localization. Abingdon, UK: Routledge.

Mansfield, H. (1996). Machiavelli's virtue. Chicago, IL, USA: University of Chicago Press.

Mansuri, G. and Rao, V. (2004). Community-based and-driven development: a critical review. The World Bank Research Observer, 19(1), 1-39.

Martin, A. and Sherington, J. (1997). Participatory research methods – implementation, effectiveness and institutional context. Agricultural Systems, 55(2), 195-216.

Massey, D. (1994). Space, place and gender. Cambridge, UK: Polity Press.

Mathbor, G.M. (2008). Understanding community participation. In: Mathbor, G.M. (ed.), Effective community participation in coastal development. Chicago, IL, USA: Lyceum Books, pp. 7-24.

Maturana, H.R. and Varela, F.J. (1987). The tree of knowledge. The biological roots of human understanding. Boston, MA, USA: Shambhala Publications.

McDonald, G.T. (1989). Rural land use planning decisions by bargaining. Journal of Rural Studies, 5(4), 325-335.

McLaughlin, P. and Dietz, T. (2008). Structure, agency and environment: toward an integrated perspective on vulnerability. Global Environmental Change, 18(1), 99-111.

McNabb, D.E. (2013). Research methods in public administration and nonprofit management: Quantitative and qualitative approaches. Armonk, NY, USA: ME Sharpe.

McNie, E.C. (2007). Reconciling the supply of scientific information with user demands: an analysis of the problem and review of the literature. Environmental Science & Policy, 10(1), 17-38.

Meeus, J.H.A., Wijermans, M.P. and Vroom, M.J. (1990). Agricultural landscapes in Europe and their transformation. Landscape and Urban Planning, 18(3), 289-352.

Mehrhoff, A. (1999). Community design: a team approach to dynamic community systems. Thousand Oaks, CA, USA: Sage.

Meyer, P.B. and Lyons, T.S. (2000). Lessons from private sector brownfield redevelopers: Planning public support for urban regeneration. Journal of the American Planning Association, 66(1), 46-57.

Michener, V.J. (1998). The participatory approach: contradiction and co-option in Burkina Faso. World Development, 26(12), 2105-2118.

Mielke, K. and Hornidge, A.-K. (2014). Crossroads studies: from spatial containers to interactions in differentiated spatialities. Crossroads Asia Working Paper Series, 15.

Mikkelsen, B. (1995). Methods for development work and research: a guide for practitioners. London, UK: Sage Publications.

Miller, G.J. and Yang, K. (eds.) (2007). Handbook of research methods in public administration. Boca Raton, FL, USA: CRC press.

Miller, H.T. (2002). Postmodern public policy. Albany, NY, USA: Suny Press.

Mintzberg, H. (1987). Crafting strategy. Cambridge, MA, USA: Harvard Business School.

Mkandawire, T. (2001). Thinking about developmental states in Africa. Cambridge Journal of Economics, 25, 289.

Mohan, G. and Stokke, K. (2000). Participatory development and empowerment: the dangers of localism. Third World Quarterly, 21(2), 247-268.

Mol, A. (2002). The body multiple: ontology in medical practice. Durham, NC, USA: Duke University Press.

Mollinga, P., (2010). Boundary work and the complexity of natural resource management. Crop Science, 50, 1-9.

Morgounov, A. and Zuidema, L. (2001). The legacy of the Soviet agricultural research system for the republics of Central Asia and the Caucasus. ISNAR report 22.

Morton, J.F. (2007). The impact of climate change on smallholder and subsistence agriculture. Proceedings of the Natural Academy of Sciences of the USA, 104(50), 19680-19685.

Moseley, W.G. (2007). Collaborating in the field, working for change: reflecting on partnerships between academics, development organizations and rural communities in Africa. Singapore Journal of Tropical Geography, 28(3), 334-347.

Mosse, D. (2005). Cultivating development: an ethnography of aid policy and practice. London, UK: Pluto Press.

Munnich, L.W. Jr., Schrock, G. and Cook, K. (2002). Rural knowledge clusters: the challenge of rural economic prosperity. Reviews of Economic Development Literature and Practice, 12.

Murphy, A. and Williams, P.W. (1999). Attracting Japanese tourists into the rural hinterland: implications for rural development and planning. Tourism Management, 20(4), 487-499.

Murray, M. and Dunn, L. (1995). Capacity building for rural development in the United States. Journal of Rural Studies, 11(1), 89-97.

Nelson, N. and Wright, S. (1995). Power and participatory development: theory and practice. London, UK: Intermediate Technology Publications Ltd. (ITP).

North, D.C. (1990). Institutions, institutional change and economic performance. Cambridge, UK: Cambridge University Press.

North, D.C. (2005). Understanding the process of economic change. Princeton, NJ, USA: Princeton University Press.

North, D.C., Wallis, J. and Weingast, B. (2009). Violence and social orders. a conceptual framework for interpreting recorded human history. Cambridge, UK: Cambrigde University Press.

Nowotny, H., Scott, P. and Gibbons, M. (2001). Re-thinking science: knowledge and the public in an age of uncertainty. Cambridge, UK: Polity.

Nygren, A. (1999). Local knowledge in the environment-development discourse. Critique of Anthropology, 19(3), 267-288.

O'Brien, K., Hayward, B. and Berkes, F. (2009). Rethinking social contracts: building resilience in a changing climate. Ecology and Society, 14(2), 12.

Oberkircher, L. and Hornidge A.-K. (2011). 'Water is life' – farmer rationales and water-saving in Khorezm, Uzbekistan: a lifeworld analysis. Rural Sociology, 76(3), 394-421.

OECD (2010). The OECD Innovation Strategy. Getting a Head Start on Tomorrow. Paris, France: OECD.

Old, G. (2014). Constructing private governance: the rise and evolution of forest, coffee and fisheries certification. New Haven, CT, USA: Yale University Press.

Ostrom, E. (1990). Governing the commons: the evolution of institutions for collective action. Cambridge, UK: Cambridge University Press.

Ostrom, E. (2009). Understanding institutional diversity. Princeton, NJ, USA: Princeton University Press.

Otto, J.M. (2009). Rule of law promotion, land tenure and poverty alleviation: questioning the assumptions of Hernando de Soto. Hague Journal on the Rule of Law, 1(1), 173-194.

Outshoorn, N. and Pinch, T. (eds.) (2003). How users matter: the co-construction of users and technology. Cambridge, MI, USA: MIT Press.

Pašakarnis, G. and Maliene, V. (2010). Towards sustainable rural development in Central and Eastern Europe: Applying land consolidation. Land Use Policy, 27(2), 545-549.

Patton, C., Sawicki, D. and Clark, J. (2012). Basic methods of policy analysis and planning. Chicago, IL, USA: Pearson.

Paulson, S. and Gezon, L.L. (eds.) (2004). Political ecology across spaces, scales, and social groups. New Brunswick, NJ, USA: Rutgers University Press.

Petrini, C. (2013). Slow Food nation: why our food should be good, clean and fair. New York, NY, USA: Rizzoli.

Phillips, M. (1998). The restructuring of social imaginations in rural geography. Journal of Rural Studies, 14(2), 121-153.

Pierre, J. (2000). Debating governance, authority, steering, and democracy. Oxford, UK: Oxford University Press.

Pierre, J. and Peters, B.G. (2000). Governance, politics, and the state. Basingstoke, UK: Macmillan.

Pierson, P. (2000). The limits of design: explaining institutional origins and change. Governance, 13(4), 475-499.

Pinstrup-Andersen, P. (2003). Eradicating poverty and hunger as a national security issue for the United States. ESCP Report 9, 22-27.

Platt, R. (2004). Land use and society. Geography, law and public policy. Washington, DC, USA: Island Press.

Pollan, M. (2006). The omnivore's dilemma: a natural history of four meals. New York, NY, USA: Penguin.

Potter, C. and Tilzey, M. (2005). Agricultural policy discourses in the European post-Fordist transition: neoliberalism, neomercantilism and multifunctionality. Progress in Human Geography, 29(5), 581-600.

Pressmann., J.L. and Wildavsky, A.B. (1973). Implementation. Berkeley, CA, USA: University of California Press.

Pressmann, J.L. and Wildavsky, A.B. (1979). Implementation: how great expectations in Washington are dashed in Oakland (2 edition). Berkeley, CA, USA: University of California Press.

Pretty, J., Sutherland, W.J., Ashby, J., Auburn, J., Baulcombe, D. and Bell, M. (2010). The top 100 questions of importance to the future of global agriculture. International Journal of Agricultural Sustainability, 8(4), 219-236.

Pretty, J.N., Williams, S. and Toulmin, C. (eds.). (2012). sustainable intensification: increasing productivity in African food and agricultural systems. International Journal of Agricultural Sustainability, 9(1).

Przeworski, A. (ed.). (2000). Democracy and development: political institutions and well-being in the world, 1950-1990 (Vol. 3). Cambridge, UK: Cambridge University Press.

Putman, R. (1993). Making democracy work. Civic traditions in modern Italy. Princeton, NJ, USA: Princeton University Press.

Radomski, P.J. and Van Assche, K. (2014). Lakeshore living: designing lake places and communities in the footprints of environmental writers. East Lansing, MI, USA: MSU Press.

Rahnema, M. (ed.) (1997). The post-development reader. London, UK: Zed.

Randeria, S. (2007). De-politicization of democracy and judicialization of politics. Theory, Culture & Society, 24(4): 38.

Ranger, T. and Vaughan, O. (eds.) (1993). Legitimacy and the state in twentieth-century Africa. London, UK: Macmillan Press.

Rap, E. (2006). The success of a policy model: irrigation management transfer in Mexico. Journal of Development Studies, 42 (8), 1301-1324.

Rapley, J. (2002). Development theory in the wake of structural adjustment. In: Rapley, J. (ed.), Understanding development. Theory and practice in the Third World. Boulder, CO, USA: Lynne Rienner Publishers, pp. 113-130.

Rappaport, J. (1995). Empowerment meets narrative: Listening to stories and creating settings. American Journal of Community Psychology, 23(5), 795-807.

Redclift, M. (2005). Sustainable development (1987-2005): an oxymoron comes of age. Sustainable Development, 13(4), 212-227.

Rhoades, R.E. and Booth., R.H. (1982). Farmer-back-to-farmer: a model for generating acceptable agricultural technology. Agricultural Administration, 11, 127-137.

Rhodes, R.A.W. (1996). The new governance: governing without government. Political Studies, 44(4), 652-667.

Richards, P. (1985). Indigenous agricultural revolution: ecology and food-production in West Africa. London, UK: Hutchinson.

Rivera, W.M., Qamar, M.K. and Van Crowder, L. (2002). Agricultural and rural extension worldwide: options for institutional reform in the developing countries.

Robertson, H.A. and McGee, T.K. (2003). Applying local knowledge: the contribution of oral history to wetland rehabilitation at Kanyapella Basin, Australia. Journal of Environmental Management, 69, 275-287.

Robinson, G. (1990). Conflict and change in the countryside. Rural society, economy and planning in the developed world. London, UK: Belhaven Press.

Rogers, E.M. (1988). The intellectual foundation and history of the agricultural extension model. Science Communication, 9(4), 492-510.

Rogers, E.M. (2003). Diffusion of innovations (5 ed.). New York, NY, USA: The Free Press.

Rogers, P. and Hall, A.W. (2003). Effective water governance. Stockholm, Sweden: Global Water Partnership.

Röling, N. (2005). Gateway to the global garden: beta/gamma science for dealing with ecological rationality. In: Pretty, J. (ed.), The Earthscan reader in sustainable agriculture. London, UK: Earthscan.

Röling, N. (2009). Conceptual and methodological developments in innovation. In: Sanginha, P. C., Waters-Bayer, A., Kaaria, S., Njuki, J. and Wettasinha C. (eds.), Innovation Africa. Enriching farmers' livelihoods. London, UK: Earthscan, pp. 9-34.

Roling, N.G., and Wagemakers, M.A.E. (eds.) (2000). Facilitating sustainable agriculture: participatory learning and adaptive management in times of environmental uncertainty. Cambridge, UK: Cambridge University Press.

Rose, G. (1997). Situating knowledges: positionality, reflexivities and other tactics. Progress in Human Geography, 21(3), 305-320.

Rose, M. (2002). The seductions of resistance: power, politics, and a performative style of systems. Environment and Planning D: Society and Space, 20, 383-400.

Rosenboom. J. and Rutten, H. (1999). Financing agricultural R&D in the Netherlands. The changing role of government. In: Alston, J., Pardey, P. and Smith, V.H. (eds.), Paying for agricultural productivity. Baltimore, MD, USA: Johns Hopkins University Press/IFPRI.

Rostow, W.W. (1956). The take-off into self-sustained growth. The Economic Journal, 66, 25-48.

Rostow, W.W. (1959). The stages of economic growth. The Economic History Review, 12, 1-16.

Ryan, B. and Gross, N. (1943). The diffusion of hybrid seed corn in two Lowa Communities. Rural Sociology, 8, 15-24.

Ryan, R.L. (2002). Preserving rural character in New England: local residents' perceptions of alternative residential development. Landscape and Urban Planning, 61(1), 19-35.

Sachs, J.D. (2012). From Millennium Development Goals to Sustainable Development Goals. The Lancet, 379(9832), 2206-2211.

Said, E.W. (1995). Orientalism: Western conceptions of the Orient. Harmondsworth, UK: Penguin.

Sandercock, L. (2003). Out of the closet: the importance of stories and storytelling in planning practice. Planning Theory & Practice, 4(1), 11-28.

Sanoff, H. (2000). Community participation methods in design and planning. New York, NY, USA: John Wiley & Sons.

Schetter, C. (ed.). (2013). Local politics in Afghanistan: a century of intervention in social order. New York, NY, USA: Columbia University Press.

Scholtes, F. and Hornidge, A.-K. (2010). Waiting for the water to come? – Poverty reduction in times of climate change. Bonn, Germany: Care International Germany-Luxembourg e.V. and Center for Development Research (ZEF).

Schwachula, A., Vila Seane, M. and Hornidge, A.-K. (2014). Science, technology and innovation in the context of development – An overview of concepts and corresponding policies recommended by international organizations. ZEF Working Paper, 132.

Scoones, I. (2009). Livelihoods perspectives and rural development. The Journal of Peasant Studies, 36(1), 171-196.

Scott, J.C. (1985). Weapons of the weak: everyday forms of peasant resistance. New Haven, CN, USA: Yale University Press.

Scott, J.C. (1995). State simplifications: nature, space and people. Journal of Political Philosophy, 3(3), 191-233.

Scott, J.C. (1998). Seeing like a state. How certain schemes to improve the human condition have failed. New Haven, CN, USA: Yale University Press.

Seabright, P. (2010). The company of strangers: a natural history of economic life. Princeton, NJ, USA: Princeton University Press.

Seidl, D. (2005). Organizational identity and self-transformation. An autopoietic perspective. Aldershot, UK: Ashgate.

Seidl, D. and Becker, K.H. (eds.). (2005). Niklas Luhmann and organization studies. Malmö, Sweden: Liber.

Selim, M. (2009). Notes from Tashkent: an ethnographic study of Uzbek scholarly life. New Left Review, 55, 73-86.

Selin, S. and Chevez, D. (1995). Developing a collaborative model for environmental planning and management. Environmental Management, 19(2), 189-195.

Sen, A. (1999). Democracy as a universal value. Journal of Democracy, 10(3), 3-17.

Sen, A. (2006). What is the role of legal and judicial reform in the development process? The World Bank Legal Review, 2(1), 21-42.

Shafer, R.J. and Bennett, D.H. (1969). A guide to historical method. Homewood, IL, USA: Dorsey Press.

Sharp, L. and Richardson, T. (2001). Reflections on Foucauldian discourse analysis in planning and environmental policy research. Journal of Environmental Policy and Planning, 3(3), 193-209.

Sheppard, E. (2002). The spaces and times of globalization: place, scale, networks, and positionality. Economic Geography, 78(3), 307-330.

Shutt, C. (2006). Power in aid relationships: a personal view. IDS Bulletin, 37(6): 79-86.

Sillitoe, P. (1998). What, know natives? Local knowledge in development. Social Anthropology, 6(2), 203-220.

Sillitoe, P. and Marzano, M. (2009). Future of indigenous knowledge research in development. Futures, 41, 13-23.

Simonds, J.O. and Starke, B.W. (2006). Landscape architecture: a manual of land planning and design. New York, NY, USA: McGraw-Hill.

Slicher van Bath, B.H. (1963). The agrarian history of Western Europe, AD 500-1850. New York, NY, USA: St. Martin's Press.

Smith, A. and Stirling, A. (2010). The politics of social-ecological resilience and sustainable socio-technical transitions. Ecology and Society, 15(1), 11.

Spear, T. (2003). Neo-traditionalism and the limits of invention in British colonial Africa. The Journal of African History, 44, 3-27.

Spivak, G. (1995). The Spivak reader: selected works of Gayati Chakravorty Spivak. Abingdon, UK: Routledge.

Stavrakakis, Y. (1999). Lacan and the political. Abingdon, UK: Routledge.

STEPS Centre (2010). Innovation, sustainability, development: a new manifesto. Brighton, UK: STEPS Centre.

Sterner, T. and Coria, J. (2013). Policy instruments for environmental and natural resource management. Abingdon, UK: Routledge.

Stichweh, R. (2000). Die weltgesellschaft. Soziologische analysen. Frankfurt, Germany: Suhrkamp.

Stöhr, W.B. and Taylor, D.R.F. (eds.) (1981). Development from above or below?: the dialectics of regional planning in developing countries. Chichester, UK: Wiley.

Swatuk, L.A. (2005). Political challenges to implementing IWRM in Southern Africa. Physics and Chemistry of the Earth, 30(11), 872-880.

Swyngedouw, E. (2000). Authoritarian governance, power, and the politics of rescaling. Environment and Planning D, 18(1), 63-76.

Swyngedouw, E., Moulaer, F. and Rodriguez, A. (2002). Large scale urban development projects and local governance: from democratic urban planning to besieged local governance. Geographische Zeitschrift, 89(2+3), 69-84.

Szerszynski, B., Heim, W. and Waterton, C. (2003). Nature performed: environment, culture and performance. Oxford, UK: Blackwell Publishing.

Talen, E. (1999). Sense of community and neighbourhood form: an assessment of the social doctrine of new urbanism. Urban Studies, 36(8), 1361-1379.

Taubman, W. (1973). Governing Soviet cities. Bureaucratic politics and urban development in the USSR. New York, NY, USA: Praeger.

Teampau, P. and Van Assche, K. (2007). Sulina, the dying city in a vital region. Social memory and nostalgia for the European future. Ethnologia Balkanica, 11(1), 257-278.

Teubner, G. (ed.) (1988). Autopoietic law: a new approach to law and society. Berlin, Germany: Walter de Gruyter.

Teubner, G. (1989). How the law thinks: towards a constructivist epistemology of law. Law & Society Review, 23(5), 727-758.

Thelen, K. (1999). Historical institutionalism in comparative politics. Annual Review of Political Science, 2(1), 369-404.

Theobald, R. (1990). Corruption, development and underdevelopment. Durham, NC, USA: Duke University Press.

Thompson, I.H. (2000). Ecology, community and delight: sources of values in landscape architecture. Abingdon, UK: Taylor & Francis.

Thorbeck, D. (2013). Rural design: a new design discipline. Abingdon, UK: Routledge.

Thrift, N. (2009). Space: the fundamental stuff of human geography. In: Clifford, N.J., Holloway, S.L., Rice, S.P. and Valentine, G. (eds.), Key concepts in geography. London, UK: Sage Publications, pp. 95-107.

Throgmorton, J.A. (1996). Planning as persuasive storytelling: the rhetorical construction of Chicago's electric future. Chicago, IL, USA: University of Chicago Press.

Thucydides and Crawley, R. (1874). History of the Peloponnesian war, Pericles' Funeral Oration, Book II, 2.40. Available at: http://www.gutenberg.org.

Tipps, D.C. (1973). Modernization theory and the comparative study of societies: a critical perspective. Comparative Studies in Society and History, 15, 199-226.

Tischbein, B., Manschadi, A.M., Conrad, C., Hornidge, A.-K., Bhaduri, A., Ul Hassan, M., Lamers, J.P.A., Awan, U.K. and Vlek, P.L.G. (2012): 'Adapting to water scarcity: constraints and opportunities for improving irrigation management in Khorezm, Uzbekistan'. Water Science & Technology: Water Supply, 13(2), 337-348.

Trubek, A. (2008). The taste of place: a cultural journey into terroir. Berkeley, CA, USA: University of California Press.

Turaeva-Höhne, R., A.-K. Hornidge (2013): 'From Knowledge Ecology to Innovation Systems: Innovations in the Sphere of Agriculture in Uzbekistan', Innovation: Management, Policy & Practice, 15(2), 183-193.

Turner, T. (2004). Landscape planning and environmental impact design. Abingdon, UK: Routledge.

Turnhout, E., Van Bommel, S. and Aarts, N. (2010). How participation creates citizens: participatory governance as performative practice. Ecology and Society, 15(4), 26.

Ul-Hassan, M., Hornidge, A.-K., Van Veldhuizen, L., Akramkhanov, A., Rudenko, I. and Djanibekov, N. (2011). Follow the Innovation: participatory testing and adaptation of agricultural innovations in Uzbekistan – guidelines for researchers and practitioners. Bonn, Germany: Center for Development Research.

United Nations Educational, Scientific and Cultural Organisation (UNESCO) (2010). Science policy for sustainable development. The power of science to empower society. Paris, France: UNESCO.

United Nations Educational, Scientific and Cultural Organisation (UNESCO) (2010). UNESCO Science Report 2010. Paris, France: UNESCO.

United Nations Educational, Scientific and Cultural Organisation (UNESCO) (2010). World Social Science Report 2010. Paris, France: UNESCO.

Urry, J. (2007). Mobilities. Cambridge, UK: Polity Press.

Vaccaro, I. and Norman, K. (2008). Social sciences and landscape analysis: opportunities for the improvement of conservation policy design. Journal of Environmental Management, 88(2), 360-371.

Van Ark, R.G.H. (2005). Planning, contract en commitment: naar een relationeel perspectief op gebiedscontracten in de ruimtelijke planning. Delft, the Netherlands: Eburon.

Van Assche, K. (2007). Planning as/and/in context. Towards a new analysis of participatory planning. METU JFA, 27(1), 110-119.

Van Assche, K. (2008). Va'Amenez-nous les citoyens et incluez-les!' Les chemins tortueux de la participation citoyenne dans les theories et les pratiques de l'urbanisme contemporain. In: Hubert, M. and Delmotte, F. (eds.), La cite administrative de l'etat a la croisee des chemins. Des enjeux pour la ville et l'action publique a Bruxelles. Brussels, Belgium: Editions La Cambre.

Van Assche, K. and Djanibekov, N. (2012). Spatial planning as policy integration: the need for an evolutionary perspective. Lessons from Uzbekistan. Land Use Policy, 29(1), 179-186.

Van Assche, K. and Hornidge, A.-K. (2012). 'Knowledge in rural land governance in Uzbekistan: evolutions, institutions and couplings'. ZEF Working Paper Series. Vol. 98. Bonn, Germany: Zentrum für Entwicklungsforschung.

Van Assche, K. and Hornidge, A.-K. (2014). Hidden mobilities in post-Soviet spaces. Boundaries, scales, identities and informal routes to livelihood. Crossroads Asia Working Paper Series, 20.

Van Assche, K. and Lo, M.C. (2011). Planning, preservation and place branding: a tale of sharing assets and narratives. Place Branding and Public Diplomacy, 7(2), 116-126.

Van Assche, K. and Van Biesebroeck, J. (2013). Governing the ice. Ice fishing villages on Lake Mille Lacs and the creation of environmental governance institutions. Journal of Environmental Planning and Management, 57(8), 1122-1144.

Van Assche, K. and Verschraegen, G. (2008). The limits of planning: Niklas Luhmann's systems theory and the analysis of planning and planning ambitions. Planning Theory, 7(3), 263-283.

Van Assche, K., Bell, S. and Teampau, P. (2012). Traumatic natures in the swamp. Concepts of nature and participatory governance in the Danube delta. Environmental Values, 21(2), 163-183.

Van Assche, K., Beunen, R. and Duineveld, M. (2012). Performing success and failure in governance: Dutch planning experiences. Public Administration, 90(3), 567-581.

Van Assche, K., Beunen, R. and Duineveld, M. (2014). Evolutionary governance theory. An introduction. Heidelberg, Germany: Springer.

Van Assche, K., Beunen, R. and Duineveld, M. (2014). Formal/informal dialectics and the self-transformation of spatial planning systems: an exploration. Administration & Society, 46(6), 654-683.

Van Assche, K., Beunen, R., Duineveld, M. and De Jong, H. (2013). Co-evolutions of planning and design: risks and benefits of design perspectives in planning systems. Planning Theory, 12(2), 177-198.

Van Assche, K., Beunen, R., Holm, J. and Lo, M. (2013). Social learning and innovation. Ice fishing communities on Lake Milles Lacs. Land Use Policy, 34, 233-242.

Van Assche, K., Beunen, R., Jacobs, J. and Teampau, P. (2011). Crossing trails in the marshes: rigidity and flexibility in the governance of the Danube Delta. Journal of Environmental Planning and Management, 54(8), 997-1018.

Van Assche, K., Devlieger, P., Teampau, P. and Verschraegen, G. (2009). Forgetting and remembering in the margins: constructing past and future in the Romanian Danube Delta. Memory Studies, 2(2), 211-234.

Van Assche, K., Djanibekov, N., Hornidge, A.K., Shtaltovna, A. and Verschraegen, G. (2014). Rural development and the entwining of dependencies: transition as evolving governance in Khorezm, Uzbekistan. Futures, 63, 75-85.

Van Assche, K., Duineveld, M., Beunen, R. and Teampau, P. (2011). Delineating locals: transformations of knowledge/power and the governance of the Danube Delta. Journal of Environmental Policy & Planning, 13(1), 1-21.

Van Assche, K., Hornidge, A-K, Shtaltovna, A., Boboyorow, H. (2013). Epistemic cultures, knowledge cultures and the transition of agricultural expertise. Rural development in Tajikistan, Uzbekistan and Georgia. ZEF Working Paper 118. Bonn, Germany: ZEF/Bonn University.

Van Assche, K., Salukvadze, J. and Duineveld, M. (2012). Speed, vitality and innovation in the reinvention of Georgian planning: aspects of integration and role formation. European Planning Studies, 20(6), 999-1015.

Van Assche, K., Shtaltovna, A. and Hornidge, A.-K. (2013). Visible and invisible informalities and institutional transformation. Lessons from transition countries: Georgia, Romania, Uzbekistan. In: Hayoz, N. and Giordano, C. (eds.), Informality in Eastern Europe. Frankfurt< Germany: Peter Lang, pp. 89-118.

Van Assche, K., Teampau, P., Devlieger, P. and Sucio, C. (2008). Liquid boundaries in marginal marshes. Reconstructions of identity in the Romanian Danube Delta. Studia Sociologia, 39(1), 115-138.

Van den Brink, A. and Molema, M. (2008). The origins of Dutch rural planning: a study of the early history of land consolidation in the Netherlands. Planning Perspectives, 23(4), 427-453.

Van der Ploeg, J.D., Renting, H., Brunori, G., Knickel, K., Mannion, J., Marsden, T., De Roest, K., Sevilla-Guzmán, E. and Ventura, F. (2000). Rural development: from practices and policies towards theory. Sociologia ruralis, 40(4), 391-408.

Van Dijk, T. (2007). Complications for traditional land consolidation in Central Europe. Geoforum, 38(3), 505-511.

Van Haute, P. (2002). Against adaptation: Lacan's 'subversion' of the subject. New York, NY, USA: Other Press.

Van Huylenbroeck, G., Coelho, J.C. and Pinto, P.A. (1996). Evaluation of land consolidation projects (LCPs): a multidisciplinary approach. Journal of Rural Studies, 12(3), 297-310.

Van Lier, H.N. (1998). The role of land use planning in sustainable rural systems. Landscape and Urban Planning, 41(2), 83-91.

Van Schendel, W. (2002). Geographies of knowing, geographies of ignorance: jumping scale in Southeast Asia. Environment and Planning D: Society and Space, 20, 647-668.

Vandermeulen, V., Verspecht, A., Van Huylenbroeck, G., Meert, H., Boulanger, A. and Van Hecke, E. (2006). The importance of the institutional environment on multifunctional farming systems in the peri-urban area of Brussels. Land Use Policy, 23(4), 486-501.

Verdery, K. (2003). The vanishing hectare: property and value in postsocialist Transylvania. Ithaca, NY, USA: Cornell University Press.

Von Glasersfeld, E. (1995). Radical constructivism: a way of knowing and learning. London, UK: Falmer Press.

Voß, J.P. and Bornemann, B. (2011). The politics of reflexive governance: challenges for designing adaptive management and transition management. Ecology and Society, 16(2), 9.

Wade, R. (1996). Japan, the World Bank, and the art of paradigm maintenance: the East Asian miracle in political perspective. New Left Review, 3.

Walker, G. (2010). Environmental justice, impact assessment and the politics of knowledge: the implications of assessing the social distribution of environmental outcomes. Environmental Impact Assessment Review, 30(5), 312-318.

Wall, C. (2008). Argorods of Western Uzbekistan: knowledge control and agriculture in Khorezm. Münster, Germany: Lit Verlag.

Walsh, C. (2010). Development as Buen Vivir: Institutional arrangements and (de)colonial entanglements. Development, 53(1), 15-21.

Walzer, N. (ed.) (1996). Community strategic visioning programs. Portsmouth, NH, USA: Greenwood Publishing Group.

Wang, H. and Rosenau, J.N. (2001). Transparency international and corruption as an issue of global governance. Global Governance, 7(1), 25-49.

Webster, C.J. and Lai, L.W.C. (2003). Property rights, planning and markets: managing spontaneous cities. Cheltenham, UK: Edward Elgar Publishing.

Weingast, B.R. (1995). The economic role of political institutions: market-preserving federalism and economic development. Journal of Law, Economics, & Organization, 11(1), 1-31.

Whitehead, L. (2002). Democratization: theory and experience. Oxford, UK: Oxford Univeristy Press.

Winslade, J. and Monk, G. (2000). Narrative mediation: a new approach to conflict resolution. San Francisco, CA, USA: Jossey-Bass.

World Bank (1988). Targeted programs for the poor during structural adjustment. A summary of a symposium on poverty and adjustment. Washington, DC, USA: World Bank.

World Bank (1997). World development report: the state in a changing world. Oxford, UK: Oxford University Press.

World Bank (1998/1999). World development report, knowledge for development. Washington DC, USA: World Bank.

World Bank (2010). Innovation policy: a guide for developing countries. Washington, DC, USA: World Bank.

Yanow, D. (ed.) (2000). Conducting interpretive policy analysis. London, UK: Sage.

Young, I.M. (2000). Inclusion and democracy. Oxford, UK: Oxford University Press.

Ziai, A. (2004). The ambivalence of post-development: between reactionary populism and radical democracy. Third World Quarterly, 25(6), 1045-1060.

Ziai, A. (2012). Postcolonial perspectives on 'development'. Working Paper 103. Bonn, Germany: Center for Development Research, University of Bonn.

Zimmerer, K. (2006). Globalization & new geographies of conservation. Chicago, IL, USA: University of Chicago Press.

Zizek, S. (1989). The sublime object of ideology. London, UK: Verso.

Zizek, S. (2006). The parallax view. Cambridge, MI, USA: MIT Press.

# About the authors

This book is the result of a long collaboration between the two authors. Since 2010, they have worked together on a variety of projects, some theoretical, some more empirical and applied, in and on Uzbekistan, Georgia, Tajikistan, Romania, Ukraine and more recently East Africa. The theoretical framework and general narrative of the book are the result of their gradually accumulating insights in these projects, and of a history of often animated discussions with academic colleagues, policy makers, bureaucrats, consultants and the vaguely defined yet ever important 'locals'.

**Kristof Van Assche** (Associate Professor, Planning, governance & development, Faculty of Extension,University of Alberta/ Canada; Visiting Associate Professor Strategic Communication, Wageningen University) holds a PhD in planning from Wageningen University. Mr Van Assche is interested in innovation and evolution in governance, with special interest in spatial, environmental and development policy & planning. As researcher, teacher and consultant he has worked in and on Central Asia and the Caucasus, Europe, the Americas and, more recently, Africa.

Mr Van Assche authored and edited several books, among which can be noted *Evolutionary Governance Theory: An introduction,* and *Evolutionary governance theory: Theory and Applications* (Heidelberg, Springer, 2014 and 2015, both with Raoul Beunen and Martijn Duineveld). Articles appeared in numerous journals, among which *Public Administration, Land Use Policy, Planning Theory, Europe- Asia Studies, Journal of Environmental Policy & Planning.* Recent work focuses on dependencies in rural development, place branding and urban development and the governance of communities in rapid development or decline.

**Anna-Katharina Hornidge** (Director and Professor, Department of Social and Cultural Change, Center for Development Research, University of Bonn/Germany) holds a PhD in Sociology from Berlin and Singapore and a post-doctoral degree (Habilitation) in Development Research from Bonn. In her research Ms. Hornidge specializes in knowledge and development sociology with a substantial part of her work being related to and contributing to current debates in sociology of natural resources, environmental sociology and development-oriented innovation creation and diffusion processes. She has extensively worked on processes of the social construction of our social as well as ecological environments, on the construction of 'knowledge societies', the development of agricultural innovations for change, but also on how people deal with different types of change. Her most current work looks at global discourses of knowledge and development and their local consequences in Central and Southeast Asia.

Ms. Hornidge is internationally well published in journals such as *Geoforum, Journal of Southeast Asian Studies, Natural Resources Forum, Rural Sociology, the Asian Journal of Social Sciences, the Journal of Social Issues in Southeast Asia (Sojourn), Journal of Environmental Policy & Planning* and *Futures*. Furthermore she has been authoring and co-editing several books on Central and Southeast Asia, among which can be mentioned *Environmental Uncertainty and Local Knowledge. Southeast Asia as a Laboratory of Global Ecological Change* (together with Christoph Antweiler; Transcript Publishing, 2012) and the soon to be published volume *Agricultural Knowledge and Knowledge Systems in Post-Soviet Societies* (together with Anastasiya Shtaltovna and Conrad Schetter, Peter Lang Publishing, 2015).

# Index

## A

access 29
accountable 99
action 234
actor
    18, 42, 44, 98, 99, 120, 125, 126, 127,
    130, 132, 134, 138, 180, 190, 192
actor/institution configuration 119,
    133, 138, 140, 152, 158, 171, 184,
    216, 222, 237, 266, 298, 300, 321
actor/knowledge position 317
adaptation 169, 173, 306, 338, 341
adaptive
    – governance 86, 89
    – management 89
adaptivity 306
agricultural extension 144
agriculture 28, 29, 322, 326, 327, 338
agro-food business 322, 334
agro-industrial complex 264
ambiguity 30
anti-colonialist 84
Arabica 218, 287
archaeology 302, 303
area-based 139
Arendt 203
asset 84, 116
    – based approach 158
authority 131
autonomy 222, 236

## B

backward area 35
Belgian Farmers Association 148
blank slate 33, 34
blue print approach 200

Boerenbond 148
boundary 53, 128
    – objects 274
branding 201, 281, 291, 316
breeding 311
Bretton Woods 76
bricolage 22
Brundtland 86
bureaucracy 34, 37, 76, 79, 152, 153
business 97
busts 248

## C

Canada 256
capitalism 48, 152, 226
capitalist 196
    – state extension 152
Carlo Petrini 334
catastrophe 88
Center for Development Research 104
centralized 235
CGIAR 323
change 20, 127
checks and balances 167, 249, 260, 285,
    313, 317, 341, 343
citizen 69
citizenship 36
city 28, 32, 338
civic
    – engagement 280
    – republican 313, 317
    – republicanism 69, 101, 116, 264,
    281, 286, 313, 316, 319, 320, 325
civilization 338
civil society 66, 313, 319
    – model 286, 316, 320, 325
    – system 318
clean slate 38
clean-up phase 250
climate 57
    – change 86